THE MANAGER'S TROUBLESHOOTER

2nd Edition

CLAY CARR • MARY ALBRIGHT

PRENTICE HALL
Paramus, New Jersey 07652

Library of Congress Cataloging-in-Publication Data

Carr, Clay.
    The manager's troubleshooter : pinpointing the causes and cures of
125 tough day-to-day problems / Clay Carr and Mary Albright.
      p. cm.
    ISBN 0-13-240318-8—ISBN 0-13-240300-5 (pbk.)
    1. Supervision of employees. I. Albright, Mary. II. Title.
HF5549.12.C358   1996   96-34328
658.3'02—dc20   CIP

Printed in the United States of America

10 9 8 7 6 5 4 3 2   10 9 8 7 6 5 4 3 2 1

ISBN 0-13-240318-8   ISBN 0-13-240300-5(PBK)

ATTENTION: CORPORATIONS AND SCHOOLS

Prentice Hall books are available at quantity discounts with bulk purchase for educational, business, or sales promotional use. For information, please write to: Prentice Hall Special Sales, 240 Frisch Court, Paramus, New Jersey 07652. Please supply: title of book, ISBN number, quantity, how the book will be used, date needed.

PRENTICE HALL
Paramus, NJ 07652

A Simon & Schuster Company

On the World Wide Web at http://www.phdirect.com

Prentice-Hall International (UK) Limited, *London*
Prentice-Hall of Australia Pty. Limited, *Sydney*
Prentice-Hall Canada Inc., *Toronto*
Prentice-Hall Hispanoamericana, S.A., *Mexico*
Prentice-Hall of India Private Limited, *New Delhi*
Prentice-Hall of Japan, Inc., *Tokyo*
Simon & Schuster Asia Pte. Ltd., *Singapore*
Editora Prentice-Hall do Brasil, Ltda., *Rio de Janeiro*

We affectionately dedicate this book to

Bryan Carr
Heather Arsham
Lisa Conant
Chris Erdman
Lynn Marker
Michael Fletcher
and
Matthew Fletcher

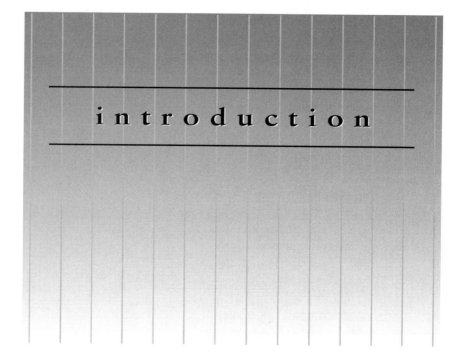

introduction

Picture this situation. You're driving through an unfamiliar part of the city, late at night. Suddenly, your car coughs and dies. There's no service station nearby, not even a public telephone. You have no idea what direction to walk for help. Then you suddenly remember the troubleshooting manual in your trunk. It takes a few minutes, but you find the problem, fix it, and get under way again. Whew!

Being a manager can seem like that sometimes. Problems come up that don't have quick and easy answers. The standard solutions you've been taught or read about don't seem to work. You feel stuck, like someone whose car has stalled in a strange part of town.

That's where the revised edition of *The Manager's Troubleshooter* can help. Six years ago, we published the first edition of the *Troubleshooter* to deal with just those sticky day-to-day issues that you never learned about in basic supervisory training. Thousands of managers have read and benefited from the first edition, as we helped them deal with some of the thorniest problems they face as managers.

But in the six years since the first edition of the *Troubleshooter* was published, there's been a revolution in the way organizations operate. Economic factors have forced downsizing in many businesses and industries, as well as in government operations. Organizations forced to produce more with fewer workers have increasingly turned toward teamwork and empowerment as ways to leverage the human resources they have remaining. So we've updated and improved the *Troubleshooter* to reflect this new organizational climate.

Managing people remains the most challenging part of managing an organization. But the specific problems managers encounter differ depending on the environment in which they work. That's why we've added 27 new problems to this edition of the *Troubleshooter* and revised 16 of the problems from the first edition—to meet the challenges of today's business world.

Much of the new material is focused on downsizing and on teamwork and empowerment issues. These are grouped together in Chapters 9, 10, and 11. Chapter 9 addresses issues that arise specifically when your company is downsizing. These include problems in keeping up production and morale—at the same time you're trying to deal sensitively with the fact that some of your staff will soon be out of work. We give you ideas about how to deal with displaced workers' needs to find other jobs and with the guilt and anxiety felt by the "survivors."

In Chapter 10 we discuss problems that are made worse in a downsizing environment, but that arise in many different work situations. We tackle issues like workers' refusals to cooperate, unreasonable corporate demands for more production, workers' defensive reactions to criticism, and the drain of your best talent to other organizations. These are all problems that arise in almost any work environment. They're especially tricky (and dangerous), though, when your company is downsizing, because that's when it's most important that the people who are left pull together to support one another.

If your company has signed up to the new culture of teaming and empowerment, Chapter 11 can help you with the problems that arise in making the transition from your old hierarchical structure. The problems in this chapter can help you work with employees who don't want to be part of a team, or who think that being in an empowered environment means they can do whatever they want. The chapter can also help if *you've* decided that you could operate more effectively in an empowered workplace, but other managers in your company (including your own boss) won't support you.

But this revision isn't just about downsizing and teamwork. We've updated other chapters to reflect even more changes in the work environment—such as the flexible work schedule and work-at-home problems discussed in Chapter 5 and your own personal work issues discussed in Chapter 13.

We've also kept the most valuable problems discussed in the first edition. These cover some of the toughest situations you'll encounter as a manager—from performance problems to personal issues to problems with your boss and your peers. We attack head-on issues such as substance abuse, workers who try to beat the system, challenges to your authority, workers who can't keep up with the team, and other managers who make themselves look good at your expense.

The second edition of *The Manager's Troubleshooter* combines the most challenging, continuously relevant management problems addressed in the first edition with discussions of the new and exciting workplace developments of the last few years. We're sure that you'll find this edition even more helpful and useful than the first.

HOW TO USE THIS BOOK

How many times have you had to read pages and pages—perhaps even chapters and chapters—to find how to deal with a problem you faced? You won't have to do that with *The Manager's Troubleshooter*. Like all good troubleshooting manuals, it will help you find the cause and cure of your specific problem quickly and easily.

Here's how you use it:

- The manual describes 125 difficult people problems, grouped into 17 different chapters. Each chapter deals with a specific theme (such as "Problems Caused by Downsizing" or "Ethical Problems"). This helps you zero in on the right topic and the right problem in a hurry.

- Find the chapter that deals with the type of problem you have to handle. Then look down the list of problems in that chapter. Find the problem that sounds closest to yours and turn to it.

- Each problem begins with a brief description or vignette. Read the description carefully. If the vignette describes a problem similar to yours, keep going.

- But what if it isn't similar? Look at other problems in that chapter, or even in other chapters. Find the problem that's most like yours. If it isn't quite the same, don't worry—many problems suggest other similar problems you might want to look at.

- Once you've found the right problem and read its description, read about its possible causes. We spell out for you the most common causes of each problem. It's important to read this carefully. Why? Because problems that look the same can have very different causes and cures. You have to find just what caused them before you can successfully cure them.

- Once you understand the cause of the problem you need to know the cure. That's the next part of each section. It's also the longest, because we talk you through all the steps you need to take. If you've identified the cause of your problem and follow these steps, you're on your way to curing it.

- In most cases, there are two or three different sets of steps to take, depending on the cause of the problem. Read and think about each set carefully before you decide which one to use. Then use it.

- What if a problem in the manual sounds like yours, but turns out to be not quite the same? You're not stuck. We've also included a number of checklists in the back of the book that you can use instead of, or in addition to, the steps in a specific problem. You might look on these checklists as general problem-solving processes. There are eight checklists: a General Checklist that can be used with any problem and seven specific checklists for problems such as poor performance and substance abuse.

We've even included a feature to help you prioritize your problems. Not all people management problems are equally important. When you have more than one problem to work—and you usually do—it's crucial to work the most serious one(s) first. (Just in case you haven't found it out yet, a manager can get into trouble just as quickly by setting the wrong priorities as by doing the wrong thing.)

We've provided specific guides to help you choose which problem(s) to deal with first. These guides aren't hard and fast; they're our best guess about how critical the problem will be in *your* unit. This is the way we identify how serious a problem is:

If a problem is a *Shark*, it requires your total attention right now! Postpone it, work something else first, and you're history.

 If it's an *Elephant*, it will trample you to death if you let it, but you have a little time to deal with it. Elephants are what you concentrate on as long as you don't have any sharks.

 If it's a *Wolf*, it lurks around, just waiting to jump you. If you're lucky, wolves are the most serious problems you have day in and day out. If you have sharks and elephants, work them first. If you don't, work on your wolves. Don't ignore the wolves, though, or they'll eat you alive.

A FINAL SUGGESTION

This is *your* book, and it will help you solve your people management problems efficiently and effectively. It's written around problems, and its goal is to help you solve these problems, but we'd like to give you this hint:

When you solve a people problem, don't settle just for getting things back as they were. Use the problem to develop a *better* situation. What does that mean?

- It might mean solving the problem in a way that increases the trust between you and the worker. The more you trust each other, the easier it is to solve problems.

- Or solving it in a way that helps workers manage themselves more effectively. The better your workers are at managing themselves, the fewer the problems that will come to you.

- Or in a way that increases the worker's sense of responsibility for and commitment to the job. A strong commitment to the job prevents many problems from occurring.

You can think of more ways to improve things as you solve problems. The important thing is to keep looking for ways to make the situation better and the worker more effective. The more you do this, the fewer problems there'll be for you to solve in the future.

Clay Carr
Mary Albright

table of contents

Introduction   iv

CHAPTER 1   1
Troubleshooting Problems with Your Employees

1–1: Your employees frequently produce unacceptable work (ELEPHANT)   2

1–2: Your workgroup won't stick with new methods long enough to learn them (ELEPHANT)   5

1–3: Your workgroup doesn't like to deal with its internal customers (ELEPHANT)   8

1–4: There's serious in-group fighting among your employees (WOLF)   12

1–5: Your workgroup is demoralized and produces only so-so work (WOLF)   15

1–6: Your workgroup has a very low (self-imposed) production bogey (WOLF)   18

1–7: Your employees respond to suggested changes with "We've always done it this way" (WOLF)   20

1–8: Your workgroup has a poor reputation in the organization (WOLF)   23

1–9: Your employees are openly resentful of a newer employee you've just promoted to a senior position (WOLF)   26

CHAPTER 2   30
Troubleshooting Problems Caused by Today's Social Environment

2–1: An employee brags to others (falsely) that she's your lover (SHARK)   31

2–2: An employee tells you that another employee (one of your best) is using cocaine on the job (ELEPHANT)   34

2–3: An employee complains that her team leader is sleeping with another employee (ELEPHANT)   37

2–4: An employee accuses another employee of racism or sexism (ELEPHANT)   39

2–5: An employee brings his children to work whenever his babysitter can't take them (WOLF)   43

2–6: Two new employees speak very poor English (WOLF)   47

2–7: You've just hired a minority group member with very high ratings who turns out to be a poor performer (WOLF)   50

2–8: Your employees seem to be dressing more sloppily every day (WOLF)   53

2–9: Your employees complain that work isn't fun (WOLF)   56

CHAPTER 3   61
Troubleshooting Problems Caused by the Personal Life of an Employee

3–1: An employee has serious health problems (ELEPHANT)   62

3–2: An employee appears to be under the influence of alcohol or drugs on the job (ELEPHANT)   64

3–3:   An employee takes a lot of time off from work because of serious problems in his personal life (WOLF)   67

3–4:   An employee comes to work frequently with alcohol on her breath (WOLF)   69

3–5:   One of your employees was involved with another employee and they've broken up, very messily (WOLF)   71

CHAPTER 4   **74**

Troubleshooting Problems Caused by the Current Performance of an Employee

4–1:   An employee has angered a key supplier by his offensive manner (SHARK)   75

4–2:   A worker is new to the workgroup and properly qualified, but is very poorly motivated (ELEPHANT)   78

4–3:   An employee has been an average performer but is slipping to the point that he's now unacceptable (ELEPHANT)   81

4–4:   An employee who usually does outstanding work has just fouled up an important job (ELEPHANT)   85

4–5:   An employee is new and not doing well, but won't accept help at doing better (WOLF)   88

4–6:   A worker is new and can't seem to learn the harder parts of the job (WOLF)   92

4–7:   An employee meets a deadline by producing a substandard report (WOLF)   94

4–8:   A new employee started out well, but his performance is deteriorating (WOLF)   99

CHAPTER 5   **103**

Troubleshooting Problems Caused by the Continuing, Intentional Performance of an Employee

5–1:   An employee is a poor worker because she won't follow work procedures (ELEPHANT)   104

5–2:   An employee on a flexible work schedule has falsified his work hours (ELEPHANT)   107

5–3:   An employee gives priority to the work she likes, not to what needs to be done (WOLF)   110

5–4:   A good worker consistently violates company rules to get his work done (WOLF)   113

5–5:   An employee refuses to use new work procedures or technology (WOLF)   115

5–6:   An employee continually gives other employees substandard work (WOLF)   119

5–7:   An employee tries to win customers by bad-mouthing your competitors (WOLF)   122

5–8:   An employee uses his work-at-home schedule as an opportunity to do no work (WOLF)   126

CHAPTER 6   129

Troubleshooting Problems Caused by the Continuing, Unintentional Performance of an Employee

6–1:   An employee is poorly organized and consistently misses deadlines (ELEPHANT)   130

6–2:   An employee has a tremendous attitude, but isn't producing satisfactory work (ELEPHANT)   133

6–3:   An employee doesn't deliver what he promised (WOLF)   136

6–4:   A good performer goes to pieces under pressure (WOLF)   139

6–5:   An employee produces a high volume of low-quality work (WOLF)   142

6–6:   An employee produces high-quality work, but too little of it (WOLF)   145

6–7:   An employee is technically your best worker but has a tremendously negative attitude (WOLF)   148

6–8:   An employee is a marginal performer, but an informal leader in the group (WOLF)   151

6–9:   An employee clearly isn't suited to the job (WOLF)   155

CHAPTER 7   158
Troubleshooting Problems Caused by the Intentional Misbehavior of an Employee

7–1: An employee is one of your best workers but has lied under oath in an investigation (SHARK)   159

7–2: An employee embarrassed you in front of your boss (ELEPHANT)   163

7–3: An employee may have lied about having completed an assignment (ELEPHANT)   166

7–4: An employee is trying to discredit a coworker (ELEPHANT)   168

7–5: An employee uses company property at home for his personal use (WOLF)   171

7–6: An employee is habitually late for work (WOLF)   174

CHAPTER 8   178
Troubleshooting Problems Caused by an Employee Who Challenges Your Authority

8–1: An employee publicly refuses to follow an order (SHARK)   179

8–2: An employee ignores your directions to cooperate with a manager he doesn't like (ELEPHANT)   182

8–3: An employee goes over your head when you give him an order he doesn't like (ELEPHANT)   185

8–4: An employee publicly criticizes you (ELEPHANT)   189

8–5: An employee brags that you can't do anything to him because of his friendship with your boss (ELEPHANT)   191

8–6: An employee tries to sabotage you with other employees (ELEPHANT)   194

8–7: An employee refuses to work emergency overtime (WOLF)   197

CHAPTER 9   202
Troubleshooting Problems Caused by Downsizing

9–1:   An employee is negotiating with your competitors to go
to work for them with her customer list (SHARK)   203

9–2:   A group of employees tells you they've heard that the
company is going to continue to downsize (ELEPHANT)   206

9–3:   An employee tells you that if your workgroup has to take
on any more new work because of downsizing they will
deluge you with grievances (ELEPHANT)   209

9–4:   An employee who expects to be caught in the next
downsizing stops producing (ELEPHANT)   213

9–5:   Your workgroup has been given a new function that
you don't understand (ELEPHANT)   217

9–6:   You have to take a displaced worker from another area
when you desperately need someone who's fully trained
in your unit's work (ELEPHANT)   219

9–7:   An employee is using company information with his own
private clients (ELEPHANT)   223

9–8:   An employee spends most of her work time looking for
another job (WOLF)   226

9–9:   You have a new manager who's been assigned your
workgroup to manage but refuses to learn anything
about its work (WOLF)   230

CHAPTER 10   235
Troubleshooting Problems Made Worse
by Downsizing

10–1:   Because of the high-pressure work environment, your
employees are competing with one another when they
need to cooperate (ELEPHANT)   236

10–2:   An employee seems to be becoming unbalanced from
work stresses (ELEPHANT)   239

10–3:   Your manager makes unreasonable demands for quality
or quantity of work (ELEPHANT)   243

10–4: Your boss tells you she's going to downsize your group, even though the workload is increasing (ELEPHANT) 247

10–5: Your manager refuses to let you fire nonperformers (ELEPHANT) 250

10–6: Your best workers are leaving for other jobs (WOLF) 254

10–7: Your manager takes credit for what you do (WOLF) 258

Chapter 11 262

Troubleshooting Problems Involving Empowerment and Teamwork

11–1: Your employees think being empowered means they don't have to listen to you (ELEPHANT) 263

11–2: Another manager won't cooperate with you on a joint project (ELEPHANT) 268

11–3: Your manager keeps telling you to turn your workgroup into a self-managing team, with no guidance on how (WOLF) 271

11–4: Your manager overrules you every time you try to empower your workgroup (WOLF) 275

11–5: An employee is a "loner" who won't work with the group (WOLF) 280

11–6: An employee won't tell you when something's bothering her, then disrupts the group (WOLF) 284

11–7: Another manager refuses to deal with anyone in your work unit but you (WOLF) 288

11–8: Another manager accuses your unit of undermining her authority with her unit (WOLF) 292

Chapter 12 296

Troubleshooting Ethical Problems Caused by Your Boss

12–1: He tells you to "fudge" the figures on a report you prepare (SHARK) 297

12–2: He tells you to destroy a report that identifies serious safety hazards in the work area (SHARK) — 299

12–3: She asks you to lend her a large amount of money (ELEPHANT) — 302

12–4: He refuses to accept work from a senior worker because she's female (ELEPHANT) — 305

12–5: He tells you to fire a good employee whom he doesn't like (ELEPHANT) — 308

12–6: He asks you for a date, even though he's married (WOLF) — 310

12–7: She tells you to give a high rating to an employee who isn't very good (WOLF) — 314

CHAPTER 13   318
Troubleshooting Your Own Personal Problems

13–1: You let your boss get caught with a problem you should have warned him about (SHARK) — 319

13–2: An employee accuses you of sexual harassment (SHARK) — 321

13–3: You missed the deadline on a major project (SHARK) — 325

13–4: You've taken over a supposedly well-run unit that's actually on the verge of disintegration (SHARK) — 328

13–5: You lied to your boss about finishing a project and now she's found out about it (SHARK) — 332

13–6: You often can't answer your boss' questions about work status (ELEPHANT) — 336

13–7: You never find out how your workgroup is doing unless you get into trouble (ELEPHANT) — 340

CHAPTER 14   345
Troubleshooting Problems with Another Manager

14–1: A manager is trying to take over one of your functions (SHARK) — 346

14–2: A manager keeps criticizing you to your boss (ELEPHANT) — 350

14–3: A manager lets his unit keep giving you substandard work (ELEPHANT) 353

14–4: A manager complains constantly about your workgroup's output (ELEPHANT) 356

14–5: A manager is trying to recruit your best employees (WOLF) 359

14–6: A manager won't cooperate with you unless you give his projects special priority (WOLF) 363

CHAPTER 15   367
Troubleshooting Internal Management Problems

15–1: The new employees you're getting aren't doing well (ELEPHANT) 368

15–2: You can't promote a talented, ambitious employee who is already looking for jobs outside the company (ELEPHANT) 372

15–3: One of your best workers has asked to go part time so she can attend college just as an important project is starting (ELEPHANT) 375

15–4: One of your best employees has asked you to make an exception to a rule for her (WOLF) 378

15–5: Your unit's supplies are being pilfered, but you don't know who's doing it (WOLF) 382

CHAPTER 16   385
Troubleshooting Problems That Your Boss Causes

16–1: He assigns you a high-priority project that you have no one capable of working on (SHARK) 386

16–2: She gives you a poor performance rating (ELEPHANT) 388

16–3: He gives a major new project that should have been yours to another section (ELEPHANT) 392

16–4: He isn't clear about assignments (WOLF) 394

16–5: She keeps pitting you against another workgroup you need to work closely with (WOLF) 397

16–6: He chews you out in front of other managers (WOLF) 401

CHAPTER 17   404
Troubleshooting Problems With Your Boss

17–1: He wants one of his people in your job (SHARK)   406
17–2: He's talking about abolishing your job (SHARK)   409
17–3: He complains about you to your peers and his boss
       (ELEPHANT)   412
17–4: He thinks you're out for his job (ELEPHANT)   414
17–5: He "micro-manages" you and won't delegate
       (ELEPHANT)   417
17–6: He refuses to support your decisions when they're
       unpopular (ELEPHANT)   420
17–7: She doesn't like you (ELEPHANT)   423
17–8: She's a good friend of one of your hard-to-manage
       employees (WOLF)   427
17–9: He bypasses you to your workgroup (WOLF)   430

PROBLEM-SOLVING CHECKLISTS   435

The General Checklist   436
Checklist #1: Performance Problems   437
Checklist #2: Conduct/Behavior Problems   439
Checklist #3: Acceptance Problems   440
Checklist #4: Problems with Your Peers   441
Checklist #5: Problems with Your Boss   443
Checklist #6: Your Personal Problems   444
Checklist #7: Substance Abuse Problems   445

INDEX   449

chapter one

TROUBLESHOOTING PROBLEMS WITH YOUR EMPLOYEES

1-1 THE PROBLEM

Your employees frequently produce unacceptable work

THE SCENE

Sunday morning finds you seated at the breakfast table with a cup of tea and Paul Strauss's latest work report. You eagerly begin to read, then note to your dismay that most of it doesn't make any sense. You can't follow his logic; sentences aren't clear; and you have no idea where his conclusions came from. You're especially disgusted because this is the third major product you'll have to return to one of your employees this month. Can't just *one* of them do something right?

POSSIBLE CAUSES

Your employees may not know what's expected of them.

This is most likely if you're new to your work unit or if requirements have recently changed in some way.

Your employees may not see any advantage to themselves in doing a better job.

Is there any reward to them for doing better work? What happens when the work is unacceptable? Do you rework the product for them, or are they required to fix the problem themselves?

The work environment may discourage good work.

Do your employees have access to all the materials they need to do their jobs well? How hard is it to get new tools or resources? Does your organizational structure facilitate the right people doing the right parts of a project?

Hint: Poor performance by an entire organization requires different treatment from poor performance by an individual. You may have a situation where the poor performance is the result of a number of different individual performance problems. It's more likely, though, that your problem is systemic; something in the way your work is organized, or communicated, or reviewed *as a whole* is causing large numbers of your people to produce substandard work.

If most of your people are producing poor quality work, don't be misled by the one or two who do well. They don't necessarily prove that you don't have a systemic problem. Some people will perform well in spite of almost any adversity.

CURES

If your employees don't know what's expected of them:

Review the unit's work products again to see if there are aspects that are consistently being done poorly. Identify two or three changes in work procedures or processes that would correct the most common problems.

Determine the training method that would best teach your employees how to do those two or three things better. Maybe a local training source for formal training? Or an employee who does one of those aspects well and could do some on-the-job training?

Tell your employees what you plan to do to help them learn the job better and that you intend to concentrate on specific items. Then provide regular feedback to them on how well they're doing and what *specific* areas they still need to work on.

If your employees don't see any advantage in doing a better job:

Set up an informal system of recognition for each job that's done well. This can be a public "pat on the back" or a more tangible form of recognition such as a certificate, a bonus, a gift certificate, or some other item that says "Good job!"

Discuss with your employees what motivates them. If they trust you, they'll probably tell you what turns them on. As much as possible, try to devise rewards intrinsic to the job (better assignments) rather than extrinsic rewards like time off work.

While you may have limited authority to set up your own recognition-and-reward systems for your employees, you can see to it that they, not you, are the ones who suffer the consequences of their unacceptable work. Give your employees regular feedback on what they're doing well and not so well. When it's not done well, make sure *they* do the work over again until it's right. Devise other "natural consequences" for their poor quality, even if that means denying them a vacation day so they'll have time to rework an important assignment.

If the work environment is discouraging good work:

Review your work situation to see just what's getting in the way of doing a good job. Talk to your staff; they know better than you do what's getting in their way.

Examine the work flow and your organizational structure. Restructure the work if necessary to see that tasks are done in a logical sequence and that segments once completed don't require rework by another person or function. Make sure that someone is ultimately responsible for the quality of every product and that that person sees the final result before it goes to you or to the next section for review.

If materials or equipment are getting in the way of quality work, make a friend of your local supply department. Visit them to see what bureaucratic roadblocks stand in the way of their serving you. Offer to help, and follow through, in whatever way your position allows, to make their job easier.

SOMETHING TO THINK ABOUT:

Most employees don't like to work in an organization that does poor work. If your employees do know what's expected of them and how to perform to those expectations, they'll probably be the best source of information on barriers to improved quality. But before they tell you what those barriers are, they need to trust you and believe that you have their best interests in mind. That trust takes some time to develop, but it's worth the effort.

1–2 THE PROBLEM

*Your workgroup won't stick with
new methods long enough to learn them*

THE SCENE

"Well, that certainly was a fiasco," Stefan remarks. "One more 'quick fix' that broke more than it fixed. Now we'll spend even more time getting everybody back in sync with our old supply procedure when we could have just left it alone in the first place."

"Wait a minute," you reply. "That new process could have worked, and could have worked better than the old one if you'd just given it a fair trial. But you can't change a whole process one week and have it working smoothly the next. If we keep giving up on new ideas before we even give them a chance to work, we'll never be able to improve anything!"

POSSIBLE CAUSES

Your workgroup may resent having new ideas imposed on them.

They may believe that they are the people in the best position to come up with new work methods and resent outside intrusion.

The group may not be accustomed to trying new methods.

They may actively resist changes or they may just not know how to deal productively with them.

The group may not be comfortable with the decreased production that almost inevitably accompanies the first implementation of a process change.

Or they may think they'll be held responsible, by you or higher management, for producing at the same rate during the change period. That's a near-impossible task.

Hint: Any change needs time to take root. First, people have to become comfortable with the *idea* of change, then they have to have time to implement the change itself. Whenever you introduce new methods or processes, you need to be sure your group understands that a reasonable "learning curve" is not only tolerated, it's *expected*.

CURES

If your workgroup resents having new ideas imposed on them:

Is this a change you've been *forced* to make because of a change in the company's policy or a decision that has been made somewhere above you in the hierarchy? If not, back up a little.

Explain to your workgroup what problems have been identified with the current process. What is it you're trying to correct? Get their ideas and suggestions. Make clear to them that this isn't just a perfunctory question. You genuinely want their input and will evaluate both their ideas and the solution that's already been proposed.

Especially if the new methods are entirely of your creation, be sure that at least some of the group's ideas are included. Even better if they come up with an overall solution that's better than yours was. Demonstrating to them that you're not only interested in listening to their ideas, but that you'll implement them whenever you can will improve the situation in two ways: Not only will you come up with a better solution, but when you *have* to impose something without their input, they'll probably be more understanding and accepting.

If this is a change you've been forced to make without input from your group, make sure you explain to them the situation and the reason for the change. Then brainstorm with them to see if together you can come up with ways to make the new methods work—to everyone's advantage.

If the group isn't accustomed to trying new methods:

Look ahead at problem 1–7 for some suggestions on introducing changes to the organization. Consider especially the three questions we list. If the change is going to work, you (and your group) must be able to answer "yes" to all three: (1) Will it pay off for me? (2) Can I do it successfully? and (3) Is it worth the effort it will take? Once you've figured out how to make all three answers "yes," you have the basic strategy for convincing your group to give the new methods a fair trial.

If the group isn't comfortable with the loss of production that accompanies the implementation of any new process:

What's the goal of the new process? Is it to increase the amount your unit can produce? Does it focus on improving quality? Does it implement some new technology or make your process more compatible with others inside or outside your organization?

Your primary focus, at least initially, needs to be on implementing the new methods in such a way that the goals of the new methods are met—or at least given a reasonable test. Be sure your workgroup knows what they need to concentrate on and that other aspects of the work will be given less priority during this transition period.

Develop an estimated timetable by which you and your group think the new methods should be up and running smoothly. The length of time may be as short as a few days, but could run for several months if the process is a complex one or if it interfaces with many other processes. *Be conservative* in your estimates. Nothing *ever* goes as smoothly as planned, and it's better for morale and for your management statistics to implement earlier than expected, rather than later.

Do you know for sure that the new methods *will* be better than the old ones? Can you try implementing them in a small way at first, then going for full-scale implementation once all the bugs are worked out? This kind of "beta testing" is often used in introducing new technology and can help identify trouble spots before your entire operation comes to a grinding halt.

Finally, be encouraging during the entire process change. Expect foul-ups, roadblocks, frustrations, and occasional short tempers. Your continued calm encouragement will go a long way toward ensuring that your group sticks with the process changes long enough to see them through.

Something to Think About

Implementing a new work process is a lot like learning to ride a bike. When you first start out you fall down a lot and you can go only a few feet before you lose your balance and have to start all over. Your little brother or sister walking beside you seems to be moving a lot faster than you are. But once you get through the frustrating experience of mastering the new technique, you can speed along faster than you ever imagined. Patience is important for the person who's learning, but it's even more important for the coach on the sidelines.

1-3 The Problem

Your workgroup doesn't like to deal with its internal customers

The Scene

"Why do you keep harping on dealing with the people down in financing—and why do you keep calling them 'customers'? They're employees just as we are, and their job is to take what we give them and use it the way they're supposed to. If they don't like it, they can tell us so and we can talk about it. In the meantime, we don't have time for all this 'customer' junk. Just let us do our job—and heaven knows we have enough to do!"

Ben looks around and most other members of the workgroup nod. He turns back, a "See, I told you so!" look on his face.

Possible Causes

The organization has never stressed internal customers.

It uses the traditional model, where a workgroup produces not what some "customer" wants but what higher management tells it to.

The workgroup is used to applying its own standards of what makes a good product.

It believes it understands what makes its products successful and uses that standard. It doesn't need any more information from other people in the company, even if you call them "customers."

The goals of the two units conflict, so your unit isn't willing to treat the other as a customer.

Your workgroup simply doesn't agree with what the other workgroup thinks is a successful product, so it ignores it.

Hint: To many people, even those who are very much oriented toward satisfying external customers, the notion of an "internal customer" seems odd. They believe that the focus of the entire company should be on satisfying that external customer and that everyone within the company should be a part of the team effort. That's a legitimate stance, but it's only one way of looking at complex internal interactions.

The notion of internal customers is useful for focusing the attention of your workgroup on what *someone else* needs from the products and services they produce. As we will discuss, it's easy for units to get caught up in their own definitions of "quality work" and "successful performance," while overlooking the real needs of the people who will use their work products. By thinking of other units in the company as "internal customers," you can refocus your workgroup's attention on what those other people need in a positive way, by using the "carrot" of customer satisfaction rather than the "stick" of performance complaints.

CURES

If the organization has never stressed internal customers:

In this circumstance, you will get very little help from higher levels if you try to get regular feedback from the other people in the company who use your work products. In fact, your manager may think you're wasting time and tell you to get back to "real" work.

What do you do? Obviously, you can't start a big "customer" relations program with people in your own company. But you can attempt to find two or three workers who would be interested in dealing with the other units and work out a small program with them. For instance, you and this small group might schedule a brief visit with one of your internal customers. It doesn't have to be anything fancy to begin with, just a "How are you? How are things going? Anything we can do to help?" kind of visit.

You may find all kinds of dissatisfaction on the first visit, which certainly gives you the excuse you need to pay systematic attention to them. Or nothing may happen. That's fine. Visit another unit that your workgroup deals with. Be patient. The odds are very good that if your internal customers have no complaints it's because they don't really believe you'll pay attention to them. So, to test the way, a member of another unit may bring up a minor problem or two she's been having with your workgroup. That's your opportunity to demonstrate your responsiveness. Commit your workgroup to solving the problem, along with a date by which it will be solved—and keep your commitment.

You can be absolutely confident that, if you demonstrate concern and responsiveness to the other units in the company who interact with yours, you will begin the find more than just a few opportunities to change your relationship with them. And when your boss asks you why you're going to all this trouble, explain that one of your goals is to cut out the unnecessary work you're sure your unit is performing.

If the workgroup is used to applying its own standards of what makes a good product:

Traditional organizations promoted this approach. So do the professions. Accountants know what makes a good report, programmers know what makes a good program, college recruiters know what makes a good hire. And human resources departments have to live by EEO laws and regulations. Increasingly, whether because they are professionals, want to be professionals, or are bound by an increasing volume of laws and regulations, workers and their workgroups have and use their own definitions of successful products.

But internal standards are never enough, because they don't incorporate the legitimate needs of the people who will use your products and services. So what do you do? If you can find a few willing workers, follow the suggestions in the paragraph above. Now, though, you add another level. If a "customer" unit is dissatisfied, your workgroup may be able to make a change and satisfy him or her, or it may not because the change would violate an internal standard. For instance, a manager might want his or her accounting data stated in a way that the accounting unit believes distorts the real situation.

What you can do in each case, however, is discuss and try to negotiate the disagreements. The more the two units understand each others' work and each others' issues, the easier it will be for them to work together and the easier it will be for your unit to satisfy the other. In the long run, your unit will be more productive, will waste less time and effort, and will be more confident that it is satisfying real needs for its internal customers.

If the goals of the two units conflict, so your unit isn't willing to treat the other as a customer:

Now we add yet another dimension. Your workgroup believes that if it gives its customers in other units what they want, they will want the wrong thing. Managers will try to bypass the EEO regulations to get a job filled quickly. The manufacturing people will screw up the design so they can make the product more easily. So "we" have to insist on our standards because "they" will screw things up if we don't.

That's a difficult attitude to change. It's even extremely difficult to get a workgroup to *consider* changing the attitude. If the organization strongly supports customer orientation and cross-functional teamwork, that will help. Make use of all the support the company can give you. Even then, expect to take a long time, do a lot of discussion, and endure a lot of emotional outbursts. These issues matter to many workers.

SOMETHING TO THINK ABOUT

Customers are very important, whether they're internal or external. If you and your workgroup believe this, here are two ideas that will make customer relations even more effective:

Work at *being a good customer*. You have suppliers you depend on, perhaps both internal and external. You may not believe they treat you well, and they may not. But it's worth spending some time and effort to find out how to be good customers for them; it really will make your relationship with them both smoother and more effective. And when they see you're willing to spend time and effort on being a better customer, they will probably begin asking what they need to do to be better suppliers.

Work at *educating your own customers*. There are certain things you just can't do; if your customers understand what these are and don't expect them, you will be able to satisfy them better. There are other things that sound good at first hearing but don't really work very well; you can see that your customers know what these are and why they don't work well. And there are some exceptions you can make occasionally that you can't even think of making routinely; it's important that your customers don't expect them routinely.

1-4 THE PROBLEM

There's serious in-group fighting among your employees

THE SCENE

"I should have known I'd pay for this later," you remark wryly to no one in particular as Bill leaves your office. "*One* afternoon off to do some shopping and now half the staff's mad at me."

Unfortunately, most of the rest of the staff had been gone too, including the senior employees you usually left in charge during your absences. So you told Pete to take over the office while you were gone, and now you've spent most of the morning hearing about "favoritism" and that it's not fair that you're "grooming Pete for the next promotion." With three hours of supervisory experience!

"But if it weren't this, it would just be something else," you muse. "Such a talented group of people, but they're always fighting about something!"

POSSIBLE CAUSES

Some occasional dissatisfaction among your employees is probably inevitable. If what you're faced with is this sort of "annoyance bickering," the best thing you can do is nothing. Any attempts on your part to make things better will probably make them worse by giving the behavior a prominence it doesn't deserve.

However, there are two cases where you can't afford to ignore infighting:

- when it's caused by real or perceived inequity in the way employees are treated, or
- when it's the result of serious dissatisfaction and employees' perception that they're trapped in meaningless work with no potential for advancement.

In those cases, you *must* analyze the situation and take action. Otherwise, things will only get worse.

CURES

If the infighting is caused by real or perceived inequity in the way employees are treated:

First determine the source of the apparent inequity. Is it the system itself (e.g., the way work is assigned, the way raises and promotions are given)? Is it something you're doing? Or something someone higher up the chain is doing?

The next step is education. Often, employees don't even know that there *is* a system or a set of rules for making certain decisions. Let your employees know what the rules are and how you've applied them in the past. (In this case, you put Pete in charge because he had the next highest level of seniority with the company, though some of the others had more seniority in their positions. If you explain how the decision was made and show that you'll be consistent in applying that rule, things will improve noticeably.)

If there are no rules, consider drawing up a set of guidelines for your own unit that covers the situations that most often cause contention. You can't make a rule for everything. And you shouldn't try. But you can identify for employees the criteria you use in making some decisions. Once the staff know what criteria you use and are convinced that you're following them, much of their dissatisfaction will cool.

And of course, if there are rules and they're not being followed, the solution is obvious: Follow them. If it's someone farther up the chain of command who's the source of the inequity, you can point out to them the impact on morale and productivity. But if you can't change your boss' behavior, you may need to make some adjustments at your level to mitigate the damage.

If the infighting is the result of your employees' dissatisfaction with their jobs, the solution is not nearly so straightforward (and you may have less satisfactory results):

If you can change the way work is structured to make it more meaningful or increase advancement potential for even *some* of your employees, as long as you're not hurting the others—do it!

Manufacture opportunities for your employees to increase their direct contact with their customers. All work products should be of benefit to someone—either within the company or outside. (If they're not, you'll want to consider whether that work ought to be done at all.) As your employees have greater contact with the recipients of their efforts, the work will become more meaningful and the group can unite around the common purpose of serving the customer.

Let your employees know you're on their side. If the work truly is boring and dead-end, let your staff know you're aware of their dissatisfactions, that you'll do what you can to make things better, and that if they do a good job for you you'll help them to move on to better jobs. If your staff knows you as an empathetic boss, it will be harder for them to imagine you treating them unfairly.

Something to Think About

Don't confuse infighting with honest disagreement. In any group made up of strong, talented individuals, there is bound to be disagreement and conflict. In this situation, the proper cure is to manage the conflict creatively, not try to suppress it. (If you're not sure how to do this, there are a number of good books that will help you.)

1-5 THE PROBLEM

Your workgroup is demoralized and produces only so-so work

THE SCENE

Your new boss was right; the performance of this group of employees is mediocre. Their work always meets the minimum standard—just barely—but never gets much better. If you try to get them to improve, they ask you to tell them what to do in detail, or come up with a dozen reasons for why it can't be improved. Worst of all, they don't seem to care.

POSSIBLE CAUSES

Their last manager was no better than marginal.

Managers who are barely competent don't take long to pass their shortcomings on to their employees.

Their last manager refused to support them.

This is another effective way to wreck a group of employees. If managers never stand up for their employees and always side with the people who criticize them, it doesn't take long for the employees to get the word and hunker down.

Hint: Once in a rare while, you may find employees from whom even an effective supervisor can't get good performance. Most of the time, though, an ineffective work unit is the result of ineffective supervision.

CURES

If their last manager was marginal:

Your number-one task is to prove your competence at the same time that you build up their self-confidence and willingness to produce.

Make it clear from the beginning that you know your job. This doesn't mean that you have to have all the answers; you don't. But you do need a clear sense of how to do the job, and you need to act on this sense.

Make it clear to the group what level of performance you expect from them. Do this at a group meeting and explain it carefully. Invite them to ask questions (though they probably won't at this stage). If it's necessary, put your expectations in writing. The important point is for them to know what you want and that you're serious about it.

Insist on getting the performance you want. If a job isn't acceptable, explain what's wrong and have it redone until it's right. Depending on the group, this may be a long struggle. For both your sake and theirs, you need to win it.

Keep your eyes peeled for one telltale sign. Managers sometimes get into the habit of accepting substandard work and (bad) having someone else redo it or (worse!) redoing it themselves. If you see signs that this was how the last manager did things, make it clear that you don't work this way, that you expect jobs to be done right the first time. Then work the situation until they are done right.

There's another bad habit work units fall into: not getting things done on time. There is virtually no excuse for this, period. If your employees have too much work to do, it's your responsibility as their manager to get the workload adjusted. Except for that, your employees should expect to meet every deadline or to renegotiate the deadline *in advance* with you.

Are you doing all of this to be hard on your employees? Not at all. You're doing it because it's the only way they'll ever be able to take pride again in what they do.

If their last manager refused to support them:

Normally, this is the only situation other than marginal management that can demoralize employees. Some otherwise competent managers always side with the people who complain about their employees.

The group is probably hoping that you'll be different, but afraid you won't be. In other words, they'll be cautious and wait for you to prove yourself.

Your basic tactics here are easy. When someone comes to you with a complaint about your employees, listen carefully to him, get all the facts as he sees them, and tell him you'll look into the situation and get back to him. If he's in a hurry, or very upset, promise to get back to him quickly, but don't make any commitments until you've talked with the employee(s) he's complaining about.

Talk to the employee or employees. Get their side of the situation. If you can back them, do it (always, not just in the beginning). If possible, let them take care of the problem with the individual who complained. If you have to come up with a different solution in order to satisfy a reasonable complaint, do it, but let them present the solution to the individual if you can.

In other words, see that the situation is resolved, but don't make your employees the bad guys. If they were careless or unresponsive or otherwise did a poor job, let them know it and let them know what you expect. But do it in private. And never correct them because someone complained; correct them because what they did was inadequate, whether anyone complained about it or not.

SOMETHING TO THINK ABOUT

If you want your employees to trust you and really produce for you, you need to protect them from outside harassment. This doesn't mean that you overlook it when they screw up; it does mean that you deal with their screw-ups in private and help them be good guys to the rest of the organization.

There's one last, very important point. To succeed as a manager, you have to delegate effectively. When you delegate, you let the person act for you. Whatever she does, as long as she does it conscientiously—she does for you. Support it and support her (even if you have to undo her decision). This is the only way that your delegations can be successful.

1–6 THE PROBLEM

Your workgroup has a very low (self-imposed) production bogey

THE SCENE

As you stroll unobtrusively through the claims section, you notice the same lack of industry that you've observed before. No one is really "goofing off," but no one seems to be working very hard either. The whole atmosphere is relaxed and laid back.

Back in your office, you review the last two months' production figures. As you suspected, the other sections doing claims processing all had higher output than yours. Of course, employees in those sections complained more too. "But maybe," you muse, "it was worth it. My people do what they have to, but not one claim more."

POSSIBLE CAUSES

If employees are producing acceptable work at an acceptable rate, but nothing more, it's probably because they see no advantage in working harder. If it's important that they begin to produce at a higher rate, there are two areas you should examine as potential sources of improvement:

Employees may not see any benefit from increased production.

Some things in your operation may even *discourage* higher production. Are there rewards for doing more work?

There may not be any penalty for producing at the low level and there may be positive reasons for not doing more.

Employees may feel they'd be exploited if they did more work for what they're getting paid.

Hint: Before you rush full tilt into a production improvement program, there's one other statistic you should check—acceptance rate. If other sections are producing at higher rates, but there are more appeals of settlements on claims their sections processed, then the company as a whole hasn't really gained. First make sure your quality level is where you want it to be, then you can work on improving production (and show your boss how higher quality, even with slightly lower production, helps the company in the long run).

CURES

If employees see no benefit from enhanced production:

Look at your compensation system to see if there's any way employees can share in the gains from increased production. Establish specific production goals at several levels and link some form of recognition to each level. This recognition, particularly for small production improvements, need not be monetary. An essential ingredient, though, is that the recognition must be public; it should serve as a stimulant both to the recipient and to other employees who see how they can benefit from production improvements.

Discuss with your employees what you might do to increase production. Ask them what they see as benefits worth striving for and then implement as many of their suggestions as you can.

As you implement these recognition systems, be sure that they're administered fairly and impartially. Let your employees know what the criteria are for recognition and don't change the rules without letting them know and telling them why you're making the changes.

If employees see some positive reason to continue their low level of production:

Identify what it is that's encouraging employees to produce at a low level and what's discouraging higher production. Review employee complaints over the past couple of years. Is there a common theme (or underlying message) in many of the grievances you've received?

Do what you can to remove the barriers to higher production and let your employees know what you can do and what you can't. If the disincentive is something as basic as the pay scales for their jobs, over which you have no control, talk with them about what you might be able to substitute for a change in pay rates.

As when your employees see no incentive to higher production, look at your compensation and recognition system to find ways to let employees share in the company's gains. If employees feel that the company's fortune is their own, they'll be much more interested in increasing its profitability.

Something to Think About

Employees have many different reasons for setting production bogeys lower than the level management believes is a "fair day's work." There are many reasons for this, but they all boil down to one: This is what pays off best for them. To change the bogey, you have to change the payoff.

1–7 The Problem

Your employees respond to suggested changes with "We've always done it this way"

The Scene

You bite your tongue to keep from yelling at Floyd and stalk back to your office. He's the third employee this week who's answered "We've always done it this way" when you suggested doing things a different way. You thought you were taking over a conservative group of employees, and, boy, were you right!

Possible Causes

The employees really don't know any other way to do things.

The group may have been so stable and done things the same way for so long that no one has ever thought that there might be another way to do them.

The employees like the way they do things and are resisting change.

Employees often see a new manager as someone who's going to force a lot of new ideas on them, and they "dig in" to resist the changes.

The employees are actively fighting specific changes you want to make.

They may be fighting the changes not because they don't want to change, but because they don't like the changes you want to make.

Hint: These three situations sound similar, but are actually different. You need to listen carefully and ask effective questions to find out what your problem is. Then you'll be able to solve it.

CURES

No matter what the cause is:

It's not true that people don't want to change. Most people choose to change many times. But they do so only when they can answer "yes" to these three questions: (1) Will it pay off for me? (2) Can I do it successfully? and (3) Is it worth the effort it will take?

When *someone else* wants the change, it's necessary to have a "yes" answer to a fourth question: Do I trust the person who wants me to change?

These four criteria are what everyone uses to decide whether to change or not. When anyone, including you, us and your work unit, can't answer "yes" to all four questions, we'll resist the change. On the other hand, when a proposed change meets all four criteria, we will change.

Your basic job, then, is to establish trust with your employees and show them "yes" answers to the first three questions.

If they really don't know any other way:

Find a change that you're sure meets the first three criteria and then explain to your employees what you're going to do and why. Give them a chance to ask questions. Be patient. No matter how good you think your idea is and how good they may later decide it is, making the change is going to make them uncomfortable.

If you can, wait to make more changes until the first change has "taken" and the group is comfortable with it. If it was an effective change, they'll be happy you did it. This will make the next change easier. If you string a succession of successful changes together, you'll probably get them to the point where change becomes natural to them. Then they'll begin suggesting changes, and you'll know that you've done your job.

If the employees are actively resisting change:

Don't get angry at their stubbornness. If you let the situation disintegrate into you versus them, you'll both lose.

Select a change that meets the three criteria. In this circumstance, it helps if the change is in response to a clear problem. ("We've got to do something to reduce the number of errors or we're going to be in big trouble.")

Here's a technique that often works. Start with the compelling reason to change. (Perhaps you've been directed to cut copier expenses by 10 percent by the end of the month or else.) Call the group together; tell them that it has to be done and how you propose to do it. Then tell them that if anyone has a better idea you'll be glad to consider it. If you don't get any ideas from them, go ahead and do what you said you'd do. If you do get ideas—and sooner or later you will—do your best to implement them (at least in part).

Remember, pick changes that clearly have to be made and make sure they're effective. This will start to build employee trust in you. Then you can start persuading employees to make changes that aren't required and may not be so obvious.

If the employees are actively fighting specific changes you want to make:

First, examine the changes you're trying to make. Are they really going to help? Are they what the work unit needs now? Will they make the group more effective or efficient, or are you just changing to make the situation more comfortable for you? In other words, do the changes meet the first three criteria?

If they do, try to persuade your employees that they do. If you can't, but try to force the change through, you'll create a situation where it's you versus your employees. Don't do this unless the change is absolutely essential (or absolutely required).

If you can't convince them the change will help them, at least convince them you're going to do it, no matter what.

If their opposition is really strong, you might try this: Agree to stop pushing the change if they'll come up with a better way to do it. That gives them an out and puts the ball in their court, without your backing down from the change.

Do whatever is necessary to make sure the change succeeds. Forcing through a change that doesn't work is disastrous.

SOMETHING TO THINK ABOUT

You may be forced to make a change that doesn't meet all three of the tests or before you can build up trust with your employees. If you must do this, do it as gracefully as possible. But don't ever initiate a change on your own when this isn't true.

The more experienced your employees get at changing successfully, the easier it will be. Getting those first few successes is the hard—but very necessary—part.

1–8 THE PROBLEM

*Your workgroup has a poor reputation
in the organization*

THE SCENE

Angered and hurt, you slam down the phone. "That's totally unfair," you fume. "What kind of a statement is that, 'I knew this proposal would be garbage as soon as I saw your unit's name on the cover'? I've worked hard with my group to make sure we put out only products we can all be proud of. It doesn't make any difference how good a job we do, Analysis and Design has had some bad press, and now nobody will give us a chance!"

POSSIBLE CAUSES

Your unit may have produced substandard work in the past.

It may be that your poor reputation is at least partially deserved. Customers (including internal customers) will not be likely to take a risk with you again if they've been burnt in the past, unless you can convince them that they won't be disappointed again.

Your unit may have produced technically adequate work that failed to satisfy your customers' expectations.

Customers don't necessarily know what's accurate or correct, but they do know what they want. Your job is to provide them with what they want or convince them that what you're offering them meets their needs even better.

Your unit may truly have gotten "bad press" for something that wasn't their fault.

No one wants to admit error, and we're all falsely blamed at one time or another. An organization that really was at fault for poor products may have passed the blame on to you, or competitors may have made misleading comparisons between their offerings and yours.

Hint: As your mother probably warned you, reputation is a fragile thing. That's true corporately as well as personally. And much of the business we get is on the basis of our reputation—for solid, accurate, reliable, responsive work. The best way to safeguard your reputation is never to allow it to be sullied in the first place. Corporate image is not just the concern of the Public Relations department; it must be a concern in every customer contact.

CURES

If your unit has produced substandard work in the past:

Be honest with potential customers and clients who are worried about your previous performance. Tell them what you've done to improve and show them examples of good work you've produced since the problems have been remedied. While you're in the process of reestablishing yourself, consider offering services on a contingency basis: You'll get paid only if the client accepts your work.

Try to expand your customer base. Approach people you haven't dealt with before, who may not have preconceived notions about the quality of your work.

Bite off only as much as you can chew. Start small. Be willing to spend a little extra effort at first producing a "perfect" product. You can use those first samples to show new customers (or to convince previous customers to give you another chance), and your "ultra-satisfied" customers can give good testimonials to your later prospects.

If your unit has previously produced technically adequate work that failed to satisfy your customers' expectations:

Work out in advance with your customers exactly what you intend to do for them. Listen closely to their needs and wants and articulate back to them what you think you hear them saying. Tell them (in a formal contract, if it's appropriate) exactly what you're offering them and which of their concerns your offering will satisfy. Make sure you both agree on the product or service you'll supply and what it will do for them, before you provide the product or service itself.

If you're offering a product that will take some time to produce, set up a series of checkpoints along the way. These can be meetings with the customer or they can be sets of formal specifications. But whatever form they take, you'll need periodic points where you and the customer examine progress to be sure that he or she is satisfied. That way you can clear up any misunderstandings early, before they become major disconnects.

If your unit received some "bad press" for something that wasn't their fault:

As closely as possible, identify the source of the erroneous information. It's tough to tackle an opponent you can't see. If the bad press appears to be the result of innocent misinformation or misunderstanding, confront the source directly. Explain the true situation and try to enlist his or her aid in repairing the damage.

Consider an information campaign aimed at your most crucial customers. Through any of a variety of media and methods, public and individual, you can provide information to counter the "disinformation."

Contact some of your most loyal customers to explain the poor publicity you've received and to ask them for references or testimonials that you can use with prospective new customers. Develop, through special attention and high quality of delivery, a cadre of customers you can count on for support even if times get tough.

SOMETHING TO THINK ABOUT

When a work unit is accused of poor work, it attacks the reputation and self-esteem of each employee in it. If the accusation turns into a poor reputation, the employees' self-esteem may drop sharply. One of your priorities should be to help them increase their self-esteem by demonstrating your confidence in your workers and identifying and praising (on the spot) every improvement they make.

1–9 THE PROBLEM

Your employees are openly resentful of a newer employee you've just promoted to a senior position

THE SCENE

"Does anyone here know anything about the problem we're having with Mason Brothers?" you ask in a staff meeting.

"Why don't you ask Petra?" is the sarcastic reply. "She obviously knows everything that goes on here."

You bite your tongue to keep from replying sharply, but this is just one comment of many. You promoted Petra to a senior job in the work unit only a few weeks ago, even though she has been with the organization for less than a year. The employees who've been there longer—and that's most of them—are openly resentful of her promotion. The resentment is so strong that it's beginning to affect productivity.

POSSIBLE CAUSES

You've violated the group's expectations for who should get promoted.

All groups have "norms" for who should get ahead. If there are few opportunities to get ahead in the unit, these norms become even more important.

Your employees may believe she doesn't know the job well enough.

In other employees' eyes, it often takes a long time for an individual to "prove" himself or herself on the job. Your workgroup may think she hasn't been there long enough.

You may have promoted her for the wrong reasons.

These include a personal friendship with Petra or liking for her as a person without regard for how well she performs, or to meet EEO goals.

Hint: Whenever you decide to take an action that isn't what your employees expect, be prepared for an adverse response. That doesn't mean you shouldn't take the action, it just means you need to think about how you'll explain the action to your workgroup in advance of their asking.

CURES

If the basic reason is your employees' expectations:

This is a common situation in all organizations. If promotions are few and far between, most employees expect them to go to the experienced, proven employees. There is a sense that employees have to "pay their dues" before they can get ahead.

If you made your choice carefully (and there's no excuse if you didn't), stick by it. Some of the resentment is meant as pressure to get you to change your decision. Make it clear that you won't, that you fully support her.

Make sure that you have clear performance-based reasons that you can explain to your workgroup for Petra's promotion. It's important to reward those employees who are able to learn new jobs quickly and take on additional tasks without detriment to the work they're already assigned. Let your workgroup know what makes Petra stand out from the others. Then, if your budget will allow, offer incentives for others who learn to perform to the same high standards. Either a promotion to a more responsible, diverse position or an award for high-level work can serve as an incentive to others. Make Petra's achievements a model to which other employees can aspire rather than a prize that only one person can win.

Help Petra be successful quickly. If the position she's been promoted to is basically an extension of the work she was doing before, this may be easy. If there's a longer learning curve, you'll have more of a problem. Even in this situation, you can assign her projects that she can handle most effectively. Make sure she's a success and that the other employees know it.

Let them see her *demonstrate* her successful performance though; don't preach to them about how well she's doing. Just as a picture is worth a thousand words, Petra's successful performance will be much more persuasive than your words of praise. Your workgroup will see for themselves that she was the right choice for the promotion, and they won't hear your "I told you so"—whether you say it out loud or not.

If they believe she doesn't know the job well enough:

As in the first situation, the keys here are making sure your workgroup knows why Petra was promoted and helping her become successful in the new job as quickly as possible.

For many jobs, especially in a period of downsizing, it's more important to be flexible, versatile, and a quick learner than it is to know the details of the work. General problem-solving abilities are often more critical than in-depth knowledge of a specific subject area. If that's true for your jobs, Petra's selection wasn't based that heavily on how well she knew the job. It was based on how quickly she could master it and then move on to other assignments.

That's not what an employee wants to hear who's been in the same line of work for 10 or 15 or 20 years and then was passed over for promotion in favor of a newcomer. But once he gets past his anger and resentment, he may actually learn more about how to operate in today's work environment than if you'd talked to him about it. And today's environment is definitely *not* the one he entered when he came to work a decade or two ago.

As before, help Petra be successful quickly to demonstrate to the workgroup that she was the right choice. This doesn't mean doing her work for her or giving her simpler jobs so she'll look good. You promoted her because she was good; now give her the support she needs and challenge her to perform.

If you did promote her because of favoritism or other nonperformance reasons:

It's probably too late to change the action, so you'd better do whatever you can to make Petra successful.

And it would be a really good idea if you learned from the situation and never let it happen again.

SOMETHING TO THINK ABOUT

All work units develop their own "norms" about who should get promoted and why (and about who should get awards and why). If you're going to change them, lay the groundwork for your action in advance.

In this situation, it would have been helpful for you to have identified the qualities you wanted in the senior position loud and clear *before* you filled the job. That way, all the employees who wanted a shot at the promotion would know what was expected of them. And if Petra was the one best suited, you'd have a clear rationale for her promotion.

chapter two

TROUBLESHOOTING PROBLEMS CAUSED BY TODAY'S SOCIAL ENVIRONMENT

2-1 THE PROBLEM

An employee brags to others (falsely) that she's your lover

THE SCENE

You sit dumbfounded as Sheila Smith, another manager and a friend of yours, walks out of your office. She's just told you that Alice McKenzie, one of your employees, is hinting to others that she's having an affair with you. You're sure you haven't done anything that she could have interpreted as an advance.

POSSIBLE CAUSES

Alice may be more immature than you had realized and is looking for attention.

She may have found that claiming to be her manager's lover gets her attention she needs but can't get otherwise.

She may be setting the stage for a sexual harassment charge if you try to deal with her poor performance.

She may be a poor employee, but nothing says she has to be dumb, too. She may believe that if she can get enough people believing the story, she can prevent you from doing anything about her performance. If you don't act quickly and well, she may be right.

She may also be setting the stage to try to trade sexual favors for advancement.

She may have decided that since her performance won't make points with you, setting you up for an affair might.

Hint: Even though you're innocent, this is an extremely serious situation and a very sticky one to deal with.

CURES

No matter what the cause is:

Go to your boss immediately and tell him or her the situation. Ask your boss to help you with rumor control.

Talk to someone in your firm's EEO office. Take your boss with you if he or she is willing to go.

Schedule an appointment with Alice. *Do not* meet with her alone; have another woman with you. (If you need to keep counseling her about performance, make sure you do it where someone else can see the two of you at all times.)

Confront Alice with what you've been told. If possible, have Sheila or someone else with firsthand knowledge with you. (You may want to have someone from the EEO office there also.)

Don't let yourself become emotional. Confront her with the situation and let her know how serious it is. Give her a chance to explain herself.

If she's apparently doing it from immaturity:

Evaluate very carefully whether she's salvageable as an employee. How honest is her response? Is she willing to correct the damage immediately?

If she seems worth saving, make the terms of it clear. She must agree to tell the truth immediately and to work on her performance. She must also understand that if anything like it happens again, she'll be dismissed—period.

If there's any question at all about her salvageability or honesty, give her the opportunity to resign and terminate her if she doesn't.

If she's apparently doing it to set you up:

Be prepared for a rough session, perhaps even a rough few days or weeks. If she was willing to lie originally to get what she wanted, she'll be willing to keep on lying.

Before things are over, the whole issue may depend on your demonstrated integrity. If you've been straight with female employees in the past, it will pay off now. If you've had serious complaints before—even if they've not been proven—you're in deep trouble now.

The organization may believe your story but still want to settle with Alice to prevent notoriety. Try to prevent any settlement that would make it sound as if you had done something improper.

If she may also be setting the stage to try to trade sexual favors for advancement:

This may be very difficult to spot. After all, if you're sitting with someone else, she'll hardly make overtures to you there.

Think about her actions over the past few weeks and observe her carefully for a few days. Is she doing anything that might be interpreted as coming on to you? Have you perhaps been overlooking it, or been flattered even though you've not responded?

If she is dropping subtle hints, you need to respond to them, clearly and cleanly. You don't have to be harsh or angry; just make sure she gets the message.

Now's a good time to think about your relationships with your women employees in general. Have you been doing anything that might encourage Alice or any others to think you might be interested in a physical relationship? If you have, this would be a dandy time to stop.

If you did make any advances to Alice that others saw or know about:

Salvage as much as you can from the situation. If you keep a supervisory job, you'll probably be lucky.

SOMETHING TO THINK ABOUT

It's often tempting to "kid around" with attractive, willing employees. Sometimes it's tempting to go further than that, particularly if the other party seems agreeable. Just remember that there are "Alice McKenzies" out there, and if your reputation is a little tarnished before she shows up it will be midnight black when she leaves.

This is written as though you're male and "Alice McKenzie" is female. That's not at all necessary. Nor is it necessary that you be of the opposite sex. The pattern and the dangers are the same no matter the sex of the participants.

2-2 THE PROBLEM

An employee tells you that another employee (one of your best) is using cocaine on the job

THE SCENE

You sigh dejectedly. Tom Vasary has just told you that Wilson Edwards is using cocaine on the job. You don't want to believe it, but Wilson *has* been acting differently lately. Maybe he really is a user.

POSSIBLE CAUSES

Tom is trying to discredit Wilson for some reason.

With today's emphasis on drugs, Tom may have decided to use the story to get rid of Wilson or settle an old score with him or . . .

Tom is being honest but is mistaken about what he saw.

Again, with the emphasis on drugs, people may see abuse in innocent situations. Mistaken or not, their perceptions have to be dealt with.

Wilson is using cocaine or some other illegal drug on the job.

Of course, this is the worst situation. It's hard to prove it, but absolutely essential to stop it.

Hint: Your natural tendency may be to delay dealing with the situation. After all, you don't really know. *Don't* put it off. If Tom was mistaken, you need to get the situation cleared up as quickly as possible. If he wasn't mistaken, every day you put it off makes the habit more dangerous to Wilson and increases the prospect that he will begin to be a performance problem.

CURES

No matter what the cause is:

Question Tom in detail about just what he saw. If there's any doubt, ask why he thinks that what Wilson was doing was using cocaine. Be careful; you need to communicate to Tom that you need these facts to act on the situation—and you're not trying to put him on the spot.

If possible, talk to one or two employees who you believe will level with you. Have they noticed anything unusual where Wilson is concerned? Are they perhaps worried about him? This will be awkward. It will require great tact on your part. Your employees must trust you for this to work, and you must make it clear you're doing this because of your concern for Wilson. But do it. The penalty for not doing it is too great.

If they're sure that Wilson is clean, check to see if anyone knows why Tom might want to discredit him.

If you're not absolutely sure that Tom was distorting the situation, talk with Wilson. You don't have to identify your source, but tell him what you've heard. Be prepared for him to react emotionally, no matter what the situation is. Stick with it until you find whether or not he has a fully believable explanation.

If Tom is apparently trying to discredit Wilson:

You have a sticky situation on your hands. If you have clear evidence that Tom was lying, take disciplinary action against him for defaming an employee. (You can find some more guidance for this situation in Problem 7–4).

If you don't have good evidence, follow the guides in the next few paragraphs.

If Tom appears to have just been mistaken about what Wilson was doing:

Call Tom in and tell him what Wilson's explanation was (if an explanation is necessary). Let him react to that.

If Tom reacts with relief (or another appropriate response), thank him for sharing his concern with you and counsel him gently on being careful about what he says.

If Tom reacts defensively, try to find the reasons for his defensiveness. For instance, he may feel you're attacking him and trying to protect Wilson. Or he may be reacting to your having caught him at trying to discredit Wilson. Counsel him strongly on being careful about what he says about others.

If it appears that Wilson may be using cocaine or a similar illegal drug on the job:

Tell your boss about the situation immediately.

Contact your company's employee assistance program (EAP) manager, or whoever is responsible for assisting with employees who have problems. Ask for his or her advice and follow it. Also find out from that person exactly what your firm's policy is in regard to employees who possess and/or use illegal drugs on the job.

If you don't have enough evidence to confront Wilson, make it a point to have contacts with him throughout the day. Does his mood change significantly? Does he sometimes act secretively? See that your EAP manager knows about anything significant.

If you believe that Wilson is abusing an illegal drug, don't give up until he seeks help or you have to separate him for using or for poor performance.

SOMETHING TO THINK ABOUT

In a situation such as this, you need to be sensitive, alert, and forceful. On the one hand, if Wilson does have a problem the best thing you can do for him, yourself, and the company is to get him to seek help. On the other, you can't take formal action unless you get usable evidence that he's breaking the law, or his performance becomes unacceptable.

Be patient but persistent. Cocaine addiction is a powerful, destructive force.

2-3 THE PROBLEM

An employee complains that her team leader is sleeping with another employee

THE SCENE

Jenny Critchlow leaves your office looking relieved, while you sit looking at your desk as if a bomb had just dropped there. And in a figurative sense, it had. Carol Kadenski, one of your best leads, sleeping with another employee! How could she risk everything like that? Her great work record, a good chance at the next promotion—all for some fling.

Well, now you know, and your employees know you know, so the monkey's on your back.

POSSIBLE CAUSES

Why Carol is having an affair with another of your employees isn't particularly important here.

It's not even entirely relevant whether she'll admit the affair or not. But there are some questions you need answers to in deciding how to solve this problem:

- Is the person Carol is sleeping with one of her employees, or is it someone in another group? Affairs between leads or supervisors and subordinates require significant intervention—both because of the possibility of coercion in the relationship and because of the possible effects on the lead or supervisor's other employees.

- Particularly if the person she's sleeping with is on Carol's team, do other employees in the unit feel they've been harmed by the affair? Is Carol giving preferential treatment to her lover—either tangibly in better ratings, bonuses, and promotions or less visibly in better assignments, better work space, time off?

Hint: Many companies have specific policies about relatives, including husbands and wives, working together. Fewer have policies about affairs between coworkers. If your company has such a policy, your task is much easier. Explain to Carol what the rules are and give her an alternative: either she fixes the problem—or you will. Then follow through.

CURES

If the person sleeping with Carol is someone who works for her:

Let Carol know immediately that you're aware of the situation. If she denies that she's having an affair with anyone on her team, tell her that her employees are concerned enough that even the *perception* that the relationship exists is causing problems.

Decide whether you need to move Carol or her lover so they're no longer in a superior-subordinate relationship. This isn't always necessary, and it's not always the best solution—but it always needs to be considered. If Carol's people believe they've been harmed by her affair, it's essential.

If Carol's people have been harmed, that is a serious mishandling of her supervisory authority. You'll need to consider whether to take some further action against Carol, including moving her out of supervision/lead duties altogether or firing her.

Make sure you let Jenny Critchlow know that you checked out her concerns and acted on them. It may not be appropriate to tell her specifically what you've done about Carol, but she does need to know that you've responded to her.

If the person Carol is sleeping with is not in her unit:

Consider whether any action is required at all. If the person Carol is sleeping with isn't in her unit, the relationship probably isn't hurting the work or the employees, and if they're being discreet (so there's no harm to the organization's reputation), you might not have any reasonable basis for doing anything. (Of course, if there's a company policy on the subject, follow it.)

Any action should start with telling Carol about the report you've received, without revealing the source of the information. Encourage her to reconsider whether the affair is in her best interests—or her lover's—and counsel her to be discreet if she decides to continue the affair.

If Carol denies the affair, tell her that perceptions can be just as damaging as real events and, again, counsel discretion.

Whenever there is any hint that Carol has misused her authority (for instance, using her position or favors she might award or deny to coerce her lover's cooperation), strong measures are in order (see above).

SOMETHING TO THINK ABOUT

One of the essential ingredients in a successful superior-subordinate relationship is trust. This situation is a particularly delicate one because it acts specifically to undermine that trust. Your primary aim in solving this problem is to set up an environment in which that trust can be rebuilt—either between Carol and her employees or, if that relationship is beyond repair, between the unit and its new lead.

2-4 THE PROBLEM

An employee accuses another employee of racism or sexism

THE SCENE

"Mr. Jones, I know that you haven't had many women employees here, but that's no excuse. Conrad has been discriminating against me."

"How?" you ask.

"He always gives me the dirtiest assignments," Madeleine replies. "When I ask him for help, he tells me to get it on my own, but I hear him explaining to all the men just how to do things. He's made two notes in my file this month—for things I couldn't do anything about. If you don't get him to change, I'm going to have to file a complaint!"

Possible Causes

Madeleine is overly sensitive because she is the only woman in the unit right now.

When you're part of a minority, it's easy to interpret situations as discriminatory, even if no one intends them to be.

Madeleine is a poor or lazy employee who wants an excuse not to have to perform.

It's all too easy to settle for this kind of an explanation, and in most cases it would be the wrong one. But it does happen.

Conrad isn't used to having women employees and isn't treating Madeleine appropriately.

This may be happening even if Conrad has no intention to discriminate at all. He needs educating, quickly.

Conrad really is discriminating against Madeleine because she's a female.

Needless to say, this situation has to be resolved immediately.

Hint: The days of obvious discrimination are almost over. Racism and sexism are more subtle these days. They're almost never overt and easy to spot. But they're often there, and they're just as dangerous and as illegal as they were before. The moral? No matter how clear-cut things seem on the surface, don't throw discrimination out as an explanation until you've looked more deeply into the situation.

Cures

No matter what the cause is:

You have a potentially serious situation on your hands. It's important to find out—quickly—all the facts you can.

Begin by having Madeleine tell you in detail what has happened that she believes is sexual discrimination. Be careful; don't give the appearance of putting her through the third degree. Make it clear that you want the facts so you can investigate what she's telling you. Then get all the facts you can.

If you can, try to observe Conrad for several days to see if he does seem to be treating Madeleine differently from the other (male) employees. Also observe Madeleine herself, to see if she's doing anything that might be causing Conrad's actions.

At some point you'll need to talk with Conrad. How open you are and just how you conduct the conversation will depend on your relationship with him, your confidence in him, and your observation of his behavior.

If Madeleine appears to be a poor or lazy employee who wants an excuse not to have to perform:

Investigate and observe carefully before you reach this conclusion. Ask yourself if it's consistent with Madeleine's performance. If she's new, you may not know. If she's been an employee for long, though, has she always been like this? If not, avoiding work probably isn't the reason for her behavior.

If you're convinced she's trying to find an excuse not to perform as she should, tell her this, make your expectations clear, and then treat her as you would any other employee whose work and/or motivation were questionable. She may file a complaint against you, but you'll just have to deal with that.

If Madeleine seems to be overly sensitive because she is the only woman in the unit right now:

This is another alternative that you should accept *only* when you've checked out all the other alternatives and believe that none of them is true.

Talk with Conrad and, if sensible, other men employees. Explain to them how Madeleine is feeling and ask for their help to make life in the unit easier for her.

Talk with Madeleine. Explain to her all you've done to check out what she said and the conclusions she's reached. Explain that you believe Conrad and others genuinely want to treat her as an equal and that you've asked them to be sensitive to her feelings. Ask her to be understanding. Suggest that any time she believes she's being mistreated by anyone she come talk to you (and if she does, be just as thorough as you were this time).

If Conrad is sensitive and willing to do it, you might include him in the conversation in the preceding paragraph. His assurances to Madeleine might mean more than yours.

If Conrad isn't used to having women employees and isn't treating Madeleine appropriately:

You have a serious situation on your hands, but at least it appears to be unintentional. Act quickly and decisively, but be tolerant and understanding of Conrad (and others, if they're also involved).

Talk clearly and firmly with Conrad. Point out what he's doing. Give him a chance to explain himself and expect that he may be defensive. But this isn't a discussion; your clear objective is to get him to change his behavior. See that he understands this and follow up to see that he has changed.

Tell Madeleine what you've done to investigate her complaint and the action you've taken. See that she understands you believe Conrad didn't do it on purpose, but that you've directed him to change. Ask her to tell you any time he repeats his sexist behavior, and if she does, follow up on it.

If Conrad really is discriminating against Madeleine because she's a female:

Act immediately. If the discrimination is clear and has harmed Madeleine's performance or advancement opportunities, discipline Conrad. If it's just been a correctable irritant—and this is his first offense—counsel him pointedly and tell him exactly what changes you expect. He'll probably be defensive and complain about reverse discrimination. Let him, but make it clear that he's to change, or else.

Follow up with both Conrad and Madeleine to see that the situation is corrected. If Conrad hasn't changed, take whatever action is necessary.

SOMETHING TO THINK ABOUT

Before you begin, make sure you know what equal opportunity laws and your company's own policies require. Once you understand these, think about how you want your unit to operate within the framework they establish.

The preceding analysis and actions above are equally valid whether the allegation is racism or sexism or any other illegal discrimination. Check to make sure you have the facts. If possible, observe. Then take the appropriate action quickly.

Even if you believe Conrad has discriminated, you may be tempted to treat him as though it was unintentional. This may work, but be careful. If you take this course of action, he may not realize the seriousness of the situation. And you may subject yourself to a complaint because you didn't act to resolve the problem effectively.

If there is discrimination, you need to deal with more than this specific occurrence. One solution is to arrange for an experienced facilitator to conduct workshops to help your employees understand the law, company policy, and (perhaps) their own prejudices. If there are pockets of resistance to cooperation and inclusion of all employees, schedule the workshops so that these people are separated from one another and intermingled with employees who are already moving in the right direction.

Above all, fight discrimination through your personal example. If you treat everyone evenhandedly and sensitively and expect each employee to do the same, most discrimination won't occur.

2-5 THE PROBLEM

An employee brings his children to work whenever his babysitter can't take them

THE SCENE

You look up from your papers to see a freckled little face peering around the door frame.

"I know you. You're Saul Freeman's son. Did your dad bring you in to help around the office?"

"Yeah. My babysitter's sick, so Dad said I could come spend the day with him. Whatcha doing? Can I watch?"

Possible Causes

Saul may have his children infrequently and so not have regular babysitting backup arrangements.

Even though Saul's babysitter seems incredibly unreliable, he brings them into the office only every few months—it just seems more often.

Saul may not have adequate arrangements for his children and brings them to work frequently.

If the situation is one that occurs often, or if your work situation is particularly inappropriate for children (for example, because it requires work around machinery or direct customer contact), you'll need to take a much stronger stance with Saul.

Hint: Some companies (although not many) do have specific policies about bringing children into the work environment. Places where children are almost *never* allowed include production lines in factories, warehouse and transportation facilities, health-care facilities, high-security environments, and workplaces that involve regular customer contact, especially in a professional setting. Even offices and retail stores may have specific rules about when and how often children may visit. Check with your personnel department to see if your company has such rules.

Note, too, that many companies now have on-site day care for workers' children. In that case, the company probably does have policies governing children in the work areas—and, for the most part, workers should be able to see their children in the day care facility rather than in the work environment.

Cures

Regardless of the cause:

Whatever your policy or your company's policy about employees' bringing their children to work, whenever children are allowed to visit, you must have a *standard* set of rules for their behavior. Some of the most disruptive children we've seen are the ones who visit least frequently. They roam the halls, walk unannounced into workers' offices, whine for money for the snack machines, and generally disrupt the entire office.

Make clear to your workgroup that, when children are welcome, it's only if they use their "company manners." While we all recognize that children, especially young children, are incapable of acting like little adults, their parents are responsible for ensuring that they cause as little turmoil to the rest of the staff as possible. And keep in mind that not all of your workers will necessarily jump for joy at the idea of little ones prancing through the aisles. Adults who are not accustomed to having children around aren't always prepared for the noise and activity level of even well-behaved children. Your rules should be sensitive to the needs of all your workers, parents and nonparents alike.

Note that we suggested that you have a *standard* set of rules for children's behavior. If you allow some children to roam the halls, but require that others stay in their parents' offices, or if you allow some children to congregate in the snack room, but not all children, you're inviting hard feelings from the parents whose children are excluded. And it's best to let your workers know in advance what your expectations are. That way, parents whose children aren't capable of conforming to the rules will know (we hope) to keep them at home, or at least you can remind them gently when the children cause a nuisance.

If Saul brings his children in only infrequently:

Unless there are specific reasons for *not* allowing Saul to bring his children into the office occasionally (such as those we mentioned above), there's probably no harm done, as long as the children are well-behaved. Let Saul know what your expectations are for children's behavior and how often you can tolerate having the children in the office (and for how long at a time).

How often is too often is a judgment call and is very much dependent on the specific environment in which you operate. In an office setting where workers have their own private work spaces, with few outside visitors or customers, it's probably acceptable to allow school-aged children to come to the office *briefly* every couple of weeks or so. Certainly many children are expected to call their parents when they get home from school, and a visit of 15–20 minutes every few weeks is no more disruptive. However, younger children should be allowed to visit the office only infrequently. Their activity level and the need for more intensive care make their visits much more disruptive.

How long is too long is also a judgment call. In general, we suggest that children be allowed to visit for only an hour or two at a time. On special occasions, such as designated children-at-work days or for the company picnic, longer visits are acceptable. But children tire much faster than adults, and the strain of extended "company manners" is often more than they can handle. Further, you *don't* want to create the impression that the worksite can substitute for regular day care. And extended visits can easily become a substitute for finding more acceptable babysitting arrangements.

If Saul brings his children in fairly frequently:

Talk to Saul about the disruption to the work (his and others') caused by having his children in the office. You can empathize with his babysitting dilemma, yet remain firm on your position that children do not belong at work. Emphasize that, even if his children are well-behaved and relatively self-sufficient, you cannot reasonably draw a line between allowing his children to come regularly to the office and not allowing others to bring their children. Give Saul a deadline to make reliable babysitting arrangements. Explain that, if he's still bringing his children to work after the deadline has passed, you'll have to send him home until he can arrange a suitable alternative. Then follow through.

If company policy allows, and if Saul's work assignments are appropriate, explore with him the possibility of working at home occasionally. If this alternative is a useful one, you'll need to set limits for the amount of time he can work at home (for example, no more than six hours each week) and establish work expectations for his work-at-home assignments. If his work is repetitive, these can be standard expectations (such as seven documents processed for every hour of home work time). If his assignments vary, you'll need to negotiate production requirements for every work-at-home period. (Of course, if Saul is a marginal worker who needs closer supervision even when he's at work, work-at-home is *not* a good idea.)

Something to Think About

Not only child care, but also "elder care," are important concerns to a large percentage of workers. If your company does not have on-site day care facilities, you might want to suggest to the management staff the possibility of arranging a partnership with a nearby provider. This need not involve any outlay of company funds and need not include subsidies for the day care costs. Many providers will be willing to offer at least nominal discounts to your employees in return for your publicizing their facilities in your company newsletter, or providing transportation from the company to the facility, or donating occasional time or talent. This very small investment can give your workers security and peace of mind that will allow them to concentrate on the work at hand, rather than worrying about the welfare of children or parents.

2–6 The Problem

Two new employees speak very poor English

The Scene

"Can't you understand simple English?" George nearly bellows in exasperation.

"I try—I really try hard!" Nguen says, obviously fighting back tears."

"I know you do," George replies, softening. "But we just can't go on having this many misunderstandings. Somehow you and Tvat have just got to learn English quickly, or we're never going to meet our deadlines." He shakes his head and walks away.

Possible Causes

The cause seems simple enough: America continues to receive thousands of new immigrants each year, and many of these immigrants can't speak English effectively. Almost all of them learn English, but in the meantime they have to work, support themselves, and get by in an English-speaking country.

Hint: It's extremely frustrating to try to communicate with individuals who can't speak English, and all too easy to take the frustration out on them. Don't. Immigrants have initiative, or they wouldn't have uprooted themselves to come to this country. Most of them are hard-working and will turn into productive citizens. When you feel the frustration of the language problem, it may help you to keep in mind what the ultimate payoff will be. And it may not take that long for the payoff; it's remarkable what good English many immigrants speak within 18 months or two years.

CURES

Help them learn English:

Of course, you can encourage them to study English formally. Your organization may even permit them to take time off from work to do so. Support their study of English in any reasonable way you can. But that's just part of the solution.

What else can you do? Have the two of them work together and make them responsible for helping each other understand the English they read and hear. Being able to translate English terms and ideas to and from their native language will help ease the transition. But make it clear that they are to use English and that the goal is to learn it as quickly as possible.

Some of the individuals in your workgroup may have a better "ear" for language than others. They can understand heavily accented language better than others and communicate back more clearly. If possible, have them work with Nguen and Tvat. It may lower everyone's frustration level and speed up their learning English in the process.

You should also maintain close contact with them. In all probability, they came from a culture where superiors were deeply respected and looked up to (no matter how anyone really felt about them). If they know that you care about them and want them to adapt quickly, it will strengthen their resolve not only to learn English but to fit into the workgroup.

Interact with them patiently and kindly:

You and the rest of the workgroup won't be able to take all of the pain away as your new members learn English—either for you or for them. But you can prevent unnecessary pain and frustration. Encourage all your workers to vent their emotions to you, and not take them out on each other. Be prepared to be a peacemaker much more often than you're accustomed to for a while.

You and every member of the workgroup can take one step that will dramatically influence the speed with which your new members learn English and fit in. You can recognize every improvement each one makes toward that goal. At first it may be a small thing, such as learning to pronounce a word correctly. Don't be picky or wait for great improvements. Look actively for small improvements to recognize and then recognize them. This may not sound like much to you and other members of the workgroup, but we promise you that it will bear results well beyond either your expectations or the little effort you spend.

SOMETHING TO THINK ABOUT

As has been said so many times, we are a nation of immigrants. When you confront an immigrant as his or her manager, especially if the individual speaks poor English, your job is clear and simple. Help the individual fit in as quickly as possible, and that means doing whatever's reasonable to help him or her learn English. If it raises the group's frustration level for a short while, let that be and move on.

What do you and the workgroup get for the extra effort? Good new workers. And, if you're really open and flexible, some new ideas that may help make everyone's job easier and more productive. And perhaps some interesting new friends.

2–7 THE PROBLEM

You've just hired a minority group member with very high ratings who turns out to be a poor performer

THE SCENE

You slam down the phone, your suspicions confirmed. Your newest employee, a minority group member who got excellent ratings from his last two supervisors, is a nonperformer. Here you are, in the middle of a production crunch—and now you have to deal with this!

POSSIBLE CAUSES

He may really want to do well and have ability.

But he may be lacking in self-confidence or may never have gotten the proper training. (Individuals in minority groups usually get formal training but may be missing informal "This is how you really do it" training from other employees.)

He may really want to do well but lacks the ability.

He may lack one or more key abilities for this kind of work. Or he may not be temperamentally suited to it.

He may be a poor performer because that's what he wants to be.

He may be content to "get by" with as little work as possible. (Remember, though, this could be a symptom of lack of self-confidence, lack of training, or lack of a key ability.)

Hints: Listen carefully and ask probing questions. An employee's first answers in any confrontation are likely to be very different from his real thoughts and feelings.

If you settle for the surface answers, you won't find the real cause, and that means you won't be able to cure the problem.

CURES

If he really wants to do well and seems to have ability:

Give him routine but meaningful work to do. You might want to assign another employee to help him. See that help is available to him, but also make sure that no one else will do his work for him. If necessary, provide formal or on-the-job training.

Follow up regularly and frequently, anywhere from every day to once or twice a week. Praise his progress and use his mistakes to help him learn.

Gradually increase the variety and difficulty of what he's assigned until he's performing the full scope of his job. This may take weeks or months. It will be easier and faster if the rest of your employees are willing to work with him.

If he really wants to do well but doesn't seem to have the ability:

Make sure that this really is the case. It's painful to admit it if you have lingering stereotypes, but it's a fact of life. If he really wants to do well, don't decide he can't until he's had a real chance.

Give him routine tasks with plenty of help (as in the cure above), until you have a clear idea of what he can do. This may take several weeks or months, if you have the time.

When you're sure he can't do the job, discuss the situation realistically with him. Try to arrange a change to a less demanding job in your unit or elsewhere. As long as he's conscientious, support him in every way you can.

Don't "carry" him, or overrate him in hopes you can pass the problem on. It may solve this particular problem in the short run, but you may not want to live with the long-range consequences.

You can find more guidance for this situation in Problem 4–6.

If he's a poor performer because that's what he wants to be:

Again, make sure this is really the case and not just a cover-up for lack of self-confidence, and so on. Remember to be careful about the stereotypes you may have about that minority group.

Assign him a regular, routine workload, the kind of work his job grade is expected to perform. Give him assistance when appropriate (but make sure no one else does the work for him).

If he gives in and performs, so much the better. If not, follow your organization's procedures for dealing with nonperformers. But deal with him.

If you push him and he threatens to file a discrimination complaint:

Double-check your expectations. Make sure you're *not* treating him differently from non-minority workers.

From a purely practical standpoint, some battles just aren't worth fighting. You may be convinced that what you're doing is right and nondiscriminatory. If you think you're likely to lose in a discrimination complaint or that the fight will tear apart your work unit, you need to think hard about the situation. Will the benefits of success outweigh the negative consequences?

If the benefits outweigh the dangers, confront the EEO issue head-on. Tell him that although he has the right to file a complaint, you're convinced that what you're doing is best for him and for the organization. Then document every action or discussion with him and start building your own case.

And what if you think the outcome isn't worth the effort? You have a serious problem on your hands. You can't let him just "slide by" because of his threat. Our best advice is to keep constant pressure on him to perform at the same level as the others. If that's not practical, see if you can assign him meaningful, useful duties that he can perform. The critical point is to somehow see that he becomes a productive member of your work unit.

SOMETHING TO THINK ABOUT

Other people let the situation develop for months or years; you don't have to resolve it overnight. Be careful and cautious—and *sensitive*—in your approach to it. Just remember that *not* dealing with it will probably create the greatest number of problems in the long run.

No matter how you deal with the EEO implications, don't forget that this is first of all a *performance* problem. The situation will never be completely resolved unless and until the performance issue is resolved.

2–8 THE PROBLEM

Your employees seem to be dressing more sloppily every day

THE SCENE

You walk down the hall, intent on making it to the weekly managers' meeting. But the first person you see is Jerry, striding along in khakis and a sport shirt. Then you pass Rosalinda, wearing jeans and an overshirt.

"Oh, this is fine," you think, "next we'll all be wearing cutoffs and halter tops!"

POSSIBLE CAUSES

Your employees believe that casual dress is appropriate in your work setting.

Maybe your company's policies allow occasional "dress-down" days and they've extended them.

Your employees don't care how they look at work.

This is especially likely if you have a group of relatively inexperienced workers or workers who are new to your work environment. They may not have a clear understanding of acceptable norms.

Hint: This is only a "Wolf" problem in some work environments. If your workers deal with customers or members of the general public in a structured setting, their appearance matters—a lot! What outsiders see in their first encounter with your organization will color all their later interactions for a long time to come.

CURES

If your employees believe that casual dress is appropriate in your work setting:

What have you done to encourage that idea? Do you always wear the kind of clothing you expect your employees to wear? Do you have "dress-down" days often? Are they designated days, or just whenever someone feels like dressing casually?

If the problem seems to be limited to just a few employees, you can deal with each person individually. But if the problem seems to be a common one, you'll need to get the message out more formally.

But that's not as easy as it sounds. Very few companies can get by these days with explicit dress codes. Certainly, you can't require suits and ties (or the equivalent) every day. You'll be deluged with grievances and complaints, or, perhaps worse, completely ignored.

Instead, you need to develop a policy that addresses the overall image you want your workgroup to present to customers and the public. That includes not only dress, but also the way visitors are greeted, the way you'll deal with complaints, and other customer-relations matters. The policy should link the specific behaviors you expect from your employees to the overall image that the company is trying to project. If at all possible, your policy should be coordinated with other groups in your company who have similar customer or public contacts, so your employees aren't singled out with special requirements. Better yet, try to get your company president, CEO, or even department head to sign a general policy statement that applies to all, or a large segment, of the company.

The next step, as always, is to follow through. Make sure that you model the behavior you want your employees to follow. And coach those who seem to have trouble with the new policies, so they understand exactly what's acceptable and what isn't. When you single out for recognition employees who have been outstanding in customer service, be sure that they're also models you want others to follow. If one of your workers did a terrific job in solving a customer's problem but comes to work inappropriately dressed, *and if that matters,* then that worker shouldn't be rewarded.

And, as a last resort, you can consider sending workers home who have real customer or public contact but who report to work too sloppily attired.

If your employees don't care how they look at work:

It's increasingly true that new employees, especially those fresh out of school, have often not learned basic workplace skills. These include not only how to dress appropriately, but also such basic rules as showing up for work (and on time), doing a full day's work for a full day's pay, letting someone know when you're sick or have an emergency that keeps you from coming to work, and other essential work skills.

But these *are* skills. While many of us learned those skills from our parents or at school, and so seemed (at least in retrospect) to have learned them effortlessly, we also weren't born knowing that it was important to show up for work on time, or that slashed jeans aren't appropriate office attire.

So your task here is simply to teach the new or inexperienced employees what the expectations are for the kind of work your group does. Especially if they do appear to be acting from lack of knowledge rather than from lack of interest in the job, you'll need to be sensitive to the way you approach the subject. Matters of dress and appearance are very personal; criticisms in these areas are often much more crushing than criticisms of the work itself.

Talk separately to each of the employees who's dressing inappropriately. Explain the image the company needs to project and how that image is made up of many components: the way you address customers (for example, "Ms. X" versus "Ann"), the way you respond to their questions and complaints, whether you are outgoing or reserved in your approach, as well as the way company representatives dress. For each of those components, describe your expectations and how those expectations contribute to the company's overall image.

In most cases, that simple explanation will be enough. If it's not, coaching and reminders should help. But if you encounter workers who take pride in not conforming and refuse, by words or actions, to dress appropriately, you should deal with them as you would with any other performance problem. The problems in Chapters 7 and 8 can give you some ideas.

SOMETHING TO THINK ABOUT

Because dress and appearance are so personal, it's a good idea to limit your dress requirements to those situations where it really does matter. Some studies have shown that workers actually perform more productively when they can dress casually and comfortably, rather than in conformance with some standard. And if you limit your requirements to situations where there's a clear link between the company's image and its performance with customers or the public, you're more likely to get willing compliance rather than grumbles and workers' testing the limits of what's appropriate. The payoff will be much more clear for them and for the company.

2-9 THE PROBLEM

Your employees complain that work isn't fun

THE SCENE

"What?!" You spin your chair around and look at Kevin and Andrea.

"We thought we owed it to you to tell you," Kevin says. "Work here just isn't very much fun. Most of the time, it's a drag. And we really don't like that. I'm not sure yet, but a couple of us are seriously considering quitting—including her." He jerks his thumb at Andrea, who nods. "I don't know if you can do anything, but at least we told you."

You sit open-mouthed as he and Andrea walk out.

POSSIBLE CAUSES

Kevin and the others have unrealistic expectations for work.

Business magazines and books often quote managers, even CEOs, who say that work should be fun. So, new workers expect that it will be.

They miss the socializing they've been used to on other jobs.

Many of the companies that offer temporary, low-skilled jobs to teenagers—fast-food chains pop to mind here—emphasize the social interactions on the job. When these teenagers move into permanent jobs, they often expect the same camaraderie there. Often, they don't find it.

Their jobs are truly boring.

"Generation X" individuals have MTV and Nintendo; they absolutely hate to be bored.

Hint: As much as it may surprise (and perhaps even irritate) you, many workers today expect their jobs to be fun. Regardless of which of the causes above is creating the problem, you must deal with their expectations.

Note also that none of the causes rules out any of the others.

CURES

If Kevin and the others have unrealistic expectations for work:

We list this first because we expect that it is the conclusion you're most apt to jump to. And it may be right. But we hope you won't jump to it until you've at least considered the other two causes. You can perhaps do something about them. You can't do much about this one.

If their expectations really are unrealistic, the best you can do is to attempt to help the individuals become more realistic about what's available in the job market. If they're unskilled or semi-skilled, most companies aren't going to worry about whether they're having fun or not. They're going to hire them, keep them as long as they want to work under the company's conditions, and then replace them when they leave in a few weeks or months.

As part of this, you can help them understand the real problems that individuals with low skills have and that the most reliable way to avoid these problems is to learn marketable skills. Being a computer operator, a medical technician, or a legal assistant won't guarantee anyone a fun job. But it will increase their control over their work—people *need* their skills—and let them have some meaningful choice in where they'll work and what they'll do.

If they miss the socializing they've been used to on other jobs:

Many companies with low-skilled jobs intentionally make up for low pay and even poor working conditions by not only permitting but encouraging workers to socialize on the job. Often, individuals form very close friendships on the job. Some companies sponsor bowling leagues and softball teams. Done right, this creates a work environment in which individuals with low skills, and compensated at comparably low levels, choose to remain on the job for years.

Listen carefully to Kevin, Andrea, and the others. Is this what they're really saying, or is it at least a big part of it? If so, what can you do about it? Is the group's work low-skilled? Then can you arrange it so that individuals can have social contact with one another while they're doing it—without reducing productivity? Do it.

But you may not be able to permit much socialization. In this case, your basic strategy is to be very careful about the people you hire. Make sure they understand that they won't have much social contact on the job. If you communicate this clearly and they understand it clearly, you will at least have workers who will be willing to work without the chance to socialize. They will probably remain on the job longer and be at least somewhat more satisfied than Kevin and Andrea.

If their jobs are truly boring:

Many jobs are simply boring in their current form, but what can you do about that? You can help workers develop more realistic expectations, hire workers who understand the work is boring and are willing to do it, and attempt to let workers socialize on the job as much as possible. Each of these will help, and all of them are relatively short-term solutions.

There are other solutions. Here are a few:

- When organizations understand and practice Total Quality Management (TQM), they normally make jobs more interesting for their workers, particularly if they're willing to let workers "own" (have full authority over) their work processes.

- Organizations that can effectively use self-directing work teams often make work far more interesting at the operating level. Team members often learn and use new skills and get the opportunity to work together to solve problems.

- When supervisors are willing to train workers fully and then delegate fully to them, they help make work more interesting for them.

None of these really make work "fun," but they do help to make it interesting, and for most people an interesting job is as good as a fun one. And very often it pays better. Check with your manager, the human resources department, or anyone else who might have some answers to see if your company uses TQM or self-directed workgroups. If so, you may be able to implement it in your workgroup. If not, see if you can make the workgroup's jobs more interesting by using effective training and effective delegation.

SOMETHING TO THINK ABOUT

First-level managers need to understand the work they supervise in depth, including understanding the kind of workers who will perform the work with the least strain. If your work is truly boring, hire people who're willing to do boring work for months or years. On the other hand, if your work can be made more challenging, reorganize it and find the people who want more of a challenge.

You probably know this by now. Just in case you don't, let us state it: People are very different from one another in what turns them on from nine to five. There are no universal motivators at work, no matter what the proponents of the current fad want you to believe. In general, you will come out best if you make your work and your work environment as interesting as possible. Do that to the extent you can, and be realistic about what you can do. Then hire people who want to do that kind of work and supervise them as well as you can.

chapter three

TROUBLESHOOTING PROBLEMS CAUSED BY THE PERSONAL LIFE OF AN EMPLOYEE

3–1 THE PROBLEM

An employee has serious health problems

THE SCENE

Gloria Singer, one of your most experienced employees, just confided to you that she has a serious illness. She's been absent for days at a time; even when she comes in she doesn't perform as well as she used to. Sometimes you wonder if there's a point in her being there at all, but she's not so sick you can justify sending her home. Your boss is pressing you for the assignments Gloria usually does, and other employees have begun to complain about having to cover for her.

POSSIBLE CAUSES

She may have a serious illness from which she'll recover.

There are many illnesses that are very debilitating, but from which individuals do recover.

She may have a serious illness that won't get better.

This is a real possibility and a very different problem from a short-term illness.

She may be trying to hide other problems.

She may be covering up for serious family troubles, severe depression, or substance abuse. People are often embarrassed by situations such as these and find it easier to pretend they're physically sick.

Her doctor may limit what she can do.

This will limit what she can contribute, no matter how much she wants to do her job.

Hint: Be careful not to discuss her problem with other employees or to make a point of treating her "special." If she told you about her illness in confidence, respect that confidence.

If you need to talk to someone, talk to a health professional or your organization's employee assistance program counselor.

CURES

If the illness is a legitimate, long-term one:

Work out with Gloria how much work she can do and a reasonable reduced-hours schedule that you're both confident she can meet.

Identify the specific job tasks Gloria will keep and which ones she will give up (even if temporarily). Reassign the tasks she's giving up to other employees or hire a partial replacement (temporary help, part-time employees, and the like) if company policy permits.

Establish a regular schedule (maybe once every month or two) for you and Gloria to discuss her condition again and make any adjustments (upward or downward) in her work schedule.

Help Gloria identify any sources available that might help her make up her lost income (disability benefits, employee assistance program, and so forth).

If the illness appears to be a cover-up for another problem:

Insist on talking personally with her doctor; don't accept a written statement.

If there really is another problem, insist that she get help for it. If your organization has an employee assistance program, offer it to her. Don't let her continue on as she is. If she gets help, assist her in any reasonable way back to full performance. If she doesn't get help, insist that she perform fully or else.

If the illness is short-term:

Insist that she not work unless her doctor clearly okays it. She should do whatever is necessary to help herself recover.

Explain the situation to the rest of your employees and ask them to help carry her workload for a short while. Follow up regularly—every week or so—with Gloria and, if necessary, her doctor. Make sure that she's recovering as expected. If she's not, look at the first alternative above.

SOMETHING TO THINK ABOUT

If the employee has been a good, productive worker, you have an obligation to treat her as compassionately as possible. On the other hand, she has the obligation both to be completely honest with you and to take the responsibility for her recovery.

3–2 THE PROBLEM

An employee appears to be under the influence of alcohol or drugs on the job

THE SCENE

Ben Morgan, your lead technician, pokes his head in your office door, whispering, "Boss, can you come here a minute? There's something I want you to see."

You follow Ben quietly, pausing at the corner of the open office area.

"Watch Leo," he says. "See how loud and talkative he's being on the phone? A few minutes ago he said something to Krista and actually giggled. *Leo!* He's been acting strange ever since the last break, about an hour ago. Donna said his eyes are kind of glazed, and, look—he's drenched with sweat. I think he's on something, but I thought you'd want to handle this one!"

POSSIBLE CAUSES

There are a number of reasons why employees may appear to be under the influence of alcohol or drugs on the job, but none of them have much to do with the steps you need to take immediately. They *will* affect the way you follow up after this incident is over, but your first concern must be for the impaired employee—for his or her well-being and safety and for the well-being and safety of the rest of your employees.

There's only one piece of information you need immediately: You need to decide if this employee really is physically or mentally impaired, whether by drugs, alcohol, or some other influencing factor. For the short term, it's the *impairment* that's important. You may know positively that it's caused by drugs or alcohol, but it could be caused by a lot of other things too, including dangerously low blood sugar or a circulatory blockage. Your first course of action is to decide whether there is an impairment, not its cause.

If you decide there is an impairment, and there seems to be no immediate danger to the employee, then you can take the time to figure out if drugs or alcohol are the cause. If they are, then it's also a good idea for you to find out, now or later, through discussions with the employee, *trusted* co-workers, and your own observations whether the employee has a continuing pattern of substance abuse.

CURES

Whenever you suspect that an employee is impaired by drugs or alcohol on the job, there are two things you need to do immediately:

- First, get him out of any situation where there could be harm to the employee or to others. If the employee is working with a piece of machinery, get him off it! If he refuses, make it a firm order—with physical assistance from you or your company's security personnel if necessary. You already have an impaired employee; you don't need to compound the problem by having somebody hurt.

- Second, observe the employee personally. Describe to him the behavior that makes you think he has a problem. Ask if he knows what's causing it. If it's a medical problem not related to drugs or alcohol, he may recognize the symptoms and be able to offer an explanation or a solution.

Important: If the employee is incoherent or displays any of the classic signs of physiological shock, get him to medical help right away. Even if he's drunk or stoned, he may be in physical trauma requiring immediate treatment. This is a situation where it's better to err on the side of caution.

Of course, all this should be done as quietly and with as little fanfare as possible. Although the employee may become confrontational, your calm, rational approach will help keep everyone from getting more upset. As you observe and talk to the employee, don't make accusations. Even if you're sure he's on drugs or alcohol, telling him, "I think you're drunk," is only likely to start an argument.

If you decide the employee is physically or mentally impaired:

Decide whether treatment is necessary immediately, and, if so, make arrangements for the employee to get treatment. In a large company, you probably have some medical staff, and you can escort the employee to them (or call them to your unit). In a smaller company, an urgent care facility is a good place to go if you can't arrange treatment through the employee's own doctor.

If medical care isn't immediately necessary, see that the employee gets home safely and explain to him why he's being sent home.

After the employee returns to work, follow up with him. Explain again what led you to deal with the situation as you did, and if you suspect repeated drug or alcohol abuse, refer the employee to your company's employee assistance program or to a rehabilitation specialist. Document the referral. If this problem persists and you have to fire the employee, the courts may want to know what you did to help him.

If you decide the employee is not impaired:

You need to decide next whether his behavior is unacceptable or just unusual. If it's within the bounds of acceptability, stop there. No further action is necessary. If it's not acceptable, explain to the employee what he's doing wrong, why it's wrong, and if it's not obvious, what he should do differently. Then follow up to see that the problem is corrected.

SOMETHING TO THINK ABOUT

As we say over and over, watch carefully for signs of drug abuse in any performance or behavior problems you face. If you suspect that abuse is there, deal with it quickly. The longer you let an employee continue to abuse drugs, the harder it will be for him or her to stop.

3–3 THE PROBLEM

An employee takes a lot of time off from work because of serious problems in his personal life

THE SCENE

Your heart is breaking for Harley. He and his wife have always been very close, and now she has terminal cancer. You don't have the heart to refuse his requests for time off to be with her.

But you also need him on the job. He's one of your most experienced employees, and the work is falling behind because of his absence. You don't know how much longer you can take not only his absences but his reduced efficiency when he is at work.

POSSIBLE CAUSES

It doesn't require much speculation to see what the cause is. Grief at the thought of losing a loved one is one of the most universal human emotions. It's also one of the most powerful, and frequently disabling to those who experience it.

CURES

For this situation:

It would be wonderful if we could give you an easy answer to the situation. We can't.

We can tell you that becoming angry or impatient with Harley won't work. He knows the problem he's causing you—he probably feels guilty about it. But none of that helps assuage his grief.

Be as supportive as you can. Grief is emotionally very draining. Support from people who care eases the pain and helps an individual cope more effectively with his or her situation.

There are several actions you can take that may help both Harley and the work situation.

- First, very strong emotion—of any kind—is often very disorganizing. (Think, for instance, of how you responded to things the last time you were extremely happy or extremely sad.) It may be useful to insist gently that Harley set a regular schedule, if possible, and follow it. This may help him be more available for work and to concentrate more effectively on work when he's there. It may also help him deal with his grief, by giving him some basic structure he can depend on.

- Another possibility, if the work situation and Harley's frame of mind permit, is to let him do some work at home. You have to be careful about this, of course—he may be even less able to concentrate at home than at work. But if he can concentrate and produce an adequate quantity of satisfactory work, it may help both of you to let him work some at home. If you try this, you should agree in advance on what he's to accomplish and how much time you expect him to take.

- If the illness is a very lingering one, you may have to look at giving Harley an official leave of absence. This permits you to replace him temporarily with someone who can produce the work you need, but the job is there for Harley when he's ready and able to return.

For similar situations:

You have basically the same situation when an employee has to stay home often with a chronically ill child or parent, or otherwise keeps losing time from work because of a demanding personal situation.

- The "work-at-home" solution may be a good one in many of these situations (if your company permits it). A mother who has to take care of a sick child, for instance, may still be able to put in almost a full eight hours of work.

- If that won't work, you may be able to divide the work between the employee with the problem and another employee. Another employee could share the work, and they could get together periodically to review their progress. (You can see how this could be combined with the work-at-home alternative.)

- As we have suggested, the length of the situation is a critical factor. If it's going to be short, you can afford to make significant accommodations to the individual. If it's going to drag on, your alternatives will be fewer. No matter how long it will be, give the employee every consideration you can.

SOMETHING TO THINK ABOUT

When an employee has a serious personal problem, be available to listen to him. Don't begrudge him the time he needs to talk about it. But *don't* give him "pep talks" or try to talk him out of his emotional responses. He needs companionship and compassion—not advice.

3-4 THE PROBLEM

An employee comes to work frequently with alcohol on her breath

THE SCENE

"Whew! You don't want to get downwind of Carla," remarks Jane to Leila, one of her coworkers.

"Is this the first time you've noticed?" replies Leila. "For months, she's been coming back from lunch reeking like a brewery. Somebody ought to say something to her, but it's not going to be me!"

This isn't the first time you've heard this conversation; only the speakers have changed. Everybody seems to have noticed Carla's luncheon habits. But what can you do? Isn't it Carla's business what she does on her own time?

POSSIBLE CAUSES

Carla may just enjoy having a drink at lunchtime.

It may not affect her performance, and while her coworkers may discuss her habits among themselves, it may not impair her relationships with them.

Carla may enjoy having a drink, with no impairment of her performance, but the obvious odor of alcohol may put off some of the people she deals with at work.

Carla may come back from lunch under the influence of alcohol—to the point where it impairs her ability to concentrate and to handle her work assignments.

CURES

If Carla is not impaired by her lunchtime drinking, and it seems to have no negative effect on her interactions with customers or co-workers:

It's best to leave it alone. It *is* Carla's business what she does on her own time, unless her off-the-job activities affect her on-the-job effectiveness. If there is clearly no connection, then you have no basis for intervening.

If Carla is not impaired, but her interactions with others suffer:

Take her aside quietly and explain that her relations with customers, or others around her, are affected by the alcohol on her breath. Emphasize that she can do what she wants at lunch—except when her activities interfere with her effectiveness later on. And this does. Explain that the odor of alcohol is offensive to some people and that diminished relationships with customers and co-workers harm her job performance.

Make clear to Carla the possible consequences of not changing her luncheon behavior, whether that's a change of assignment, or disciplinary action, or firing.

Take this opportunity to make her aware that assistance is available if she needs it. Refer her to your employee assistance program or, if your company doesn't have one, an outside source of help for substance abuse problems.

If Carla's ability to do her work is impaired:

Deal with the problem immediately and firmly. See Problem 3–2 for specific instructions for dealing with employees who are under the influence of alcohol or drugs on the job.

SOMETHING TO THINK ABOUT

Be sure you separate the problem of alcohol on an employee's breath from the completely separate problem of an employee whose level of performance is impaired by alcohol or another drug. While the former may be part of an abuse problem, it need not be, and it requires action whether it is or not.

3–5 THE PROBLEM

One of your employees was involved with another employee and they've broken up, very messily

THE SCENE

Germaine is the last to arrive at staff meeting, and all the places are taken except the one beside Don.

"Well," you say to yourself, "this should be interesting. The hot office romance decays to smoke and ashes. Let's see how uncomfortable it gets in here today."

A pleasant surprise—there are no sharp exchanges and no overt hostilities, but it's obvious that the rest of the staff is on edge, probably because of the blow-up the two of them had just a few days ago. The situation is awkward for everyone. So what happens now?

POSSIBLE CAUSES

As in a few of the other cases we've looked at, it's not necessary here to know what *caused* the problem, but it is necessary to have some information about the situation:

First, are the employees in any kind of superior-subordinate relationship?

If so, look at Problem 2–3 for advice.

Second, does the breakup seem to be affecting the performance of either of the two people involved?

Third, regardless of how well the principals themselves are coping with the situation when they're at work, is it having a negative effect on the rest of your staff?

Do you expect the negative effects to be short-lived and to resolve themselves, given a little time, or do they require your intervention?

Hint: We've said this before, but it bears repeating: You're justified in involving yourself in your employees' personal lives only to the extent that what they're doing *off* the job affects what happens *on* the job. If these two former lovers hurl epithets at one another, slander each other, or worse, when they're not at work, but are models of decorum on the job, then you have *no* basis for getting involved. But as soon as what's happening in their personal lives begins to affect their work, or that of others, you should step in firmly and swiftly.

CURES

If the breakup is affecting the performance of either of the two people involved:

Have a talk with the affected employee, explaining in some detail the deterioration you've noticed in his or her work performance. Let the employee know that you're aware of his or her personal situation and delicately inquire if that situation could be the cause of the performance problems.

Offer to refer the employee to a counselor or to provide other appropriate assistance to help him or her work through the situation. At the same time, make it clear that you expect the performance problems to be corrected. Make it clear that the situation you're concerned about is *not* the breakup, but the deteriorating performance.

If it's appropriate, consider offering the employee a reassignment, permanent or temporary, to allow time for emotions to cool and for the two employees to reach some kind of equilibrium.

If the relationship is having a negative effect on the rest of your staff:

Observe carefully to see whether the actions of the two employees are the cause of the disturbances in your staff, or whether it's the staff's *anticipation* of trouble that's affecting them badly. If the problem isn't due to anything the two employees themselves are doing (or not doing), then you can't hold them responsible. In that case, time and continued civil relations between the parties will probably solve the problem.

If you can attribute the negative effects on the staff to either of the two employees involved in the breakup, then talk to the employee(s), explain what behaviors are causing strained relations among the staff, remind them of their responsibility to establish and maintain effective work relationships, and see that they take whatever steps are necessary to mend the relationships.

SOMETHING TO THINK ABOUT

Several problems in the book deal with strong emotional attachments between employees. One of the problems in any relationship like this is what happens when and if the relationship ends. Keep that in mind whenever you're evaluating the effect of any relationship.

chapter four

TROUBLESHOOTING PROBLEMS CAUSED BY THE CURRENT PERFORMANCE OF AN EMPLOYEE

4-1 THE PROBLEM

An employee has angered a key supplier by his offensive manner

THE SCENE

"Charlie, I can't believe I have anyone who would pull a dumb stunt like that. I can absolutely, certainly promise you it won't happen again. My God, I'm mortified!"

And you are. You slam the receiver down and start for the door. You've known that Art Mayfield wasn't the greatest in the world at dealing with people, but yelling at the manager of Eastern Manufacturing and then hanging up on him is too much.

POSSIBLE CAUSES

Charlie (or someone else at Eastern) did something that provoked Art.

So far, you've heard only one side of the story.

Bad blood has been building between Art and Eastern.

It may be that this is a "last straw" encounter.

Art really did "blow his stack" without reason.

Hint: What Art did was wrong, regardless of its cause. The question isn't whether to take strong corrective action. The question is whether you can remedy the situation short of firing Art.

CURES

No matter what the cause is:

Make sure that your own anger is under control. This is going to be a rough situation, and you need a clear head to deal with it. That doesn't mean you shouldn't be mad. You should, and Art should know it from the word go. But it should be controlled anger. If it isn't, take a walk, kick some file cabinets, do whatever you have to do to get back in control.

Then call Art in. Tell him exactly what you've heard. Don't exaggerate. Don't pull punches. Let him see how angry the call made you. He needs to know that he's in trouble.

Now, here comes the really hard part. Give him every chance to explain his side—and listen, listen, listen. This is hard to do, but in this serious a situation it's absolutely necessary. If the encounter gets too emotional, break it off and get back with Art later.

If someone at Eastern really did provoke Art:

This is where you consider Art's record with the company. If he's been a good worker, and this is the first time something like this has happened, give him the benefit of the doubt. If possible, let him get back with Charlie and mend the situation. You keep close tabs on it, though—both to support Art and to make sure that he's doing what needs to be done.

If Art can restore the relationship effectively, go lightly on him. Perhaps a short, clear chewing out will be enough. But he needs to understand clearly that, regardless of what anyone at Eastern did, his conduct can't be tolerated. If he understands, leave him working with Eastern.

If Art is too involved in the situation, or lacks the skills, you get back with Eastern and Charlie, quickly. If you can do it in person, that's the first choice. If not, get on the phone. See if Charlie realizes the contribution he made to the problem. If he's calmed down and is willing to cooperate, see if you can get him to talk with Art. If they can smooth out their relationship, fine. If they can't, move Art and get someone else to work with Eastern.

If Art won't face the problem and/or can't help you solve it, take strong action. Just what's best will depend on your firm's policies. Suspension without pay, cut in pay, reassignment—any of these might be appropriate.

If bad blood has been building between Art and Eastern:

Art has helped create an extremely serious situation. He should have informed you of what was happening long ago. His not doing so is just as critical as the incident.

Again, take prompt action with Eastern. Try to work with Charlie or anyone else at Eastern to find out what went wrong and remedy it. At this point, you do whatever you have to do to resolve the situation. If Art can be any help, use him, but carefully.

Evaluate your options with Art. Unless there were mitigating circumstances—*very* mitigating circumstances—you can't trust him to deal with suppliers again. If you can find a position where his skills can be used without the danger of alienating others, do so.

Take strong disciplinary action. Regardless of his past record, what he did is indefensible. Your action should communicate that to him, clearly and unambiguously. Whatever happens, he should have the definite feeling that he just barely avoided disaster.

If Art lost his temper and alienated Eastern without reason:

Forget Art for the moment and get back with Charlie. Do *whatever* you must to reassure Eastern that this was an isolated incident, one that won't happen again. Assure them that they won't have to deal with Art again. If necessary, cry real tears and promise them your first-born as a hostage.

Then take care of Art. The basic question is: Has he been so good an employee in the past, and is he apt to be so valuable in the future that he shouldn't be fired?

If you can answer "yes," take forceful action just short of firing him. The action should include moving him into another job, probably one at lower pay.

If the answer isn't "yes," fire him. That may sound inhumane, but it's necessary.

SOMETHING TO THINK ABOUT

A great deal has been made—and justly so—about pleasing customers. Maintaining good relationships with suppliers is only slightly less important. You cannot tolerate employees who do anything less than deal effectively with the firms you depend on for your raw materials.

But suppose you hadn't made this clear to Art? Suppose you didn't take the relationship with Eastern seriously enough? In that case, slack off on Art, he's not the main culprit. Then look in the mirror and decide what kind of action's necessary to shape up the person you see there.

4–2 THE PROBLEM

An employee is new to the workgroup and properly qualified, but is very poorly motivated

THE SCENE

"I just don't understand about Janine," you remark to Harry at lunch. "Loretta over in Stock Accounting said she was her top producer, and Ruben in Inventory Control thought she was great. But as soon as she was transferred over to my shop, she just sat down on the job. She's developing an "attitude" too. I don't need another problem like that, but I also don't know what I can do to get her motivated here."

"Sorry, I can't help you with this one," responds Harry. "But it sounds as if you'd better think of something or things will only get worse."

POSSIBLE CAUSES

Janine may not like the work in her new assignment.

She may have interests or aspirations in another direction and not be interested in the work she's doing now.

She may have been comfortable in her old job and be fearful that she won't perform well for you.

That kind of anxiety drives some people to work harder, but for some people (Janine may be one of them), the normal response is to admit defeat immediately and give up trying.

She may not know how to do the work.

Many people equate ignorance (which is simply not knowing something) with stupidity (or the inability to learn). Fearful that they will appear stupid if they admit they don't know how to do the work, they never tell you what the real problem is. So lack of knowledge *appears* to be lack of motivation.

Hint: Whenever an employee is not fulfilling your expectations for performance in a job, it's very tempting to blame his or her lack of motivation. But many times, apparent lack of motivation masks the real cause. Before you place all the blame for poor performance on the employee, consider what else could be contributing to the problem. Then do what you can to remove those impediments. Your efforts don't let the employee off the hook for improving his or her own work, but they will improve his or her chances of success. And it's much better to salvage a current employee than it is to start all over again with a new, and unknown, worker.

CURES

If Janine doesn't like the work:

Talk to her to find out what kind of work she's most interested in and point out to her those parts of her new job that are most similar to the things she likes to do.

Let Janine know that if she does well in her current assignments, you'll try to arrange for more of the work she finds interesting or help her find a job that's closer to what she's looking for.

Make it clear to Janine that your offers to help her don't substitute for her hard work and diligence in her current job. Be sure she understands that the responsibility for good performance is hers and that she'll still be held accountable for what she does (or doesn't do) in the job she has now, whether she likes it or not.

If Janine is afraid she won't do a good job in her new position:

Talk with her to let her know that you don't expect her to know how to do everything exactly right when she first walks into a new job. Express your confidence in her skills, pointing out that she wouldn't have been placed in the job if you, or your personnel department, didn't think she was qualified.

Make sure Janine gets to know everyone in the new office and has a special introduction to people in other organizations with whom she may have to interact in the course of her assignments.

Encourage her to come to you if there are parts of her job she's not sure how to handle, or identify a coworker who can be a good resource person (especially if you think she feels threatened by having to admit her imperfections to her boss).

Try to structure the job so that Janine's first few assignments are fairly simple ones that will give her an idea of what her job is and how to get things done in your organization without overwhelming her.

Most important of all, give Janine some time. You've told her you don't expect her to know everything right away, so don't act as if every mistake is a major failing. Let her know when she could have done better, but be patient.

If Janine doesn't know how to do the work:

Find out from Janine's previous supervisors, from the personnel department's files, and from Janine herself what kind of work she's done in the past and any training she's had that would equip her to do your job. Identify the skill deficiencies she has that interfere with her performance. To do that, you'll need to keep some records of the things she does right and the things she does wrong. Fairly soon a pattern should emerge that will point to specific areas where she needs improvement.

Check with your personnel department to see if there are any formal classes available that will teach the skills Janine needs. Formal classroom training, if it's directly related to what happens back on the job, is frequently the fastest way to gain knowledge or skills.

Try to identify a "mentor" for Janine to whom she can go when she has questions or problems and who can check her work and help her correct her errors. It's better if the mentor is someone in the organization other than her supervisor or leader so she can feel free to admit problems without feeling threatened.

If there are several parts of the job Janine will need to learn, parcel out some of the work to several other employees and give to Janine first the few things that are *essential* to the job. As she masters those, you can add in the rest later.

Encourage Janine and give her all the positive feedback you can. At the same time, let her know that you *expect* her to pick up on the job and that doing well is ultimately her responsibility, regardless of the amount of assistance you're able to give her.

SOMETHING TO THINK ABOUT

Note that every cure we've discussed begins with a direction like "Talk with Janine . . ." *Whenever* you have a problem with an employee, performance or otherwise, one of your first actions should be to talk to the employee. You may find that the answer is simpler than you'd thought.

4–3 THE PROBLEM

An employee has been an average performer but is slipping to the point that he's now unacceptable

THE SCENE

"Boss, I hate to complain—but I just can't live with this!"

Ellen Wegner has just dumped Ollie Berlin's latest run on your desk. Once again, a high percentage of the sheets are smeared or out of register. Once again, Ollie is going to have to do a job over.

In the last couple of months, Ollie's work has clearly slipped from average to unacceptable. You've been living with it and hoping it would improve. But now you've run out of hope; it's time to do something.

POSSIBLE CAUSES

Ollie has a personal problem that's distracting him from his work.

Some painful situation outside work may be worrying him to the point that he can't concentrate on work.

Ollie may have a physical problem that is preventing him from doing work correctly.

Ollie may be abusing alcohol or another drug, and it's gotten bad enough that he can no longer perform effectively.

Ollie may be "burned out" on his job.

He just doesn't care anymore.

Hint: While the cause of Ollie's poor performance is important, you need to focus your action on the performance itself.

CURES

No matter what the cause is:

You're going to have to talk with Ollie, of course. First, though, you might want to talk with Ellen and other employees who work with him. Anything you can learn from them about Ollie's performance and its deterioration will help.

Then talk with Ollie. Deal with the performance, and be very straightforward with him. You can't accept this level of performance, and he needs to know it. But don't attack him, or be angry with him for it, or threaten him. Just start with the bare fact that his performance isn't satisfactory.

Give him every chance to reply and listen carefully. The more he can tell you about why he's slipping, the better. The reverse is also true: if he evades the problem or can't come up with any reason for it, or if he just makes promises to do better without explaining it, the situation's going to be harder to deal with.

If Ollie seems to have a distracting personal problem:

We deal with these problems in several places, especially in Problem 3–3. Turn to it for suggestions on how to deal helpfully with Ollie.

If Ollie seems have a physical problem that's interfering with his performance:

We also deal with physical problems, particularly in Problem 3–1. This should give you the information you need to deal with Ollie's situation.

If Ollie appears to be abusing alcohol or another drug:

You'll find guidance for this situation in Problems 3–2 and 3–4.

In this case, whether Ollie drinks or uses drugs on the job is only one aspect of the problem. No matter when he's using them, his performance is suffering. You have the right to require him to do whatever is necessary to improve his performance—or else.

If Ollie owns up to his drug-abuse problem, work through your employee assistance program coordinator to develop a plan for Ollie. Every firm has a slightly different approach, and you want to follow yours.

Suppose your company doesn't have a formal program, and there's no one to help you? Many hospitals have rehabilitation units, and someone there will probably be happy to work with you. If the problem is drinking, talk to someone in a local chapter of Alcoholics Anonymous. Somewhere in the community there will be people who can help.

Wherever help comes from, remember this: Insist that Ollie perform satisfactorily—starting now, and without relapse. If he doesn't, "keep book" on him. Document his poor performance. Keep putting pressure on him. The worst thing you can do with an addict of any kind is to make his addiction less painful for him. Keep the pressure up without relief. It's the kindest action you can take.

If Ollie is burned out on the job:

This may be the hardest situation of all to deal with effectively. Job burn-out probably happens to most of us at some time or another. But you can't accept it as a continuing reason for poor performance.

Don't deal with job burnout by blaming Ollie or by trying to "motivate" him out of it. Neither will work very well. You might see some improvement for a little while, and then things will be back just as they were.

One of the first solutions to think of, if it's available, is finding another job that Ollie could be reassigned to. Of course, it would have to be a job that he'd be motivated to do; reassigning him to another job that's equally as boring to him won't help for long.

Another solution might be to add extra duties—more interesting ones—to Ollie's job. This should be done as a reward; he gets to do them *only* if he performs his basic duties well. The result might be both that Ollie performs acceptably and that he produces more work.

Another solution is more demanding, but might be the best one. Do your employees often burn out on their jobs? Are several of the jobs the kind of boring, dead-end ones that produce burnout? If so, can you reorganize your work so that each employee does a greater variety of the duties? If the work is done piecemeal, can you rearrange it so that each employee does all of the steps necessary to produce a final product?

This last approach is called "job enrichment." We don't have room to go into it in greater detail here, but it has produced excellent results in some companies. If it sounds as if it might work for you, find out more about it.

SOMETHING TO THINK ABOUT

It's easy to react emotionally to the *causes* of poor performance, to get angry at an employee who drinks too much or feel sad for one with serious problems at home. As a manager, though, you need to keep focused objectively on the poor performance itself, and to deal with it. In the long run, that's the way you're most helpful to the company *and to the employee*.

4–4 THE PROBLEM

An employee who usually does outstanding work has just fouled up an important job

THE SCENE

"I can't believe this!" you exclaim with dismay. "Clark usually does such a great job on everything I give him. He's the one person I can count on to do things right when no one else knows how. And now this, this, this . . ."

Words fail you. A report due to your boss tomorrow, and what Clark has given you is *garbage*. Well, the immediate problem is to get this fixed so you can present it on time. But next—what to do about Clark?

POSSIBLE CAUSES

Clark may not have understood what you wanted in the assignment.

Especially if Clark is usually a good worker whom you can rely on, you need at least to consider that part of the problem was a failure to communicate.

Clark may not have set his priorities effectively.

He may have had a number of tasks and didn't give this one enough priority to get it done well on schedule.

Clark may have had personal issues that distracted him from performing this assignment as well as the others he's done in the past.

He may have a sick child, marital problems, worries about finances. He may be getting ready to leave for a long-awaited vacation. Your best employees may be able to put those distractions out of mind to concentrate on the job at hand. But not everyone can, and no one can *all* the time.

Clark's performance in general may be slipping, with this foul-up just the first sign you've noticed.

Think about the other things he's done recently. They may not have been this dramatically awful, but have they been up to Clark's usual standard? If not, consider that this may not be a single incident of poor performance, but may be the start of a trend.

Hint: This list doesn't even begin to cover all that could be wrong. Clark could have had too little time to devote to this assignment; he may not have understood what you wanted; he may not have wanted the assignment and saw this as a way to "get back" at you; or there could be even more causes. One thing you can be sure of, though, when an otherwise good employee delivers a substandard product, you need to get to the bottom of the situation fast.

In each case, you have two distinct, and distinctly different problems. The first is the substandard report. The second is the conditions that led Clark to produce it. Each needs to be dealt with, but the underlying conditions are almost certainly more important and more serious than the report itself.

CURES

If Clark misunderstood what you wanted in the assignment:

Ask Clark to tell you what he thought he was assigned to do in this project. Note the areas that differ between his ideas of what the assignment encompassed and what you intended.

For each area of misunderstanding, identify for Clark how the overall assignment would have come out differently if he had done things the way you intended.

Then, for each area of misunderstanding, try to find out from Clark what he thinks you said to him. If you can figure out what you said (or what he thought he heard) that caused the misunderstanding, you'll be better able to avoid a repetition.

If Clark didn't set his priorities effectively:

There are actually two problems here. First, he didn't set the right priorities. Second, he didn't tell you he couldn't produce a quality report by the deadline you set. Both have to be dealt with.

Deal with his failure to set priorities right by reviewing his work with him regularly and helping him readjust his priorities as necessary. Don't redo the priorities for him. Help him go through them and develop the judgment necessary to set them effectively for himself. (If you set them for him, you may have found yourself a job for life.) These sessions should be fairly frequent at first, then further and further apart until they become unnecessary.

Clark's failure to tell you he couldn't produce a quality report on time is a separate problem, and one that's just as serious. Every employee should know that he or she has to let you know *in advance* if a deadline can't be met. No exceptions! Enforce this. But also make sure you listen when they tell you they can't meet a deadline and help them readjust the deadline (or their other priorities). It takes *both* a firm requirement and a willingness to listen.

Give him back his work product and set the priority it should have. Meet with him as frequently as necessary to see that he gets it done.

If Clark had personal problems that detracted from his performance:

Discuss with Clark his *performance* deficiencies. If he offers the personal problems as a reason for his failure on this assignment, offer him your understanding and your help in getting outside counseling or assistance (if he needs it).

Let Clark know that because he's been such a good employee in the past you'll stick with him through the tough times too. But let him know also that there are limits to how much the organization can handle and that you expect him to take responsibility for working his personal problems out so that he can resume his productive role in the company.

Then follow up. If things get better, let Clark know that you've noticed and give him a pat on the back. If things don't get better, make sure Clark knows the consequences of continued poor performance, continue to counsel him, and take action if necessary.

If Clark's overall performance is slipping:

There are a lot of reasons why Clark's overall performance could be deteriorating. See Problems 4–3, 6–2, 6–3, and 6–6 for possible solutions.

SOMETHING TO THINK ABOUT

Performance problems can have many causes. This scenario and discussion illustrate several of the most common ones: misunderstanding requirements, lack of knowledge, and personal problems. If you really want to save a good worker, you'll probably need to help him or her identify what's causing the poor performance. Many times workers themselves don't know what the problem is because they're too close to it. But especially if an employee has been a good worker and begins to have problems, it's important to step in as soon as you see that there is a problem. The more times an employee fails, particularly if he or she doesn't know *why* the failure occurred, the more likely he or she is to get frustrated and give up.

4–5 THE PROBLEM

An employee is new and not doing well, but won't accept help at doing better

THE SCENE

Abel Resnick came to your outfit right out of technical college. He has a two-year degree in drafting, and he seems plenty sharp enough to do the job. He's been with you for almost four months now, though, and he hasn't learned as much about the job as he should. The big problem is that he insists on learning it on his own; he won't let anyone else help him.

Possible Causes

Abel is trying to establish himself in the unit.

New employees often feel they have to prove themselves. Sometimes they do this by refusing to admit they have to learn.

Abel has always had to learn on his own and doesn't know how to accept help gracefully.

The way that the others are trying to help him isn't effective.

They may (or may not) mean to be helpful, but don't do it very well.

Hint: There's one other possibility you need to consider. Abel may not *know* he's not doing well. Sometimes, employees are so engrossed in trying to learn everything at once and are so overwhelmed that they don't know what it is they don't know. So Abel, with his still very superficial understanding of the work, may believe everything is just fine. In that case, your first task is to explain to Abel just what the problems are and that he *does* need help. Maybe then he'll accept the assistance that's been offered and your problem will be resolved.

Cures

No matter what the cause is:

As in so many of the situations a supervisor encounters, you need to talk with Abel and try to find out how he sees the situation. Since he's a new employee, though, he may be very defensive about his behavior. If he is, don't get angry; just deal with him calmly and learn all you can.

You also need to talk with your other employees. How do they see it? Just as important, how do they feel about it?

One other point. In each of the following situations, there's a choice to be made. *You* can always take responsibility for helping Abel. That may solve that problem; Abel may be willing to accept help from you because you're the supervisor. He may feel less threatened by getting assistance from you, or he may feel that he can't refuse it. This isn't normally an acceptable solution for very long; you want him to get used to working with other employees to solve his problems. But it may help him and the group get over an initial impasse.

If Abel is evidently just trying to establish himself in the unit:

Help your other employees understand what's happening. They may feel that Abel "ought" to want help from them. If they do, explain how hard it is for him to ask for it and accept it and why.

Help them become more skilled at offering help in a way he might accept. Offering effective assistance requires interpersonal skills as well as technical ones. They may be doing fine on the technical level but need some coaching to develop their own coaching skills. (The last "cure" in this section has more ideas on this.)

At the same time, try to build up Abel's self-confidence. Assure him that he will be accepted by the group. Suggest gently to him that it's all right to admit he needs help while he's learning the work of the unit.

If Abel has evidently had to learn on his own and doesn't know how to accept help gracefully:

This may seem strange, but it happens. His parents may have felt that he would learn best on his own, or may not have been available to help him. He's always learned by himself. He may even feel that it's wrong or a sign of weakness to have to accept help.

You probably can't change Abel's approach quickly. He's had a long time to develop this trait, and it will change slowly. But it will change, if you and your unit have the skills to help him.

Put your attention on the group. Help them develop a very "low-pressure" approach to helping Abel. If one of your employees is particularly good at this, you might want to let him or her offer most of the help. Remind them that it will take time, but that they probably will see results.

If the group is trying to help him in ineffective ways:

The group may not have the interpersonal or communication skills they need. They may feel that it's Abel's "place" to let them help him, or expect him to ask them. Then, when he won't accept help, they get angry. They may even feel that their own expertise is being challenged.

Obviously, you need to help them deal with these feelings. If they're upset with Abel, they play a part in creating a vicious circle that has nowhere to go but down. You need to work with both Abel and them to reverse this vicious circle.

All of the ideas in the preceeding "cures" may be useful here. But you may need some others. Here are some possibilities:

- Get training for some or all of your employees in how to do on-the-job training. (Get it for yourself, too, if you need it.)
- Help them remember how it was when they were new. If they really understand Abel's anxieties, it will help them be more patient.
- Get them training in communications skills. Maintaining effective communication in a stressful situation is difficult for everyone. Training can help.

SOMETHING TO THINK ABOUT

Your main job here is to help everyone "stay cool" and not overreact to the situation. If everybody accepts the situation without getting emotional, it'll be far easier to resolve.

All the preceding suggestions assume that Abel shows the basic skills and attitudes he needs to be a good employee. In that circumstance, it's best to be patient and help him develop. If he seems to lack the necessary skills and attitudes, though, much less patience is called for. Try to understand him, try to help him, but insist that he put forth the effort to become a good employee. If he doesn't, take action to reassign him to a more suitable job or help him find a job elsewhere.

4–6 The Problem

An employee is new and can't seem to learn the harder parts of the job

The Scene

Rosemarie came to work for you about six months ago. She's a good worker, dependable, friendly, and cooperative, but she consistently messes up your unit's time and attendance records. It shouldn't be that hard—just a few simple arithmetic computations and entries in an automated system—but for some reason Rosemarie just can't get it right. You don't want to have to fire her, but things can't go on like this much longer. Last week two employees were short on pay because of her mistakes.

Possible Causes

Rosemarie may lack basic skills she needs to learn the job.

She may not know basic arithmetic or may lack keyboard skills or knowledge of the automated system. These skills are prerequisite to learning the more complicated time and attendance system, and she'll need the basic skills first.

The tools you're using to teach Rosemarie may not be appropriate for her learning style.

If you're using a manual or written instructions, they may be hard for her to understand. If another employee is teaching her, that employee's explanations may not be meaningful to Rosemarie. You may need to find another way to get the message across.

Rosemarie may not be able to learn this particular task.

She may have a learning problem that interferes with her ability to learn the arithmetic skills or other parts of the job.

CURES

If Rosemarie lacks basic skills she needs to learn the job:

Identify what the skills are that she's lacking. What does she consistently do wrong? For a while, check each step in the process as she completes it. Does she do the arithmetic right? Does she make mistakes entering the information into the automated system?

Once you've identified Rosemarie's specific skill deficiencies, decide the best way to train her in those areas. Your company may have classes in basic arithmetic and keyboard skills or you may have arrangements with a local school for remedial training. Software vendors often provide training on the systems they sell. You may decide that the knowledge Rosemarie lacks is so specific that you can best train her right on the job.

After you've completed the basic skills training, review how the whole job assignment is to be performed so she can see how her new skills fit in.

Follow up. Continue to check Rosemarie's work to see if she still has problems. If the work is not performed very often, she may lose the skills for lack of practice. Consider a job aid she can use to walk her through the process each time she performs. If training and job aids don't help, then look at some of the other possible causes.

If the training method you're using doesn't work with Rosemarie:

Consider some alternative ways of presenting the information. If she's been reading a manual, then do some one-on-one tutoring. If she's been working with another employee, listen to that employee explain the process to you. See if he or she is explaining it well enough that someone not already familiar with the work can understand. Put together a step-by-step instruction sheet. Some people learn better by *seeing* what they're learning; others learn better by *hearing* it. Try to match the learning method to the learner.

If your company has a training department, ask the professionals there to help you figure out the best way to organize and present the material Rosemarie has to learn.

If Rosemarie is finally unable to learn this part of her job:

Decide how important this task is to successful performance in the job as a whole. Is this something you could assign elsewhere without detriment to the job or the efficiency of the organization? If so, consider giving the work to someone else and assigning Rosemarie work where she can make valuable contributions.

If the task is integral to Rosemarie's position, then decide how important Rosemarie is to the company. Is there another job she could be assigned where she could work productively (even at a lower pay rate)? If so, and Rosemarie is someone who's valuable to the company, offer her the other assignment. If she refuses, or if she's not that valuable, then her poor performance warrants termination.

As tactfully and sensitively as you can, explain to Rosemarie why she's being fired. Let her know that you appreciate the good work she's done for the organization and explain why her performance deficiencies require that you terminate her. If she really has been a good, hard-working employee who just couldn't learn the job, offer her the opportunity to resign and work out with her what you'll tell any prospective employers who contact you for a reference.

4-7 THE PROBLEM

An employee meets a deadline by producing a substandard report

THE SCENE

You told Edwina Ellis you wanted the report today, and you got it today. Lot of good that did you—it's going to have to be redone. Superficially it looks good, but the organization is poor and the conclusions aren't well supported. Edwina isn't your strongest employee, but she usually does better than this. So what do you do now?

Possible Causes

Edwina is beginning to slip from acceptable performance to substandard performance.

This may be a result of personal problems, health problems, substance abuse, job burnout—any of a wide variety of conditions.

The deadline didn't give her enough time.

She did her best, but it wasn't possible to get out a quality product in the time she had.

She didn't set priorities effectively.

She may have had a number of tasks and didn't give this one enough priority to get it done well on schedule.

She's angry at you about the deadline, and this is her way of showing you.

She's just waiting for you to complain so she can tell you how unfair (or dumb, or rigid) you were when you forced the deadline on her.

You weren't clear about what you wanted.

All too often, employees produce the wrong product because they didn't understand clearly what was wanted.

Hint: This list doesn't even begin to cover all that could be wrong, though it covers the most likely candidates. One thing you can be sure of, though—when an otherwise good employee delivers something substandard like this just to meet a deadline, you need to get to the bottom of the situation fast.

In each case, you have two distinct and distinctly different problems. The first is the substandard report. The second is the conditions that led Edwina to produce it. Each needs to be dealt with, but the underlying conditions are almost certainly more important and more serious than the report itself.

CURES

No matter what the cause is:

If you're angry, get over it. Then call Edwina in, tell her how dissatisfied you are, and ask for an explanation. *Don't* be judgmental or accusing.

If she feels she has an explanation, listen carefully to it. If she doesn't have a ready explanation, probe a little bit. If the explanation is too glib, probe a little bit. Keep digging, if necessary, until you have a "feel" for the situation.

If she may be beginning to slip into substandard performance:

Look back at Problem 3 in this chapter; it will give you the information you need to deal with this situation.

If the deadline didn't give her enough time:

Here the underlying problem is lack of communication, lack of trust, or both. The first question to be answered is *why* she didn't have enough time. Did you impose the deadline without listening to her objections? Were you afraid she was "padding" her estimate? Did she know she didn't have enough time, but was afraid to say so? It's critical to find the answer.

Once you find the answer, there's much work to be done. You both need to agree that you won't repeat the actions that led to the bad deadline. Then you need to stick to your agreement. The next time you assign work with a deadline, you need to help each other live up the agreement.

Give her the report back, set a mutually acceptable deadline, and expect a fully acceptable product by the deadline.

If she didn't set her priorities effectively:

This *isn't* the same problem as the one above. In that case, she did what she should but didn't have time. In this case, she put her time on the wrong projects.

There are actually two problems here. First, she didn't set the right priorities. Second, she didn't tell you she couldn't produce a quality report by the deadline you set. Both have to be dealt with.

Deal with her failure to set priorities right by reviewing her work with her regularly and helping her readjust her priorities as necessary. Don't redo the priorities for her. Help her go through them and develop the judgment necessary to set them effectively for herself. (If you set them for her, you may have found yourself a job for life.) These sessions should be fairly frequent at first, then further and further apart until they become unnecessary.

Her failure to tell you she couldn't produce a quality report on time is a separate problem, and one that's just as serious. Every employee should know that he or she has to let you know in *advance* if a deadline can't be met. No exceptions! Enforce this. But also make sure you listen when they tell you they can't meet a deadline and help them readjust the deadline (or their other priorities). It takes *both* a firm requirement and a willingness to listen.

Give her back the report and set the priority it should have. Meet with her as frequently as necessary to see that she gets it done.

If she's angry at you about the deadline:

This may be based on any of the situations we've already described. Realistically, she may not have had enough time. Or she may not have handled her priorities well. Deal with that situation. But that's not enough.

The question that most needs answering is: *Why* was she so angry that she chose to set both you and herself up for failure this way? Is she so frustrated because you won't listen to her that she's decided to do this in hopes it will get your attention? Is it because of a completely unrelated grudge she has with you? Is she reacting in this manner because she didn't get her way with the deadline in the first place?

Spend the time you need to find out why she was angry and what the two of you need to do about it.

If this action got her anger off her chest, give her back the report and agree on a time when she'll finish it. If she's still angry, you may want to give the report to someone else to finish. If so, make it clear to Edwina that, regardless of the cause, this was a performance failure on her part. If necessary, write her up formally on this.

If you weren't clear about what you wanted:

One reason you need to listen carefully to Edwina's reasons for the poor report is that this may well be one of them. Actually, this isn't just one failure. It may reflect one or several of these:

- You don't explain projects carefully to employees. If you get back many projects that aren't done as you want, this is probably one of the major causes.

- You don't ask effective questions to see if the employee understands what you want.

- The employee doesn't know to ask for clarification, or is afraid to do so. She may not think that you want her to. Just saying the words isn't enough; you have to communicate in your response that you want her to ask.

- You don't trust the employee, so you discourage her from asking questions. Or she doesn't trust you enough to ask. (This is very much like the one above—but when lack of trust is a cause, the problem is more serious.)

Spend however much time you need to understand what's happening and start to correct it. If you and the employee can't agree at the beginning on what's wanted, you will both lose at the end.

SOMETHING TO THINK ABOUT

When a good employee stumbles on one product, it's easy to overlook the stumble. That's a judgment call. Remember, though, that every problem is easier to solve if it's caught quickly and dealt with quickly. Most of the time, the best course of action is to surface the problem calmly and objectively as quickly as possible.

4-8 THE PROBLEM

A new employee started out well, but his performance is deteriorating

THE SCENE

"Did I make a mistake, or what?" you ask one of the other section supervisors in bewilderment. "Pete Herkemer seemed like such a good candidate when I interviewed him, and his first few weeks on the job he was like a house afire. But in the last several weeks, it's as if he's run out of steam. He's slower, he's making more mistakes, and he's not learning the new stuff nearly as well anymore. I just can't figure out what's going on."

POSSIBLE CAUSES

Pete could be in over his head.

Assuming that you structured his learning the new job so that he learned the simpler parts first, he may have reached his learning saturation point. He may never get much better at the work than he is right now.

Pete could have run into a particular part of the work that he can't get a handle on.

It may have him stymied so that it's interfering with the parts of the job he's already mastered.

Pete might be disillusioned with the work.

He may be having second thoughts about having accepted your job offer, and his performance is beginning to reflect his disillusionment.

Hint: Whatever the cause of the problem, don't give up on Pete too soon. Learning is *not* a continuous upward curve. People learn incrementally—in fits and starts. Figure out what the cause is and deal with it. But maintain your faith in Pete. Chances are that this is just a temporary roadblock, and he'll still live up to your expectations. But if you begin to treat him like a loser already, he'll give up on himself too. And then you'll both lose.

CURES

If Pete is in over his head:

What kind of recommendations did you get about Pete when you checked his references? (You *did* check his references, didn't you?)

Did his former supervisors say he was a quick learner, that he was slow but once he learned something he knew it backwards and forwards, that he learned enough to get by but didn't stick with the details?

What kinds of jobs did Pete hold before yours? Were they equally responsible or complex? Or is this a significant step up for him?

If Pete's former supervisors tell you that he's had learning difficulties in the past, or if this is a major job change for him, you should talk to Pete to probe more deeply into his skills and aptitudes. You might want to consider asking your personnel department to administer a battery of aptitude and interest tests to Pete to see if he's suited for the kind of job he's been placed in.

If Pete really has reached the limits of his abilities and you are convinced that he won't be able to learn parts of the job that are critical to his successful performance, you need to take action to move him out of the position. If he has other skills that you want to retain, try to find some other work, in your group or elsewhere in the organization, where he can make a contribution. But if you decide that Pete's not going to work out anywhere, then it's best to let him go now. Once you've decided that his skills and aptitudes aren't sufficient for your organization, you've spent your time (and his time) needlessly delaying the inevitable.

If Pete has met a temporary roadblock:

First, don't panic. And don't let Pete panic. Let him know that you expect there to be some areas he'll have more trouble learning than others. Especially if your reference checks revealed that Pete has had some initial problems grasping new tasks in the past, you need to reinforce your faith in his ability eventually to learn the work.

Try to figure out what he's having problems with. Is it the volume of work (does he need help in organization skills)? Is it the complexity of the work (can you break the work down into smaller segments that he can master one by one)? Is the problem in specific subject areas (can you provide some on-the-job mentoring or some formal training to help him)?

Look also at Problem 6 in this section. Temporary roadblocks are often in just those harder-to-perform parts of the job.

Work with Pete to develop a specific "get well" plan. If necessary, give him some slack on the parts of the job he's already mastered so he can concentrate on the areas in which he's having problems.

But, above all, repeat, over and over, your continued confidence in Pete's ability to learn the job. We know from personal experience that it can sometimes take months for some employees to learn specific tasks, even tasks you think they should be able to master in days or weeks. Every employee learns at a different pace. And, in most cases, it's more important to learn to do the job well than to learn it quickly.

If Pete's become disillusioned with the job:

This will be most obvious from the attitude and enthusiasm (or lack) he shows toward the work. But be careful! Some people also show frustration (like from not being able to learn) by "tuning out." While you may be more accustomed to seeing frustrated employees react with anger or impatience, apparent indifference is not an uncommon response either.

But if your observations and your discussions with Pete reveal that he's not happy with the way the job is turning out, it's time to have a frank discussion with him about your expectations for his performance and the consequences of poor performance. Explain that if he's really unhappy in his work it's better for him to leave of his own volition (or to decide to put up with his disillusionment and perform anyway) than to be taken out of the job. Offer him whatever help he needs to learn the job and to be successful. Describe the *realistic* opportunities available for recognition and for advancement. But be clear that the choice is his. Your job is to see that his job gets done and gets done well. Ultimately, he needs to understand that your overriding concern is for the health of the organization.

And if he neither "shapes up" nor "ships out"? Treat his performance problems as you would any other in your workgroup. Chapter 6 illustrates a number of approaches.

SOMETHING TO THINK ABOUT

Moving to a new job, especially if it's with a new company, is a traumatic experience. All the security and comfort of the old environment is gone, and an employee who's used to feeling competent and knowledgeable suddenly becomes a novice all over again. We can't stress too often that the most effective cure for many early apparent performance problems is *time*. Time to learn the work, time to learn the organization and how to work with the people in it, and time to adjust and become more comfortable in the new environment. Encouragement from you is important, but often that's all that's needed. Before you jump in to help with any of the cures we've described, give your new employee a little time. Then if things don't improve you still have an opportunity to intervene.

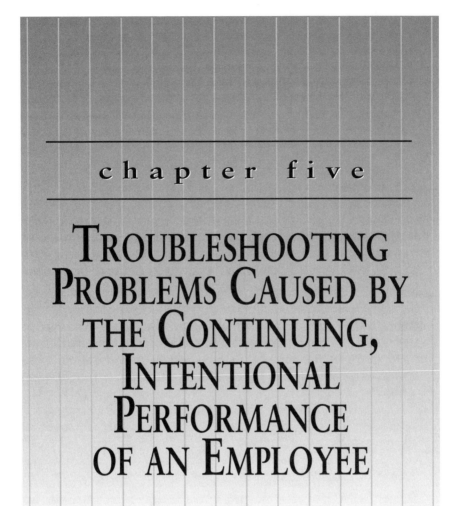

TROUBLESHOOTING PROBLEMS CAUSED BY THE CONTINUING, INTENTIONAL PERFORMANCE OF AN EMPLOYEE

5-1 THE PROBLEM

An employee is a poor worker because she won't follow work procedures

THE SCENE

Carlotta did it again! She handled that problem with Mrs. Woods beautifully—tactful, conciliatory, just the right note of urgency. She can charm suppliers out of almost anything. But when it was all over and Carlotta hung up the phone, did she document the call and let the shop floor know when they could expect the next shipment of supplies? *No, she did not!* She went on to make another call, so now no one knows when the material is due. And when someone else calls the supplier, not knowing that Carlotta already has, they're likely to get angry and not send anything. She *could* be such a good worker, if only she'd follow procedures.

POSSIBLE CAUSES

Carlotta may not see any value in doing things your way.

Particularly if there's no negative consequence to her for not following instructions and plenty of positive consequences for *not* following them (like positive experiences with the suppliers), Carlotta may view the established procedures as a waste of her time.

Carlotta may not know how to perform the particular procedures you're concerned about.

She may know a lot about how to wheel and deal on the telephone, but may have problems with the paperwork. In that case, she's most likely to do the things she knows well and skip the things with which she's less comfortable.

Carlotta may see herself as a free spirit who can't be bothered with your petty requirements.

She may consider that her failure to follow procedures "makes a statement" and sets her apart from her fellow workers, which it certainly does, but not in a positive way.

CURES

If Carlotta doesn't see any value in doing things your way:

Explain to her the importance of the procedures you've established and how her failure to perform them impacts the rest of the unit.

Walk Carlotta through the other parts of your operation so she can see for herself how her failure to follow procedures makes it harder for other people.

Look at the way you've organized the work and the consequences to Carlotta of not following procedures. Wherever possible, arrange positive consequences for following the procedures and negative ones for not following them. At the very least, you can make sure that following procedures is an item that's specifically addressed in your performance reviews.

Make sure Carlotta knows the consequences to her personally of failing to follow proper procedures (for example, poor performance appraisals, low [or no] raises, possible reassignment or termination).

If Carlotta doesn't know how to perform the procedures:

Talk to Carlotta to try to find out what parts of the job she's having problems with. Keep in mind that she may not tell you. She may prefer to disguise her lack of knowledge as a *refusal* to follow instructions rather than an inability. In that case, treat the situation as if she didn't see the value in doing things your way (as described above). Let her know the serious consequences of her continued failure to follow procedures and encourage her to tell you about any parts of the job she's having trouble performing.

If through your discussions with Carlotta or through your own observations you're able to identify specific areas where she needs help, find the best way to teach her those skills. There may be formal courses that will teach her the skills she lacks (particularly for things like basic literacy skills or keyboard skills). Or it may be better for her to work with an experienced employee who can coach her through the process until she gets it right.

Follow up with Carlotta. Congratulate her on her successes, and continue to identify and help her overcome her difficulties. Be sure she understands, though, that the ultimate responsibility for doing a good job is hers.

If Carlotta sees herself as a free thinker who can't be bothered with following your bureaucratic requirements:

This cause is somewhat like the first one, but not exactly. In this case, Carlotta may objectively understand the value to the organization of following procedures, but may not see their applicability to her.

Review with her the reasons for establishing the procedures and their importance to her job and to the rest of the organization. Try as much as possible to describe the effect of failure to perform on other *employees* rather than on the organization. Oftentimes, the object of a rebel's actions is the impersonal bureaucracy; pointing out the harm her actions do to *people* may help Carlotta see the procedural requirements in a new light.

Emphasize to Carlotta the personal consequences to her of her failure to perform, including poor performance reviews and possible termination. She may still see her "cause" as more important and make a conscious decision not to follow your instructions. In that case, be prepared to follow through with the consequences you've outlined. If the procedures and employees' willingness to be team players are important to your organization, then, for the sake of the organization, you will have to "make a statement" of your own—by terminating Carlotta if necessary.

Something to Think About

In many ways, intentional poor performance is harder to deal with than is poor performance that results from employees not knowing how to do the work or from their being unable to do the work. If someone doesn't know how, you teach them. If, after training, they are still unable to do the work, you find something else for them to do or terminate them. Intentional poor performance is particularly troublesome because employees may *sometimes* perform as you want them to, but you can't predict when.

And since the problem is one of *willingness* to do the work, there's nothing you can do to make someone want to do things your way.

If all this sounds terribly discouraging, remember that you are not ultimately responsible for your employees' performance. They are. You can coach, encourage, exhort, praise, reward, and correct them. But eventually, your responsibility ends. Not every employee will work out. Congratulate yourself on the successes. But don't beat yourself up about the failures. In the end, it's all up to the employee.

5-2 THE PROBLEM

An employee on a flexible work schedule has falsified his work hours

THE SCENE

"Betty, this is serious. Are you sure Arnie left at 3:30 last Wednesday?

"I promise you there was no mistake. He came out and checked to see if you were here. When he saw you weren't, he went back, turned off his computer, and left. I waited till today to tell you so he'd have turned in his time sheet—and I'll bet it shows he worked until 5:30 or 6:00."

"It does. I've been afraid this was happening, but this is the first concrete evidence I've had. Are you willing to put this in writing and sign it?"

"Sure—I don't want him or anyone else screwing up flexible scheduling—I need it too much."

Betty isn't your best worker or the easiest one to manage, but she's completely honest. If she said Arnie left early, Arnie left early.

POSSIBLE CAUSES

The workgroup is very sloppy about flexible work hours.

You haven't been paying much attention to how accurately workgroup members record their time. You don't really know to what extent anyone's been abusing flexible work hours.

Arnie has been abusing his flexible work schedule.

He's simply been using the freedom it provides to get paid for more work than he puts in.

Hint: Note that both of these may be causes.

CURES

If the workgroup is very sloppy about flexible work hours:

Flexible work hours are a tremendous benefit for workers that costs the organization nothing and often enables it to retain workers it would otherwise lose. But the benefit doesn't police itself. Unless workers know that management is paying attention, someone is going to start taking advantage of the situation. If he or she gets away with it, others will take advantage. Soon productivity drops and the organization decrees an end to the flexibility.

While Arnie may be guilty, he may simply be taking advantage of your inattention. How do you correct the situation and correct it quickly? Talk about it at group meetings. Make it clear that workers can enjoy the benefit only as long as they use it responsibly. Review everyone's time sheets periodically and question any time that looks out of line.

Most important, though, be there at the beginning and the ending of the workday. If you typically come in later but your earliest workers log in at 6:00 or 6:30, come in at that time occasionally. You don't need to do a lot. You might get a cup of coffee and wander around enough to chat briefly with everyone. No big deal. And if you don't usually stay until the end of the scheduled workday, adjust your schedule to remain until then. And make sure your workers know you're there.

If Arnie has been abusing his flexible work schedule:

Get Betty's written statement, then call Arnie in and show it to him. Don't start by lecturing at him or accusing him of anything.

Ask him what he has to say. Listen carefully and if necessary draw him out. Regardless of how certain you are he's falsified his time sheet, you want to give him every opportunity to present his side of the matter.

What if he denies that he left? Now it's his word against hers, and if you believe she's telling the truth you take her word. (Be careful, though, that she doesn't have any reasons to lie or to "get" Arnie.) Talk to your human resources department or whoever else handles discipline to find out the appropriate discipline in this case.

Suppose he admits it, but claims that everyone else is doing it? Ask him for evidence. If he has some, consider it. If it really is the case that large numbers of workers have been abusing the flexible schedule, you may want to take lesser action against Arnie (as well as taking all of the steps described in the first section). But you do want to take action, even if it's only an informal reprimand and/or taking him off flexible scheduling for several months.

If he can't produce real evidence that "everyone is doing it," proceed as though he were the only offender, because he's the only one you have concrete evidence on. And while you don't want necessarily to make an example of Arnie, he and others have to understand that taking advantage of the system simply isn't permitted.

A final comment. Anyone who abuses flexible work hours should be removed from the flex schedule for a long enough period of time to get his or her attention. How long? Normally, at least a month and quite possibly longer. This is too important a benefit to treat lightly.

SOMETHING TO THINK ABOUT

It's unfortunate, but a supervisor's job always has something of the policeman in it. Most of the time, most workers are going to abide by the rules and manage themselves. But there's always the one individual who believes the rules are for someone else, and so he or she tries to take advantage. Shaving the work day here and there, taking extended breaks, getting and making private telephone calls—the list goes on and on.

It's important that you catch these abuses and stop them. The important point isn't punishment, though you may have to discipline individuals. You want to communicate clearly that the rules are meant to be followed and that you won't tolerate individuals breaking them simply for their own benefit. In the long run, this keeps workers out of trouble. It may also persuade individuals who would have cheated on the system if they had the chance to remain productive and employed.

5–3 THE PROBLEM

*An employee gives priority to the work
she likes, not to what needs to be done*

THE SCENE

When you passed Marybeth's desk, you couldn't help but look at what she was working on. Sure enough, it was the new office layout. She's doing it again! You've told her at least three times that the end-of-month reports need to be done before anyone works on office improvement. What do you have to do to get her to follow the right priorities?

POSSIBLE CAUSES

Marybeth honestly believes that the office layout is more important than the reports.

This doesn't make her right, but at least she's being conscientious.

Marybeth is getting burned out on her regular duties.

She'll turn to anything that will relieve the boredom of them.

She's undisciplined and sets her priorities by what interests her.

Hint: One of the basic skills of a fully competent employee is the ability to set appropriate priorities. When an employee can't do this, you (the manager) can't fully delegate work to her.

CURES

No matter what the situation is:

If you've lost your temper, wait until you cool down. Then call Marybeth in. Tell her you saw what she's working on; don't play games.

Be sure you give her the opportunity to explain her side of the situation. While it might not seem so, the time it's most important to listen carefully to an employee is when you believe she's in the wrong.

If she honestly believes that the layout is more important than the reports:

This requires skillful listening. You told her to set other priorities, but she believes she should do the layout instead—why? If you don't listen carefully to her, you may end up seeming arbitrary to her, which will probably make her angry and the problem even harder to solve.

If she convinces you she's right, agree with her. Work out a satisfactory set of priorities for the reports and the layouts and agree that she'll follow them.

If she set her own priorities because you wouldn't listen to her, assure her that you'll listen next time—and do so. But counsel her that she's not to go her own way again.

Suppose she had the chance to persuade you but couldn't, and then set her own priorities regardless of what you said? Counsel her clearly and firmly: That's not acceptable behavior. Warn her that if it happens again you will discipline her. (Then, if it does happen again, be as good as your word.)

There's one more option. She disagreed with you but didn't say anything. What now? Would you have listened if she had said something? Are you sure? If you're sure, counsel her strongly that you won't put up with that again. If you wouldn't have listened, or give people the impression that you wouldn't, that's something you need to work on.

If she's getting burned out on her regular duties:

She may want to do what you told her, she may even think the reports are more important, but they've gotten so boring and empty for her that she'll do almost anything else instead.

In Problem 2–9, we discussed how to deal with an employee who's bored with his job. Look at it for some suggestions that might apply to Marybeth's situation.

There's one other point to consider. Is Marybeth a relatively new employee? If so, a basic problem may be that she isn't cut out for the job she's doing. Perhaps you can reassign her, or help her get reassigned to a job that fits better. At the least, you should show her how—*if she does her current job well*—she might get promoted to more interesting work.

If she sets priorities by what interests her:

This may be a good characteristic for an inventor or tinkerer, but it's a sign of immaturity and lack of discipline in most other jobs.

It's not necessary to know why Marybeth is this way, but it may help to know. Is she just young and inexperienced? Has she been working for an ineffective supervisor who let her do what she wanted? Or is she simply so hard to deal with that no one has wanted to tangle with her?

Whatever the situation, you do need to exercise some care—especially if she's a good worker (or potentially so). Her preference for the layout work may indicate that she's in the wrong job or doesn't do well at some of the duties. When the immediate problem is solved, you need to see if job changes are warranted (as in the "cure" immediately above).

Now that we've said all that, the problem is that Marybeth isn't doing what she needs to be doing and what you told her to do. You need to call her in and explain clearly that you expect her to follow the priorities you set. If she complains about the work or disagrees with your priorities, offer to discuss that further with her—*after* she completes the reports. Make it clear that you expect her to follow the priorities you set and that you will discipline her if she doesn't.

After this situation is settled, you may need to have one more talk with Marybeth. If you think she'd be receptive, you need to explain to her the problems she'll create for herself if she gets the reputation of wanting to work only on jobs she finds interesting. Show her that from a manager's point of view the best and most promotable employees are those willing to do whatever the organization needs done.

SOMETHING TO THINK ABOUT

In the long run, workers (including you and us) are happiest and most productive doing duties they like. One of the fundamental tasks of management is to get the right people in the right jobs. But this has to be balanced against the immediate need to get the work out, whether it's interesting or not. A good manager needs to keep both short-run and long-run factors in mind in all his dealings with his employees.

5–4 THE PROBLEM

A good employee consistently violates company rules to get his work done

THE SCENE

Monday morning finds you on your way to an important meeting in the farthest section of the warehouse. As you stroll briskly through the busy sections, you see Tim whip around a corner on his forklift, narrowly missing the corner of the stacks and another worker.

Tim always gets the job done—often faster than others—and has never had an accident. But he's had several near-misses. It doesn't seem to matter how many times you stress safety rules in your staff meetings; Tim just ignores them and does his work his way.

POSSIBLE CAUSES AND CURES

This situation is a lot like that described in Problem 1 of this chapter. The main difference is that Carlotta is a poor worker *because* she won't follow the rules, while Tim is a good worker *in spite of* the fact that he won't follow the rules.

The causes and cures for the two problems are about the same, with these differences:

It is less likely in this case that Tim doesn't follow the procedures because he doesn't know how. If he's a good worker who ignores rules to get his work done, chances are that it's because he sees a positive benefit (reaching his production goals) in not meeting your requirements and sees no benefit in doing things your way.

In Carlotta's case, there is a clear consequence of her failure to follow the rules (her poor performance). In Tim's case, there is no demonstrable result. He gets his work done, and he hasn't had any accidents. So the sole issue here is the violation of company rules.

Decide how important it is that Tim follow the rules. While he may be able to ignore safety requirements without having an accident, does his behavior set a bad example for other workers who may not be as skilled as he is? Does the nature of the work itself require that employees follow rules without question, even ones they don't agree with (as for example, when you're dealing with hazardous materials, security items, or in other sensitive situations)?

If you decide that it is critical that Tim follow the rules, then first explain to him your rationale. Acknowledge his good performance, stressing that truly good performance requires not only that the end product be right, but also that the procedures be followed correctly. Invite him to tell you if following the rules prevents him from meeting his production requirements and to suggest ways to rearrange assignments so that the rules don't get in the way.

Explain also that, regardless of how well he's performing, following company rules is also a bottom-line issue. Remind him that violation of the rules may result in disciplinary action against him—even termination. Express your confidence in his ability to get the work out *within* the rules, and point out examples of employees who manage to accomplish a lot without violations.

Then follow up. If Tim changes his behavior, congratulate him. If the rules really may interfere with production, then overlook for a time slight performance slippages that may occur as he readjusts his mode of operation. If he fails to conform to the rules, remind him again—then take whatever corrective action is warranted (an annotation in his file, a disciplinary action, or termination).

SOMETHING TO THINK ABOUT

You always have a problem when a worker—good or poor—refuses to follow work rules. If the rules are inefficient, change them. If they aren't, explain and enforce them. In short, have as few rules as possible, and then see that they're followed by everyone. Insist that they do.

5–5 THE PROBLEM

An employee refuses to use new work procedures or technology

THE SCENE

"Mac, you don't seem to be using your new personal computer very much."

"Nah—it just doesn't do that much for me. I still get all my work done, just like always."

Mac does get his work done, but only because Marty, your office clerk, knows how to turn his sketchy handwritten notes into contracts. Mac is the only one left that Marty has to do this for, and before long she's not going to be available to help him. How do you get him to start using his computer so there won't be a blow-up when that happens?

Possible Causes

Mac thinks the new technology is demeaning.

For him, actually "typing" the contracts is clerical work that's beneath him.

He thinks that it will make his job less interesting.

Many people associate new technology, especially automation, with boring jobs.

He thinks it may make him unnecessary.

It's hard to get someone to be enthusiastic about new equipment that may replace him.

He may simply be afraid he can't *learn it.*

If he doesn't try, he doesn't have to face the embarrassment of failure.

Hint: In Problem 1–7 we dealt with the problem of a work unit that didn't want to change. What applies to groups of employees also applies to individuals: People will change only when they believe that (1) the change will help them; (2) they can successfully produce the change; and (3) the change is worth the effort it will take.

Whenever you want someone to change, you need to show him or her that the change will help him or her, is practical, and is worth it. When you do that, the person will usually change.

Cures

If Mac thinks the new technology is demeaning:

For many people, using computers or fax machines or other office technology means doing their own "clerical" work. This is particularly true when they have to use a keyboard. Many of us were brought up to believe that only clerks use typewriters. When someone puts a computer with a keyboard on our desk, it looks like they want to make clerks out of us.

If that's how Mac looks at the situation, your first objective is to see that he understands the difference between using a personal computer and doing typing. A personal computer lets him do more of his job; it really means that *no one* does the clerical work.

You may also have to see that he has the skills necessary to use the new technology. No matter how he feels about computers in general, Mac may be uncomfortable because he doesn't have good keyboarding skills. Getting him self-paced training in keyboarding, or sending him to a class (made up of other nonclerical employees) will help.

If the problem is attitude, though, skills training alone won't solve it. You need to explain to Mac how personal computers can make it easier for *everyone* to do their job. Perhaps you need to have another employee, one whom Mac trusts, show him how useful it can be. If he understands that his using his computer will help Marty move up to a better job, that may help, too.

If he thinks it will make his job less interesting:

Unfortunately, organizations have often used computers in ways that *do* make jobs less interesting. Most of us have seen rooms full of data input clerks, punching data into terminals hour after hour. It's easy to believe that a computer on our desktop will do the same thing to us.

What you have to do is show Mac that this isn't the case. If you have another employee who's using a computer effectively, have him or her show Mac how helpful it is. Perhaps there's a training course available that shows how to use personal computers effectively.

In general, personal computers make jobs easier and, often, more interesting. You need to see that Mac understands this. Once you can get him actually using it, he'll probably find it out for himself.

If he thinks he may be replaced by the new technology:

This is a common reaction to new technology, since technology is so often justified as a way of reducing the workforce.

If your company is intending to reduce workers because of this new equipment, you need to be honest with your employees about it. See if the company has a program for retraining and reassignment inside for displaced workers. If not, see if they at least have an effective outplacement program. They may also be planning to offer early retirement, and Mac might qualify for that. If there's nothing else, explain to Mac that learning to use the new technology will make him more employable elsewhere.

Normally, new office technology *won't* reduce workers. If this is the case, see that Mac—and every other employee—knows it. He may still think it's demeaning or will make his job less interesting, but this will relieve him enough to let you work the other problems with him.

If he doesn't want to try because he's afraid he can't *learn it:*

"You can't lose if you don't play." Many people avoid new and challenging situations to avoid the possibility of failure. Perhaps that's what Mac is doing.

If his fear is relatively mild, the combination of a little pressure and a lot of reassurance may be enough to get him to try the new technology. Other workers might help him and apply a little bit of peer pressure, too.

If his fear is strong, his avoidance of new challenges is probably a deep-seated character trait by now. Look at the second "cure" in Problem 6–9 for some ideas on how to deal with that.

SOMETHING TO THINK ABOUT

A situation such as Mac's may require a manager to walk a fine line. On the one hand, you need to accommodate each employee's personality and preferred way of working. On the other, you can't do this to the extent that it disrupts the production of other employees. Finding the right balance is often difficult, but always rewarding.

5–6 THE PROBLEM

An employee continually gives other employees substandard work

THE SCENE

"I was very disappointed in the feedback I got on your design layout for Coultrey Systems. Their office manager told me that the public areas looked great, but the cubicles you designed for each of their workers were so small they couldn't back their chairs away from their desks without stretching out into the aisles. What kind of a design is that?"

"Well, boss, you know I'm not one to pass off blame on other people. But my group only assembled the pieces into the overall design plan. Marge is the one who designed the individual work-stations, and she assured me that *this* time she got it right."

This same problem seems to crop up over and over again. Every time a design plan goes wrong, Marge's name comes up. Too small, not enough power, inadequate lighting . . . The list goes on and on. But you can't review every component as it's designed. So how do you know until the end of the project that Marge has messed up again?

POSSIBLE CAUSES

Marge may not know how to do the work correctly.

Since her work isn't always reviewed separately, she may not receive adequate feedback to know what her performance problems are.

Marge may think it doesn't matter what the quality of her work is, since it becomes part of a larger product.

She may figure that someone else along the line will catch (and correct) her mistakes, or she may have decided that her errors will be compensated for somewhere else in the design plan.

Hint: Although at first glance this problem looks a lot like the one you'll read about in Problem 14–3, in this case the causes of your worker's poor performance are probably much different from the causes of another manager's lack of cooperation. And there's a lot more you can do directly to fix the problem on your own staff.

CURES

If Marge doesn't know how to do the work correctly:

Often, the performance of even well-trained workers can deteriorate over time because of lack of continuing feedback. Especially if Marge works independently and her input is accepted without review for inclusion into an overall product, she may lose touch with what's expected of her. Lack of some exterior objective criterion against which she can measure her performance means she has only her own subjective impressions to fall back on. And, with changes in the products she's working with, changes in technology, and even changes in others' expectations of her, she may fall further and further out of step.

So the first step to curing the problem is to establish some kind of immediate, ongoing review process for Marge's work. Explain to her that you've received a lot of complaints about her work from the people who use her work products, and that you'll need to check out for yourself to see how she's doing. (That doesn't mean that you need to do these reviews yourself. Particularly if Marge works in an area in which you're not technically skilled, you should ask a senior member of your staff to go over Marge's work and provide you the results. You and your senior worker can then work together to mentor Marge.)

Be aware that Marge may get defensive when you tell her that you've received complaints from others. She may demand to know who said what and deny that there's any problem. She may even claim that they're "out to get her." It is *not* necessary to reveal the names of the people who've complained; it's probably not even a good idea to reveal their names unless you let them know first that you intend to.

On the other hand, if Marge is in denial, it's often very effective to have one or two of the people who use Marge's products meet with her, and you, to discuss in detail their complaints. That will help convince Marge that there really is a problem and that the complaints are legitimate ones. If your other workers aren't comfortable participating in that kind of meeting, well-intentioned as it is, it's probably useless to insist on their attendance. They won't be very helpful in explaining the problems to Marge, and they'll just resent your insistence.

After you've spent some time reviewing Marge's input to the larger product and given her feedback on her performance, you will have some idea what's causing any remaining performance problems. Chances are that they'll fall within the situations we'll describe in Chapter 6. Look there for help with solving any performance issues that don't cure themselves once Marge begins to receive regular feedback.

If Marge believes that the quality of her work doesn't matter:

How have you handled other complaints about the substandard work Marge has given your workers? Have you fixed the problems yourself? Have you had the other workers in your group fix the problems for Marge? Or have you sent them back to Marge for correction?

If there are no consequences to Marge herself for poor performance, it's inevitable that she'll decide that it doesn't matter whether she does good work or not.

Begin immediately to hold Marge, and every other contributor, accountable for the input they make to the final product. Send back work that isn't acceptable and reward work that is completed especially well or quickly.

Consider establishing specific teams for each product your group prepares. Hold the entire team accountable for the results. They'll quickly adopt self-policing practices that will make it unnecessary for you to personally review each component of the final product. Remember that teams don't have to be full-time assignments. Marge and your other group members can work with two or three teams at one time in the same way they might have worked before on two or three independent assignments at once.

Be sure, too, that Marge and other contributors have an understanding and appreciation of the entire production process. Each person doesn't need to know all the jobs that go into making the final product. But they should all understand where all the components come from, who does what, how the final product is put together, and what use it's put to. It's easy for people who work only part of a process or product to believe that their contribution doesn't matter when in fact *every* contribution is important to the success of the whole.

SOMETHING TO THINK ABOUT

It's not possible to design a perfectly seamless organization, one where every process is "owned" by a single person or group who isn't dependent on anyone else to get the work done. But problems such as this one point out that it's best to have as few critical interfaces between individuals and groups as possible. No matter how well people work together, every interface becomes a potential source of miscommunication and error.

5–7 THE PROBLEM

An employee tries to win customers by badmouthing your competitors

THE SCENE

Mr. Samuelson, your boss, motions you to a chair. "Jamie Seguin just called from Progressive. Guess what she had to say about Ronnie Mitchell?"

"He's been badmouthing Progressive again."

"You better believe—and this time is the worst yet. Not only did he point out one or two of their genuine faults, but he made up several. You know as well as I do that we and Progressive have to depend on each other as well as compete with each other. I promised Ms. Seguin that we were going to shut Ronnie up one way or another—and that's your job. You either get him to lay off our competitors' backs or you get rid of him. Am I clear?"

POSSIBLE CAUSES

This is how Ronnie has always sold.

When he learned to sell, he learned to sell negatively. He thinks this is how it's done.

Ronnie is insecure as a salesperson.

He's afraid that if he doesn't sell negatively he won't be effective at selling.

Ronnie enjoys tearing down other firms and people.

He maintains his self-esteem by attacking others.

Hint: The three causes don't exclude one another. Two, or even all three, of them may be part of the problem.

CURES

No matter what the cause is:

Knowing something about the cause of Ronnie's problem will help you devise the most effective solution. It doesn't change your goal—to get Ronnie to stop attacking competitors or else.

If this is how Ronnie has always sold:

Ronnie may believe that attacking competitors is the most effective way to sell. When you tell him he can't sell that way, he thinks you're telling him that he has to be less effective. That's a basic hurdle you must overcome.

What about your other salespeople? Are there several of them who are very effective but don't sell negatively? Use them to point out to Ronnie that it can be done. That in combination with a clear explanation of what will happen if he doesn't change (he'll be fired) may be enough to get him to start changing.

If this happens, you need to stay on your toes. Schedule regular meetings with Ronnie to check on his progress and ensure that he keeps the goal clearly in mind. Otherwise, he'll probably slip back into his old ways and you'll be on the spot again.

It may not be that easy. He may not think that anyone else sells as well as he does (and he may have the figures to prove it). He simply refuses to change. If that happens, the two of you have a very straightforward talk. The subject: Does he want to keep on selling negatively and work for someone else or does he want to keep his job by changing his approach? If he decides to leave, and he's been a generally good worker, give him time to find a new job and arrange an amicable parting.

That's probably not really what you want. Presumably, you want him to stay. Remind him of the many benefits of his current job (it's hoped there *are* a number) and promise him that you'll work with him to help him change the way he sells. Assure him that as long as he'll work sincerely to change you'll support him.

If he agrees to change, here's something you might try. Go with him on a few calls. Don't go as his boss; that telegraphs that you're looking over his shoulder for some reason. Let him explain that you're a new and inexperienced salesperson and he's showing you how an experienced salesperson sells. Then he proceeds to sell positively. Surprisingly enough, in this circumstance he may really get into it.

If Ronnie is insecure as a salesperson:

This may be driving his insistence on selling negatively: he simply believes that he's not good enough to sell otherwise. Your task is to demonstrate that he is good enough. How? You can use some of the ideas in the section just above. Whatever you do, though, your goal is to get him into a situation where he sells positively and successfully and then make sure he understands that he did so and how he did so.

You may need to play customer with him. Have him make a presentation to you in his usual way, negativity and all. Then have him change it to leave out the attacks and emphasize the positive points of your company's products and give the presentation to you again. The two of you work on it until it's polished. Then he uses it with a customer and reports back to you on the results. (If he won't get too nervous, use the idea in the preceding section and go along as a trainee. For the first few times, though, this will probably be too stressful for him. Then it may be a possibility.)

Remember to notice and recognize him for each improvement he makes, no matter how small. This is especially important just when he's beginning to change and it's hard for him to see progress. If he knows that you see and appreciate his progress, it will help him immensely.

If Ronnie enjoys tearing down other firms and people:

This may be the hardest cause to deal with because Ronnie has developed a strong habit of attacking others. From his point of view, the fact that Progressive is a competitor gives him every excuse he needs to do so. Subtlety will probably get you very little in this circumstance. The situation needs to be met head-on.

Tell Ronnie how you see things and give him every chance to answer. Listen carefully and ask leading questions. You want to understand as clearly as you can just how he sees the situation and why he sees it that way.

Then you make your point of view clear—he changes or else. He won't like that. He may accuse you of picking on him or trying to make him look bad. Let him. Your job here is to get him to stop attacking competitors or else. Make sure he understands this clearly. Then let him make a choice. If he's a good salesperson, offer to support him and help him change, though the responsibility for change remains his. But the choice is his. If he decides he wants to change, use the ideas from the preceding sections, but use them firmly. (For instance, you may want to insist on going with him on calls.) Have regular follow-ups with him and accept nothing less than clear improvement.

SOMETHING TO THINK ABOUT

When a worker (or manager) needs to change his or her behavior or else, the situation is always stressful. Changing is hard work. If the individual can see a payoff from the change that's worth the effort, the change is easier. If he or she doesn't like the change or doesn't believe it will work, it's harder.

How do you aid the process? Try not to let workers get into situations like the one in this case where they must make major changes or else. Don't try to threaten them into changing unless absolutely necessary. Threats are normally the least effective motivators for change. Give them a positive reason for change, preferably a clear payoff for them. Above all, convince them you are serious about the change and that it *will* happen.

5-8 THE PROBLEM

An employee uses his work-at-home schedule as an opportunity to do no work

THE SCENE

You try very hard to be a good manager. It's obvious that your work-at-home schedule is a real boon to many of your workers, and to the workgroup. People appreciate being able to work around other commitments, and the kind of document processing you do can be accomplished anywhere. It doesn't have to be in a particular office or a particular building.

But what about Christie? She's going to spoil this arrangement for everyone. You can tell she's not doing much during her work-at-home hours, but you're having a hard time proving it. When you ask her what's she's getting done, she just smiles and says everything is "on target." What's that supposed to mean?

POSSIBLE CAUSES

Christie may not know what your expectations are.

She may have the idea that work at home is a kind of bonus for which she's not really accountable.

Christie may see work at home as a means of taking advantage of the system.

She may think there's no way you can tell whether she's producing or not, so she's free to do as much (or as little) as she chooses.

Hint: At least in most organizations, work-at-home arrangements (also known as flexiplace) are not a normal condition of employment to which workers have any entitlement. The ability to work at home is often conditioned on special circumstances, such as physical disability or unusual dependent-care arrangements, or it's treated as a privilege that employees earn. If you find that your employees are abusing their work-at-home time, you can usually take strong and swift action with little fear of grievances or employee reprisals. But, to be sure, check with your personnel department to see just what the company's work-at-home policies cover.

CURES

If Christie doesn't know what your expectations are:

You, and she, may have assumed that work-at-home hours could be handled just like work hours in the office. She gets assignments, she completes assignments, she turns in assignments. And for some kinds of work, that's true.

If Christie is responsible for processing documents, or for preparing textual or graphical materials, or for making telephone contacts, or other work where there's a clear production standard, it's fairly easy to hold her to the same production level out of the office as in. And you can make it clear to her that if her overall level of production drops, you'll have to reduce or eliminate her work-at-home hours.

But what if Christie's work output is not so easily measured? You can still set performance goals, either for her work-at-home time specifically or for a particular period of time (maybe a week or two at a time). If Christie can tell you in advance what she intends to accomplish in her flexitime hours, and you agree that it's a reasonable expectation, you can have her report her progress to you when she returns to work. In that way, you can keep a close watch on what's going on.

If she can't tell you what will be accomplished in each work-at-home period, you should at least be able to establish milestones and goals for her overall work, keeping in mind her full work schedule (not just the hours she spends in the office), and hold her accountable for producing work against those milestones. Milestones that aren't met then become the basis for changing her work-at-home flexibility.

If Christie sees her work-at-home time as an opportunity to take advantage of the system:

The cure described above will solve most of these problems also. Make clear to Christie what your expectations are and how you intend to ensure that she really does produce when she's working out of the office. If her work isn't easily quantified, you can at least compare her production to that of other workers in similar positions (with or without work-at-home privileges).

The reminder that her output is monitored may be sufficient to change Christie's attitude toward her work-at-home responsibilities. If not, by having a system in place to keep track of her production, you've laid the foundation for taking whatever corrective action is necessary to improve her production rate. Problems 5–6, 6–2, and 6–6 can give you some ideas for dealing with continuing problems.

SOMETHING TO THINK ABOUT

As you undoubtedly know already, some workers have better self-management skills than others. Arrangements such as flexible work schedules and work at home are great for employees whose self-management skills are well developed, but can cause real difficulties for employees who have trouble keeping themselves together in even a traditional work setting. Some workers *need* structure in order to operate most effectively; others work best when they can develop their own structure.

Though you need to be consistent in your policies and requirements of workers who choose to use flexible work hours and work place arrangements, you also need to build in sufficient controls to be able to rein in those employees who have trouble with the lack of structure. The balance is a delicate one.

chapter six

TROUBLESHOOTING PROBLEMS CAUSED BY THE CONTINUING, UNINTENTIONAL PERFORMANCE OF AN EMPLOYEE

6-1 THE PROBLEM

*An employee is poorly organized and
consistently misses deadlines*

THE SCENE

"Gladys, do you mean to tell me that you're going to be late
with the newsletter again this month?!"

"I'm sorry, Mr. Cuzak, I really am. I took the material home
with me every night this week and worked on it, but I just can't
seem to get it together. If you could just get someone to help
me . . ."

You sigh. Gladys doesn't need someone to help her. She needs
to get herself organized and quit spinning her wheels. But how to
do it . . . ?

POSSIBLE CAUSES

Gladys may not realize that she's not organized.

Perhaps she's never worked with anyone who was really well
organized.

She may never have had to learn how to organize herself.

In her previous jobs she may never have had to do anything but
get the work done as it came to her.

She may not believe that it's important to organize herself.

It may seem too trivial for her to spend time on.

Hints: As you've probably realized already, none of the causes
excludes the others. She may not believe it's important to organize
herself because she's never had to *and* never worked around anyone who did it well. One of the critical steps here is knowing just
where to start.

Remember, organizing your time and your work is a *learned* skill. Because of their past history, and perhaps their personalities, some people are better at it than others will ever be. But everyone can learn to organize himself or herself well enough to do what has to be done.

CURES

No matter what the cause is:

Spend some time observing Gladys and talking with her. Your goal is to find out *how* she's disorganized. Does she put things off until the last minute? Does she spend too much time on the unimportant parts of the job? Does she start on something, work on it for a little while, and then leave it unfinished while she goes on to something else? It's important to get a feel for the specific ways that she's not being efficient.

If she doesn't realize that she's not organized:

This is good news and it's bad news. The good news is that once she realizes she's not organized, she'll probably want to learn how to get organized. The bad news is that it may be difficult for her to see that she's not organized.

The easiest, least-threatening way for her to learn she's not well organized is to work with someone who is. Can you arrange a joint task that she and one of your best-organized workers can do together? (The other worker also needs to be one who can be helpful and not get frustrated.)

If you're good at organization and there's no one else to work with her, you can do it. (You're the second choice because it's going to be harder for her to relax and learn from you, her supervisor.) You may just need to tell her what to do, but you'll be more effective if you can ask questions and make suggestions.

Once she realizes that she doesn't have the self-organization skills she needs, she'll probably be happy to have you or someone else help her gain them. It would probably be a good idea to send her to a formal course on work organization, too.

If she's never had to learn to organize herself:

She may have had jobs before where she wasn't required to do much organizing. Perhaps she did the work as it came to her. She didn't have to organize it, so she never learned how.

This may not be as difficult as the situation above. If you can explain the difference between the work she did and her current work, with some examples, she may see the difference quickly. Having her work jointly with a well-organized worker can also help her see the difference.

Once she sees the difference, having another worker help her and/or sending her to a formal course should get her going in the right direction.

If she doesn't think that organizing herself is important:

If this is the case, it's helpful to understand why she thinks this way. Does she see herself as a "creative" person and believe that being organized would get in her way? Does she think that "organizing" is something only clerks and secretaries do? Or does she just not realize that she's disorganized (back to cause 1)?

If she insists that she's as organized as she needs to be, deal with her performance. Instead of talking about being organized, insist that she get her work done on schedule. If she feels pushed enough, she may ask someone else to help her get organized.

Having another person who's organized work with her is also a good idea here, particularly if she begins to feel pressure to meet deadlines. Once she sees that someone else can handle the same kind of work more easily and skillfully, she'll probably want to learn the skills.

When she accepts the need to organize herself, see that she gets the on-the-job and/or formal training she needs.

What if she still refuses to learn how to get organized? Deal with the problem as a performance problem and take whatever steps are necessary. See Problem 6–2 for suggestions.

Something to Think About

Everything in this problem assumes that *you* are organized. Be sure that's the case. If it's not, your disorganization may be spilling over onto Gladys and other employees. You may actually be making it harder for them to organize themselves. You can figure out what the solution is to that, can't you?

Have you been accepting it when employees are late with assignments? Do you fuss and fume a little, then give up and take the assignment when you can get it? If so, *you're* a major part of the problem. See Problem 3 in this chapter and Problem 13–3 for suggestions on how to handle this.

It's important in this case, and in so many others, for the employee to believe that there really is a better way. As long as Gladys thinks her problem is just overwork—or lack of ability— she's stuck in it. Once she sees that she can get out of the situation by learning some new skills, the battle is almost won.

6–2 THE PROBLEM

An employee has a tremendous attitude, but isn't producing satisfactory work

THE SCENE

Glenda has done it again—given you a report you couldn't use. You thought you had done everything right: You called her in to explain exactly what you wanted, where the numbers came from, how to compute the percentages, the way to format the columns. She nodded in all the right places and even asked a couple of questions that sounded as if she understood what you were talking about. "Right away, Dan," she had said as she left your office.

But the report she gave you is nothing like what you had in mind. Glenda tries so hard, but it's just not working out.

POSSIBLE CAUSES

Glenda may not understand what you want.

Especially if she is obviously trying very hard to do a good job, she may not know what it is you're looking for.

She may not know how to do the work.

Even if she understands what you want, she may not know how to get there. This is particularly likely if she's recently been assigned new duties or is new to the organization and if what she's doing now doesn't bear much resemblance to the work she's done in the past.

Glenda may be the sort of person who starts out well, but then doesn't deliver.

You may think she has a great attitude because of her apparent enthusiasm when you give her assignments. But that enthusiasm may be feigned to get you off her back so she can go back to whatever it is she really wants to be doing.

Hint: If you decide that Glenda's intentions are good, but she's still having trouble producing, then it's particularly important that you step in *quickly* to help her solve her performance problem. One of the unfortunate consequences of repeated failure is that even employees who want to do a good job eventually get beaten down so badly that they give up, don't care anymore, or even become resentful and hard to manage. By stepping in as soon as you discover the difficulties, you may be able to overcome them in time to avoid the demoralizing effect of continued unsuccessful performance.

CURES

If Glenda doesn't understand what you want:

Talk with her about your expectations. Her lack of understanding may stem from one of two causes: Either she's been misinterpreting your instructions *or* you've been unclear in explaining what you need. In either case, your first step should be to have Glenda tell you what she *thinks* you told her to do.

In those areas where Glenda's interpretation and your expectations don't match, identify for her what she should have done differently. Show her some examples of work that's been completed to your expectations and how it compares with the products she's submitted.

Try to put Glenda's work in context. Show her who the customer is for her products and how her work affects other people's performance. By learning how her work is used by others, she'll be better able to identify the things it's critical that she do well and the parts that are just "nice-to-haves."

Review Glenda's work closely for a while. Look at her work each time she turns in an assignment or sample her products every day or two if they're things that don't normally flow through you on their way to the customer. Identify the things she's doing correctly and the areas that still need work.

An even better idea is to have Glenda work with another employee who can review her work and give her pointers on how to do things better. She may be more willing to go to a peer for advice than to you, since she may believe that you'll hold her lack of knowledge against her at appraisal time.

After you've given Glenda what ought to be sufficient opportunity and assistance to improve her performance, review her progress to decide if she's showing satisfactory improvement. She probably won't get better all at once, but you should begin fairly soon to see signs that she's catching on to what you want. If not, you'll need to make some hard decisions. Not only is it not fair to the organization and your other workers to carry Glenda in a job she can't perform; it's not fair to her either. Try to find her another position in which she can perform satisfactorily, but, failing that, you must be prepared to terminate her as tactfully and sensitively as you can. Your personnel department should be available to help you and Glenda get through both the paperwork and the emotional upheaval.

If Glenda doesn't know how to do the work:

Identify the specific areas in which she makes mistakes to isolate those parts of the job where she needs help. Decide what kind of training is best to give her the knowledge or expertise she needs (e.g., classroom training, on-the-job training), and arrange for her to get it.

Work with her closely for some time to review each product and to identify the things she's doing correctly and the areas that still need improvement.

Encourage Glenda and let her know that you have confidence in her ability to learn the work. At the same time, make sure she understands that it's her responsibility to do well, regardless of the amount of assistance you're able to give her.

As before, be optimistic but realistic. If, after your best attempts to teach Glenda the job, she still doesn't improve, be prepared to remove her from your organization or to help her find another position. That doesn't mean you've failed. *No* worker is equally good at every job.

If Glenda starts out enthusiastically, but then doesn't deliver:

See Problem 3 in this chapter for help in dealing with an employee who doesn't deliver what he or she promised.

6–3 THE PROBLEM

An employee doesn't deliver what he promised

THE SCENE

"R.B., this is just a summary of the overdue accounts. You told me you'd have an analysis of them for me by today."

"I really meant to—but you know how busy we've been lately. I'm sure I can do the analysis by Wednesday."

"You'd better!" you fume as you walk off. Will R.B. *ever* come through on time?

POSSIBLE CAUSES

~~R.B. is disorganized.~~

He means well but can't produce.

You accept it when employees don't deliver what they promise.

If this is the case, you've got to change yourself before you can change them.

R.B. worked for another supervisor who accepted it.

You haven't caused the problem—you've inherited it.

R.B. makes promises to "get people off his back," whether he can deliver or not.

Hint: Unless the problem is R.B.'s lack of organization, you have a serious problem here of work discipline. Don't confuse this with "discipline" for misconduct. Work discipline is simply what good workers make it a point to do, always. And good workers *always* deliver what they promise, when they promise it—or they let you know in advance.

CURES

If R.B. is disorganized:

Look back at the first problem in this chapter for suggestions.

If you accept it when employees don't deliver:

First, accept something else: *You're* the cause of their failure to come through for you. If you don't care about promises and deadlines, why should they?

There's a simple way to deal with this: Stop! Now! Get your employees together, explain the change and then enforce it.

You'll probably get a great deal of static at first. Employees will say that you're being unfair and expecting too much. Change is painful; you can accept that. But *don't* accept work that isn't done as promised, when promised. You may have to counsel them a little, perhaps even write an employee or two up for not delivering. Do it. They'll get the word. And your unit will start to run considerably better.

Don't go to the other extreme and insist that they deliver no matter what. Something may happen that genuinely has a higher priority or that causes an unavoidable delay. If this happens, if the employee can't produce on schedule, he lets you know *as soon as he knows.* Then the two of you work out a realistic new schedule.

If R.B. worked for another supervisor who accepted it when he didn't deliver:

First, make sure you don't have the same problem (see above).

Then have a talk with R.B. Say to him essentially what we suggested you say to all employees in the situation above. Make it clear that your standards are different from those of his former supervisor.

R.B. may feel that you're being unfair to him. If you've set clear standards and enforced them, though, your other employees will set him straight quickly. They deliver, and they'll expect him to deliver. (Yes, it usually is that simple.)

If R.B. makes promises to keep people from pressuring him:

Unfortunately, too many employees (and their managers) fall into this trap. Somebody pushes them, so them promise anything to get the pressure off. Then the day comes to deliver what was promised, and the individual who did the promising is in trouble.

If the cause seems to be one of the other ones above, keep your eyes open to see if this is also the case. Employees who'll promise anything to get out of a tight spot feel right at home with supervisors who don't insist that commitments be kept.

This problem will probably take a bit more time and attention. First, make your position clear to R.B. Then be equally clear that you won't force unrealistic commitments on him and that you don't want him to let others do it, either. (There's a good chance that he won't believe this, so be prepared to have him test you on it.)

Follow up to ensure that he stops making unrealistic commitments and that he keeps those he makes. When he makes a commitment and delivers, praise him for it. If he doesn't deliver, counsel him. Be patient, but be firm. It may take a few times, but he'll get the message.

SOMETHING TO THINK ABOUT

It's worth repeating: if your employees don't deliver what's promised, when it's promised, *you're* the culprit. Be realistic about what you expect from them and insist that they're realistic about it, too. Then expect that they deliver or tell you in advance why they can't. With no exceptions.

There's a very simple truth at work here. Most employees will produce what their supervisor will settle for. Even good employees will get sloppy if the supervisor has sloppy standards or (the same thing) has high standards but doesn't enforce them. Enough?

6–4 THE PROBLEM

*A good performer goes to pieces
under pressure*

THE SCENE

"What's wrong with Brendan?" asks Sally. "He's normally so calm and easygoing. But today we've had complaints from three different people who said he gave them bad information and didn't seem to know what he was talking about. I know the line out at the reception desk is getting longer by the minute, and Keith said he'd help out as soon as he finishes with this client. But Brendan's just going to have to hold on until we can get somebody else out there!"

"I guess this isn't really a new problem," you reply ruefully. "Brendan falls apart whenever the going gets rough. He's such a good worker most of the time, I hate to get on his back about something that doesn't come up that often. But, unfortunately, when it does, he makes a bad situation even worse."

POSSIBLE CAUSES

Brendan may not have the skills to deal with stress and pressure.

He may know the job itself well enough, but may not have learned coping strategies to keep from panicking when the pressure's on.

Brendan may not be that good at the work he's assigned.

He may be able to get along okay when he has plenty of time to figure out what to do, but when things move along too quickly, he gets lost.

Brendan may have learned to fall apart under pressure to get himself out of an unpleasant situation.

If falling apart under stress in the past has resulted in people feeling sorry for him and bailing him out, he's likely to repeat the behavior in similar situations. Your job is to help him unlearn that behavior.

Hint: There are very few jobs that don't require the ability to work under pressure at least some of the time. Brendan may be a good worker when he has little stress to contend with. You can try to structure his environment so that the pressures are reduced or so that they occur infrequently, but sooner or later it's almost inevitable that he'll be asked to perform under some kind of pressure—whether from deadlines, or an angry client or co-worker, or the boss looking over his shoulder on an important project. So regardless of how infrequently the situation occurs, it's in both his and your best interests to help him prepare ahead of time, not in the middle of the crisis.

CURES

If Brendan hasn't developed his own mechanisms for coping with stress:

Start by talking to Brendan and explaining why it's important that he not let the pressure get to him. Make sure he understands the impact on other people when he falls to pieces—that he's not getting just himself worked up but others too and that his lack of coping skills only makes tense situations worse.

Find a good commercially available course on stress reduction that includes not only relaxation techniques but also specific tactics for planning around stressful situations. Send Brendan, then ask for his feedback both on the content of the course and what he plans to do to put the things he learned into practice.

Take some time to work out scenarios with Brendan in which you describe some of the kinds of pressure he's likely to encounter in his job (like having 16 people lined up at the reception desk, all of whom want answers *now*). If you're both comfortable with the technique, role play the situations with him until he's practiced in dealing constructively with the pressure. If you're not comfortable with role playing, at least have him describe to you how he would handle the situation. Go over similar situations in several different sessions until you're confident that his appropriate response has become well ingrained.

If Brendan's work skills aren't strong enough for him to operate effectively under pressure:

Talk with Brendan to find out what skills require his unstressed time and attention. Then have him practice those skills over and over until he can perform them to mastery. *Note*: Mastery requires that he be able to perform the task both *accurately* and *quickly*. If he has learned the tasks to mastery, he is less likely to fall apart under pressure since mastery is reached only when the responses become semi-automatic.

If it's appropriate, you may want to see that Brendan gets some remedial training or you may want to review, step-by-step, what's involved in his assignments. He may know how to perform each individual task, but may get muddled when he has to sequence steps rapidly.

If falling to pieces is a learned response to get him out of stressful situations:

Explain to Brendan, tactfully but firmly, why you have to count on him when the pressure's on and how his inability to cope hurts others in the organization. Let him know that you'll do whatever you can to help him develop coping strategies (including the actions we've discussed), but that you need his cooperation.

Give Brendan some time to come to terms with your requirements. Send him to stress-reduction courses and work out ways of coping with the stresses he's likely to encounter, as we mentioned before.

The next time a stressful situation occurs, don't rush in to help him out. Give Brendan a chance to use the techniques he's learned.

Once he sees how you're counting on him, he may do fine. If not, and you have to step in, be sure to do a "post-mortem" with him to review how he handled the situation and what he could have done differently.

If Brendan improves his ability to perform under pressure, no matter how slowly, congratulate him on his improvement and stick with him. If he seems not to be improving, you can try a referral to your employee assistance program or another counseling service for more individual professional attention. You may be able to restructure the job to minimize the pressure. Or you may want to help him find another job where ability to deal with pressure isn't so critical.

While termination is always a possibility when employees don't perform to your expectations, it's less likely to be necessary in this situation. If the ability to work under pressure is a real necessity in Brendan's position, and if he continues not to cope well, chances are good that he himself will be uncomfortable enough that he'll look for another job.

6–5 THE PROBLEM

An employee produces a high volume of low-quality work

THE SCENE

"Sarah, I see that Emile is your top producer again this month. Is he still making bunches of mistakes?"

" 'Barrels of mistakes' is more like it! I've spoken to him about it several times, but he just points out how much he produces. He won't listen to me, because I'm not his supervisor. I need you to take care of it."

POSSIBLE CAUSES

You set low standards.

Alternatively, you set high standards but don't insist that people meet them.

Emile learned how to work fast but not accurately.

He's continuing to do what he knows how to do best.

The real rewards are for quantity, not quality.

In many organizations, quantity is what's tracked and paid for.

Hint: On the surface, this is an individual problem. If you let Emile get away with fast, sloppy work, though, others may start copying him. (This is particularly apt to happen if the pay system stresses quantity at the expense of quality.) Now you have an additional reason to act quickly and effectively.

CURES

If you set low standards (or high ones you don't enforce):

Let's be realistic here. What really counts in your company? In your division? In your unit? Is quality critical, or important, or an also-ran to quantity? Yes, "quality" is still a buzzword, but that doesn't mean that it's what's wanted, fought for, and rewarded.

If quality is a low priority for your company, your problem is much bigger than Emile. He may be producing exactly what the organization rewards. See the last "cure" for this problem to get some ideas on this.

Suppose the company wants quality, but you concentrate on quantity instead? The first question, of course, is why your boss lets you get away with sloppy work. Perhaps we'd better talk with him.

Since we can't, we'll just have to suggest that you get your act together. There's not room to talk about it in this book, but there's broad agreement that the best way to get high productivity is to do the things that lead to high quality first.

We can give you this: In a well-run organization, everything is done right the first time—*everything*. If you believe, live, support, and reward this, most of the sloppy work will vanish. Then it will be easy to deal with the occasional employee who hasn't gotten the word.

If Emile learned how to work fast but not accurately:

He's doing what most of us do—what we know how to do. In fact, even if he slows to half speed he may still make just as many errors.

What sounds like the sensible thing to do? Retrain him. Retraining is always harder than training, but it can be done. If Emile doesn't see the need for it, refuse to accept sloppy work and make him redo all of it. Make it crystal clear that you expect the work done right the first time.

That should get him in the right frame of mind to do some relearning. This is when you need to be patient, because he may have to begin over almost from the beginning. He'll have to establish new work habits, and they'll be difficult at first. Keep insisting, keep encouraging, and keep persisting.

One other thing: Make sure he understands that he can work just as fast without errors. Sound too good to be true? It's not. If he's trained properly, that's what will happen.

If the real rewards are for quantity, not quality:

Anyone who's worked for long in an average American firm has run into the dilemma. The company advocates quality and encourages its employees to produce quality. Then, when the dust has cleared, the people who get the rewards are those who meet or exceed their quantity targets, without regard for quality. (Just in case you haven't noticed, the time it takes to produce something is out in the open and measured; the time it takes to *redo* it is usually hidden.)

If this is your situation, you're caught in a real bind. Unlike the first cause above, you're not the reason for the sloppy work. If the firm pays for quantity at the expense of quality, you probably can't change that.

Does this mean there's nothing you can do? No. You can encourage Emile and others to produce quality work, which may help a little. If you have some discretion over bonuses or the amount of pay increases, announce that you'll give them for quality, not quantity. Then do it.

Make sure your boss knows how the company's preference for quantity over quality is affecting your unit. Perhaps you can enlist his or her help. Sooner or later, maybe managers like you and your boss can change the company's compensation policies.

SOMETHING TO THINK ABOUT

In some organizations, inspectors, senior workers, or leaders review everyone's work and redo any of the work that's substandard. Don't, DON'T, *DON'T* ever fall into this trap. Every individual should be responsible for his or her own work; if it wasn't done right, he or she redoes it. If the person has to do the rework and it detracts from the bonus he or she or the group gets, watch how quickly the rework will drop off.

Some companies still think you get productivity by emphasizing quantity at the expense of quality, if necessary. That's been proven wrong. The way you get productivity is by organizing for quality. When your people and your processes get it right the first time, then you'll get quality *and* quantity.

6–6 THE PROBLEM

An employee produces high-quality work, but too little of it

THE SCENE

Camille is one worker you can always depend on—slow and steady. Very, very steady—and *very, very* slow. In the three years she's been packing here, she's never had a package returned for breakage, or incorrect address, or falling apart in shipping. *But* as slowly as she goes, she might as well be wrapping fancy Christmas presents. The wrapping has to be just so, and the tape, and the filler, and the label, and everything else. You admire her meticulousness, but she takes twice as long as she should. How can you hurry her up?

Possible Causes

Camille may lack confidence in her abilities.

She may fear that if she goes any faster, she'll begin to make mistakes (whether that's true or not).

Camille's skills may not be well developed enough to allow her to go faster without making errors.

She may do fine as long as she goes slowly, but may begin to make mistakes once she speeds up.

Camille may have a mental or physical disability that makes it impossible for her to go any faster.

Hint: If you're not sure whether Camille will begin to make mistakes when she speeds up or just *thinks* she'll make mistakes, the only way to find out for sure is to test her. Tell her exactly what you're doing (finding out how fast she can go without increasing her error rate) and why (because her current production isn't satisfactory). Then instruct her to pack as many boxes, start to finish, as she can in a given amount of time (half an hour, an hour, two or three hours—whatever seems reasonable in your situation). Stand nearby during the test, giving her encouragement (and checking to make sure she really is increasing her speed). Then measure her production and error rates at the end of the specified period.

Cures

If Camille lacks confidence:

Encourage her as much as you can. Let her know that you appreciate her attention to the quality of the product, but stress that quality also means on-time production, and the company won't be on time if everyone works at her rate.

Help Camille set goals for incrementally increasing her rate. If you want her eventually to pack eight boxes an hour and she's now at four or five, begin by increasing her requirement to six, then seven, and finally eight. Congratulate her on each success and reassure her of your confidence that she can make the next increment at the same high-quality rate.

Make sure your incentive system rewards production rate as well as quality, if that's what's really important in this job. Camille may not lack confidence as much as she lacks incentive to go any faster. If pay and rewards are based only on error rates, then there's no good reason, from Camille's standpoint, to go any faster, especially if her errors are likely to increase.

If Camille lacks the skills to go any faster:

Observe her as she packs several different kinds of items. Are there particular areas where she seems to have some trouble, where she hesitates or seems to have to think about each step as she completes it?

Wherever you find those hesitations or problem areas, isolate those tasks and teach them specifically. This is an area where you can probably delegate the teaching and practice-monitoring to one of your better workers. Have Camille practice the tasks to mastery, that is, until she can complete them both *accurately* and *rapidly*. Once she's mastered those isolated tasks, then she can begin to combine them with the other steps in the process to speed up her overall rate.

Don't stop when she's mastered the individual steps, however. She may still have problems when she tries to put them together. In that case, you can combine the individual tasks into larger and larger units, until she has the whole process down. You may find, as you observe her combining the individual steps into a whole process, that there are parts of the job that aren't organized as well as they could be. Are all the steps in the most logical sequence? Does she have to "undo" things she's already completed to complete another step? Are the materials she needs organized so she can get to them when she needs them, or are they in the way of something else? As you observe Camille, you may find that her production problems are simply an exaggeration of difficulties everybody's having.

If Camille has a mental or physical condition that prevents her from working faster:

Decide how important speed is to the success of the operation. Can you afford to let Camille continue at her slower pace? Does her lack of errors compensate for her lower production level?

If the organization will suffer by allowing Camille to continue at her current production rate, look at alternatives. Can she be assigned to some other work where speed isn't as important, or where her condition won't interfere with her production? Does your company have an employment program for handicapped employees that would allow Camille to remain in your unit, working at her own speed, but that would give you some relief from work-year quotas?

If you cannot accommodate Camille within the company, be as tactful and sensitive as you can in terminating her. Explain exactly why you're taking the action and offer her as much assistance as possible in outplacement efforts.

6–7 THE PROBLEM

An employee is technically your best employee but has a tremendously negative attitude

THE SCENE

Paula isn't exaggerating when she tells you how frustrating Maury is. He's consistently one of your top two or three producers, but he's so full of negativity that no one wants to work with him or even around him. He fights every change, he assures everyone constantly that the company is about to downsize the workgroup out of existence, and he criticizes even the smallest mistake to death. He just plain brings everyone down, constantly.

POSSIBLE CAUSES

Maury doesn't realize he's being so negative.

Sounds too simple, but it may be true. He just thinks he's giving his honest opinions.

He simply doesn't care about the others.

If his pay is based on his individual production, he may not see any reason to worry about his impact on them.

He has a serious emotional problem.

He's "trapped" in his negativity, and his work provides him a way to escape it for a while.

CURES

No matter what the cause is:

You know what the problem looks like from outside; now you need to talk with Maury. More accurately, you need to listen to Maury, as carefully as possible. Don't be judgmental, but describe how his negative attitude appears from the outside. Then listen to how he sees it. Ask helpful questions, but don't put him on the spot.

The cures concentrate on dealing with the specific problem of a specific employee. Be sure to read "Something to Think About" at the end of this problem for a suggestion on how to turn negatives like this into positives.

If he doesn't realize he's being so negative:

If you think this is the problem, be as tactful as possible, but point out to him the effect he's having on others. This may be all you need to do to get his attention. He may be a little offended by what you say, but he'll probably understand how others are affected. (This may take several talks.)

This may not significantly change his negativity, but he may not voice it so much at work. This may be all you need. Make sure that both you and the other employees notice any improvement and recognize him for it. If you don't, he may conclude no one really cares and go back to voicing his negativity.

If he doesn't care about his effect on others:

Most employees are sensitive to other employees' reactions and want their approval. But not all employees. Some will do what rewards *them*, with little or no thought for others. This is particularly true if the individual is a "loner," or someone the group doesn't particularly like.

One approach is to assign Maury duties that don't bring him into contact with others, if the group's work permits that. Then he can continue to be as negative as he wants and still produce what he needs to. Everything considered, this may be the simplest and quickest solution. (It also works if you try the solution in the section before this one and it fails.)

If you can't assign Maury duties separate from others, can you make at least part of his pay dependent on working effectively with others? No matter how negative he is, if he and other workers see that they have to work together or else, everyone will find a way to deal with the negativity.

If he has a serious emotional problem:

Don't play amateur psychologist and don't anyone else in the workgroup do so. If this is an emotional problem, it's beyond your capabilities to correct. If an opportunity presents itself, you might suggest that he get professional help.

Then limit yourself and the group to being as supportive as possible. Don't let his negativity frustrate you and other workgroup members or make any of you angry. That just makes it harder for everyone and makes it harder for him to control. On the other hand, don't agree with his negative statements. Accept what he says, explain how you see the same situation if you want, then drop the matter. Don't get into arguments or extended discussions.

Once again, any time you or a workgroup member see even a small improvement, be sure to notice it and recognize it. If he can change, that will help him do so.

SOMETHING TO THINK ABOUT

You want a workgroup filled with "can do, will do" workers—individuals with a genuine positive mental attitude. But you also need individuals who will be honest about proposed changes and who are picky about the quality of their and others' work. Their approach may be labeled as negative when they're really trying hard to help.

How do you manage the situation? Let's take a product that one of your "negative" workers thinks isn't good enough. Why isn't it good enough? How can he or she communicate to the individual(s) who produced it how to fix the problem or how to avoid it the next time? Try to get the individual to link suggestions for improvement with any problem he or she identifies.

Encourage this approach in general. Whenever someone sees a problem in a product or proposed change, ask him or her to identify the problem as specifically as possible and then propose one or more ways the problem could be overcome. If you have some really negative workers, they may resist this. Let them, but insist on it as the price of voicing their negativity. It could turn around even someone like Maury.

6-8 THE PROBLEM

An employee is a marginal performer, but an informal leader in the group

THE SCENE

Gretchen is a real challenge. She's hardly one of your best workers—in fact, she's marginal at best. But people listen to her. She's never admitted to you that she's unhappy about anything, but the rest of the staff have certainly heard enough about it. And, unfortunately, they listen to her. She's stirred up resentment about your overtime schedule and your project assignments and your travel procedures—and probably a lot of other things you haven't even heard about yet. Not everyone pays attention when she complains, but enough do to cause you trouble. So how can you deal with her marginal performance without causing more discontent in the ranks?

POSSIBLE CAUSES

Neither the cause of Gretchen's marginal performance nor the source of her influence with the workgroup are of particular concern here. We've discussed the causes and cures of poor performance, intentional and unintentional, elsewhere. (See particularly Chapter 5 and other problems in this chapter.) And it doesn't matter *why* the rest of your staff are willing to listen to Gretchen's complaints; the fact is that they do, and that's causing you problems.

Your intention here is twofold: You want to help Gretchen improve her performance and you want to stop her negative influence with your staff. This is *not* a situation where you can take the justified, but entirely ineffective, step of dealing with the performance difficulties while ignoring Gretchen's leadership role in the workgroup. That approach will just result in Gretchen's complaining more to her peers about your "unreasonable" demands and will do nothing to improve her performance. You *must* deal with both the performance and the influence at the same time.

This is a tough situation, and it's not one in which we can give you a neat set of steps to follow that, if performed correctly, will solve the problem successfully. What we *can* do is offer a number of suggestions, some of which will apply to your problem, some of which won't. Consider them in light of the specific characteristics of your "Gretchen" and your workforce, use the ones that you think will work, disregard the ones you think won't—and good luck!

CURES

If your other workers are not aware of the quality of Gretchen's work:

They may accept her leadership more readily than they would if they had little respect for her technical competence. In that case, it may be effective to let your other employees see for themselves the kind of work Gretchen does. It's unlikely that they will have much faith in her critical remarks if they perceive them as a cover for her own lack of production.

Note: Your intention here is not to discredit Gretchen; that's underhanded, unworthy of you as a manager, and likely to backfire. Your intention is to structure opportunities for your staff to work with Gretchen and make their own informed decisions about her ability to form objective opinions about you and your management of the office.

To the degree it's possible, given the kind of work your unit performs, assign some work to teams rather than to individuals. Make sure Gretchen is a part of the team and that one or two of your best workers are too. Make your expectations clear to the team members, both in terms of the product you expect at the completion of the assignment and in terms of the level of participation you expect from each of the team members. If Gretchen isn't carrying her fair share, the team will discover that quickly.

Again to the degree possible in your particular work situation, let some decisions be made by teams rather than by individuals or by you. If your unit is supposed to develop schedules (e.g., for inventorying, for review of other units' work, for customer visits), assign a team to develop those schedules and make sure Gretchen is part of it. The degree of cooperation she exhibits in her dealings with you will probably be reflected also in her interactions with the team members.

Establish a peer review system. Instead of checking all your employees' work yourself, set up a system in which workers review each others' products. Include Gretchen as part of the peer review group. When you set up the system, establish regular rotation dates so that employees do not become so accustomed to reviewing the work of specific individuals that they lose their objectivity. Rotating review assignments also ensures that every employee gets the chance to review and evaluate the worth of every other employee's contributions (including Gretchen's).

If Gretchen is a marginal employee in a group made up largely of marginal workers:

In this case your challenge is a different one. The group itself will probably not be able to see that Gretchen's contributions aren't all that great, because they're all performing at about the same level. Problems 1–1 and 1–6 discuss variations on the basic theme of *organizational* productivity problems. In correcting the organization's performance deficiencies and improving their over-all morale, you may solve your specific problem with Gretchen. If the rest of the group responds to your efforts, but Gretchen does not, then the steps outlined above may help after you've improved the productivity of the majority of your staff.

If Gretchen's performance and attitude problems stem from a dislike of the job:

Her perception of your management style and decisions will be distorted by her own unhappiness. That doesn't mean that other employees are less likely to listen to her. On the contrary, she is more likely to be listened to if she's bright and articulate and tal-ented but simply misplaced in her current assignment. Problem 9 in this chapter discusses steps you can take when an employee clearly isn't suited to the job.

SOMETHING TO THINK ABOUT

An employee who is unhappy can make life miserable for you and the rest of your staff. When that employee requires correction, either because of poor performance or unacceptable conduct, the "noise" level is almost invariably going to increase, and everyone will be even more discontented. But both the unhappiness and the performance or conduct issue are problems that you can't ignore. They won't go away; they'll only get worse.

Your first approach should be to reduce the level of influence the employee has with the rest of the workgroup. Then, when you deal with the performance or conduct problem, the employee's attempts to stir up the workgroup against you won't meet with much success.

If you can't reduce the employee's negative influence, you still will have to address the performance or conduct problem. You may precipitate a crisis. But if you're being fair, reasonable, and have ensured the support of your superiors, both you and the organization will survive—a little bruised perhaps, but ready to forge ahead.

6–9 THE PROBLEM

An employee clearly isn't suited to the job

THE SCENE

It doesn't seem to matter what you do. Chuck has managed, one way or another, to mishandle every single assignment you've given him in the past six months. Sometimes his work seems to be acceptable, but then you find out later that something was missing or just slightly off course. And he's not rude to your customers, but somehow he always manages to irritate them. He doesn't fit in with the rest of the group, but his problem isn't something you can get a handle on. You don't know whether he doesn't like the job or can't handle the work, but clearly this isn't the job for him.

POSSIBLE CAUSES

Chuck may not feel comfortable with the assignment he has.

He may be accustomed to being the "star" in the office—either because he's the best at what he does or because he has a unique role—and this assignment doesn't offer that opportunity. Chuck will either have to adjust to this new role or be miserable until he can find something else.

Chuck may not find the work interesting.

It may just not be in a field that he has any interest in. It may be an administrative position—when Chuck's really a "people person." It may involve a lot of travel—when Chuck would rather be at home. Or it may just involve a subject area that Chuck doesn't care about—and so he's bored.

Chuck may not feel that he fits in with the rest of the staff.

They may have different interests or styles of interaction than he's comfortable with. And so he separates himself from the group and tries to think of ways to get out.

Hint: Often it's hard to tell whether a person is going to be suited to a job when you hire him for the position. He may come in with excellent credentials and appear to be just whom you're looking for. But somehow or another, he never works out. Over time, the employee will become discouraged and stop trying. He'll decide the fault is yours or the company's. ("This is a dumb job, anyway. Who cares whether it's done well or not?" he may say to reassure himself.) While you may believe that employees are responsible for their own happiness or unhappiness (and they are), it is still in your best interest to help them adjust to the situation or find another job. An employee who doesn't like what he's doing 8 hours a day, 250+ days a year isn't likely to be very productive and may develop more serious performance or conduct problems over time.

CURES:

If Chuck doesn't feel comfortable with his assignment:

Make sure he knows how to do the work. Problem 4–6 provides some tips on working with employees to be sure they learn what they need to know to do the job. If Chuck has been a "star" in the past and has the opportunity to learn the new assignment, he's got a good chance of being a star again.

Talk to Chuck about the aspects of the assignment he's not comfortable with. Think about how you can change the emphasis of the job a little to accommodate his specific goals. If it's not possible to restructure the position, let Chuck know up front and help him in his efforts to find a more satisfactory assignment.

If Chuck isn't interested in the work:

See Problem 4–2 for steps to take when an employee is assigned work in which he's not interested. Offer your support to Chuck in finding an assignment that more closely matches his interests, but make it clear that you expect him to continue to do his best for you until the new job comes through.

If Chuck doesn't feel that he fits in with the rest of the staff:

See Problem 11–5, which offers advice on situations when an employee doesn't relate to the group. You'll be working with the rest of your unit as well as Chuck to try to help him become more a part of things.

SOMETHING TO THINK ABOUT

An individual may not fit a job for three reasons:

- He may not have the native ability to do it.
- He may not want to do it.
- He may not have an affinity for that kind of work—that is, no matter how good he is or how hard he tries, the work just isn't satisfying to him.

When you have a real mismatch between a person and his or her job, your best bet is to help the person get a job that fits him or her as soon as possible. Don't waste your time verbally beating on the individual or otherwise trying to "motivate" him or her.

chapter seven

TROUBLESHOOTING PROBLEMS CAUSED BY THE INTENTIONAL MISBEHAVIOR OF AN EMPLOYEE

7-1 THE PROBLEM

An employee is one of your best workers but has lied under oath in an investigation

THE SCENE

You stare sadly at the report lying open on your desk. It's all too clear that Jeremy Cook lied in the investigation. The report says that on at least two occasions Mike Murgaty, one of your subordinate supervisors, approached Jeremy to try to talk him into participating in his land development scheme. But Jeremy denied that Mike had ever discussed the subject with him. Jeremy's one of your best workers—reliable, hard-working, and trustworthy—or so you thought. But a lie is a lie, isn't it?

POSSIBLE CAUSES

A lie is a lie? Well, yes—and no. Anytime an employee lies, it chips away at the bond of trust that is the basis of all of the relationships we form, at work and elsewhere. And the answer to that breach of trust is usually fairly automatic: An employee who lies is fired, since you never know, from now on, when you can believe him and when you can't.

But there are some extenuating circumstances that require that you at least *consider* an exception to that rule. You may still decide that you can't afford to keep the employee on the payroll any longer, either because you can't trust him or because you have to make a clear statement to the rest of the staff. But in certain situations, you owe it to the employee to at least consider some alternatives.

Jeremy may have believed he was expected to lie in the investigation.

Particularly if the employee being investigated is in a sensitive or highly visible position, or if he's one of the company favorites, Jeremy may have thought that he was supposed to protect the employee and the organization. His dishonesty may actually have been misguided loyalty to the company.

Jeremy may have been pressured to lie.

He may not have decided on his own that he was expected to lie; others in positions of influence over him may have fostered that impression. He may even have been threatened with loss of pay or stature or position—or with physical harm.

Jeremy may have lied to protect himself.

This is the most likely situation, and the least forgivable. Jeremy may have been implicated in the wrongdoing being investigated, or in some other wrongdoing that is likely to be revealed in the course of the investigation. He may have lied simply to keep his own transgressions from being discovered.

Hint: In deciding on the appropriate action to take, you need to consider not only the employee's motivation, but also the effect of your decision on the company (including the rest of the staff). Your bottom-line position *must* be that lying, or any action that undermines your trust in an employee, is intolerable. If it's well known in the company that the employee lied, then you have no choice but to take some corrective action. Regardless of the employee's misguided loyalty or perception of outside pressure, you must make it clear to the rest of the staff that you expect them to be open, honest, and trustworthy. If your staff can't trust one another, you can't expect customers to trust you either.

CURES

If Jeremy believed he was expected to lie:

First, be sure that Jeremy really did believe he was expected to lie and that this isn't an excuse for his unacceptable actions. Even if Jeremy has been entirely trustworthy in the past, remember that he has broken that trust, so anything he says is suspect until he has proven himself again.

If you're convinced that Jeremy is being honest with you about his reasons, explain to him what you would have expected of him in this situation and why his attempts to be a loyal employee were misguided. Make sure he knows that he can come to you if a similar situation arises for clarification of your expectations and support for his honest testimony.

Decide what corrective action is appropriate. If Jeremy lied about something relatively minor that had no material effect on the outcome of the investigation, if his false testimony is not a matter of public knowledge, and if it's clear that he gained *in no way* from his lie, you may be able to let him off with a warning. If any of those conditions are not met, take corrective action in accordance with your company's disciplinary policies. Your personnel department will be able to help you decide on an appropriate penalty and work through the required procedures.

If Jeremy was pressured to lie:

You will need to do an investigation of your own here. Find out who Jeremy felt was pressuring him. Get names, dates, places, records of conversations. Have Jeremy document his contacts in writing. Talk to other witnesses in the original investigation who may have been pressured by the same person(s) to see if they were approached. If your company has an investigations or security division, ask for their help in following up. Your personnel department may also be able to help you investigate Jeremy's allegations. If, at any point, it looks as if there is possible criminal activity involved, go immediately to your legal department or to the police in your location to report what you've discovered.

After you've collected all the information you can, make a decision about whether Jeremy had good reason to believe that he was being pressured to lie in the investigation. Remember, there are many kinds of pressure, some more subtle than others. It doesn't take a direct threat to convince an employee that he needs to listen, but you do need some reasonable basis for Jeremy's perception of outside pressure.

If it appears that Jeremy was pressured and reasonably expected some harm to come to him if he didn't lie, explain to him how you would have wanted him to handle the situation. Make it clear to him that he could have come to you, that you would have supported him and taken action against those who were pressuring him. Some minor corrective action may still be appropriate (for example, a reprimand), but it could also be appropriate to let Jeremy off with a warning.

If Jeremy misperceived pressure where none existed, you will need to take stronger measures. Explain clearly and firmly the standards of honesty to which you expect your employees to adhere. Make sure Jeremy understands what he did that was wrong and why it was wrong. To make sure other employees get the message, you may still need to take some disciplinary action against Jeremy—perhaps write up the incident for his personnel file.

Decide what corrective action is appropriate. If Jeremy has been a good employee and trustworthy until now, it may not be necessary to fire him. A suspension or a demotion to a position of lesser trust may be sufficient. But if there's any doubt about your ability to trust him in a similar situation again, terminating his employment is the appropriate action.

If Jeremy lied to protect himself:

The appropriate course here is clear. Make sure Jeremy knows what he did that was wrong and why it was wrong. Then separate him from your organization.

Let him know that his dishonesty is a matter of record and, subject to your company's policies, that you'll let his prospective employers know the reasons for his termination when they do reference checks.

Particularly if you work for a large company with multiple offices, make sure your personnel department has documentation to support the termination and a recommendation that Jeremy not be rehired within the company. Ask them to keep the records on file so that he isn't inadvertently rehired by another division that doesn't know his history with the organization.

Something to Think About

While it should go without saying that employees are expected to be honest and trustworthy, this might be a good time to issue a policy letter on the subject. Have it signed at as high a level in the company as you can, then present it to your employees with your own personal endorsement.

7–2 THE PROBLEM

An employee embarrassed you in front of your boss

THE SCENE

You can't believe it! You assure your boss that everything is on track for the Smithson job, then call Joe Esch in to confirm it. Instead, Joe tells you pointedly that he isn't doing anything on it because you haven't gotten him the spec sheets you promised. You get rid of Joe, mumble the best excuse you can think of to your boss, and try to look calm as he leaves. Now it's time to deal with Joe.

POSSIBLE CAUSES

Joe was just giving you an answer.

For some reason, he didn't understand what its consequences would be.

Joe is angry because you're holding up a project you assigned him.

Maybe he really has to have the spec sheets before he can go on.

Joe's been holding a grudge against you and this was his chance to "get" you.

Sometimes employees have long memories.

Joe wants to get you replaced as his boss.

Hint: Watch your anger! This kind of situation really gets under the skin of most managers. That's okay, but don't take any action to resolve it until you've cooled down.

CURES

No matter what the cause is:

You guessed it—you begin by talking with Joe—after you've calmed down. Give him every chance to tell you why he did it.

Then, no matter why Joe did it, make it clear that he's not to do it again. How clear you have to be depends on the situation, but don't leave any question in his mind about what will happen if he repeats the behavior.

If Joe was just giving you an answer:

As painful as it is, this is the easiest situation to deal with. Explain to Joe just what his response caused and how he should have handled it. Then make sure he knows not to do it again. Finally, explain that you're not angry with him since he acted out of ignorance.

If Joe is angry because you're holding up his project:

Perhaps Joe is a conscientious worker. Perhaps you really emphasized the due date when you assigned it to him, and he wants to get it done on schedule. Whatever the cause, to Joe you're holding up his work.

You have two issues to deal with here. First, face up to your failure to give him the materials he needed. Perhaps he could have reminded you that you promised them, but if you made the commitment he has no responsibility to serve as your memory. You blew it. Give him the spec sheets, or tell him exactly when you'll have them for him.

Second, tell Joe clearly that he's not to do that to you again. This may make him angry, but stick to it. Explain how it hurts himself as well as you.

If Joe's been holding a grudge against you:

You may have to probe a bit to find this out. But it's important that you do.

When you find out what caused the grudge, try to work it through. Is Joe unhappy over work assignments, or over a chewing out you gave him? This can be an opportunity to surface the issue and lay it to rest.

While you may not deal with it now, there's a question you need to ask: Does this point to a continuing problem in your relationship with Joe and perhaps with others in your unit? If it does, take this incident as the occasion to deal with the underlying problem.

If Joe wants to get you replaced:

This specific incident is probably the least of your worries. But you have to deal with it. If what Joe did was really blatant, you may want to take some disciplinary action.

The deeper issue is Joe's wish to get rid of you. Is there something specific you did that offended him and that you might be able to settle now? Sounds as if you need to do it. Any manager who has employees working to get him removed has a serious problem, one worth every reasonable effort to resolve.

What if no resolution is possible? You'll hope Joe is the only one who really wants you out of your job. If that's the case, you might want to see about getting him reassigned. (His behavior in front of your boss may help you get your boss's support for this.) If there's no realistic step you can take, just stay aware of the situation and be prepared. Joe may go too far, and then he may be the one who leaves, whether he wants to or not.

Suppose most of your employees would like to see you taken out of the job? Why? If it's because you're carrying out your boss's direction to "shape up" the unit, make sure they know that you have his support. If it's because your supervisory style creates unnecessary friction—well, do you have any good reasons not to change it?

SOMETHING TO THINK ABOUT

We've been concentrating on how you handle Joe, but there are two other issues you can't overlook. First, it's important to handle your boss. You can't undo the damage that Joe's comments did. You can make sure that you get the spec sheets to Joe, revise any dates that you have to, and then assure your boss that everything is okay. If Joe had an ulterior motive, mention it to your boss, but not as an attempt to get yourself off the hook. (By the way, is Joe behind, so that the project due date will have to slip? Don't let it; do whatever you have to do. Remember, you said it was on track—your credibility is at stake here.)

The other problem is you. *Why* didn't you get the spec sheets to Joe? You intended to but it just slipped your mind? Remember what good intentions pave the way to. Do what you have to do to see that this kind of thing doesn't happen again. From now on, when you make a commitment, keep it—period.

7–3 THE PROBLEM

An employee may have lied about having completed an assignment

THE SCENE

"Charlene, are you sure you don't have the production report?"

"Weldon, I *know* what a production report looks like, and I can promise you it never got to us."

"Dammit! I specifically asked Vic if he'd finished it before he left yesterday and he told me he had. I'd never have let him take the day off today if I'd known it wasn't done. I'll grab him as soon as he walks in tomorrow and get him to finish it."

POSSIBLE CAUSES

There's been a mistake somewhere.

Vic finished the production report, but it didn't get to Charlene.

There was no mistake—Vic lied.

Vic may have lied.

The situation looks suspicious, but . . .

Hint: This may seem like a small thing. After all, it was only one report, and it was only one day late. That's almost beside the point. Employees need to live up to their commitments, or you won't be able to rely on them. You also don't want employees around whom you can't trust. This is serious, and Vic needs to understand how serious it is.

CURES

No matter what the cause is:

Once again, begin by calming down, then call Vic in and confront him with the situation. Give him every chance to explain, but ask the hard questions if you have to.

If there's been a mistake somewhere:

Find out what happened to the production report and get it to Charlene. Do whatever you have to do to see that the problem isn't repeated. (This could mean revising an office procedure.)

If the mistake happened because Vic was sloppy or didn't follow through, counsel him. The problem was embarrassing to you and the unit—as well as to him—and he needs to make sure it never happens again.

If Vic lied:

The only serious question you're facing is whether to keep Vic or fire him. This may seem like a harsh approach to one small lie, but now you don't know how many times in the past Vic lied and you didn't catch it.

If Vic is a good employee and this is the first time anything like this ever happened, it may be enough to give him a couple of weeks off without pay. It's also possible—though not likely—that there were extenuating circumstances that might permit a lesser penalty. Be understanding, but don't forget how serious the offense was.

In this circumstance, you also have to remember the effect of your action on others. If you merely "slap Vic's wrist," it will communicate to the rest of your employees that you don't think lying is too serious. They may decide to try it, and then you and they will be in real trouble.

If Vic may have lied:

Suppose this is what happened. You're deeply suspicious of Vic, and no one can find the report. Then, three hours after he returns to work, he "discovers" the report in a desk drawer and immediately carries it to Charlene's unit. He apologizes, explaining that he thought he'd put it in the office mail but that it got stuck in some other material. Did he really misplace it, or did he rush and get it done as soon as he got back?

There's no way you can find out for sure—this time. You can talk with Vic, and you can make two points loudly and clearly:

- The situation looks extremely suspicious. Even if he did misplace the report, he's raised a question in everyone's mind. It will be that much harder for you and others to trust him the next time.

- Even if he's being completely honest, he dropped the ball. He knew finishing the report before he left was a condition of taking the day off. He should have made absolutely sure that either Charlene's unit or you had the report.

Whichever is the situation, he's put a question mark by his performance. Now it's up to him to perform so well that the question mark gets removed.

SOMETHING TO THINK ABOUT

Lying is an extremely serious offense. It not only destroys the trust between employee and manager, but it calls the whole past performance of the individual into question. Its effect is far beyond the immediate incident.

This works both ways. If you lie to your employees and get found out—and sooner or later you will get found out—it destroys your credibility and any trust they have in you. There's virtually nothing you can accomplish by lying that's worth that.

7-4 THE PROBLEM

An employee is trying to discredit a coworker

THE SCENE

"You'll never believe what Vivian just did," Ross confides at lunch. "She told the people on the Willenbacher account that she could get them a 20 percent price break if they signed a contract in 15 days! Can you believe it? That's the only reason she got that contract in so fast. She thinks she's 'Queen of the Hill' right now, but I'd never stoop to a trick like that!"

Oh, no? *You* know why Vivian closed that deal so quickly; you've been working with her on it since the beginning. And there was nothing underhanded about it. So who does Ross think he's fooling? And why is he out to get Vivian?

POSSIBLE CAUSES

Ross may be jealous of the attention Vivian is getting.

He may crave the same attention and think it's easier for him to shoot down someone else than to prove himself.

Ross may be trying to sabotage Vivian's chances for advancement—whether a promotion or a reward such as a bonus or public recognition. This cause is related to the first, but the intent to harm is greater.

Ross may have misunderstood the facts.

He may be repeating a version of the story he heard from someone else. That version may have been distorted either intentionally or unintentionally farther up the line.

Hint: Unless Ross genuinely misunderstood the situation and is inadvertently passing on bad information, it doesn't make a lot of difference what his true intentions are. Just as the trust between supervisors and subordinates is critical to the operation of any group, the trust among the members of the group is also critical. Whenever you have a situation in which one of your employees is trying to discredit another, there are two things you need to accomplish: (1) You must make it clear to the employee at fault that you will not tolerate that behavior, and (2) you must do all you can to repair the damage to the offended worker's reputation.

CURES

If Ross intended to discredit Vivian, whether because he's jealous of the attention or because he wants to keep her from getting some benefit:

Let him know *immediately* that you're aware of what he's doing and order him to stop spreading the falsehoods.

If this is the first time he's engaged in this behavior and if the damage to Vivian is minimal, you may let him off with just a warning, preferably a documented one. Make sure he understands that you consider his conduct unacceptable and that you will deal harshly with any repetition of this behavior.

If he has a history of similar conduct, or if Vivian has really been hurt by his rumors, you'll need to take much more severe action. Termination wouldn't be out of line, especially if yours is a business where cooperation and teamwork are essential. If competition among employees is encouraged in your line of work, lesser measures are appropriate. But even then, it's important that Ross learn from this experience the limits of acceptable behavior—that you can compete just as well, if not better in the long run, by improving yourself rather than by discrediting others.

If Ross was inadvertently passing on bad information:

Let Ross know that his information is incorrect, tell him the real story of how Vivian pulled off this brilliant feat, and enlist his help in undoing the damage he's done. Require that he talk again to people to whom he repeated the wrong story and give them the right version.

Give Ross a warning about trusting everything he hears "on the street." Especially if he's new or if yours is a competitive business, make sure he knows the dangers of turning into a dupe for someone else's plans to discredit others. Express your confidence in his own good intentions and his ability to learn to distinguish those sources he can trust from those he can't.

In either case:

You need to take some positive steps to restore Vivian's good reputation. You can begin by spreading the word among your staff of Vivian's good work, perhaps offering it as an example of a strategy others might want to copy.

You might consider also some public recognition of Vivian's achievement. If the circumstances are appropriate, your repetition of the true story and stated approval of Vivian's actions will go far in overcoming the negative effects of others' gossip.

7–5 The Problem

An employee uses company property at home for his personal use

The Scene

"Nice poster," you observe as you walk past the bulletin board. "I see Steve's neighborhood association is having a rummage sale next weekend."

But wait! That type style and those graphics look terribly familiar. Steve took the computer home to finish that design proposal a couple of nights ago; it looks as if he finished something else while he was at it. That's not supposed to happen. One thing they're firm about here is company property for company use—only.

Possible Causes

Steve may not be aware of company policy.

Especially if he's new to the company or if he just began taking the equipment home to work, he may not know what the rules are.

Steve may not agree with the rule.

He may have made a conscious decision to violate this company policy.

Steve may have a disregard for rules and restrictions in general.

This may not be an isolated incident, but Steve's usual mode of operation.

Hint: As with any suspected violation of company rules, it's critical that you get the facts before you act. Is the software that Steve used commercially available? Might he have bought software identical to what you're using at work for his own use? Can you prove that Steve used company property? Especially if he made an honest mistake or if he made a conscious decision to break the rule, he may tell you. But you can't do anything until you know what the real situation is.

CURES

If Steve isn't aware of company policy:

A word of instruction is probably the only action you need to take in this situation. Tell Steve what the company's rules are and, as clearly as you can, explain why the rules exist. If you have any authority to make exceptions to the rules, explain what the limits of your authority are and how Steve should request an exception.

You might also take this opportunity to make sure *everyone* in your unit knows what the company's policies are—on this and maybe one or two other things that people seem to have trouble remembering. The rules may not be all that meaningful to the employees who have to follow them, so a friendly reminder now and again doesn't hurt.

If Steve doesn't agree with the rule:

Discuss with Steve his reasons for not following the company's policy. Explain the purpose of the rule and what it is intended to accomplish; listen to any ideas Steve has about how the same purpose could be accomplished differently. Let him know that you'll try to push for changes in those areas where his ideas show promise. (If your company has a formal suggestion program, encourage Steve to submit his ideas through that channel so he can get credit for them.)

At the same time you're listening to Steve's criticisms and recommendations for improving the current system, remind him of his obligations as an employee. Regardless of his opinions about company rules and policies, as an employee of the organization he's expected to follow directions first and then question them. Make sure he understands that refusal to obey a company rule or policy is insubordination and is subject to severe penalties.

If this is the first time Steve's failed to follow the rule, your warning and explanation are probably sufficient. If this is a repetition of similar behavior, however, you'll need to take stronger disciplinary action. (See the cure described next.)

If Steve has a general disregard for rules and restrictions:

This is a serious problem. Organization without rules and limits is disorganization and confuses and disturbs people—it doesn't "free" them from anything except a sense of purpose and order. If Steve does have a general disregard for rules and restrictions, chances are this isn't the first time he's exhibited it. You may even have warned or disciplined him in the past for similar behavior. Your specific actions in this case depend considerably on his history with the company.

If this is the first time you've personally had to deal with Steve in this kind of incident, and if this offense is relatively minor, a warning is appropriate, preferably one documented in his employee records, either in your office or in the personnel department.

If this is not the first problem of its kind you've had with Steve, harsher measures are necessary: a formal write-up in his personnel file, a suspension, or maybe even termination if this has happened several times before and lesser remedies haven't corrected the misconduct.

In any case where you have to warn or discipline an employee (whether for failing to follow rules or for something else), it's crucial that you explain why you're taking the action. The purpose of discipline is almost always to correct behavior rather than to "punish" employees. At the same time you impose the penalty, make sure Steve understands not only what he did wrong, but what behavior you expect in the future.

7–6 THE PROBLEM

An employee is habitually late for work

THE SCENE

As you walk through the work area, you notice that Larry's desk is empty. You glance at your watch; it's already 15 minutes past starting time. He didn't ask for any time off, so there's only one likely conclusion you can draw—he's late again. Sure enough, as you finish your errand and walk back, there's Larry rushing in. This has got to stop.

POSSIBLE CAUSES

Larry has family responsibilities that take time in the morning.

You've been letting him and others get away with being late and not saying anything.

He's concluded it doesn't matter to you if he gets in late.

He's beginning to develop a bad habit.

This is the first sign of a serious personal problem.

He may be drinking to excess or abusing other drugs.

Hint: Just one employee coming in "a little late" may not seem like much. When this happens and you don't seem to care, it sends a message to other employees. The message may be that you don't care, or that you're a "weak" supervisor, or that you play favorites or . . . All of the messages are bad ones.

CURES

No matter what the cause is:

Need we say it yet again? Begin by talking with Larry—and don't put it off. The rest of the office is probably watching already, to see whether you're going to deal with the problem.

If you're really angry, though, put off talking with him long enough to cool down. It doesn't hurt for Larry to know you're unhappy with him, but you want to be able to listen objectively to what he has to say for himself.

If Larry has family responsibilities:

It wasn't too long ago that mothers were the ones who were late because they had to get kids off to school. Not any longer. Many husbands perform these chores, either because they want to or because their wife has to leave before they do. And it's not just kids anymore; more and more working people have to take care of aging parents.

If that's the situation, and Larry is otherwise a good worker, make whatever accommodations you can to his situation. Will it help if he starts his workday later and then puts in a full day? Can he start a little late and make up the difference by taking a short lunch? Could you even consider "flexitime" for the entire unit?

The important point is that if Larry has honest reasons for not getting to work at the normal time, it's proper to fit his work schedule to his personal schedule. If you can't, of course, then you have to deal with his tardiness as a performance problem. But try very hard to avoid that.

There's one other important aspect of the problem. Why hasn't Larry told you? He's been late several times; he should have taken the initiative to explain this to you. Even if his reasons for tardiness are the best and you do accommodate his situation, you need to counsel him on this point.

If you've been letting him (and perhaps others) get away with being late:

You've been sending them the message that it's okay to be "a little late"—whatever a little late is. Larry figures that if you don't care, he doesn't care.

It's time to stop that foolishness—*your* foolishness—right away. That doesn't mean chew out Larry and then ignore the problem again until it hits you in the face. It means having an honest talk with him, admitting that you've been getting lax, and then making it clear that you won't permit tardiness in the future. If you've been letting others get away with it, talk with them, either singly or in a group.

Larry or one of the others will probably test you on this, quite possibly the next morning. Be ready for it. There's no point in getting mad; after all, you helped cause the problem. But confront the situation and be firm about it. That will probably end the testing. If it doesn't, do some serious counseling, even writing up the offenders.

If Larry is beginning to develop a bad habit:

He may have been a good worker, so you didn't want to push him the first time or two. But now his tardiness is turning into a habit, and it's time to stop it.

Talk to Larry, make it clear what your standards are. If he makes excuses, brand them as excuses and reject them. If he has poor work habits, he may not think that tardiness is that important. Make it clear to him that it is.

Don't be surprised if he resents this and gets angry. Just accept it, but repeat that you won't tolerate the tardiness. Then, if he's tardy again, counsel him immediately. You'll probably want to write him up this time.

Keep the pressure on. If Larry likes his job, he'll start getting there on time. If he doesn't, treat it as a performance problem and deal with it that way.

If this is the first sign of a serious personal problem:

Larry may be drinking too much, so it's hard for him to get going in the morning. He might be producing the same result by abusing other drugs. Perhaps his home life is bad, so that it's emotionally difficult for him to start the day.

There are dozens of possible causes. If Larry is a normally good worker who's suddenly starting to have bad work habits, or if the excuses he gives you don't hold up at all, he may well have this kind of problem.

Look at Chapter 3 for suggestions on how to deal with an individual who has a serious personal problem.

SOMETHING TO THINK ABOUT

It's only natural to give a good worker some slack. If Larry is a good worker, you don't want to hassle him just because he's late a time or two. No—but you don't want to let him set a pattern either. It's possible to talk about his tardiness without being angry. That's what you need to do, as soon as you see it's not an isolated case.

chapter eight

TROUBLESHOOTING PROBLEMS CAUSED BY AN EMPLOYEE WHO CHALLENGES YOUR AUTHORITY

8-1 THE PROBLEM

An employee publicly refuses to follow an order

THE SCENE

"I don't care what you do, I *will not* touch that mess in the collection room. You get somebody else to do it, or you do it yourself." With that, Jolene stalks out of your office.

POSSIBLE CAUSES

Jolene may believe you've asked her to do something that's unsafe.

Jolene may believe you're picking on her. As she sees it, you've unfairly singled her out for the job.

She may believe that what you want her to do is "beneath" her.

She may see that as menial, humiliating work.

She may not like the work and isn't going to do it.

Sometimes, people's reasons are no more complicated than that.

Hint: There are two distinct problems here. The first is Jolene and her motives. The second is the impact of her action on other employees. You have to consider both.

CURES

No matter what the cause is:

You may have a good idea of the cause, or you may not. Either way, wait until you and Jolene have both calmed down and then talk with her. Don't jump to the conclusion that she's wrong. Listen with an open mind and give her every chance to explain what she did.

If Jolene honestly believes you asked her to do something unsafe:

This is sticky, but there's broad agreement in our society that an employee may refuse to carry out an order that she believes endangers her health or that of others, is illegal, or violates common moral standards. An employee is at risk whenever she refuses to obey an order, but if it's for one of these reasons the disobedience may be justified.

It may be difficult to tell whether Jolene means this or is just using it to get off the hook. This is where skillful listening comes in handy.

If she genuinely believes what you told her to do was unsafe, then accept that as a sufficient reason for not doing it. But it doesn't answer everything. There are still questions like:

• Did she tell you she thought it was unsafe at the time? (And, if she did, why didn't you pay attention?)

• Did she ask you to let her explain? (And, if she did, did you refuse to let her?)

• Did she tell you *why* she thought it was unsafe? (Again, if she did, did you listen?)

If you were ready to listen to her, but she didn't give you a reason for disobeying, she didn't do what a conscientious employee should. Counsel her on that. Then make sure the two of you agree on how you'll handle the situation (if it may reasonably come up again).

If Jolene believes that you're picking on her:

This is also sticky, but for different reasons. How do you tell if this is the case, or just a convenient excuse?

Here's where you have to be really clean with yourself. What is your relationship with Jolene? Were you trying to "show her who's boss," or force her to change a "poor attitude"? Were you angry with her before the situation came up? Or—we hate to ask, but we have to—were you influenced by the fact that Jolene is a woman or (perhaps) a minority?

If you're convinced you treated Jolene as you would have anyone else, you still have to deal with her feelings that you were picking on her. And you should deal with them, regardless of what else you do. As long as she feels that way, situations like this can occur at any time.

What if you may have picked on her? Discuss it openly. If it was based on her personal characteristics or traits, discuss these with her. Give her plenty of room to express herself. See if you can get the situation behind both of you.

If she honestly believed you were picking on her, it's not really appropriate to discipline her—*this time*. Agree that if it comes up again, you'll call a halt to what's happening and go somewhere that you can talk it over.

Regardless of all this, make it clear that if she refuses to follow an order again, you *will* discipline her. Her honest feelings buy her one pardon, but only one. Make sure she understands the options open to her the next time such a situation occurs (see the last part of the preceding "cure").

If she believes the work is "beneath" her:

Golly—another sticky one! This dances right on the border between excusability and lame excuse.

Here past practice may help you decide. If there's a clear practice that employees in Jolene's job do that kind of work, *and if she knows it*, she has no excuse. If they don't usually do it, or if she's never been told, what she did may not have been quite so bad. If there is no consistent practice—well, back to square one!

If employees in her job don't normally do this kind of work, both of you need to understand why you expected her to do it. If you've decided to change how things are done and just didn't tell anyone, you shouldn't be surprised when she reacted as she did.

Now, suppose employees in that job regularly do what you ordered her to do. Would she reasonably have known that? If she wouldn't have, make sure she knows now. If she should have, use the suggestions in the next cure.

Again, no matter the situation, use the suggestions at the end of the first "cure" to make sure the situation never happens again.

If she doesn't like the work and isn't going to do it:

She picked the wrong place and time to make her point. This is where you and she have a heart-to-heart talk about how much she wants to continue to have a job. It should be a *serious* talk; clear insubordination is one of the reasons for severe discipline—including termination—accepted by almost everyone.

If she's an otherwise good worker and appears to have learned, you may want to close off the situation by giving her a few days off without pay. If she's marginal, or she clearly has learned nothing, look into terminating her. (Sound cruel? Remember, the rest of your work unit is looking over your shoulder, waiting to see what you're going to do.)

Something to Think About

There are two reasons for firing an employee:

- She's demonstrated that she doesn't intend to follow workplace rules. In other words, she's past reasonable rehabilitation.
- She may or may not be salvageable, but you have to take the action to maintain discipline in the work unit. When an employee is openly insubordinate, just this reason may be a sufficient reason to fire her.

Always consider *both* reasons when you're faced with a serious offense.

8-2 The Problem

An employee ignores your directions to cooperate with a manager he doesn't like

The Scene

"What's wrong with that Sartini woman on your staff?" Joe asks indignantly. "All I asked for was expedited handling of *one little supply requisition*, and you'd think I'd asked for the moon and the stars. I thought you told me you were stressing customer service to that group of yours upstairs!"

Well, actually you can empathize a little with Elaine Sartini; Joe's not the easiest manager to get along with. *On the other hand*, you explicitly told her to cooperate with him since you're trying to get *his* cooperation on something else. Wasn't she listening?

POSSIBLE CAUSES

Elaine may have misunderstood your directions.

She may not have meant to be uncooperative, but simply didn't know what you were asking her to do.

Elaine may not realize why it's important to cooperate with the other manager.

Even if she knows why it's essential to keep customers satisfied, she may not have grasped the concept of "internal customer" or the importance of peer relationships.

Elaine may be deliberately ignoring your instructions.

She may not agree with you; she may not respect your decision-making capabilities; she may have let her dislike of Joe interfere with her good judgment; or she may be out to get you. But regardless of her underlying motive, in this case she's clearly made a conscious decision *not* to follow your direct order.

Hint: As we'll discuss in more detail in a later chapter, good peer relationships are critical to a successful career. But that fact is often not obvious to your employees who are most concerned about protecting their own parochial interests. Regardless of any individual employee's attempts to undermine your efforts to establish and maintain those relationships, it's important that your staff in general understand why they're important and what they can do to foster good relationships between units.

CURES

If Elaine didn't understand what you were asking her to do:

Review with her the limits of her authority—to bend the rules or to make other accommodations in response to "special requests." Make sure she understands which rules or procedures *may not* be violated and why, as well as those over which she exercises some discretion.

Then discuss with her the particular case with Joe. Explain what she could have done better and how. Rehearse with her how she should handle similar situations in the future and how to decide whom she should make special efforts for.

Suggest that she consult with you the next time this kind of situation arises. And when she does, instead of *giving* her an answer, ask first how she thinks it should be handled. That way you'll foster her own independent resolution of cases, while ensuring that there are no more foul-ups while she's developing her judgment-making skills.

If Elaine doesn't understand why it's important to cooperate with the other manager:

Describe to her the relationship between Joe's unit and yours. Explain what benefits you get from him, either as a regular part of the work or because of special efforts he may make for you. You may have to go into considerable detail here, especially if Joe and his unit don't affect Elaine directly. In that case, you'll need to make sure that Elaine also learns something about the different functions of your unit and in particular the areas where Joe can help, or hurt.

If the message doesn't seem to be getting across, you might ask Elaine to list the people that she personally relies on to get her work accomplished. From there you should be able more easily to generalize to the interdependence among units, including yours and Joe's.

In the end, although it's better for you *and* Elaine if she understands why it's important to cooperate, your basic concern must be that she *does* it. If you can't convince her of the necessity of fostering good relationships with other units, then be as directive as you need to be to get your instructions across. You can't afford to let one employee's lack of understanding alienate an important ally.

If Elaine is deliberately ignoring your instructions:

Failing to follow an order is tantamount to refusal to follow it. Both are forms of insubordination. Problem 1 in this chapter describes a blatant case of insubordination and describes appropriate responses.

SOMETHING TO THINK ABOUT

You can't assume that every incident in which an employee fails to follow a direction is a conscious attempt to undermine your authority. In at least some of the cases we've discussed here there's a real possibility that the employee was trying to help out—that she thought you were mistaken and could save you by doing things differently. In dealing with failures to follow instructions, it's important to explain to employees as well as you can *why* you've made the decisions you have. Of course, they also need to know that it's not acceptable for them to substitute their judgment for yours when you've required a specific course of action. But you're much more likely to get their wholehearted cooperation in the future if your decisions appear to them to be the well-reasoned judgments they are, rather than capricious whims.

8-3 THE PROBLEM

An employee goes over your head when you give him an order he doesn't like

THE SCENE

"Hello—this is Eleanor Wilkins."

"Eleanor, are you and Eddie Daniels having some sort of donnybrook?"

"I don't think so, Mr. Sugeno," you answer, with growing anxiety. "Why do you ask?"

"He came up here to see me—as a matter of fact, he just left. He was complaining about some work you assigned him, said you were loading him up and letting the others off."

"I really don't know what the story is, but I'll take care of it," you say, as bravely as you can.

"I expect you to."

"Damn!" you mutter to yourself as you hang up. You knew Eddie didn't like the assignment, but you hadn't expected him to run right to your boss.

POSSIBLE CAUSES

In Eddie's eyes, you're mistreating him so badly that he believes this is the only way he can get things straightened out.

What he did was an act of desperation.

Eddie believes that what you told him to do is so bad that your boss ought to know about it.

He isn't getting what he wants, so he tried to "end-run" you.

When Eddie doesn't get what he wants, this is his habitual way of dealing with the situation.

The difference from the one above is that this is Eddie's *pattern* of dealing with these situations.

Hint: This is irritating, of course, but there's something more. You need to deal with this one quickly and effectively so that your authority doesn't start to erode. If other employees see that Eddie can get around you, well . . .

CURES

No matter what the cause is:

This is another situation where you wait until you have your anger well under control and then review the situation objective-ly. If you've contributed to the situation, you need to realize it up front.

Then have a clear discussion with Eddie. You want to listen carefully to him, so you get a good feel for what's going on.

If Eddie believes you're mistreating him and this is the only way he can deal with it:

Be careful with this one. You need to listen carefully and be honest with yourself: Are you mistreating him? Is this something he did only out of desperation?

If he apparently believes this in all honesty, deal with that problem. Why does he believe it? What have you done? What can you—and he—do to correct it? Do your best to get to the bottom of the situation and deal with his concerns. You want to lay them to rest if you can.

Did he voice his concerns to you before? If so, why didn't you listen? If not, why didn't he? Unless he had a good, realistic reason for not talking to you, counsel him strongly that you expect him to do so next time. If necessary, tell him that if he goes over your head without talking to you, you'll write him up or take even more serious action.

You may have noticed this pattern in other problems: First make sure that you really listen when an employee comes to you with a problem or complaint. Then make sure that he comes to you before he talks to anyone else or takes any action. If you do the first, you have every right to require the latter.

If he believes what you told him to do is so bad your boss should know about it:

We don't need to tell you this is serious. Why would he believe that? Again, look at the situation calmly. Did you tell him to do something because you were angry or trying to prove a point? If so, you need to apologize, get straight with yourself about why you did it, and then not do it again.

If you really didn't, if the assignment was an acceptable one, why did he react so strongly to it? There could be any number of reasons for this; the burden of proof is on him to persuade you that his was a legitimate one. (If it wasn't, see the next "cure" for suggestions.)

Your relationship with Eddie obviously needs some work. If he believed that you told him to do something you shouldn't have, he's telling you that the relationship isn't very good. What do you have to do to correct that?

You also need to talk to Eddie about his responsibility to talk with you first. Use the suggestions in the preceding "cure."

If he tried to "end-run" you because he didn't get his way:

(The difference between this situation and the one below is that in this one Eddie is pulling an end-run for the first time. In the one below, it's a habitual way that he deals with not getting what he wants.)

When you've established that this is the case, the mildest thing you do is counsel Eddie in no uncertain terms not to repeat it. Then promise him that if it happens again you'll take much stronger action. You want to stop this before he starts to make a habit of it.

Your side of this action is to make sure that you haven't contributed to the problem. For instance, some employees—some very good ones—have a highly developed sense of what's reasonable. What looks to you like Eddie trying to get his way may seem to him like an attempt to get around your "unreasonable" assignment. (This is akin to the "cure" right above, but not really the same thing.)

You also need to speak to Eddie about the importance of coming to you first; see the suggestions in the first "cure."

If this is the way Eddie habitually deals with not getting his way:

This is where you make crystal clear that you won't tolerate his behavior. You may not be able to discipline him formally this time, but you can certainly write him up now and then discipline him if he tries it again.

Why so strong an approach? If this is the way he usually reacts when things don't go his way, he'll keep on doing it. He won't change unless the cost of doing it becomes too high.

Keep this in mind: Eddie may be used to going around supervisors because he's had one or more who wouldn't listen to his problems and complaints. What you see is the habit; the frustration that drove him to it may not be so clear. It's worth probing for. If his action was based on frustration, you can try to show him that you'll listen to him and try to deal with his problems.

SOMETHING TO THINK ABOUT

We've left out an entire element in the situation: your boss. Once you get Eddie dealt with, you need to deal with your boss. If you and he have a good relationship, be honest about the situation. If not, put the best face on it that you can. You need to assure him that it was an isolated incident that you've dealt with firmly and fairly and that it won't happen again.

Then make sure it *doesn't* happen again.

8-4 THE PROBLEM

An employee publicly criticizes you

THE SCENE

"Just who does she think she is?" grumbles Peggy to Mike in the hall outside the rest room. A group of workers begin to gather as Peggy expounds her litany of grievances: "She couldn't find her office without a map and here she is telling *me* how to manage a project I've had for years. On top of that, she's *insisting* that I coordinate with Paul Preston next door. We'll never get anything done now, and all because the old bat has to have things *her* way!"

POSSIBLE CAUSES

It really doesn't matter *why* Peggy is criticizing you in front of the rest of the staff. This is an action designed specifically to undermine your authority. You cannot tolerate it—regardless of what provocation Peggy may have had or of how limited her influence is over her co-workers.

CURES

This is one situation where immediate action is important. You overheard Peggy's remarks, and your workers know it. If you ignore the situation or put off dealing with it, they'll interpret your inaction as a sign of weakness, and you'll add another nail to the coffin Peggy is working so hard to build for you.

At the same time, you cannot stoop to the tactics Peggy has employed. Public criticism is always out of line, barring a direct threat to human life or safety. It doesn't matter whether it's Peggy criticizing you or you criticizing Peggy. You cannot allow yourself to engage in the behavior for which you're about to chastise Peggy. But you *can* make it clear to the group at large that this a serious matter with which you're about to deal *now*.

Calmly but firmly disengage Peggy from the group. A clear, "Peggy, I'll see you in my office right now!" should convey the message.

Explain to Peggy exactly what she did that you consider inappropriate. She probably already knows, but it's important that you define the specific things she did that are unacceptable. Explain also *why* they're unacceptable. Nothing long or complicated is required here, just a short statement about the need for respect and courtesy for co-workers and for proper authority.

If this is the first time Peggy has publicly criticized you, warn her that you will not treat such behavior lightly and that repetitions of this incident will likely result in severe action, including termination. Make sure she understands the consequences of a "leaderless" organization and the confusion and lack of focus that result.

If Peggy has criticized you, or other supervisors, in public before *or* if this criticism is likely to result in real damage to your credibility or effectiveness, a warning is not sufficient. You should try to obtain a public retraction from Peggy, but, even after retraction, you may decide that Peggy has done enough irreparable damage that you can't afford to keep her on the staff.

Public retraction does not necessarily mean public apology. While it's certainly desirable to get Peggy to admit to her audience that her behavior was inappropriate, this is not an opportunity for you to exact revenge. Public retraction should be done as sensitively and tactfully as you can arrange it. It should not result in Peggy's humiliation.

SOMETHING TO THINK ABOUT

While public criticism is clearly inappropriate behavior, public disagreement is not. In fact, the best managers have a clear preference for open and honest disagreement on issues that arise. The difference between unacceptable criticism and acceptable disagreement lies in the setting and the manner of presentation. Public disagreement should be in a setting where both sides of the question are represented so that there can be real debate on the merits of each position. It should not be done behind your back or the backs of other employees who hold the opposite position. And acceptable public disagreement *always* focuses on the issues, never on personalities and *never* descending to insults or name-calling.

8–5 THE PROBLEM

An employee brags that you can't do anything to him because of his friendship with your boss

THE SCENE

"Look, it doesn't really matter *what* you think I ought to do. I'm not going to do it, and there's nothing you can do about it! Ernie Eckart and I are old friends, and he'll do anything I ask—and if you push me one more time I'm going to ask him to get you off my back. Understand?"

With that, Andy turns and saunts out, leaving you even more frustrated than before. How are you going to maintain discipline when an employee openly flaunts his friendship with your boss?

POSSIBLE CAUSES

Andy is bluffing.

His friendship with Mr. Eckert is an exaggeration, or even a pure invention.

They are friends, but Eckert still expects Andy to produce like any other employee.

They are friends, and what Andy said is exactly right.

Eckert cares more about the friendship than Andy's productivity or your work unit discipline.

Hint: It doesn't sound good, but don't panic yet.

CURES

No matter what the cause is:

We often begin with the recommendation that you talk with the employee. Not this time. This time you talk with your boss—Mr. Eckert.

Your goal is to find out just what the relationship is between him and Andy. You might start the conversation something like this: "I understand you know Andy pretty well, and I was wondering if you could help me. I've been having some problems with his productivity and . . ."

Listen carefully to Mr. Eckert's response. If he's honest with you, you'll know just what to do. But he may not be completely honest. If he says "I want you to treat him just like anyone else," he may or may not mean it. Be tactful, but try to probe for his real feelings.

If Andy is bluffing:

He just tried to play hardball and failed. Now it's your turn to play hardball. Call him in, make it perfectly clear you don't buy his "friendship" routine, and tell him what you expect. Then make sure he delivers.

Needless to say, you don't take this course of action unless you're *sure* that Mr. Eckert has no interest in what happens with Andy.

If they are friends, but Eckert doesn't expect you to make exceptions for Andy:

Call Andy in. Explain that you just talked with Mr. Eckert and found that he expects the same thing you do—an honest day's work from Andy. Be tactful and reasonable and be clear. When Andy leaves, he should have no doubts about what you expect from him.

Keep in mind that Andy will probably relay his version of the conversation to Eckert. You'll help accomplish your objectives if you take these two steps:

- When you talk with Eckert in the first place, explain to him the problem you're having and what you intend to tell Andy. If any of it troubles him, change it and get his okay before you leave.
- When you've talked with Andy, give Eckert a call. Tell him you and Andy have had your conversation, and that he can expect a call or a visit from Andy. Depending on Eckert's response, you might want to summarize the conversation for him.

If they are friends, and Eckert will support Andy:

Don't conclude this until you've probed very carefully in your talk with Eckert. He probably won't ever tell you he'll side with Andy, but he may say something like "Oh, yes, he's a good man. I expect you to treat him well." A few statements like this, and you've got the picture.

If Andy can get Eckert to block you, your choices are very limited. Problem 17–8 discusses this situation at length.

SOMETHING TO THINK ABOUT

It's normally a good rule of thumb to treat employees as though they intend to do a good job. That prevents a lot of misunderstanding and helps you get the best from each of them.

There are exceptions, employees who really do intend to get away with everything they can, any way they can. When you've got one of those, take your kid gloves off. Don't do anything immoral or illegal; don't break the rules. Just be very smart and very tough.

By the way, this is where it pays off to have good working relationships with your employees. If the group as a whole thinks well of you, they'll help you take care of the people who don't want to do their fair share.

8–6 THE PROBLEM

An employee tries to sabotage you with other employees

THE SCENE

"Boss, I think you should know what's going on behind your back," offers Carolyn after staff meeting this morning. "Frank is running around the office trying to get people stirred up against you and your decision to take us off flexible hours for the next two months. Most of us know why you had to do it, and, while we're not thrilled, we're willing to go along with you. But Frank is talking about a slowdown—kind of a 'you can't make me if I don't wanna' trick. He thinks if he can make you look bad enough, he can drive you out of this unit!"

POSSIBLE CAUSES

Frank may believe that you're damaging the organization.

He may feel so strongly that what you're doing is wrong and so powerless to change it by working through "channels" that he's willing to descend to guerilla tactics.

Frank may be out to get your job.

He may see discrediting you as a way to get you out of the organization and open up chances for his own advancement.

Frank may not like you.

It may not be that he thinks you're doing a terrible job from which he has to save the organization or that he wants your position, he just wants you to be gone. Maybe you have a personality clash; maybe he doesn't like the way you dress, or wear your hair, or talk. But for one reason or another, he doesn't want you around anymore.

Hint: This situation, like most of the others in this chapter, involves overtly hostile acts toward you by your subordinates. Regardless of the motives, which may (as in the first cause listed above) be essentially good, the methods are unacceptable. Organizations can't run without leaders; someone has to set directions and make decisions about policy and values. Undermining authority never solves a problem; it only creates additional ones.

CURES

If Frank believes you're hurting the organization:

His motives are basically sound, even though his methods are not. Before you talk to Frank, you need to get your own emotions under control. It's not pleasant to realize that someone's out to get you, no matter what the reason is. So think before you act. Try to find out from trusted co-workers what it is that Frank's concerned about. Then in confronting him, deal with the issues, not your own pain.

Let Frank know that you're aware of what he's been doing and that you disapprove strongly, not just because of the personal harm it's causing you, but also because of the damage *he's* doing to the organization. Sabotage only works when it's undiscovered; once it's out in the open, it's a useless tactic.

Give Frank a chance to explain why he believes you're harming the organization. Listen carefully. If he believes it that strongly, there may be something important in what he says. Tell him specifically what you intend to do to allay his concerns, and what acceptable redress is available to him if he's still not satisfied.

Explain to Frank how his efforts to sabotage you damage the organization at least as much as anything you may have done. Talk to him about why mutual respect and trust are so critical and how his actions have undermined both your respect for and trust in him.

If Frank wants your job:

As before, the best way to get Frank to stop his campaign against you is to let him (and others, as appropriate) know that you're aware of what's going on.

Because Frank's motives are not nearly so pure in this case, it's not so important to direct your efforts toward reestablishing the relationship. Frank has made it clear that his ambition is paramount, and your reasonable, understanding approach is going to have no impact on him.

Confront Frank. Let him know that what he's done has destroyed the trust and confidence you had in him, and that you see no way for him to regain them.

He may apologize and offer to make amends. If so, it's your judgment call whether he's destroyed the relationship so thoroughly than it's unsalvageable or whether you're willing to give it another try. If you do decide to work with Frank, watch him carefully. He's betrayed you once, and he may again—especially if he *really* wants your job.

He may not offer to make amends, or he may offer and then step back into his old maneuvering. At this point, you have no choice but to offer him the door. As long as he's around to sabotage your efforts, your effectiveness will suffer.

If Frank doesn't like you:

Once again, begin by bringing the covert behavior out into the open, but as unemotionally as you possibly can. At this point, you don't know whether the underlying cause is something you can work out with Frank or not.

Make sure Frank understands why his actions are unacceptable, and their impact on the trust and confidence you have in him. At the same time, explain that you know people don't always get along and offer to discuss with him things that the two of you can do to mend the relationship.

If Frank trusts *you*, he'll probably be willing to tell you what it is that bothers him. Then you can decide whether it's something that you can, and are willing to, change. If so, work out with Frank what you're willing to do and what you expect from him. Remind him that one of the things you expect is that he won't engage in sabotage against you again and warn him of the consequences if he should.

If Frank won't talk to you about the underlying causes of his dislike of you, then you won't be able to salvage the relationship. He's already undermined your trust in him and now, in effect, has refused to do anything to fix things. Offer him a position in another part of the company if one's available and he's a worker you would otherwise want to keep. If not, let him go.

SOMETHING TO THINK ABOUT

If you find that a number of the problems in this chapter sound familiar to you, then you're probably working in an organization that is essentially sick. Disagreement and dissension among workers is not that uncommon—particularly in organizations undergoing unusual stress or change. But deliberate attempts to undermine authority, overtly or covertly, are not that common. Individual workers may be dissatisfied, not know more constructive ways to accomplish what they want, and resort to these kinds of tactics. If you begin to see patterns of this kind of behavior, either within your own unit or across organizational lines, then you need to look hard at the company itself. *Something* is operating to make employees believe that this is a good way for them to get what they want. For the good of both the company and you, it's essential that you convince them otherwise.

8-7 THE PROBLEM

An employee refuses to work emergency overtime

THE SCENE

"Ms. Johansen, we can stand here and argue until quitting time and it won't change anything. I won't work until 9:00 tonight. May I go now?"

You nod. You really need Bonnie to work late, and the example she's setting by refusing to do so may encourage other employees to refuse, too. Now what do you do?

POSSIBLE CAUSES

Bonnie has personal commitments that keep her from being flexible.

She may have to get her children at a fixed time or go home to take care of elderly parents.

She may have special plans for this evening.

She's organized her life so she doesn't have any flexibility.

Bonnie has a second job.

She starts work soon after she leaves this job.

She's not a flexible person.

Hint: Sorting out just what the situation is may be a challenge.

CURES

If she has personal commitments that keep her from being flexible:

In Problem 7–6 we looked at an employee who was late because of personal commitments. You might want to look at that problem for additional thoughts.

More and more people who work have demanding personal responsibilities. If Bonnie has to pick up an elderly parent from an "elder-care" facility and take him home, she may have to do it no matter what. There's no point in getting upset about it; she simply doesn't have flexibility.

Does this mean you let her refuse to work overtime? Perhaps. But there are other alternatives (though probably not for today). It may be she can make other arrangements if she gets advance notice of the overtime. Perhaps she could come in early in the morning instead of staying late. The important point is for both of you to know what if any flexibility she has and then make your plans based on it.

There's a moral in this story: You should know what flexibility each of your workers has *before* a situation like this comes up. That way, both your expectations and theirs will be realistic. You'll avoid these last-minute confrontations.

If she has special plans for this evening:

What you do depends more than anything else on the practices of your work unit. Is this the first time last-minute overtime has come up in months? Then it's reasonable for her to make plans like this. On the other hand, is last-minute overtime common, with the expectation that employees will be available to work it? That's a different situation. Also, did she tell you in advance she wouldn't be able to stay today?

In other words, there's a lot to take into account in this circumstance. If she knew from past practice that she was taking a gamble, she should be counseled or even disciplined for refusing the overtime. Otherwise, it's not reasonable to expect it from her.

Is the situation apt to arise again, with Bonnie or someone else? Then you (and your employees, if possible) should establish a reasonable policy that gets the work done with the least disruption to their personal lives.

If she's organized her life so she doesn't have flexibility:

Sometimes it's hard to tell the difference between this and the first cause. She may be locked in to responsibilities after work, but she may have had the option whether or not to do it that way. Does she have to pick up a child from day care? She may have been able to get a neighbor to do it for her. It's important to find out how much flexibility she really has.

If she has made most of the decisions that have taken away her flexibility and you need her to work last-minute overtime periodically, then make it clear that you expect her to reorganize her life to accommodate the overtime. This may take several discussions, and you may have to help her think it through. If she can reasonably do it, though, you have the right to expect her to.

If she has a second job:

Is this her primary job? If the answer is "yes," then this is the job she owes her primary allegiance to. You have the right to expect her *not* to refuse reasonable requests for overtime.

It's probably not wise to deal with the situation any more today. But call her in tomorrow and discuss the situation with her. Make it clear that you expect this job to come first. If you need her to work overtime, you expect her to be available to do it. If she refuses again, she could subject herself to disciplinary action.

Having said that, here's a strong qualification on it: Many people, particularly unskilled workers and/or heads of single-parent families, have to work two or more jobs to make ends meet. Even though this is Bonnie's primary job, she may need the other one to survive. This doesn't give her the right to turn down overtime based on the other job. It does mean that you and she need to look at the situation closely and work out an accommodation if possible.

If she's not a flexible person:

If she's a good, well-motivated worker who doesn't have the emotional flexibility to make last-minute changes, your options are almost as limited as in the first "cure" above.

If you can arrange the job so that she doesn't get last-minute overtime, fine. Perhaps she can work the overtime if given a day or two advance notice; can you accommodate that? Can someone else learn her job and take the necessary overtime? Can you take the duties that require the overtime out of her job and give them to someone else who can work the overtime?

If it's not possible to prevent last-minute overtime for her job, you may want to look into reassigning her to another job. If all else fails, deal with it as a performance problem.

SOMETHING TO THINK ABOUT

Everything above assumed that Bonnie would be honest with you. Suppose you asked when you hired her and she assured you that she'd work overtime? Suppose she checked "yes" when you circulated a questionnaire to your employees last month? That probably means that you need to have a serious conversation with her about why, and about her responsibilities as an employee.

There are two "deep" and somewhat contradictory issues here. On the one hand, most families are now two-worker families. This means that each spouse has more before- and after-work responsibilities and less flexibility about working extra hours. On the other hand, the organization has to get its job done; this often means last-minute changes in schedule. There's no easy solution for this, but planning ahead and being clear with employees what your expectations are will help. So will planning work so that last-minute overtime is absolutely minimized.

chapter nine

TROUBLESHOOTING PROBLEMS CAUSED BY DOWNSIZING

9-1 THE PROBLEM

An employee is negotiating with your competitors to go to work for them with her customer list

THE SCENE

"Roy, I think there's something going on with Drew that you should know about," confides Earlene one evening at the close of the day. "I've overheard some of her conversations in the past couple of days and answered the phone on some 'hang-up' calls, and, well, frankly, I think she's trying to move over to Clark, Dawes, and Somerset and take some of our best customers with her."

"Oh my gosh," you panic. "If she takes our customer list and starts courting all our clients, we'll go under like a torpedoed submarine. There's got to be something I can do to stop her."

POSSIBLE CAUSES

Drew may believe her job is in jeopardy and wants to protect herself.

Downsizing creates a climate of anxiety. Drew may believe that she's more likely to get a job if she takes her client list with her, or she may think it will be easier to get started with the new employer if she has her own customers.

Drew may be angry with you or your organization, and this is her way of getting even.

She may not have been recognized when she thought she should be, or maybe she didn't get a raise or a promotion she thought she deserved, or she may resent what she feels is needless downsizing.

Hint: This is a very serious charge you're making against Drew. Investigate as thoroughly as you can (as quickly as you can so no real damage is done) before taking action.

CURES

Regardless of the cause:

Confront Drew right away as soon as you have a reasonable basis for believing that Earlene's report is accurate. If Drew is not negotiating to take the customer lists to your competitors, you can back off. But if she is negotiating, you may be able to shock her into reconsidering. Customer lists are crucial to many organizations, and armed competitors will know exactly whom to target to increase their business and damage yours. You must take immediate action.

Regardless of the cause, as soon as you are convinced that Drew is negotiating, you should also consult your legal department to find out what protections the company already has in place. Many companies whose customer base is limited and exclusive require their employees to sign "noncompetition" contracts before they start work. These are often enforceable as regular contracts, and Drew could be liable for damages the company can prove it suffered because she used the client lists to compete.

Even if new employees aren't required to sign noncompetition contracts, are there other mechanisms in place to protect customer lists? Are they considered "confidential" or "proprietary" company lists? Is taking your company's customer lists treated like other thefts (like thefts of equipment or trade secrets)? Has the company had similar problems in the past, and, if so, how did it protect itself? Your legal department should have the answers to these questions and may even direct you to step back so that they can handle the situation themselves. But assuming the ball is still in your court . . .

If Drew believes her job is in jeopardy and wants to protect herself:

In this case, she's more likely to deal rationally with the situation than if she's out for revenge. First, tell her to stop negotiating to take the customer lists with her when she leaves. Make sure she knows that you know what she's planning, that you will deal with her actions severely if she doesn't stop her negotiations voluntarily, and that action against her will continue even after she leaves your employment—through your legal department. If Drew promises to stop, *and* if you believe her, then you can back off, let her continue her assignment and her job hunt, and just keep a watchful eye on her activities.

But if you can't get a firm commitment from her that your customer list is safe, or if you don't believe her commitment is real, you'll need to take stronger action. Move her out of the job—that's right, completely out of the job. You can move her out of the department or into a less sensitive job in the same unit, but get her into a job where she doesn't have access to your customer lists any more. Even if she promised to stop using the lists as a negotiating tool, if you can't take her at her word, then that's a sign that her actions have destroyed the trust that's essential in the employee-employer relationship. That's the only reason you need to have her taken out of the job.

If Drew is angry with you or the organization and is trying to get even:

Your first step here is clear. If Drew wants to hurt you or the company, then you have to separate her before she can do any more damage. As in the cause above, she has broken your trust and confidence in her. In addition, she's acted purposefully to sabotage the company.

As you work through the termination process, you need also to consult with your legal department, security division, or employee assistance program coordinator to see whether there is any potential for Drew to react violently to her separation. Her acts of sabotage were obviously hostile, and that hostility can take many forms. Although for many people in Drew's situation such industrial sabotage substitutes for violence, it could also be a first step toward more violent behavior.

You also need to consider what else Drew might do (or has already done) to hurt the company. Then take precautionary measures. If you believe she's dangerous enough, don't give her time to do more damage after she's been notified of her termination. Give her the notice papers, then escort her to her office to pack up her personal belongings under your scrutiny, take away her keys, company identification card, and parking pass and walk her out the door. Even if your company insists on a formal notice period before the termination is effective, you can carry Drew on paid leave and still keep her out of the office.

If you believe Drew has done other damage (like fouling up computer records or "fixing" accounts or reports), investigate the areas where she could have done some harm. If you find evidence of misconduct, talk to your legal department about whether there is some action you can take, even after Drew is terminated, to recover.

SOMETHING TO THINK ABOUT

While you don't necessarily want to publicize the *extent* of the damage Drew has done, employees need to know that you identified a serious threat to the company and dealt with it swiftly and decisively. This send two messages to your unit, both of them important: First, it lets others know that negotiations with competitors to take them the company's customer lists will not be tolerated and that you will follow up. Second, it lets the unit know that you'll do what's necessary to protect the company, and them, from such threats. They need that reassurance.

And if you don't already have a policy in place and your customer lists *are* closely-held information, you will want to suggest instituting policies (like noncompetition or nondivulgence contracts) for your workforce.

9–2 THE PROBLEM

A group of employees tells you they've heard that the company is going to continue to downsize

THE SCENE

It is midafternoon on a hot August day. You've just offered what should have been an exciting training opportunity to four of your best employees. But no one's excited. Is this the "Dog Day" blahs? Midafternoon nap time?

"I don't know why you think we should get all excited about learning something we'll never even be able to use," complains Bonnie. "We all know the company hasn't finished its so-called 'right-sizing' yet. What good is it to go to training and then come back the next day to find a pink slip in your in-basket?"

"She's right, you know," Lena adds. "We thought we were safe because we kept our jobs through the first round of layoffs. Now we don't know where we stand, and we don't know how many more times we're going to have to go through this again. That kind of anxiety doesn't make us feel like putting out any more for the company. We just want to lay low and try to keep the jobs we have."

POSSIBLE CAUSES

The rumors may reflect employees' continued anxiety about losing their jobs even though the worst is already over.

Even after downsizing and layoff actions have been completed, the "survivors" have emotional adjustments to work through, too.

The rumors of continued downsizing and layoffs may be true.

You may already be aware of the company's plans, or word may not have filtered down through official channels.

Hint: While a little suspense may be invigorating, anxiety, especially about keeping a job, can really sap employees' motivation and energy. Even if your employees are likely to be affected, they will be able to deal much better with what they know than with what they don't know. Information and support are the two most important things you can offer to anxious staff members, both to make them feel better and to keep up the performance of your unit.

CURES

If the rumors are groundless but reflect employees' continuing anxiety:

First, put your employees' immediate fears to rest by reassuring them that the rumors are false. But check out the facts before you speak. Employees expect their managers to reassure them—and then issue pink slips the next week. If you're to have any credibility with your employees, you need to be absolutely sure that they won't be affected before you attempt to allay their fears. If there will be layoffs that affect some other section of the company, explain what conditions in your unit are insulating it from the damage.

Then make sure that the employees who survived the previous downsizing actions get some professional help and counseling to help them deal with the situation. Their reactions will range from relief that they haven't been hurt to feeling guilt that they were spared although others were hit, from being too hard on themselves in an effort to protect themselves from any future cuts to being paralyzed by their fear of future harm so that they can't produce anything. These are serious emotional reactions that often can't be handled by even a sensitive and well-intentioned manager. Get your people the help they need to overcome this "survivor syndrome" and return to high-performance work.

If the rumors of continued downsizing and layoffs are true:

Make sure your employees get all the information they need to make plans for their own futures. There is a fine line here between telling them too much and too little. At any stage in the planning process, some decisions will have been made firmly, but other issues will still be under consideration. And some things that sound like firm decisions may still be subject to change. Tell your employees what you can, subject, of course, to the company's policies about release of information. And don't speculate. The worst thing you can do is feed your employees' already present anxieties; they'll pick up enough false rumors without your help.

Let your employees know also what training is available for those people who will be affected by continued downsizing. Encourage them to take advantage of whatever the company offers, either in the way of formal training or skills-enhancing job assignments. The better employees' skills are and the better they have performed during their tenure with you, the more likely they are to beat the competition in the job market. Identify available outplacement services (and if the company doesn't already have outplacement contacts, push the personnel department to develop some) and direct your employees to them. Many companies offer affected employees help in preparing resumes, in improving interviewing skills, and in identifying new employment opportunities.

Most important, keep talking to your employees. Be as reassuring and helpful as you can, but most of all be informative. One of the worst parts of any bad situation is not knowing the real story. Replacing fiction from the employee rumor mill with truth, even unwelcome truth, is probably the single most valuable service you can offer your employees.

SOMETHING TO THINK ABOUT

Much of the success of your efforts to dispel rumors and to help employees work through the effects of downsizing depends on how much they trust you. If there have been times in the past when you've not always been true to your word or when the information you've given employees has turned out not to be reliable, then your employees won't have a lot of trust in you now. And unless your workgroup trusts you, you won't be able to do anything to relieve their anxieties, for their sake or yours.

9–3 THE PROBLEM

An employee tells you that if your workgroup has to take on any more new work because of downsizing they will deluge you with grievances

THE SCENE

"Now, look, Mrs. Abrams—we don't have anything against you. You're a decent person and you're fair to us. But we just can't do any more work than we're doing now. We keep hearing rumors that the company is going to dump new work on us because of this latest round of downsizing. If it gives us anything more for at least a month or two, I promise you you'll have a dozen grievances on your desk Tuesday morning, and that's just a start. If you've got any pull with management, you'd better use it now. We're not kidding!"

When she finishes, Sandy walks out of your office without even waiting for you to answer. It's clear she means it. Now what do you do about it?

POSSIBLE CAUSES

Your workgroup is unhappy with the company because of the continuing downsizing, and this is their way of showing it.

They may or may not be able to increase their workload, but they don't intend to.

Your unit's productivity is much lower than it ought to be.

It could increase its productivity if it chose to do so.

The unit's productivity is high, but management has been increasing workload without regard for productivity.

So the workgroup is being penalized for its high productivity.

The unit's productivity is acceptable, but it could absorb another increase without being overloaded.

Hint: This is a classic example of the situation that a first-line supervisor gets caught in. On the one hand, you owe loyalty to management to support the production increase. On the other, your people think it's unfair and are up in arms against it. You're right in the middle.

Remember that all you have so far is a rumor. The downsizing and/or workload increase may or may not happen. You want to look at the sections in this case for ideas, but you also need to find out whether there really is going to be more downsizing and whether it will affect your workgroup.

CURES

If they're unhappy with the company because of the continuing downsizing, and this is their way of showing it:

This isn't so unusual a situation, but it's a difficult one. If the real cause of their anger isn't the specific increase in workload itself, nothing you do about the increase is apt to help.

You know at least something about why they're unhappy with the company, but is there more to it than just the downsizing itself? Has the company made the downsizing harder on employees (at least in their eyes) than it needed to be? Has management cut employees and cut employee pay but kept up their own pay? Be sure you find out all the factors behind their unhappiness.

Once you know the factors for sure, what can you do? If the unit's productivity is relatively low (see the next section), not much. But if it produces at a continually high level—and if you can show this—you may get any workload increase headed off. (See the second section after this one.) You need to walk a narrow path, supporting your workgroup while not appearing to be fighting higher management.

If your unit's productivity is much less than it ought to be:

No matter how strongly they may feel about the workload increase, you can't defend their reaction to higher management. Your job is to get them to accept the increased production. If you don't, both you and they will suffer.

Your most important job is to persuade your employees that they need to increase their productivity, because you're not going to be able to defend their not getting more work. You know this is going to be difficult, but it has to be done. If you have productivity statistics from other groups like your own, use them to show yours why it needs to improve. If not, do whatever you can to get the point across to the workgroup.

If the group's productivity is low, attempting to avoid more work when other groups are already producing more will be a disaster. You must avoid this at all costs and with any luck, you can convince the workgroup to do so.

If the unit's productivity is high, but management has been increasing workload without regard for productivity:

Here we have the reverse problem: Your people are productive, but they've gotten stuck with the same increase as the rest of the organization, which isn't as productive. If you don't do something, they're going to be punished for doing so well. You can figure what that will do to their productivity and motivation in the future.

How you deal with this one depends on how your company deals with productivity. If there are established goals that your people have been exceeding, you can at least show higher management that an increase isn't fair. It should also be easy to show them if your employees have a higher rate of production than other similar units.

What if there aren't records that will show how productive your unit is? Here's where your boss's confidence in you comes in. If he or she believes that you've been getting production from your unit, he or she may go to bat for you.

Your other alternatives aren't very good ones. Do what you can to talk management out of the increase and to talk your employees into being patient. Then find a way to demonstrate how high their productivity already is.

If the workgroup's current productivity is acceptable, but it could absorb another increase without being overloaded:

This is another challenging situation. You wouldn't be embarrassed if you sided with your employees and tried to persuade higher management to drop the increase. On the other hand, you wouldn't be out of line to try to get your people to accept the increase.

The basic question for your employees is this: Why should they increase their output if it's already acceptable? That's the question you'll have to answer for them if you want them to change. Will taking on the new work make their jobs more secure? Is it really just their fair share, so that other units don't see them as slackers? What if you can't find a reason for them to increase production? As you might suspect, you'll be in a difficult situation. Higher management will be expecting the increase, but your employees won't be willing to produce it. This is a true impasse, and one that's not easy to resolve. You'll have to dig more deeply for reasons for the workgroup to change. Here's where credibility with your boss and your employees will stand you in good stead. If you have credibility, both of them may be willing to give you some time to find a solution. If you don't have credibility? Sorry— wish we could help, but . . .

SOMETHING TO THINK ABOUT

When a company must increase productivity to make up for downsizing, it can easily run into trouble. Employees can fight back by filing grievances, "working to rule," refusing to cooperate with other units, and in a dozen other ways. They can also work faster and turn out more products with a higher rework and rejection rate.

How do you prevent this? One alternative is to get greater productivity by training employees more effectively. They may not know the best ways to perform their tasks even if they've been doing them for some time. High-quality training in the best procedures might enable them to produce more with no more effort or strain.

Another way: Involve workers in improving the processes and procedures they use. They know their work better than anyone else, and if they choose to do so they can improve how they do it better than anyone else. If your organization has a continuous process improvement program, find out about it and find out how your workgroup might be able to use it.

9–4 THE PROBLEM

An employee who expects to be caught in the next downsizing stops producing

THE SCENE

"Joe, I asked you to have those budget figures for me two weeks ago, and you still haven't completed them. What's the problem here?" you ask in obvious frustration. "Don't you know that with these layoffs going on all around us, this is the worst possible time for us to slack off?"

"Well, Darryl," replies Joe, "it looks to me like it doesn't make any difference one way or the other how much work we do or how well we do it. Look at Lillian over in public relations—one of the best representatives the company ever had—and she's out the door. And Bill in marketing, and a whole slew of people on the floor. I figure my number's up any way you look at it. So why should I put out for the company if they won't put out for me. I'm just making the transition from working to not working a little early."

POSSIBLE CAUSES

Joe may believe that it doesn't matter how well he works once he gets his layoff notice.

He may not recognize that, even with notice in hand, his prospects for being retained in this job or getting a good reference for another job depend on his performance in the time he has left here.

He may be using lack of production on the job as a way of venting his anger over being laid off.

And, within bounds, this may be one of the less painful possible ways (for him and for you) for him to work through that anger.

He may be using lack of production as a "self-fulfilling prophecy."

Then if he does get hit by the downsizing he can tell himself it was because he stopped producing, not because the company doesn't value him anymore.

Hint: If you didn't know before, you need to understand now that being laid off is much more than an economic blow. Government unemployment compensation and "golden parachute" deals help to soften some of the financial loss, but there isn't much of an emotional safety net for workers who lose their jobs. The loss of self-esteem and the depression and anxiety can be devastating. So workers will cope in whatever way they know how, which may not be the most productive coping mechanism for either the company or the workers themselves. There's a major difference in how you'll need to react to the fairly rational reaction described in the first situation and the emotionally driven second and third situations.

CURES

If Joe thinks it doesn't matter how well he works once he gets his layoff notice:

In this situation, a heart-to-heart chat with Joe may be all it takes to get his work back on track. If there's a chance that some of the termination notices may be withdrawn before the downsizing becomes effective (usually because other workers get placed somewhere else or because of retirements or resignations), then let Joe know that his chances of being kept on are better the better his performance is. Call-backs from temporary layoffs may also be affected by workers' performance, especially in a system that's not driven exclusively by seniority. Even if it's a virtual certainty that Joe will lose his job, you can talk to him about the effect a good reference can have on his ability to get another job, especially another job in the same industry where many of the managers know one another and rely on referrals from each other. If this is the reason Joe's been slacking off, your explanations and encouragement may be all that's needed to get him back on track.

If Joe is working out his anger at losing his job:

Your task here is harder. You're dealing not with a rational response to a situation, but with a purely emotional response. Joe may not be able to work past his anger without some professional help. Your coaching and explanations may fall on deaf ears. You may even need to be on the lookout for more than this passive response, such as Joe's sabotaging the work or acting out his anger in abusive language or even violence.

Anger is a normal and healthy reaction to misfortune. If it lasts only a few days, or even a week or two, you can be fairly sure that Joe will work through the rest on his own. Your encouragement and support will help, along with occasional reminders of the benefits to him of continuing to produce even when things get rough. But if the angry reaction seems to go on for a long time and Joe doesn't seem to be working through it by himself, then you need to make sure he gets some outside help, through your employee assistance program or referral to an outside counseling service.

If Joe is working against himself by performing poorly:

You'll need to deal with the problem on both a rational front and an emotional front at the same time. If there's still not a final decision about who will stay and who will go (and if performance *does* count in determining who stays), you need to talk to Joe to make sure he understands how the system works and that his lack of production may be hurting him. Even on an entirely rational basis, Joe may not realize that he is his own worst enemy when he doesn't produce. But then you also need to help Joe get some outside assistance to work through his anxiety and depression so that he can deal with whatever comes constructively, rather than self-destructively.

SOMETHING TO THINK ABOUT

You need to consider what kinds of messages you're sending your workgroup by your own attitude toward impending downsizing actions. If your job is also on the line and your anger or anxiety or depression are affecting how you approach the work, those emotions will be obvious to everyone you work with, just as Joe's emotional responses were obvious to you. And, as in Joe's case, you yourself may not be aware of how you're being affected. Downsizing and the changes that accompany it are traumatic for *everyone*, workers and managers alike. One of the best ways you can take care of your employees is by taking care of yourself too.

9-5 THE PROBLEM

Your workgroup has been given a new function that you don't understand

THE SCENE

"Hey, I need a minute of your time," Margaret says as she sits down across from you.

"Sure—what's up?"

"I've been looking at the files we just got with this new assignment, and I gotta tell you that I'm confused. How in the world did we end up with this stuff, anyway?"

"I wish I knew," you reply. "Supposedly it has something to do with the special projects we did last year, but it doesn't make any more sense to me than it does to you."

"So what are we going to do?"

POSSIBLE CAUSES

The organization probably gave you the new function because it was downsizing further and spreading the work of abolished units around. Did it pick your workgroup because it believed the new function was similar to work you already do? Because it believed your workgroup was talented enough to do it? Or because it thought your group didn't have enough to do? It doesn't matter. What matters is whether or not you can successfully integrate the new function.

CURES

Assign an individual or small group to learn and perform the new function:

If you can spare an individual or, if necessary, a small group, have them learn the new function. Get training for them if it's available. Have them talk to individuals who previously performed the work if you can. Just make it their mission to "get up to speed" on the task as quickly as possible.

Once they've learned how to perform the function, do you have them continue to perform it or teach the workgroup to perform it? If it is different from the rest of the work of the workgroup, it's probably better for them to continue to perform it. (You want to train a backup individual or group in the function if you can, of course.) But if it is related to the group's primary work, perhaps you want to have them gradually train everyone to do it.

Here's another way to look at the new function: Is the regular work of the group getting somewhat boring for employees? Would the new function be more interesting and challenging? Would it let them learn and use new skills? Then use the new function as a way of expanding workgroup jobs and making them more interesting. If you can do this, you can turn the new function into a plus for the workgroup.

Try to trade off the function for another one the workgroup understands better:

Don't try this unless the first is too impractical. If you really don't believe the workgroup can integrate the new function with what they're already doing, see if you can find another function— one easier to learn—that the group could pick up in place of it. Be sure that this function fits better, though; it won't help much to find another function and then discover that it's just as hard to learn as the first one.

Try to persuade the organization your workload is too heavy to accept the new function:

Don't even *think* of taking this approach unless you can show, on the basis of production reports or other solid measures, that your workgroup has more work than others. Every workgroup is probably having to take on new work, and every workgroup is probably as overworked as your own.

Suppose you can show that your workgroup has a heavier workload than others. Do you automatically try to get rid of the new function? No. First you ask if you can squeeze it in. If you can, look again at some of the potential benefits from the new function that the first section described. Are these benefits worth the extra work and stress of the new function? They may be, and if they are you want to take on the function. Remember, if higher management believes your workgroup is more productive than others, its job security increases.

If none of this seems relevant, bite the bullet and show the organization how the new function imposes a greater workload on your group than others have. But be sure you can *show* them, with objective measurements. If you can't, you'll get the reputation for not wanting to shoulder your fair share of the load, and that's a reputation you want to avoid.

Something to Think About

You need to protect your workgroup from a workload so heavy it can't produce a quality product. You don't need to protect it from improving to the point that it can handle a heavy workload effectively.

Workgroups often let themselves get caught in the trap of comparing themselves to other workgroups. If they're producing about the same as other workgroups, they're producing enough. The problem: This prevents the workgroup from distinguishing itself from other workgroups. It's just "one of the pack."

Particularly in a highly competitive environment, the workgroup may be cut or abolished for no better reason than there's no reason not to. You want to prevent that. Help the workgroup keep improving, so it can take an increasing workload in stride. Then make sure that higher management knows how heavy the group's workload is and therefore how valuable the workgroup is to the organization.

9–6 The Problem

You have to take a displaced worker from another area when you desperately need someone who's fully trained in your unit's work

The Scene

"Well, Jill," your boss begins, "I see you're looking for a new buyer." Then he drops the bombshell: "You know, we've got a lot of people here who are going to lose their jobs if we don't do something to help them. So I've arranged for Claude in sales promotions to come over to work for you. He's taken some business courses in college, and I'm sure he'll work out fine for you."

"But, Karen," you stammer, "I've got a backlog I won't be able to work through for several months even if I can find somebody who knows what he's doing. I can't afford to take someone who doesn't have any experience at all. A lot of money passes through this department. If we buy the wrong stock or at too high a price, we can lose a lot of money too. We *need* to have somebody experienced!"

"I hear what you're saying," Karen replies. "But you'll just have to do the best you can. I'm sure if you were the one being cut from the staff you'd be grateful for a second chance. And Claude might work harder for you than someone who hasn't been so close to unemployment."

POSSIBLE CAUSES

This is one of those situations where the cause is clear: Your boss has made a decision and you need to live with it. Maybe it's company policy to find jobs for displaced workers before new employees are hired. Maybe Karen has a personal interest in seeing that as few people as possible lose their jobs. Her motivation doesn't matter. Placement of unqualified or marginally qualified people in new jobs is a common side effect of downsizing. The only question you have to answer is how you're going to cope with the situation with the least possible loss of productivity.

Hint: Don't pick just one of the "cures" below. Use every one of them you can.

CURES

Provide intensive training to your new worker:

Many offices don't have established training programs. New employees learn from watching and working with experienced workers. Or the firm normally hires nothing but trained workers, so it never sees there might be a problem. If your company doesn't have an established training program, find out quickly if there are some training sources you can tap. A local college or junior college? Courses in the area given by a professional association or an organization that specializes in training? Perhaps even a video course you can rent or buy?

Don't forget books on the subject. There are dozens and often hundreds of books on almost every occupation. Can you find one or two that deal with your kind of work and see that the new employee reads them? Perhaps you and he could meet once or twice a week to discuss them.

Match your new employee with a "mentor":

Whether or not you can get formal training, you need to see that your new employee has a chance to learn the specific skills he'll need on *your* job. One good way to do that is to identify a worker in your area who does a job that's very similar to the one your new person is going into, someone who's very good at doing that job and who can explain things well to somebody who doesn't know the area, and who's *very* patient. That's a mentor.

Before your new employee arrives on the job, sit down with the mentor and explain what her role is. She will be expected to help orient your new employee to the work, show him how each task is performed, review work and provide advice and assistance, and answer questions. It's helpful if you have time to work with the mentor to break down the job into steps or processes, then decide how well your new employee should perform on one task before he goes on to learn the next. You can sequence the tasks or processes however seems most logical to you (for example, you can teach the most important tasks first, or the simplest ones first, or use some other order). Then the mentor will work with your new employee on tasks one or two at a time, teaching and coaching until he becomes proficient in those one or two before moving on to the next ones.

Be sure your mentor knows that she has some relief from her own workload and that training the new employee is important. Then follow up with both the mentor and the trainee often enough to be sure that the training is progressing on schedule and to reinforce to the mentor how important this training assignment is. If you just dump the assignment on her and never follow up, she'll think you really don't care how well she works with the new employee.

Separate out the simpler work and give it to the new employee:

When everyone in an organization is well qualified and well trained, the most difficult work is often assigned among all the jobs. That means that each employee also does some of the simpler work. If this is the case in your unit, a little job redesign will let your new employee become productive quickly.

Get together with your best workers—or perhaps even all your workers—and find the simplest and least challenging work they have to do. You can count on their help, since most of them will be happy to get rid of this work. Identify enough of the routine work to make a separate job and assign the new employee to that job.

You still want to train your new employee on the work of his job, but now he can begin making a useful contribution to the unit much more quickly. Then there's a decision you get to make after a few weeks or months: Do you leave your new employee doing just the simpler work, or do you bring him along to become a full performer? That depends on many factors, one of which is the individual's progress in the job. Keep that decision in mind as you evaluate his performance from the beginning.

SOMETHING TO THINK ABOUT

Every manager likes to have the best qualified employees possible. It generally makes life much easier. There's a down side to it, though. What happens if your people are highly qualified and motivated, but much of the work is boring? They may lose their motivation and look for more challenging jobs elsewhere.

In other words, it often makes sense to concentrate the simpler work in one or a few jobs. Then you can hire less qualified, less expensive employees to fill these jobs. If they have the ability and the motivation, they can move up into the more skilled jobs. If they don't, they can still make a contribution doing the less demanding work. You win two ways: You get your work done while keeping your best workers challenged, *and* you have an opportunity to "test" the work of newer employees before you put them into jobs with greater responsibilities.

9–7 THE PROBLEM

An employee is using company information with his own private clients

THE SCENE

What several other employees have told you is true. You pause outside George Maripolis's cubicle and listen to his phone conversation. He is clearly talking to someone who isn't a customer of the company, and he just as clearly is giving the caller confidential company information. It's bad enough that he's dealing with his private customers on company time. It's even worse that he's giving them company information. You know you can't ignore the situation any longer.

POSSIBLE CAUSES

George has been doing his own business on company time with company clients for a long time.

This is just the first time he's been caught.

George is afraid of continuing downsizing and is trying to set up a business to support himself if he's laid off.

He wants to protect himself from the threat of the organization's continued shrinking.

George has specific reason to believe he'll be laid off and is trying to provide a continuing source of income.

Hint: None of these reasons justifies what George is doing. Remember, though, that continuing downsizing and layoffs are tremendously hard on the workers who remain. If your company doesn't have a program to work with remaining employees and help them cope with the situation, at least you should talk with them and help them through the rough times. And they are rough times.

CURES

No matter what the cause is:

Your first task is to get data. Talk with George. Tell him what you heard. Give him every chance to respond. But be sure you ask the hard questions: How long has he been doing it? What makes him think it's okay to use the company client list? It may be uncomfortable for both of you for you to ask the hard questions. But your job is to ask them. Then ask other members of the workgroup who have observed him. Again, you and they will be uncomfortable, but this is your job.

If George has been doing his own business on company time with company clients for a long time:

You don't know which of the three situations is true. What you do know is that George has dealt with his clients on company time using company information. The natural assumption that goes with this is that he has done so in the past. So begin with that assumption. And go with it unless he and other members of the workgroup present clear evidence—not assertions, evidence—to the contrary.

What if he has been not only transacting his business on company time but using the company's client list to do so? He has seriously violated his employment contract with the company. The question is: Should he remain with the company any longer?

Here you need to talk with the company's human resources management office to see what usually happens in situations like this one. At the minimum, George needs to agree to stop using company time and the company customer list at once and permanently. And he needs to be disciplined, with no less than a suspension without pay. Whatever happens, the message needs to be clear to him and other members of the workgroup that the organization won't tolerate this kind of behavior. Period.

If George is afraid of continuing downsizing and is trying to set up a business to support himself if he's laid off:

George may genuinely be reacting to the company's serious reductions, though it's up to him to persuade you of that and to do so with something other than promises and contrite words. What he's done is serious, regardless of his reasons for doing it.

Suppose he does make a case that he was doing this because he was afraid of more downsizing? Is he competing with the company, offering generally the same services? That's extremely serious, no matter what his reason was. Or has he been careful to offer very different services, ones that might even lead customers to want more services from the company? How much he's looked out for the company's interest as well as his own carries a lot of weight in judging his offense.

He has to stop, unless the company is specifically willing to authorize him to do it. *You* can't authorize him to do it; that will only get you into the same trouble once the company finds out about the situation. (It will also suggest to other members of the workgroup that they can get away with the same thing.) He has to stop and guarantee you that he has done so. And he needs to be disciplined, though if he's looked out for the company's interest as well as his own, the discipline can be much less severe than in the case above. But he needs to get the message loud and clear that he shouldn't have done it and can't do it again.

If George has a specific reason to believe he'll be laid off and is trying to provide a continuing source of income:

George has still acted wrongly, but perhaps you and the organization can afford to be somewhat more understanding in this situation, especially if he has looked out for the company's interests (as in the cause just above).

Does the organization permit individuals who will be laid off to look for jobs on company time? If so, George has jumped the gun. Is the organization willing to let him look now? If so, perhaps a stern lecture is enough to cover his past behavior. And if he's genuinely taking the company's welfare into consideration, you and the organization might be willing to let him continue.

Note that we've put in a lot of "if's." Here as everywhere else, the burden remains on George to demonstrate that his actions weren't as serious as they seemed.

SOMETHING TO THINK ABOUT

Every manager must walk the sometimes narrow line between looking out for the interests of the organization and responding to the needs of his workers. Often, the two don't conflict. When workers break the rules, the only appropriate response is discipline in some form.

There are extenuating circumstances at times, and effective managers develop the ability to tell these circumstances from more ordinary ones. They also develop a feel for how these circumstances need to be handled so that they don't set precedents that someone will apply to more normal circumstances.

Always begin with the assumption that the circumstances are ordinary and breaking the rules can't be excused. When this approach doesn't seem fair in the current situation, begin considering that you may truly have extenuating circumstances on your hands and act accordingly.

9-8 THE PROBLEM

An employee spends most of her work time looking for another job

THE SCENE

Marla quickly changes her computer screen as she notices you walk by. "Well, she's at it again," you reflect silently. "Marla was always a pretty good worker, but I can't get a bit of work out of her anymore. All day long, she's either typing up a new resume or calling for job openings or taking a 'long lunch' to go on another interview. I can't afford to keep paying her for doing nothing, and I can't stand to hear another complaint about her not carrying her share of the load. I guess I need to get tough and hope I don't get a grievance in return!"

POSSIBLE CAUSES

Marla may believe she's being hit in the next round of layoffs.

She may have heard rumors or she may have reliable sources who've given her a "heads up" that she's next on the list. In either case, she's trying to protect herself.

Marla may have lost interest in your job or decided that it's time to move on to greener pastures.

Very few people stay in the same job for more than a few years anymore, and Marla may have decided she's learned all she can where she is.

Hint: There are really two areas of concern here. First, you need to address Marla's lack of productivity, since she's spending so much time job hunting rather than producing. If Marla is a good worker whom you'd like you keep, you also need to address the "why" of her job search. What made her decide it was time to leave? If her reasons are in areas within your control, you'll need to decide how much you want to change her situation to encourage her to stay. (Of course, if Marla was never a great worker to begin with, your major concern is to keep her producing for as long as she's still on the payroll.)

CURES

If Marla believes she's being hit in the next round of layoffs:

Talk to your personnel department to find out what you can about whether the information Marla is working from is accurate. Keep in mind though that sometimes the personnel office can't disclose upcoming layoff plans as a matter of company policy until all the notifications are ready to be delivered, to keep some employees from having an unfair advantage over others. If your organization has such a policy, or if you suspect that the information the personnel department gives you isn't reliable, you will need to dig deeper to find out whether Marla's concerns are well founded.

Talk to Marla about her own sources of information. Use whatever informal information network you've already developed to find out what you can about Marla's situation (and the situation of everyone in your unit). If you find out that Marla or others you supervise are likely to be hurt in the next downsizing effort, then even if you can't divulge specific information to them, you can be especially sensitive to their personal needs over the next few months.

The key here is balance. If Marla really is about to lose her job, you must balance your continuing need for production in your unit with Marla's need to find a new job. On one level, the company has some moral obligation to Marla to facilitate her job search. On a very practical level, you're limited in what you can do at this point to enforce her performance. (But Problem 9–4 suggests some techniques for keeping up production.)

Once you find out that Marla's job really is in jeopardy, discuss with her accommodations that will allow her to look for a new job while she continues to produce for you. Find out what the company's policy is concerning employees' use of computers, copiers, and other equipment to prepare job applications. Even if the company generally doesn't allow employees' personal use of its equipment, there may be special policies for workers caught in downsizing. Once Marla receives official notice of termination, refer her to the company's outplacement and job-training facilities for help.

If your investigations reveal that Marla is not likely to lose her job, and if you're confident that your sources are reliable, talk to Marla to reassure her that her employment is secure. Make sure she knows that you'll let her know if you get any information to indicate that her situation has changed and that you'll keep checking. At the same time, be sure Marla understands that since her job's not in danger, you expect her to return to her previous high level of production. Then enforce that expectation.

If Marla has decided it's time to move on to greener pastures:

In this case, it's appropriate for you to take a stronger stand. Marla is job hunting entirely for her own benefit, and the company bears no responsibility for putting her out on the street if she doesn't find a job. Remind Marla that her duty is to her current employer as long as she's on the payroll and that you expect full production during the time she's at work. If there are occasional calls to or from prospective employers, that's okay. If her job search is becoming a full-time occupation, that's not. For many companies, interviews must be taken on vacation days or personal days, not on long breaks when the employee "slips away" for an hour or two. Check to see what your company's policy is and make sure Marla understands. For most employees, a simple explanation (or reminder) of what your expectations are will serve to correct the situation.

If Marla's a good employee and you genuinely don't want to lose her, discuss what you could do within the bounds of her current position to meet her needs. Find out first what her needs are (obviously, they're not the same for every employee). Does she want more challenge and a chance to grow in her assignment? Does she want more recognition for the things she's accomplished? Does she want to branch out and learn about other areas, get some experience in a related field? Is she leaving because of the pay, or benefits, or working conditions? Once you know what's given Marla the urge to move on, you can see what it's possible for you to do within your own company to entice her to stay.

Be careful, though, that you don't give Marla "perks" that aren't available to every other employee in her situation unless you can back up her special treatment with solid reasons: higher performance levels, greater expertise, or similar job-related reasons. The fact that Marla's ready to leave, by itself, is *not* a reasonable excuse for giving her special treatment.

And if Marla is someone you'd just as soon see leave the company, you need to make a decision about how hard you want to come down on her job-hunting activities. On one hand, a strict approach toward your performance expectations may nudge her into intensifying her search. On the other, she may comply with your demands—and also not find another job. In general, you're better off to treat Marla's job search as you would any other performance problem. Other sections in this book can give you ideas.

SOMETHING TO THINK ABOUT

When you're trying to find out why Marla is looking for another job so that you can entice her to stay, keep in mind that it may take some time for *her* to figure out why she wants to leave. Many employees begin a job search whenever boredom or a vague, ill-defined dissatisfaction sets in, without knowing exactly what the problem is. Finding out the source of Marla's dissatisfaction may take some sensitive, but not intrusive, questioning, and patience.

And keep in mind, too, that the reasons Marla's leaving may have nothing to do with the job or the company or the work environment at all. She may have personal reasons for wanting to leave (like a commitment in another town) or she may be making a career switch to an area that's completely different from anything your company's involved in. Turnover is not *always* a sign of a problem with one's job. It's an item for concern only if a significant number of your best people are leaving, especially if they're reluctant to tell you why.

9–9 THE PROBLEM

You have a new manager who's been assigned your workgroup to manage but refuses to learn anything about its work

THE SCENE

"Hey, see you have a new boss," Jeff remarks as you're having coffee together. "What do you think of her?"

"Well, it's much too early to tell," you reply, "but I think there's going to be one serious problem. She called me in the first day and explained that she doesn't know much about what my workgroup does, and since she doesn't expect to manage us for that long she doesn't intend to learn. She made it clear that we're on our own."

"That may not be all bad."

"I don't know. Mr. Jones sure gave us a lot of help when he managed us. I'm not sure what will happen without that kind of help."

POSSIBLE CAUSES

You're probably getting a new boss because of downsizing, but that doesn't really matter. What we're concerned about here is how to manage effectively with a boss who (1) is new and (2) has made it clear she doesn't intend to learn your work. You need to deal with these two key aspects of the situation.

Hint: Don't forget that there are a number of things you *don't* have to worry about: You already know the work, not only your general technical area, but the specifics of how to do business in this company and how to get things accomplished. You've also already established relationships with your peers and superiors throughout the organization. So you have time to adapt to the new situation, and even without your new boss's support you can keep the work of the group on track.

CURES

First, deal with the fact that you have a new boss:

First impressions *do* count—a lot! While you can destroy a good first impression later on by screwing up something important, it's very hard to do the reverse and overcome a poor first impression. In your first few meetings with your new boss, you need to convince her that

- you're a loyal subordinate
- you're not a threat to her
- you and your workgroup know their business, and she can count on you for consistently good and timely products.

How do you do that? Well, *not* by making a sales pitch for yourself. What you need to do is *demonstrate* those things by what you say and do in the course of normal business.

These are some specific things you can do to make the transition as easy as possible for both you and your new boss:

- Find out as much as you can about your new boss before she starts on her job. Talk to other people in the organization and any contacts you have in the organizations where she's worked before. If you have a good relationship with *her* boss (your second-level supervisor), you might also ask him what to expect. Consider all of this as background information. Don't rely exclusively on other people's opinions in forming your own. But use what you learn to try to make the best first impression you can.

- Schedule a meeting where the two of you won't be rushed and you can ask specific questions about how your boss likes things done. Does she prefer information in written form; does she like to converse about the work; or does she like a combination of the two? Does she intend to hold regular staff meetings where you'll report on status, or would she prefer to meet with you individually? Does she want you to report on a scheduled basis, or just whenever you think something's going on she should know about? These questions about style preferences are legitimate questions to ask, and your boss herself is the best source of information. Better to ask now than to spend months giving her things she doesn't want (or not giving her what she does).

- This first meeting is *not* the best time to ask questions about how to handle specific work problems. If there are pressing issues, try to keep them on "hold" for a week or two. If you can't, let your boss know what the issues are and what you plan to do about them. Then let her know at what stages in the future, if any, she'll have the opportunity to reverse anything she's uncomfortable with. If she gives you specific direction, that's fine. But if you press her before she's ready, she'll probably be uncomfortable because of her lack of knowledge, and you'll have made a tactical error right at the start.

- Use the information you've gathered beforehand to identify any areas where your management style is likely to conflict with your boss's. Try to work in some opportunities during your discussion to probe those areas to see how she reacts. If there's a possible conflict (for example, she likes to control things closely, but you give your people a lot of autonomy as long as they produce), stop there. Don't press the issue. Wait until you can come up with a strategy for working out those areas with your boss that will be likely to get you what you want without causing conflict.

Then deal with her desire not to be involved in your unit's work:

Your first task, of course, is to find what she means when she says that she doesn't intend to learn your unit's work. Is she going to keep completely hands-off and basically act as though she weren't supervising you and the group? Does she want to do the administrative management, so that she expects you to clear all personnel decisions with her? Just what does she intend the relationship to be? The sooner you find this out, the better both you and she can deal with the situation.

Does she want to be briefed about your unit and what you do in the company, so she'll have a basic knowledge? Set up a summary briefing with her, preferably with your workgroup present and taking an active part. As part of the meeting, find out what kinds of reports, if any, she wants on the workgroup's work. Arrange to provide her any that she wants promptly.

Does she want to be involved in the administrative decisions? See that she meets every member of the workgroup as soon as possible and give her information on different employees whenever you get the chance. You don't want her overseeing your personnel and other administrative decisions without some understanding of the different workers as individuals.

Does she simply want to be a supervisor on paper, with no involvement at all with your unit? This places extra responsibility on you, but it also gives you extra opportunity. This might even be an opportunity to make changes you've wanted but your previous supervisor wouldn't let you make. Whatever the disadvantages of the situation, make sure that you take advantage of the opportunities it offers.

SOMETHING TO THINK ABOUT

We talk a lot in this book about how important it is that you have the confidence of your boss. When you have a new boss, you have a golden opportunity to establish that confidence from ground zero. Sure, things will never be the same as when "Good Old What's His Name" used to run things here. If you deal with your new boss as you should, they will be better.

So spend the time and attention necessary to get off on the right foot with your new boss. At the same time, make sure that she knows how good you and your workgroup are. She may not want to spend time learning the group's work, but if she thinks well of you and the group she'll support what you do.

Remember, your first job is to make your workers successful and your second job is to make your boss successful. All else is optional.

chapter ten

TROUBLESHOOTING PROBLEMS MADE WORSE BY DOWNSIZING

10-1 The Problem

Because of the high-pressure work environment, your employees are competing with one another when they need to cooperate

The Scene

You take a few minutes before the end of the day to glance through the papers accumulating in your in-basket and find, to your dismay, that the proposal you asked for on new-product designs has come in duplicate—one version from Rita and another from Chris.

"What's going on here?" you wonder, as you leaf through each submission. "These look like the same ideas, just in different words and different format. Why can't they get together on some of this stuff? They know I'm going to have to meet with them to work out whatever picayune differences there are; they know I'm going to be ticked off that I have to spend my time arbitrating between them; but they seem to think that one of them's going to come out a winner. Don't they know that when they can't work together they both come out losers?"

Possible Causes

Your unit has become accustomed to letting you work out their problems rather than working them out themselves.

If they know that they don't have to cooperate with one another because you're a willing arbitrator, then they won't cooperate.

There's no payoff for teamwork, but big payoffs for individual performance.

Whatever else may be wrong, you can be sure that this is a major part of the problem. And the problem won't go away until you solve this.

Your staff members have weak cooperative skills.

We talk about people having "interpersonal skills." Actually, there are a wide variety of interpersonal skills. Some people are very good at giving and taking orders. Others are good at the give-and-take of cooperative relationships. Your people may be short on cooperative skills.

Hint: When workers are under a lot of pressure, they tend to follow the most comfortable, least demanding paths to get the work done. Downsizing creates a lot of pressure on workers who remain because they often have to take up the slack caused by the loss of jobs elsewhere in the company. If you haven't structured the work of your unit in such a way that cooperation is more comfortable (and rewarding) than individual efforts, it will be much harder to get your staff to change at a time when demands on them are highest.

CURES

If your staff has become accustomed to letting you work out their problems for them:

Especially if this is a long-established practice, you can't just suddenly back out on them. First you need to establish a reason for them to want to change. The cause below discusses this. Then you need to develop in them the skills they will need to work together constructively. The next cause discusses this process. But then the biggest challenge comes: You need to change your own behavior.

Once your workgroup is ready to assume responsibility for their own success in teaming, you need to give them the opportunity to practice their skills. Assign group members a project that is too much for one person to accomplish in the time allotted. Then stand back.

Arrange for regularly scheduled project reports from the team to see that they stay on track. But when conflicts or questions arise and team members come to you for resolution, throw the ball back in their court. Tell them that you expect every problem presented to you to come with a recommended solution. If you continue to get multiple recommendations or reports from the individual members of a group rather than a group report, send those individual products back to the group. Stand firm that your expectations are for cooperation, not competition.

If the rewards are for individual performance rather than for group performance:

Take a cold, honest look at what the rewards really are for your people. Are the individual "stars" the ones who're selected for promotions? Do pay increases depend solely on what the individual has done with his own work?

Do you really *need* cooperation? That's not a silly question. In many circumstances, it's best to put up with the friction and let people handle projects independently. If that's the way it should be, though, don't expect them to work well together. Don't make joint assignments unless you're forced to.

If you need cooperation, reward cooperation. Revise your reward structure so it pays for cooperation. Make cooperativeness one of the factors that pay increases depend upon. Give bonuses to people who help others get their jobs done. Borrow an idea from college football teams and let your employees give stars to other employees who have been particularly helpful to them. Each month or quarter, give the employee(s) with the largest number of stars a day off, or a steak dinner.

Expect flak, listen to it, and keep on track. If individual performance is what's been paying off, your people have been "trained" to compete. It will take time for them to change, so be patient, but firm.

If your employees have weak cooperative skills:

Get your employees together and tell them how the way they work is going to change. Make it clear that cooperation will be important, that it will be rewarded, and how it will be rewarded. Make sure your employees know *why* you've decided that cooperation is now more important than individual performance—what in the work situation has changed, what has happened to change your own perceptions. Link the change in work method to some objective happening so your employees won't think you're just being fickle and try to outwait you rather than change.

Arrange with your training department to provide training support for the change. Just sending your people to one training course probably won't be enough. To make the change effectively, you'll probably need several courses or workshops spread over several months. Training will be most productive if your employees can attend the sessions together so they'll have a chance to practice in class with their own workgroup members. You may also need to identify someone who can provide after-class support—offering observations or consultation as the group puts its new skills into practice.

Identify some assignments that require your people to work in two's or three's, so they can start practicing cooperation. Tie this in as closely as you can to the training they get. Give them a chance to practice what they're learning as soon as possible after they learn it.

Expect your employees to be anxious. They're not only changing the way they work, but they're having to learn and practice a whole new set of skills. Encourage them, help them as you can, but make sure that they keep moving in the direction you want.

SOMETHING TO THINK ABOUT

People do what they have the opportunity to do and know how to do if it pays off for them. As a manager, it's up to you to provide the opportunity, the training (if necessary), and the rewards.

10–2 THE PROBLEM

An employee seems to be becoming unbalanced from work stresses

THE SCENE

You walk back to your office, shaking your head. Martin Kaminsky has always been a little weird, but lately he's been acting truly crazy. You just heard him accuse Sandra Wilson, a new clerk, of hiding the notes from his latest audit. When Sandra left the room in tears, Martin turned to the others and yelled, "You think I can't keep up with you, but I can. I'll show all of you!"

POSSIBLE CAUSES

Martin may be reacting to a temporary stressful situation outside work.

Perhaps his home life is bothering him. Perhaps it's as simple as his attempting to quit smoking or drinking.

He may have periodic episodes.

All of us go through "phases" in our emotions, more "laid-back" at times, more "up-tight" at others. Martin's swings may be more pronounced than normal.

The stress resulting from downsizing and additional work may be getting to him.

His strange behavior may be a sign that on-the-job pressures are making him irrational, that—in the language of the last generation—he's "having a nervous breakdown."

Hint: The worst reaction you can make is to get angry with Martin. Whatever is happening, getting angry with him will only make it worse.

CURES

No matter what the cause is:

First, remember what we said just above. Keep your cool. Observe carefully. Then, if necessary, find someone who's familiar with emotional disturbance and learn all you can from him or her.

Talk to other employees. Learn everything they know about Martin. How has he changed? Has this ever happened before? What happened then? How was it handled then? How quickly did he recover?

Talk with Martin. Yes, this is going to be stressful. No, you're not going to play psychiatrist. But you want to get a "feel" for his situation. You want to talk with him about the problem, if possible. If he can talk about it, that increases the chance that it can be resolved with a minimum of stress. If he can't, well, that's important information, too.

There's another side to the picture. If the situation is deteriorating, you may have to act without knowing all you need to know. It may be a tense time, for Martin, your other employees, and you. But if you act on the best information you have, trying to do the best you can by everyone, you'll bring about the best solution possible under the situation.

If he's reacting to a temporary stressful situation outside work:

How will you know this? You won't, for sure. But if the problem is a specific situation that doesn't involve work, he should at least be able to assure you that the problem has nothing to do with work. He may not want to talk about the specific problem, particularly if it's something very personal, such as a divorce or a terminally ill individual close to him. But he will probably be willing to work with you to the extent of assuring you that it's personal.

Is Martin getting help to see him through the situation? If not, you should suggest, as tactfully as possible, that he get help. While you want to support him, and his fellow employees probably will want to also, he has to take reasonable steps to keep his job performance from deteriorating.

Be as supportive as you can. Simply be a friend to him. Encourage your other employees to do the same.

Should you suggest he take time off from work? Be careful about this. He may depend on work to take his mind off his off-the-job crisis. If he does want to continue working, though, you have the opening you need to suggest that he needs to have control of himself at work. And perhaps to suggest again that he get professional help.

If this is a periodic episode:

Your best guidance is what he's done before when he's had similar episodes. How long have they lasted? How severe were they?

Remember, though, that the present one may be more or less severe.

It's important to find out whether he understands what's happening. If he does, it may be even easier to resolve than the situation above. Many people are able to realize when they're having an episode such as this and respond realistically to it.

You'll probably want to suggest that he get professional help in this case also. You may also want to encourage him to take some time off. That depends, of course, on the severity of his condition. You'll have to walk a careful line between supporting him and insisting that he take whatever actions are necessary to help himself.

If the stress resulting from downsizing and additional work may be getting to him:

He may show this when you talk to him. He may understand what's happening and describe it to you. Or he may show it by denying the situation, responding inappropriately, or becoming very defensive—all of these are signs that he feels caught in something he can't control.

If he does understand what's happening, is he taking steps to counteract it? Is he getting professional help? Or is he sinking more and more deeply into inappropriate behavior? If he's taking appropriate steps, your most effective response is to give him room and to see that other members of the workgroup do so also. Then, if he improves, fine.

But if he doesn't improve, or if he's not doing anything to prevent his on-the-job behavior from deteriorating? You need to take swift, effective action. If he's being disruptive, you may have to insist that he take sick time off, use vacation time, whatever is necessary to get him out of the work situation. If company policy permits, you may need to send him for a psychiatric evaluation. Remember, you're not doing this to punish him, but to relieve a condition that's painful both for him and for your other employees.

If Martin in any way threatens or implies violence to others or himself, respond to that *immediately*. You must assume that he means it. Get counsel from your company physician or any other professional you can reach. Call security if it seems imminent.

SOMETHING TO THINK ABOUT

Downsizing produces additional stress for most organizations, their managers, and workers. Unless individuals are accustomed to handling this level of stress, it may severely affect them, even to the point of serious emotional disturbance. One of your basic jobs is to help your workgroup deal with this stress. Find out if your company has training available in stress reduction. If it does, get it for your workgroup. If it doesn't, find a course through a commercial firm or a local community college and use it. But get help, and get it quickly. For individuals like Martin, a course is too little, too late. But it may help others in the workgroup avoid the extreme reaction that Martin had.

Stress is a real killer, especially when individuals aren't accustomed to dealing with it. Understand that managing stress in your workgroup and helping your employees manage it is now one of your fundamental job responsibilities and set your priorities accordingly.

10-3 THE PROBLEM

Your manager makes unreasonable demands for quality or quantity of work

THE SCENE

Just who does your boss think he is? It doesn't seem to matter how much the staff works themselves to death, he's never pleased. He was bad enough a year ago, but now with the company's downsizing and staff reductions he's becoming impossible. Whatever your group does, it's never fast enough, there's never enough of it, and it's never good enough. You've *never* worked for a boss who was so unreasonable. Doesn't he have any idea what you're up against? After all, your workgroup has taken its share of reductions.

POSSIBLE CAUSES

Your unit may not be producing a reasonable quantity or quality of work.

Maybe this isn't your boss's problem at all. Maybe it's yours.

Your boss may be reacting to the pressure for greater productivity from those above him.

Not every demand is a reflection of your own boss's needs or desires. Just as you may have to push your people to make the boss happy, sometimes he has to push you to make *his* boss happy. And with the downsizing, he has to do more of it now.

Your boss may not understand what it's reasonable to expect of you and your unit.

This is particularly likely if he's been transferred recently from a unit that does different work or is operating in a different environment.

Hint: Remember, when an organization has to downsize to survive competitive pressures, everyone gets affected. The old standards of what constituted a good day's work aren't valid any more. This doesn't automatically mean that everyone has to work harder, though they may have to. It does mean that everyone has to work as smart as possible. There's no room left just to do things the way they used to be done, or to use an inefficient process just because you know it. Everyone needs to be constantly engaged in process and performance improvement.

CURES

If your unit isn't producing a reasonable quantity or quality of work:

This is a major problem. You should approach your boss *immediately* and talk candidly with him about where the workgroup is falling short. Don't be defensive or argue with him; get the clearest picture you can of how he wants you to do better. What are his production goals? What does he consider adequate quality? What does he consider "complete staff work" in the assignments he gives you to perform? Maybe you've misunderstood his expectations of you.

If it's still not clear after talking to him what quantity or quality of work he expects, you might consider talking to a colleague who also works for him (or who's worked for him in the past). You might get some ideas about how much or what kind of work it takes to satisfy him.

Once you know what he's looking for, it's up to your workgroup to produce it. Maybe you're not organized as efficiently as you could be. Maybe you've let some of your own people slide and haven't expected as much of *them* as you should. Now's the time to tighten up. You can't produce any more than the people in your unit produce for you. Your leverage is through them. You can't do it all yourself. So make sure the people who work for you know what you expect and what are the consequences of their failure to meet your expectations.

If your boss is reacting to the pressure for greater productivity from those above him:

You have a narrow line to walk. You can't refuse the work, but you also have to be realistic. As in the first section, sit down with your boss and find out exactly where he believes you're falling short. Again, listen—don't argue. You want all the information you can get on how he sees you and your workgroup.

Then get together with either a few key workers or your entire workgroup. Make what your boss said clear to them. Go over each item specifically and ask for suggestions on how they can give him the productivity and/or quality he wants. If they don't believe they can do it all—and if they persuade you they genuinely can't—find out in detail what tasks they don't think they can get done and why. Don't let the group off easily, but don't let them overestimate what they can do. The best strategy: Be optimistic enough that the unit will be reasonably challenged but can get done what they commit to.

Now it's time to talk with your boss again. If you see how you can provide him what he wanted, tell him so and show him how you intend to do it. If you can't provide him everything, you need to use all of your negotiating skills. What does the workgroup need to concentrate on? What must be done well and on time? What might slide a little or be done without quite as much care without causing problems? You want to help him look good to his boss; concentrate on what you need to do to do that.

The two of you will probably be able to agree on a workable course of action. But don't dare stop there. Your workgroup will almost certainly pick up more work, so you need to start thinking about ways to do what you're doing now better and faster. Remember, every time you say to your boss, "It'll be tough, but we can do it," both your job security and his go up a notch.

If your boss doesn't understand what it's reasonable to expect of you and your unit:

Your goal is still to satisfy your boss, but you may be able to negotiate down his requirements. What kind of relationship do you have with him? Does he seem to respect you and your abilities? Or do you think he may be looking for an excuse to dump you? Will he listen to your ideas?

If you have the kind of relationship that allows you to discuss with him the problems you're having in meeting his demands, then talk with him. Find out as specifically as possible where he thinks you're falling short. If you have previous production charts or performance-review results that show other observers' satisfaction with the quantity and quality of work your unit has produced, show him. Try to find out if anything has changed in the company's priorities that changes your own unit's work priorities. And remember that he may be under pressure from those above to increase productivity (as in the section just above). Then work out the most realistic work agreement possible with him. After that, your job is to sell your workgroup on the agreement and go.

What if your boss really is being unreasonable, but isn't willing to change? You've shown him your production records and commendations from previous supervisors or audit teams, but he just won't be persuaded. He's convinced that you can do more and better than you are, and he expects you to improve. If you really can't find any way to meet his demands, then your best bet may be to try to get out of the job. This is a no-win situation, where it looks as if there's no way to satisfy him. Rely on your previous good record, go to other managers, and sell your services elsewhere. In the meantime, do the best you can to satisfy him, so he won't sabotage your efforts to find a better situation.

SOMETHING TO THINK ABOUT

While the third "cause" and "cure" are the most tempting from your point of view, they're also the least likely. (That's why they're last on the list.) Most second-line managers have worked their way up through first-level supervisory jobs. They have a pretty good idea when they become second-tier managers what's reasonable to expect and what isn't. If there's a disagreement about how much your unit ought to be producing, or what quality of work it's reasonable to expect, chances are it's your problem, not your boss's. In the interests of retaining the position you've worked so hard to achieve, it's in your best interests to assume that *you're* the one who's got to change.

It's also important to keep in mind that in a lean organization, particularly one that's still downsizing, everyone needs to look for ways to increase productivity. Don't wait for the next round of additional work to hit, or for your boss to get upset with your current productivity. Encourage your workgroup to keep finding ways to improve their quality and quantity—and help them do it.

10–4 THE PROBLEM

Your boss tells you she's going to downsize your group, even though the workload is increasing

THE SCENE

"They're at it again, Trudy. We have to cut our staff by another 10 percent, and since you have two vacancies, I'll have to start there. I'm afraid you can't fill them until at least the first of next year."

"But, Ms. Jackson, I need those people to meet all the new assignments our unit absorbed when you abolished Pete McNamara's unit six months ago. I can't do more work with fewer people."

"That's exactly what you'll have to do, Trudy. If I don't stop hiring now, I'll have to start thinking about whom to lay off later. I'm sorry about the bind this puts you in, but I'll let you know if anything changes."

Just when you thought you were going to catch up, this happens. Now what?

POSSIBLE CAUSES

Your boss is trying to set you up to get rid of you or your unit.

Other units have already been abolished. That's how you got all this extra work to begin with. If you and your group can't perform under the extra pressure, you'll probably go too. Your boss may think the easiest way to find out how much you can handle is to create a situation that taxes your resources; you'll either be a star *or* you'll self-destruct.

Your boss is making the right decision from her point of view.

Otherwise, she really would have to start letting permanent employees go.

Hint: This is one of those cases where the cause is generally less important than what you need to do to handle the situation. Regardless of why your boss is taking positions out of your unit, the consequences to you and the group are the same.

CURES

In either case, the only course you can take is to make the best of a tough situation. Here are some ideas:

- If your employees understand that the alternative was to let permanent employees go (including perhaps some of them), they may be willing to work longer and harder, at least in the short term. After a few weeks or a month or two, though, this may start to sound a little hollow to them.

- Whether your employees can produce more or not, you need to see that the highest-priority work gets done. Be sure you and your employees know what the priorities are. Talk to your boss to see that the two of you understand them the same way. Then pass this on to your employees and spend as little time as possible on the low-priority items and as much time as possible on those at the top of the priority list.

- Challenge your group to come up with better and quicker ways to get their jobs done. In this circumstance, they certainly won't have to worry about working themselves out of a job if they become more efficient. In fact, the more efficient the group becomes, the more indispensable they will be to the company. When group members come up with good ideas, see that they get recognized and, if possible, paid handsomely for them.

- Spend even more time than usual making sure your people have the equipment and supplies they need. If they've been needing some new equipment, this may be the time to try to get approval for it, as long as it doesn't cost so much that the budget cuts rule it out. If fluctuations in the work you receive from other units make it harder for your people to do their job, work with those other units to smooth out the work flow. You might try a sharing arrangement where your group helps others who have peaks in workload in return for those units helping you when your group gets overloaded.

- If you start to get seriously behind in the work, explore more formal borrowing arrangements. (After all, the cut you took may have saved jobs in someone else's group.) If your output is the input to another unit, they may be particularly willing to help you.

- If your unit really has to stretch to make up for the vacancies you couldn't fill, and especially if the group comes up with ways to really work smarter, make sure your boss knows. Nothing could be worse than her believing that you handled the cuts because you were overstaffed to start with.

Something to Think About

Like many other problems we discuss in this book, your boss's actions here put you in a real bind. Just remember that fighting the situation won't help much, but concentrating the energies of yourself and your people will. If you and your unit can successfully deal with this challenge, you may enhance your reputation significantly and ensure your long-term survival in spite of downsizing.

10-5 The Problem

Your manager refuses to let you fire nonperformers

The Scene

"Ms. Jonas, Bev simply isn't working out. She gets sloppier and sloppier every day, she accuses me of picking on her, and she's disrupting the other employees. I've got to get rid of her.

"I understand how you feel, but I'm not at all sure you've given her a fair chance. Work with her some more. I think you can bring her around."

"But I'm already short two workers. I need everyone left in my workgroup to be fully productive."

"No more. I've made my decision. Now you go back and shape her up."

Possible Causes

Ms. Jonas believes you really haven't given Bev a fair chance.

She thinks she has to intervene to see that you don't compound the problem you've caused.

She may be unwilling to fire employees.

She's concluded it isn't worth it, for one reason or another. And she may not understand how important it is in a lean organization for everyone to carry his or her part of the load. In short, she hasn't adapted to the new situation.

Ms. Jonas may have organizational reasons for not firing Bev that have nothing to do with your situation.

The organization may not yet have faced the requirement for everyone to be fully productive.

She may be friends with Bev and unwilling to let you take any action against her.

Her friendship is more important to her than any damage that Bev's poor performance can cause.

Hint: The situation has the potential to create two very undesirable results. First, it can undermine your authority in your work unit. Bev may see that no matter how strongly you talk, you can't really deliver. Second, others may ask themselves why they're working so hard if Bev can get away with poor productivity. Neither of these situations is tolerable in an environment in which you're already threatened by cutbacks (or even elimination of your unit). You want to prevent or minimize both these problems, no matter what their "causes" and "cures" are.

CURES

If Ms. Jonas believes you really haven't given Bev a fair chance:

This is serious. It means you don't have Ms. Jonas' confidence in an area that's key to your success in your job. In the other three causes, the problem is Bev and—at least in your eyes—your boss. In this situation, the problem is your relationship with Ms. Jonas, and perhaps with Bev.

First, you need to review the situation in your own mind. What's happened that might make Ms. Jonas think Bev hasn't gotten a fair chance? Then find out why Ms. Jonas thinks you haven't been treating her fairly. If possible, ask her that, in so many words. Don't argue or defend yourself; concentrate on finding out exactly how she sees the situation. Has Bev gone around you and complained to her? Does Ms. Jonas suspect that you may be prejudiced against Bev because she's female or a minority? Look for any other reasons why she thinks you haven't given Bev a reasonable opportunity to succeed.

Is there a chance Ms. Jonas is right? Is it possible that you have been treating Bev differently from other employees? Do you perhaps not like or trust her, or is she difficult for you to get along with? Once you have an answer that seems right, you can start to correct the situation. Talk with Bev and try to get her to open up with you about how she sees the situation. Then try to make a mutual agreement that both of you are willing to follow. As part of the agreement, arrange regular meetings with her where each of you can review how she seems to be doing. And then make sure that Ms. Jonas knows that the two of you are working together to ensure that she's being treated fairly. Remember, it's just as important that Ms. Jonas knows you're working on the problem as it is to work on it.

Suppose you honestly believe you've treated Bev fairly? Now you need to figure out why Ms. Jonas doesn't see it that way. The next step, of course, is to plan what you need to do to help Ms. Jonas change her mind. Perhaps you haven't mentioned to her when Bev has failed at an assignment or been late on one. See that Ms. Jonas knows that now. One word of caution: Don't give the impression that your goal is to prove Ms. Jonas wrong. Your goal is to treat Bev fairly and help Ms. Jonas see that you are. Then when she sees that you are managing as you should, she will (probably) let you take whatever action you need.

If she's unwilling to fire employees:

How would you know that this is the case? Either from your prior experiences with Ms. Jonas or from what other managers have told you. In the long run, it makes a difference whether she won't fire employees in general or is just responding to immediate organizational pressures. In this situation, it makes no difference. She has developed an approach as a manager that isn't workable in the current high-pressure, high-productivity situation. You need to deal with that.

So what do you do? You analyze your unit's work and then show Ms. Jonas as specifically as possible how Bev's failure to produce is handicapping overall productivity. If possible, explain how it almost kept the group from meeting an important deadline or almost caused them to submit an unacceptable product. You should know what Ms. Jonas's priorities are. Show her how Bev's performance is interfering with achieving those. In short, do the best possible job of showing that Bev's poor performance directly affects Ms. Jonas's success in her job. If you can get that across, you may get the authority you need to take action to get rid of Bev.

And if you can't change Ms. Jonas's mind? Ask her to take Bev off your hands and find her another job. If Bev is a poor enough performer, offer to get along without a replacement. That may persuade Ms. Jonas either to let you do something or finally to do something herself.

If none of these work, give Ms. Jonas regular updates on how Bev's poor performance continues to interfere with your work-group's ability to do its job and with Ms. Jonas's ability to succeed in hers.

If Ms. Jonas has organizational reasons for not firing Bev that have nothing to do with your situation:

She may be responding to pressures that have nothing to do with you or Bev. The organization, for whatever reason, still doesn't believe in firing people. And Ms. Jonas may not feel that she needs to tell you the reason, or that she can tell you.

Use some of the suggestions from the section just above. Ask Ms. Jonas to find Bev another job. Give her regular reports, which she might want to share with her own boss, of how Bev's poor performance is interfering with the group's productivity. Keep the issue alive.

There is one consolation in this situation: Bev probably doesn't know that you can't fire her, at least not yet. You still have some leverage with her. Use it. Keep insisting that she perform satisfactorily. If she won't, discipline her to the maximum extent that your boss permits. Who knows—if you do the most that you can do it may be enough to get her to start performing more effectively.

If she's friends with Bev and unwilling to let you take action against her:

Make sure Ms. Jonas knows exactly what problems you're having with Bev and how they affect your unit's ability to do the work. She may know Bev primarily from a social perspective. And if no one's complained to her before (with hard facts to back them up), she may really not know what the problems are. Her attempts to protect Bev may spring from her lack of knowledge rather than a conscious decision to protect her no matter what. She may decide to let you deal with Bev's performance without regard for their friendship.

But probably not. In this case, ask Ms. Jonas to find a position for Bev in another workgroup. You don't want to be caught in the middle. She may agree to try to move Bev. If she doesn't, follow the suggestions in the section just above and make sure she stays constantly aware of Bev's impact on the workgroup and on her own success.

THINGS TO THINK ABOUT

Very few aspects of your job as a manager are more important than making sure that your boss has confidence in you. This over-all confidence is more important than almost any specific situation that can arise. If you have it, you will be able to deal with any problem, even one where you may need to fire an employee. If you don't have it, you may have trouble getting your boss's support for even minor actions.

So one of your basic goals as a manager is to establish and maintain your boss's confidence. This doesn't mean becoming a "yes person," or letting your boss run your workgroup. It does mean understanding what's important to your boss and support-ing this in every way you can. In other words, one of your basic responsibilities is making your boss look good. Do that, and you'll have his or her confidence.

10–6 THE PROBLEM

Your best workers are leaving for other jobs

THE SCENE

"Well, Paul, we're sorry to see you go, but I understand how you feel. If I had kids getting ready to go to college, I'd be look-ing for more security too."

"Argghhh!" you snarl, as Paul leaves your office. Three of your best workers—gone in just as many months. Not that you can blame them; the rumors of layoffs are flying fast and furious. But how are you ever going to get all this work done? And if you can't, that makes you and the rest of your staff even more vulnerable in the downsizing.

POSSIBLE CAUSES

It's fairly clear why your best workers are leaving the company. They believe that they'll be out of a job sooner or later, and they've decided to get out while the getting's good. But how reliable are the rumors that are floating around?

If the rumors are accurate and there will be more downsizing and layoffs, including your unit, there's not much you can do to entice your workers to stay. In that case, your main concern needs to be to keep up production (and morale) in the rest of your unit.

But if the rumors are false, or if the planned downsizing isn't likely to hurt your group, then you have considerably more leverage to stop the drain of talent.

Hint: Loss of your best talent is a challenge in the best of times, even when everything else in the company is going smoothly. Talent drain during downsizing can be a real killer because you often can't do anything to replace the people you're losing. Be careful not to take out your frustration on the staff, either the ones leaving or the ones staying. The ones who leave are reacting to their situation in the best way they know how and so are the ones who stay. Your continuing support is important to both groups.

CURES

If the rumors of downsizing are true:

Recognize that there probably isn't a lot you can do to keep your workers from looking for other jobs if the ones they have now are likely to disappear. But that doesn't mean that your situation is hopeless. You have several avenues you can try to keep up production and morale in your unit in spite of the frequent departures.

- Talk to your manager or your personnel department to try to find out who's likely to be hurt in the downsizing and who's likely to be more secure. Within the limits imposed by your company on disclosure of downsizing information, reassure the people whose jobs are most secure. Emphasize the need for everyone to continue to produce and to pull together to keep that security.

- Find out also what authority you have to offer retention bonuses to workers who have other jobs lined up but who may be able to delay their reporting dates for a few weeks or months. Your company might have options available to give those workers an incentive to stay for a little longer to give you time to adjust the workload in your unit.

- Talk to other managers in your organization to see if you can arrange to borrow some workers, even part time, to get over the hump until the downsizing and reorganization is complete. Depending on the kind of work your unit does and how easily other people can learn to perform, you may even be able to offer overtime hours to workers in other units who'd be willing to do some work for you after they've completed their full-time jobs each day.

- If it looks as if your options for additional help are running out, meet with your staff to review all the functions they perform. Decide which ones are critical and which ones aren't (or are less critical). Go over each employee's work assignments. Prioritize the work within each job and move assignments around as necessary to ensure that all the high-priority work gets done and that all your workers are actively involved in the high-priority assignments. Develop some contingency plans to cover any of the less critical areas that may suddenly become "hot," but let everyone know that you don't expect the remaining group to perform everything that the full group did.

- Is being short-staffed likely to be a long-term situation? If so, consider doing a process reengineering study of some of your key functions. A reengineering analysis will look at all the work involved in each function and the process you use to perform it, then evaluate whether there are better or more efficient ways to get the same work done. There may be ways to rework your unit's processes themselves to get more work accomplished with fewer people and without burning out the ones you have.

If the rumors of downsizing are false:

Pass on to your staff all the information you can about what the company's plans are and how secure they are in their jobs. Reassure them that you'll let them know if anything changes to put their jobs in jeopardy and make sure they know that they're valued members of your staff. If you're able to get to staff members who have accepted other jobs or are negotiating with other companies for positions, see if you can offer retention bonuses to entice them to stay. Most of all, make sure that the information you give your staff is accurate and timely. If the jobs aren't secure, don't give false hope. Not only is that unfair to staff members who've been loyal to you and the company, it's also very likely to backfire once your workers find out the truth.

SOMETHING TO THINK ABOUT

Workers change jobs for lots of reasons, sometimes because they have better opportunities to look forward to elsewhere and sometimes because they're not happy where they are. If your company is downsizing and job security is in question, the reason for the mass exodus is obvious. But what if your unit's jobs are secure and your workforce is still leaving? Take a look at your work environment from your employees' point of view. Is it too structured? Not structured enough? Is the work challenging? Or are employees burnt out because there's too much work?

Sometimes several workers will decide to change jobs at about the same time just by coincidence. But sometimes it's because there's a problem where they are. Just make sure *you're* not the problem!

10-7 The Problem

Your manager takes credit for what you do

The Scene

"Look here at the company newsletter," Craig offers at lunch. "Mr. Newton's been interviewed about that new order-processing system you put in a couple of months ago. And see what he says: 'I thought we needed . . .' and 'It seemed to me . . .' and 'I decided this . . .' and 'I created that . . .' Reading this, no one would ever know you had anything to do with the project at all—and it was your idea to begin with!"

"Don't you know?" Alice adds, "Newton's been doing that to all of us lately. He seems to think he can grab all the glory for our work, and then when the layoffs come, the CEO will see he's so valuable that he'll get to keep his job while the rest of us are out on the street."

Possible Causes

He may really be trying to enhance his own image by claiming credit for what his subordinates accomplish.

This could be a strategy to make himself more competitive in a downsizing environment, or it could be because he really believes he deserves the credit for anything his staff does. In either case, the behavior is guaranteed to make him plenty of enemies and may backfire when his staff starts to fight back.

He may believe that when he speaks of himself, his listeners understand that he's referring to his staff also.

He may not realize how important it is to the people who did the work to get specific credit for it and that his superiors will give him credit for assembling a good staff, perhaps even more than for coming up with ideas himself.

Hint: This is a tricky situation. Part of the job of any subordinate is to make his or her boss look good, but preferably not at the expense of other employees. Your goal here is to make sure your boss gets lots of credit for what you and your unit do, but for his excellent leadership of the effort, not for the idea or the work itself.

CURES

If your boss is trying to enhance his own image by claiming credit for others' work:

Although his tactics are inappropriate, his strategy is not bad: During a period of downsizing, it's important that the decision makers know who in the organization is making a significant contribution. Obviously, the problem here is that your boss is taking credit for contributions that others are responsible for. So it's critical that you protect yourself some way. You need to make sure your company's decision makers know how valuable you are, and your record will look dismally bare if all *your* accomplishments appear to be *your boss's*.

Try to work out an informal arrangement with your boss that you won't complain when he takes the credit for things you do, as long as he does what he can to boost *your* career. This doesn't even have to be a spoken agreement, as long as you both know what the rules are and live up to them. Drop a few hints here and there that you're on to his game, and see what reaction you get.

If subtlety doesn't work, and if you can't come to a more open agreement about what he'll do for you, then you need to get more assertive. Document your ideas and accomplishments. When you have something new to suggest, do it in writing rather than in informal conversation. Make formal proposals rather than oral requests—and early enough in the process that it's obvious later whose idea this really was. Prepare regular progress reports that identify, specifically and in detail, what's been done and who did the work. Keep records, and whenever possible, make sure your documentation becomes part of the unit's official files.

As much as you can without appearing to brag, let others know what you've accomplished. You can always tell friends and co-workers what you're contemplating and what you've completed. If your boss's other subordinate supervisors are suffering the same treatment you are, they'll be glad to share their accomplishments with you and help you establish your own contributions. As opportunities arise in conversations with casual acquaintances, mention work you've done that's especially noteworthy. This is delicate. You don't want to look like a braggart or a "know-it-all," and it's best not to upstage your boss or contradict him too openly. But it's important to engage in a little defense publicity from time to time.

Keep your sense of humor. If you're a talented and dedicated manager, especially if you have a proven track record in the company, people will know already who's *really* doing the work. They'll soon recognize your boss for the scene-stealer he is and begin to discount his tales of great feats.

If your boss believes his listeners understand that his staff shares in the credit for the work:

Make sure that when you report progress or accomplishments to your boss you include the names of the major contributors. Give him the information he needs to pass credit along when he has occasion to talk about the project to other people.

Make gently encouraging statements to him about the positive effects of recognizing employees' contributions. Let him know how your employees react (such as with greater enthusiasm or productivity) when they know that someone above them is aware of their efforts. Your occasional hints may be all it takes to raise your boss's consciousness.

If gentle reminders don't work, and if your relationship with your boss is generally good, you might try a more direct approach. Tell him how discouraging it is—to you and to your workers—when it appears that he's taking credit for others' hard work. If he's a sensitive manager, he'll get the message. But, of course, you *won't* want to be this direct if you suspect that he really does want to claim credit for other people's efforts. It's likely to make him even more aggressive in grabbing the glory from you and your group.

SOMETHING TO THINK ABOUT

While you're concerned about the credit your boss is taking for your accomplishments, are your employees concerned about your taking credit for *their* work? You can't expect workers to do their best if all their efforts go to your greater glory. You want your boss to be generous with his praise and credit; don't your workers deserve the same?

chapter eleven

Troubleshooting Problems Involving Empowerment and Teamwork

11–1 THE PROBLEM

Your employees think being empowered means they don't have to listen to you

THE SCENE

"Hannah, I don't understand what's happened here. I asked you last week to call the Supero Group and apologize for our having taken so long to finish their order. Now I see that they've sent back their customer satisfaction questionnaire and said that we took too long and did superficial work. I thought you were going to try to mend our relationship with them. You reported back last week that everything was taken care of."

"Well, everything is taken care of. When I passed your request on to the team, they decided that since Supero was such a pain to work with, we'd be better off without them. Why, is that a problem? You told us we were empowered to handle our own accounts!"

POSSIBLE CAUSES

Your employees may not have a clear understanding of the limits of their authority.

They may truly believe that they're entirely on their own, and you may have contributed to their misunderstanding by the way you've delegated assignments to them.

Your employees may be testing their limits.

They're not sure how far empowerment stretches, and this seems like a good opportunity to find out—particularly if this customer doesn't seem that important to them. They may not believe you really meant it when you told them they were empowered to handle the accounts themselves.

Your employees may not want to be "empowered" and think that ignoring your request will force you to take charge again.

Especially if your employees have been accustomed to a fairly structured environment, the idea of taking charge of their own assignments may not be all that appealing.

Hint: If empowerment is to work, it requires a high degree of trust between you and your workgroup. When the relationship between you is strained, or uncertain, you need to introduce the notion of empowerment more slowly—maybe not even say the word "empowerment" at all until the group is more accustomed to accepting responsibility for its decisions. When empowerment begins to look like anarchy, you need to consider whether you're moving too fast for the rest of the staff to keep up.

CURES

If your employees don't have a clear understanding of the limits of their authority:

It's not too late to fix the misunderstanding. You just need to back up a little and start again.

Empowerment, just like any form of delegation, is not all or nothing. Employees can be empowered at several different levels. At one level, your employees are empowered to handle "routine" cases (and you will define for them what is routine and what isn't), and for more complicated or sensitive matters, they're expected to come to you for direction. At a higher level of empowerment, your employees handle all routine cases along with some more difficult ones and come to you with recommendations for handling the most troublesome situations. At the highest level of empowerment, your employees handle virtually everything themselves, coming to you with recommendations and seeking approval only in unusual cases. At *all* levels, your staff is expected to make sure they keep you informed well enough that you don't get blindsided. And also at all levels, you have ultimate "veto" power to override the team's decisions.

It is up to you to decide at what level of empowerment you expect your group to operate. Since "empowerment" implies a level of autonomy higher than traditional "delegation," you will want ultimately to have as many people as possible operating at the highest level, or at least the middle level. But not all employees are ready to make that leap. So you should begin by assessing the strengths and weaknesses of the members of your staff and your own comfort level to decide at what level of empowerment to start.

Meet with your workgroup to explain exactly what you mean by "empowerment," including what level of autonomy they'll have to begin with and where you want to end up. Explain what kinds of issues they have authority to resolve themselves and give them specific examples of what they can and cannot handle without consulting you. Explain also how you'll know when it's time for them to assume the next level of authority. That may take a bit of introspection on your part: It's not good enough to say you'll "know it when you see it."

Then turn them loose, but monitor their performance, especially in the first few weeks (or months, if necessary). As soon as the group has demonstrated that they can competently handle routine issues, to your quality and quantity standards, it's time to move to the next level of empowerment. It's important that you not throw them into unfamiliar waters too quickly and before they've built up your trust in their judgment. But it's also important that the group be recognized for the progress they make and that you allow them to operate with a higher level of authority as soon as they've earned your trust. If you hold them back too long, they'll doubt that you're sincere about empowerment and they'll begin to work around you.

If your employees are testing the limits of their authority:

Let's begin by assuming that your employees really do know what they're empowered to do and what they're not. In this case, they understand their limits, but they want to push further. Your first task is to figure out why they feel the need to test limits. Are they capable of working at a higher level of authority, but you've chosen to limit them? So do they think you're being arbitrary and autocratic in not giving them greater autonomy? Or is the opposite true—do they see you as a weak leader who will buckle under pressure or simply not react to their bid for more power?

How do you know whether they're capable of assuming a greater level of authority? Ask yourself two questions: Do they successfully handle the things they really are delegated authority to handle, and do you trust them to handle more difficult or more sensitive issues appropriately? It's not necessary that you trust that the group would handle these more difficult issues the way *you* would. It's only necessary that you trust that they would handle them in a way that's consistent with your policies and corporate values. Part of empowerment is trusting that other people's judgments can be good ones, even when they're not exactly the judgments you would make. If you can answer "yes" to both of these questions, then it's time to give the group greater responsibility and authority. Holding them back will only stifle their initiative and cause them to test you even more often.

On the other hand, if the group sees you as a weak leader who can be run over by a show of independence, you can reinforce the limits you've set very easily. Call the group's attention to the delegation discussion you had with them earlier when you first established the limits of their authority. Don't overreact by being too stern or authoritarian; they'll know that for the mask of insecurity that it often is. Instead, calmly and reasonably point out that they've overstepped their bounds. Then explain why it's important to ensure that *all* customers are satisfied, even those whom you don't particularly want to cultivate. Express your confidence that they'll follow your guidance in similar situations in the future and wait to see what happens next time.

If the group comes to you with recommendations, but listens to your suggestions and follows your explicit directions, they're moving in the right direction and may be getting ready to jump to the next higher level of authority. But if you have a repeat of the problem, then it's time to move *down* to a lesser level of delegation (of course, after you've explained why) until they can rebuild your trust and confidence in their judgment again.

If your employees are trying to undermine your attempts at empowerment:

Recognize that not all workgroups will embrace the idea of empowerment with open arms. Although empowerment is discussed in terms of the increased authority and autonomy it gives employees, it also shifts to employees increased responsibility for the consequences of their actions. Many of your employees won't want that increased responsibility, either because they are fearful of making mistakes or because they don't want the added burdens. If your workgroup is to successfully negotiate the transition from a traditional authority-based structure to an empowered team structure, you will need to be sensitive to this reluctance.

Look again at the levels of empowerment described earlier. Notice that at each level the workgroup assumes a little more responsibility and gains a little more autonomy. Where is your workgroup most comfortable? Find that level and begin again. Explain to your workgroup that you believe that it will benefit both them and the organization for them to operate as an empowered team, but that you realize that you have to move one step at a time. Then once again describe the level of empowerment at which you'll start—what decisions they can make on their own, which ones they need to get approval for first, and which ones you will make. Although you're decreasing the level of authority and responsibility at which you'll require them to operate, be clear that this decrease is only *temporary*. Your goal is still a fully empowered group.

As the group gets comfortable with the first level of empowerment, begin to move them toward the next level. Encourage them. Reward their successes and help them learn from their mistakes, but don't punish mistakes. Learning involves risk. When you punish errors, you discourage them from taking the risks that are necessary to their growth. Support the workgroup, but don't allow them to use you as a crutch. And that's a fine line to draw.

SOMETHING TO THINK ABOUT

There is one level of delegation that's even lower than those we've described here (and doesn't even deserve the title "empowerment"). At that level your employees make recommendations to you for almost every decision they make and very seldom take an independent action, no matter how small or insignificant. If your workgroup is operating at this level, it's likely that you either have a very inexperienced group or you have somehow made it clear to them that you want to work this way. Making all the decisions yourself isn't healthy in the long term—for you, for your workgroup, or for the organization. Examine your own management style and leverage your resources—get the most from your group by giving them the tools and the authority they need to work on their own. You'll multiply your group's productivity immensely.

11-2 THE PROBLEM

Another manager won't cooperate with you on a joint project

THE SCENE

"How do you want to handle getting these work standards written?" you ask Frances. "I can gather up some good samples and see what we can draw from them."

"Oh, just go at it however you want," Frances replies. "I'm pretty busy right now, so why don't you just draw something up and then we'll talk."

"Well, that doesn't sound much like a 'joint project' to me. I think Ms. Cryder's idea was that we would put together standards that would cover all our units' work, and I don't know enough about what your group does to be sure I cover all your projects. I feel as if you're stonewalling me on this assignment."

POSSIBLE CAUSES

Frances may really not have the time or resources to devote to the project.

It may be an area in which she'd really like to be involved, and she may be the sort of person who usually comes through, but she's just been caught at a bad time.

Frances may want to make you look bad by failing to produce on this joint assignment.

She may think that she has a good enough reputation in the organization that you'll be blamed for any deficiencies in the final product (rather than Frances). Then she'll have "proof" that you're not doing your job.

Hint: You know from your experience with your own work-group that when a team gets a project assignment that is executed poorly, the *whole* team looks bad, not just the one or two people who contributed most to the failure. Frances can make you look bad on this project, but she won't come out smelling like a rose either. And even if you want to see that Frances gets her just desserts, sabotaging the assignment won't accomplish your purpose. Regardless of the cause of Frances's lack of cooperation, it's up to you to make sure the assignment is done well and on time. Revenge, if any, has to wait.

CURES

If Frances doesn't have the time to devote to the assignment:

Talk to Frances about what she's able to do. If she can't come to meetings or devote her personal time to the assignment, does she have someone on her staff who could carry information back and forth (or even do part of the work she was responsible for)? Can she feed you information that you can put together in the final product? Can she give you some ideas on how to approach the assignment, which you can then pass along to your own people to work on? Define clearly at the beginning what Frances can contribute and what she'll have to leave up to you.

Since Frances is someone whom you can trust to do what she says she'll do, we'll assume that she follows through on the things she's promised, or at least has someone else in her unit do the work. Take what she's given you and put together the best final product you can. If there are areas you can't finish without additional input from her (because they're things only she knows about), get back to her with *specific* questions.

Allow Frances an opportunity to see the final project before you submit it to your superiors. Give her a "drop dead" date after which you'll not be able to accept any changes and still get the product finished by the deadline. Let her know in advance also that this is a technical review only. If the material is correct and she simply disagrees with your approach or your presentation, this is not the time to raise those issues. She had an opportunity to be more involved earlier and declined. By depending on you to put together the final product, she implicitly agreed to defer to your judgment.

If Frances is as good a person as you think she is, she'll give you top billing and lots of credit for the success of the project. She'll also have the grace to assume her half of the blame for any failings in the final product. If not, you'll know the next time around how unreliable she is and treat her accordingly (see below).

If Frances consistently takes advantage or wants to discredit you:

Keep track of the attempts you've made to collaborate with Frances on the assignment. Identify the parts of the project you think you should be responsible for and the parts that only Frances has the information to produce. Give the list to Frances and try to get her agreement. Chances are you won't get disagreement—just no response at all. In that case, keep a copy of your memo to her, annotated with the attempts you've made to discuss with her, and start working.

Once you've completed as much as you can without Frances's input, go back to her again to get the information you need. If she still refuses to cooperate, put together a mock report. Make it as complete as you can, but identify clearly the information that's missing and its possible impact on the validity of the final product. Give Frances a copy of your mock report with fair warning that if she doesn't do her share this is exactly what will go forward as the final product. Chances are pretty good that she'll finally come through.

What if you don't need Frances's help to do a good job on the assignment? Then keep going without her. Write frequent memos to her to ask for information or to request meetings. Call her secretary to schedule appointments and document her unavailability. But produce the best report you possibly can. Just be sure to keep all your notes and rough drafts so it's clear to anyone who wants to find out who it was that did all the work.

And whether Frances finally comes through or not, be sure that your peers know what a struggle you've had to get the assignment finally completed. A well-placed word to your fellow supervisors (maybe even to your boss in the right context) will get the message across. Keep in mind that Frances's failure to help you is probably not an isolated incident. If she hasn't cooperated on your joint assignment, she's probably let others down too, including her superiors.

Finally, be sure that when you're asked to work with someone else on a joint project, even someone you don't particularly care for, that you don't follow Frances's example. Your cooperation with others will demonstrate that if there was any flaw in the previous assignment, the fault surely wasn't yours.

SOMETHING TO THINK ABOUT

There are only so many things you can do to get your peers to cooperate with you. While good peer relations are critical to your own success as a manager, you'll inevitably run into managers who don't want to play fair. When that happens, try your best to work things out with them. But if your attempts fail, do whatever you must to protect yourself. Don't let an unsuccessful manager take you down with her.

11–3 THE PROBLEM

Your manager keeps telling you to turn your workgroup into a self-managing team, with no guidance on how

THE SCENE

"You're one of the most intelligent managers I know, and certainly one of my most intelligent direct reports. I just can't understand why you keep fighting me on this self-managing team issue!"

"Mr. Garcia, I'm not fighting you, really I'm not. I just don't have any idea how to go about making my workgroup a self-managing team."

"For someone as smart and experienced as you, that's no excuse."

"Then you tell me—how do I go about it? Where do I begin?"

"That's your job. I'm not going to do it for you. Now go and get started."

POSSIBLE CAUSES

Mr. Garcia has been told to create self-managing teams; he has no idea how to do it either.

This is how many organizations attempt to implement teams: They tell managers to do it, sometimes with minimal training, sometimes with no training at all.

Mr. Garcia understands the basics, but he wants you to exercise the necessary initiative.

He may believe that the team will be much more effective if you find out for yourself how to implement it. He may also be testing to see if you're willing to take the initiative.

Mr. Garcia needs greater productivity from your workgroup and this is how he believes he can best get it.

He sees this as a real positive step for you and your workgroup and for himself.

Hint: It doesn't really matter what the cause is—this could be a great opportunity for you and your workgroup. Approach it that way, no matter what the obstacles may seem to be.

CURES

If Mr. Garcia has been told to create self-managing teams and has no idea how to do it:

The basic approach to this cause is the same as that to the next one, with one exception. And it's an important exception. If Mr. Garcia doesn't understand much about teams, starting to make your workgroup a self-managing team may raise his anxiety level in a hurry. He may well feel that he's losing control, and managers never like that feeling in the least.

What do you do? You keep him posted at every turn. You see that he gets educated along with you and the workgroup. If possible, have him attend the training with the group. Schedule frequent conferences with him. Explain to him—probably over and over—how the team's greater autonomy is going to boost production and make him look good. Don't attempt to move the group any faster than he's willing to go.

And follow the steps in the next section.

If Mr. Garcia understands the basics, but wants you to exercise the necessary initiative:

This should mean that you can spend less time educating him and more time educating the group. Start by looking at the characteristics of a successful team in the next section. Make sure that your workgroup has or can develop these characteristics. Find a good book or two on self-managing teams at the library and read it. Make sure you understand the basics and know what you need to do.

Then start. See that the workgroup gets training in the essentials of self-managing teams as soon as possible. The entire workgroup should attend the same training, either at the same time or at successive sessions. Needless to say, you attend the training with them. Then hold a discussion session or two to compare notes on what everyone learned and begin to plan the transition to a self-managing team. You will also want to identify training in team-building and conflict management and schedule the team for it. If the organization has trained team facilitators available, arrange to get one of them to help the team get started.

By this point, you and the team should know basically what you need to do. Establish a clear mission, one that each member of the team is committed to. Begin finding ways to share leadership among team members. And you're on your way.

If Mr. Garcia needs greater productivity from your workgroup and this is how he believes he can best get it:

Teams have been oversold. They do not always improve productivity. In fact, they are not always as productive as a traditional workgroup. And if an individual can do a job by himself or herself, a team attempting to do the same job will always be less efficient.

How do you tell? There's no simple answer, but here are two key points:

- Be sure that the team has a clear mission, one that every member sees is important and worthwhile. Teams work only when each individual member is committed to the team mission.

- The team will be most effective if it produces a single product or service, manages a single process, serves a single customer or group of customers, or combines two or all three of these. Each team member can contribute a different skill to accomplish this (the team can be multifunctional), or each can learn all of the skills required (the individuals can be multiskilled). But the team must have a unity of purpose, and this is easiest if it manages a single product or service, controls a single process, serves a single customer or group of like customers, and/or combines two or all three of these.

SOMETHING TO THINK ABOUT

As the hint suggested, the opportunity to help a workgroup become a self-managing team is an opportunity worth seizing. But be aware of two critical points:

- Your role will change dramatically. You will move from being a supervisor to being a leader, then to being a teacher or coach. Depending on the degree of self-management the organization will tolerate, you may even end up as consultant and coordinator for a large group of teams. Be prepared to make these changes and take whatever steps you need to make them successfully.

- Make sure you find a role for yourself in all of this. When an organization makes effective use of self-managing teams, first-line supervisors become an endangered species. We know that you don't want a pink slip as the reward for your efforts. So, from the beginning, look for a role for yourself. You could end up as coordinator for several teams, or perhaps become a facilitator. Keep your eyes open and look for the possibilities. If necessary, ensure that the organization knows that you've supported teams from the beginning and they have an obligation to you. In short, be self-managing.

11–4 THE PROBLEM

Your manager overrules you every time you try to empower your workgroup

THE SCENE

"I don't understand what the problem is, Mark. Empowering my group doesn't mean I'll let them just fly off on their own. I'll still . . ."

"I know perfectly well what empowerment is, and I don't like it. You're in charge of this group, and I expect you to act as if you're in charge."

"But they're a good group, and they do good work. If they had a little more authority to make decisions on their own, we could get a lot more done. And our production numbers can always stand a boost."

"No, Emily, this isn't going to work. I supervise you, and you supervise your group. And we both know what that means . . ."

POSSIBLE CAUSES

Your boss may not understand what you mean by "empowerment."

Even though Mark says he knows what empowerment is, he may think this is just a way for you to make supervision easier for yourself.

You and your boss may have different ideas about what a supervisor's job really is.

Your discussion with him indicates that he's focused on what a supervisor *does*. Empowerment is more about what a supervisor can *accomplish*.

Your boss may be concerned that the group's work will deteriorate without your close supervision.

He may not be as convinced as you that the group will do good work on its own.

Hint: The three causes we've listed can be summarized as disagreements about what to do, about how to do it, and about what it means to be a supervisor. Whenever you and your boss disagree about something, chances are good that the bottom line is one or the other of those causes. So you might want to generalize the approaches we've described below for solving the problem; they apply to a multitude of situations.

CURES

If your boss doesn't understand what you mean by "empowerment":

"Empowerment" is one of those popular terms that mean different things to different people. For some managers, empowerment means allowing the workgroup to do as much as they can as independently as they can, but with continuing management responsibility for ensuring the overall adequacy of their work. But for some others, empowerment *does* mean making their own lives easier by pushing responsibility for getting the work done down into the organization, but keeping much of the authority for themselves.

So, before you resume your discussion with Mark about why empowering your employees is a good thing, you need to decide what it is that *you* mean by empowerment.

In its best form, we see empowerment as a way to "leverage your resources." It's a way to allow your workgroup to exercise as much responsibility and authority as it can competently handle.

By delegating some of the decision-making power in your group, you don't have to be involved in every decision they make. So, instead of the unit's productivity being limited by *your* capacity, it's limited by the capacity of the group, which is much greater than you alone.

In its most advanced form, we see an empowered workgroup as operating with the authority to make all routine decisions and many more difficult decisions. But they will *always* be responsible for consulting with their supervisor on issues that are particularly complex or particularly sensitive. How many of those complex or sensitive issues they must get guidance on depends mostly on the competence of the workgroup. The more practice they get in handling issues and the more comfortable the supervisor is with their judgment, the less often consultation will be necessary.

Empowerment is not about making anybody's life easier. It's about getting the most out of the resources you have. And it's a two-edged sword: It confers both authority and responsibility. The workgroup not only has the ability to make decisions, but they are accountable for those decisions. Any successful empowerment initiative has to include consequences, both good and bad, for the decisions the workgroup makes, both good and bad. And it's not just a bowl of cherries for the manager either. In some ways managing an empowered workgroup is *more* difficult than traditional supervision. You're still responsible for what the group does, but you don't have the same level of control you used to.

So, if after thinking about what you mean by empowerment and considering our suggestions you still want to empower your workgroup, what should you do to convince your boss?

First, work out a specific plan for how you intend to empower your workforce. What will be the extent of their authority? What will you do to ensure that quality and quantity aren't adversely affected? How will you review their decisions? How will you decide whether they're ready to move from one level of authority and responsibility to the next? What will be the rewards to the group for successful exercise of their authority? What will be the consequences for inappropriate exercise of their authority?

Then schedule an appointment with your boss to present your proposed plan in some detail. This should take about an hour. Begin by explaining what you see as the benefits to the organization; then go through the implementation steps. Let your boss interrupt all he wants. Be prepared to answer the tough questions such as, "What's this going to do for me?" and "If your group is so empowered, what do I still need you for?"

Don't press for approval right away. Make this an information presentation, not a decision-making session. Give your boss a few weeks to think about empowerment as you've presented it and to come up with any other objections he might have. You might even want to consider not referring to your plan as "empowerment" at all. That's a pretty radical term in some circles. It might be better to talk about "delegation" or a "responsibility matrix" instead.

After some time go to your boss and tell him how you plan to proceed, planning to take the first steps slowly. This also is not a decision meeting—it's an information meeting for your boss. Unless your authority to organize the work of your group is restricted, you're probably in a position to decide who has authority to do what within the group. So when you talk to your boss about your first steps, do it in the context of passing information, not asking permission.

As your group assumes greater authority successfully, continue to delegate more authority and responsibility to it. Keep your boss informed and stay within the limits of your own authority, but maintain a positive, active approach—and your strategy will probably *never* even be questioned.

Recognize that there are probably some "sacred cows" assigned to your unit that you will probably *never* be able to delegate to the rest of the workgroup. Those are the issues or projects that your boss (or his boss) has such a personal interest in that you need to know exactly what's happened on them and be actively involved in making decisions about them. Similarly, your group needs to know that you probably have your own one or two "sacred cows" that appear to you to be so sensitive or visible that you can't delegate them. Those issues don't destroy your entire empowerment initiative; they're just minor exceptions to your general practice.

If you and your boss have different ideas about what supervision really is:

Recognize that you're not going to change his ideas and he's probably not going to change yours (although he may change the way you implement them). Acknowledge that you understand what he says about a supervisor's role. Identify for yourself the areas where you agree and disagree. Then decide whether the span between them is too great to bridge.

If not, then prepare the detailed implementation plan described above and present it to your boss, with special sensitivity to what you know about the differences in the way you and he view supervision. If you deemphasize the notion of "empowerment" and talk instead about delegation and the continuing control you'll exercise over a broader delegation of powers, you probably won't get strong resistance to your plan. You should at least be able to implement on a trial basis. Then your workgroup and your boss (and you) can have some time to see if you're all really ready for your group's greater autonomy.

If the differences between your ideas of supervision and your boss's *are* too great to span, you need to make a decision: Do you want to back off on your idea of delegating more responsibility to the unit, or do you want to take a strong stance (recognizing that it may cost you your managerial role in the company)? You can compromise (or back off completely for a while, and then offer a compromise proposal). Most managers are in favor of increasing their units' productivity; their concern is largely with the perceived lack of accountability of an "empowered" workforce.

If your boss is concerned about deterioration of your unit's work without close supervision:

Again, the detailed implementation plan described above is one of the most powerful tools we've found. But also again, you don't want to march into your boss's office and try to steam-roll his acceptance of your proposal. The notion of empowerment seems like a big change for many managers. That may be because it's a different word from "delegation" or "authorization." But, at base, it's much the same concept: progressively greater authority with progressively more powerful consequences.

Show your boss how you will phase in decision-making authority as the group demonstrates it can handle the more extensive autonomy and how you'll pull it back if they consistently fail to handle it well. Emphasize the parts of your plan that address your continued monitoring of the group's performance and your intention to intervene if necessary. Assure him that you'll keep in touch with the work, but that the rewards for delegation of much of the decision making and responsibility will be greater productivity and efficiency.

Then, as above, begin your implementation slowly and without fanfare. Your goal is not to announce to the world that you've "empowered" your workforce. Your goal is to leverage your resources by delegating responsibility. You can accomplish the delegation without putting the group on parade.

Follow through on the phased-in implementation you promised your boss. As the group achieves successes, make sure he knows about them. As your system of controls and reviews becomes established and routine, let him know how well it's working. Nothing succeeds like success, and your successful implementation of early steps is the best guarantee that you'll be able to see the empowerment process through to the end.

SOMETHING TO THINK ABOUT

Oftentimes negative reactions to new initiatives are as much an emotional response to the words used as to the ideas being proposed. Unless you're working with a management group that's really into being on the cutting edge of management theory, you'll probably want to strip your proposals of jargon as much as possible. Focus on what you want to accomplish and what it will do for the organization. Leave the jargon for your write-up in the business magazines.

11–5 THE PROBLEM

An employee is a "loner" who won't work with the group

THE SCENE

As you leave for a staff meeting, you hear one of your group members call to another, "Hey, Walter, want to see this demo

Carlene brought back from the applied learning conference last week?"

"No thanks," Walter replies, "I'm busy on the graphics for next week's class in Houston."

Following the group down the hall, you hear them remarking on how aloof Walter always seems and speculating that he thinks he's better than they are.

POSSIBLE CAUSES

Walter may prefer to work alone rather than in groups.

Some individuals aren't comfortable in groups or just don't choose to spend their time with others.

Walter feels like an outsider.

He may not want to be a loner, but believes that the group doesn't really like him or want him to be part of its activities. This especially happens when the individual belongs to a different racial or ethnic group from the others, or is a different gender.

The group is uncomfortable with him.

He feels like an outsider because that's how the group considers him. This is also particularly common when the "outsider" is different in race, ethnic background, or gender.

The group may be discriminating against him.

There's a fine line between being "uncomfortable" with another and discriminating against him. It's important to know if that line's been crossed.

Hint: Although not "fitting in" hasn't always been much of a problem, and in the past workers who did a good job but weren't team players were still valuable employees, that's not nearly so true today. Downsizing and the requirement to do more with less, combined with the "flattening" of organizations to remove layers of supervision make it essential that every worker in the company be able to function as part of a team. So, while you may be tempted to put Walter in a corner and leave him alone, *don't.*

Cures

No matter what the cause is:

It's always important to know and understand your employees, and this is one of the times when it's particularly important. You may not know Walter well, but you should know all the people who've been with you for months or years. You should have a good idea whether or not they're excluding Walter.

It wouldn't be a bad idea, though, to talk with one or two of your workers to see how they view the situation. Have they really tried to get Walter to join them? Or are they waiting for him to come to them? When you know the answers to these questions, you'll be ready to handle the situation.

If Walter seems to prefer being alone:

Take Walter aside for a few minutes to talk to him about his work style. Explain that you value his accomplishments and understand that much of what he does requires individual effort, but also stress the importance of working as a part of a team to accomplish larger projects, to combine the expertise of several people, to help solve complex problems. Give him specific examples of work your unit has done in the past year or so that *couldn't* have been accomplished without team effort. Let him know that it is your expectation that he will begin to include himself in group efforts, that it is a part of the job for which he will be held accountable.

Consider also developing guidelines or performance criteria for your whole group that stress teamwork over individual effort. Link consequences to workers' participation in group projects, especially positive rewards for working and contributing to team efforts.

Lead by example. Do you work together with other group leaders to solve problems or develop work processes that cross unit lines? If you don't, why not? If you do have such team success stories to tell, share them with Walter and the rest of the group. Demonstrate your commitment to team efforts by assembling teams within your group to work on specific projects and join in those team efforts when it's appropriate.

If Walter appears to feel like an outsider:

Don't rush things. Walter may be very careful and cautious about the group and may want to be sure he's really comfortable with them. Even though he may want to belong, pushing him can have the reverse effect from what you or he intend.

Get to know Walter well yourself. Your goal is to get to know him, but this will also help you understand why and how he feels like an outsider.

If Walter has certain mannerisms that separate him from the group, you can discuss them with him. And if there are things in the way the group acts that he doesn't understand, you can help him.

Stay in touch with the group and their feelings about Walter. When both they and Walter are ready to move closer together, help the process. You might want to suggest going to lunch together or stopping for a drink after work.

If the group seems uncomfortable with Walter:

Again, don't rush things, but take the time to get to know Walter better yourself.

Listen to what your workgroup is saying about Walter. If necessary, ask several of them what they're uncomfortable with in Walter. They'll probably talk in generalities ("He's unfriendly," "He's just *different*"). Push them (gently) for specifics ("He never asks us to help him," "He's so *loud*").

Now, as you talk with Walter, help him understand how the group is and how they see him. Where possible, point out tactfully the mannerisms and habits that bother them. Don't push him to change, just help him understand how they see him. You're suggesting he may need to change, and that often makes people anxious. He may get defensive; if he does, don't get defensive yourself. Just stay friendly and objective and help him understand.

As you get to know Walter better, help your other employees understand him. Encourage them to talk with him, to understand him better and to help him understand them. Don't push anyone—just try quietly to help Walter and the others become more comfortable with one another. When the time is right, you might want to suggest a group activity that will include Walter.

If they are genuinely discriminating against Walter:

This is clearly unacceptable behavior and the suggestions offered above are no longer appropriate. Talk to one or two people in the workgroup who seem to be most vocal in their rejection of Walter. Remind them that discrimination in the workplace is illegal and you as their supervisor are dedicated to ensuring that no one in your workgroup discriminates against another.

Then follow through. Assign Walter to projects that require group work and hold the entire group accountable both for the quality of the results and for the quality of their team efforts. Impose whatever consequences are appropriate (written reprimand, dismissal, and so forth) for continued discriminatory behavior. And be sure that nothing in your words or behavior might lead your group to believe that you'll tolerate discrimination.

SOMETHING TO THINK ABOUT

Much of the problem we've described here is best solved by personnel selection procedures that weed out those applicants who don't have good teamwork skills. While it won't solve your problem with Walter, you can avoid other "Walter" problems in the future if you look for evidence of good (or poor) interaction skills when you interview applicants or when you check their references.

11–6 THE PROBLEM

An employee won't tell you when something's bothering her, then disrupts the group

THE SCENE

There goes Darla again! You *knew* she wasn't happy about your sending Glenda on the trip to Phoenix with her. She wanted to spend time visiting relatives, and now she'll feel obligated to socialize with Glenda at least part of the time they're out there. But did she say anything to you about it? No, of course not. She said something to Ken, and Tricia, and Curt about how insensitive and biased you are. This would have been bad enough a year ago, but now that the company is emphasizing teamwork and cooperation it's even worse. How are you going to get your group working as a team when Darla complains to everyone about you, but won't come to you with the problem?

POSSIBLE CAUSES

Darla may dislike your decisions but may not believe she has a good enough reason to challenge them.

She doesn't think she can persuade you to change, but she at least wants someone to empathize with her tough break.

Darla may believe that complaining to you won't do any good.

Have you established a relationship with your employees in which they trust you to listen to their concerns and act on them? If not, then they won't come to you when they're unhappy. They'll try other tactics.

This may simply be how Darla learned to deal with conflict.

She never learned how to deal directly with individuals who upset her. Since managers often don't like workers to complain to them, she may have had the habit strengthened on her past jobs.

Hint: While this kind of situation is rarely a serious problem in itself, it can lead to more serious problems, particularly if it gets out of hand in a workgroup that needs to work closely together. Darla and perhaps one or two others habitually complain about your decisions. First, you notice some grumbling in the ranks. Then there seems to be slightly less cooperation among the group. Then the group begins to have significant trouble working together, and productivity begins to suffer. It's best to identify the initial problem and deal with it now.

Cures

If Darla dislikes your decisions but doesn't believe she has a good enough reason to challenge them:

It's inevitable that you, as a manager, will make some decisions your employees don't like, even if they agree that they're reasonable decisions. But if a good decision inconveniences an employee or spoils other plans she's made, she's not going to be happy. And there's not much you can do to change that. If Darla limits her grumbling to ordinary, everyday griping and doesn't really disrupt the group, it's probably better to let her express her feelings, work through them with her peers, and get back to work. If that's all that's involved, you can ignore most of her grumbling.

Nonetheless, give Darla an opportunity to express her feelings to you too. Even if the decision is one you can't change, she needs to know that you, as well as her co-workers, empathize with her and that you'll listen to her with an open mind.

If Darla believes that complaining to you won't do any good:

Look first in your own backyard. Is there anything you've been doing in your relationship with Darla that would make her believe you won't listen? Or that you'll listen, and make empty promises to fix things? If so, fix your own problem before you approach Darla. Unless you change what you're doing so that employees believe that coming to you will make a difference, it won't matter how much you *say* you have an open door. Your door may be open, but is anybody really home?

If you're not aware of anything you're doing to discourage Darla from coming to you when something's bothering her, approach her about the problem directly. Ask her why she doesn't feel free to talk with you about her dissatisfaction. Listen carefully to what she says; don't argue or disagree with her.

Since Darla has a specific concern, is there something you can do to resolve the problem or at least minimize it? Could you offer to let her out of this trip entirely, since it's not working out the way she'd like? Maybe you could send Glenda for just part of the time. Or perhaps you could let Darla take some extra vacation time once the work is completed so she can mix business and pleasure. Try to find a way to demonstrate that you hear her concerns and that you're prepared to do what you can to help her.

Make sure Darla knows that you're aware of how she's been dealing with her dissatisfactions and that you don't think she's using the most productive methods to resolve them. Encourage her to come to you directly in the future, and explain that you can only fix problems you know about—that there's not much you can do in response to vague grumbling. And make sure she knows the impact her griping to others can have on the workgroup's ability to work together.

It may take a few attempts before Darla gets the message. But once she sees that coming to you really does yield results—maybe not *every* time, but often enough—she'll change. She may even encourage others who complain to her to come to you instead.

If this is how Darla learned to deal with conflict:

Of the three causes, this is by far the most serious. Darla has learned to deal with conflict not by dealing with its source but by *avoiding* its source. This kind of habitual reaction is both the most serious of the three but also the hardest to manage effectively.

What do you do? Begin by establishing, publicizing, and then living by an open-door policy. If someone in the workgroup is dissatisfied with a decision or action of yours, you want the individual to come to you with the dissatisfaction—and to come to you promptly. Then demonstrate that you'll listen and whenever possible deal with the individual's dissatisfaction. Give everyone, including Darla, the chance to use this open door.

Now if Darla persists in complaining to other group members, you can challenge her on it. (They may get tired of it, and challenge her as well.) This won't make everything right, but it will start to put pressure on Darla to change because she now has another clear alternative. If she continues to complain to others, and particularly if her complaints disrupt the group, you need to begin counseling her. Make sure she understands the damage she can do to the workgroup and that you will not permit this damage. Hopefully, she'll change. If she doesn't, follow your company's disciplinary procedures and hope that this will lead her to change before it becomes necessary to fire her. (Yes, when close teamwork is required, constantly disrupting the group could get serious enough to merit firing.)

SOMETHING TO THINK ABOUT

When workgroups were more or less loose collections of individual workers, teamwork wasn't required. In today's environment, though, the individuals in many workgroups must work closely with one another to get the group's job done. Even when a group isn't called a team, it performs more and more like one.

In these circumstances, the ability to bring up and resolve conflict is a survival necessity. Conflict will always occur. Individual workers will always have dissatisfactions with your decisions and with the decisions or actions of other workers. It won't work to cover up the conflict, to encourage a "positive mental attitude" that keeps individuals from acknowledging the conflict.

What will work? Respect for the feelings and thoughts of everyone on the team and the willingness to deal with them openly and frankly on any matter that concerns them. As the manager, you take the lead by demonstrating this attitude in your own performance. And you get the workgroup the training they need to practice it themselves.

11–7 THE PROBLEM

Another manager refuses to deal with anyone in your work unit but you

THE SCENE

You sigh as John Wolensky closes the door behind him. You've just taken 20 minutes to clear up a problem for him. That's 10 minutes longer than it should have taken. More important, it should never have happened at all. John's refusal to deal with anyone but you was bad enough before, but now that the organization is stressing teamwork it's even worse. John's unit should have dealt directly with your unit, team to team. Not only did the two of you waste the time you spent playing go-between, but you interfered with the units' ability to deal directly with each other. But John won't let his unit bring its problems directly to your unit. How do you get him to change?

POSSIBLE CAUSES

John doesn't have confidence in your people.

The dealings between his workgroup and yours in the past haven't been satisfactory from his point of view. He doesn't believe that his group will get the response it needs if it goes directly to your group.

He isn't comfortable with the team idea and is still working as though he headed a traditional workgroup.

One of the ways he can preserve his old role and authority is to monopolize the contacts between his unit and other units.

The two workgroups haven't matured to the point that they can manage their contacts yet.

They each have to pick up the skills required to deal effectively with each other.

CURES

No matter what the situation is:

Have an informal talk with John. Find out why he wants to deal with you. This may take some tact; John may or may not be willing to level with you. And you certainly don't want to seem unresponsive to him. Be patient. If he begins to tell you that he thinks you or the workgroup fall short, don't argue or get defensive. Listen. You may believe he's wrong, but this is not the place to tell him so.

Maybe you can get an idea of what his reasons are. Perhaps it's your unit's shortcomings as he sees them; perhaps it's his attempt to preserve his traditional supervisory role; perhaps it's his feeling that his unit, or both of them, haven't matured enough to handle their contacts. Make your best guess about the cause and use the information in the section below, but be prepared to switch to another "cure" if the first one isn't working.

If John doesn't have confidence in your people:

Have more conversations with him if necessary and get all the details you can. Ask him to give your people a chance to provide what his team needs. Then get with your group and go over what he said. The group may be tempted to argue or get defensive. Let them, but don't let them stop there. Help them move through their emotional reaction to planning how to meet the needs of John's team. Then see that they do so.

An effective way to help your unit mature and at the same time see that it performs effectively is to help it schedule follow-ups with John's unit. If your unit is continuing to fall short of John's unit's expectations, it will be more apt to listen carefully and take the criticism seriously if it's coming directly from the members of the unit, not from them through John and then through you to your unit.

If he isn't comfortable with the team idea and is still working as though he headed a traditional workgroup:

You may have found this out when you talked with John. Dealing directly with you may be important to him, particularly if he holds strong beliefs about protocol. Letting the two units deal directly may appear inappropriate. And no matter what other reasons he may have, he believes letting the units deal directly reduces his authority as a supervisor.

Remember, whatever his reason, and no matter how inconvenient his behavior is, this is an honestly held belief. You're not going to get him to change it by attacking it. So what can you do? More than anything else, you can model the appropriate behavior. Let him see that you trust your workgroup to deal with other workgroups directly. If the occasion arises, mention how you prepared the unit to do this and how you follow up to ensure that it's done effectively.

What will be more persuasive than anything else, though, is your own understanding of your new role as a coach, teacher, and mentor for your unit. Have you gained this understanding? If you haven't, then you need to make it a top priority for yourself. Then you can show this understanding in your everyday actions and demonstrate to John that he doesn't have to hold on to his old supervisory role. Be patient, though. This will take time, probably for you and John both.

If the two workgroups haven't matured to the point that they can manage their contacts yet:

In this case, you and John should be able to agree that this is the situation and that you will work together to help the two groups develop.

Try this. When your group has an issue with John's group, meet with the group and make sure that it both understands the issue clearly and has devised an effective way to present it. Then have the group schedule a meeting between its representatives and representatives of John's group. Both you and John sit in on the meeting, but don't intervene unless the groups are clearly getting into trouble. Two or three sessions like this should develop both groups to the point that they're ready to schedule and manage the meetings on their own.

SOMETHING TO THINK ABOUT

It's extremely important for your people to be able to deal directly with their customers. If you keep acting as an intermediary, their job commitment will start fading, as will their productivity. The ideal situation is one in which you deal only with the most unusual and complex situations. Let your workgroup handle all the others.

It's equally important, as your unit matures and becomes capable of managing more and more of its activities, that you find an appropriate new role for yourself. This case suggested that the new role is more that of a teacher, coach, and mentor. Your organization may understand this and be able to give you training and other support in the new role. Or it may not, which means that you have to find the new role for yourself. Either way, you take the initiative to find what the role requires and learn how to perform effectively in it.

11–8 THE PROBLEM

Another manager accuses your unit of undermining her authority with her unit

THE SCENE

"Just where do your people think they get the authority to screw up my workgroup?!" Myra Sanderson glares at you across your desk.

"I have no idea what you're talking about."

"Like hell you don't—you're the one who lets them get away with it, and for all I know you put them up to it!"

"At least tell me what they're supposed to have done."

"There's no 'supposed' to it. I called in Denzil, my senior worker, and told him I needed to get together with him to plan what to do about the joint visit to Global Insurance next week. He told me it was already taken care of, that he and a couple of other members of my workgroup had met with some people from your workgroup and planned the whole thing out. That's my job, and I don't want your people or anyone else interfering with it. You tell your people to back off."

POSSIBLE CAUSES

Myra is willing for her unit to become more self-managing, but isn't ready for this step yet.

She may be taking it more slowly than you are, either because of her personal preference or because her unit isn't as ready as yours was.

Myra expects her people to operate like a traditional work-group with her as the supervisor, while you've helped your work-group become much more of a self-managing team. Individually and collectively, the members of your workgroup have more freedom and authority than the members of her workgroup.

Hint: When an organization is stressing teamwork and encouraging independent, even self-managing teams, this kind of stress can easily develop. Some supervisors and their workgroups will move faster than others toward autonomy and self-management. It's almost impossible to avoid this. The key is to minimize the conflict it causes as much as possible and to move through the stress as quickly as possible.

CURES

If Myra is willing for her unit to become more self-managing, but isn't ready for this step yet:

You can hope that this is the cause, because it's much easier to deal with than the next cause, but you won't know until you listen to Myra at greater length.

If this is why she still holds her workgroup in, offer tactfully to work with her, or let your people work with hers, to develop her group. You might want to consider joint meetings in which the two units carry most of the responsibility, but the two of you sit in and take over if the groups begin to lose their way. If it helps her feel more comfortable with the situation, you can have your group prepare an agenda for the meeting that you and she agree on and revise as necessary before the meeting.

Myra may be moving more slowly than you because she doesn't understand or feel comfortable in the new management role required to manage autonomous teams. If you think this is the case, look at the material in the next section and see if you can use some of it to help her adapt more rapidly.

Myra expects her people to operate like a traditional work-group with her as the supervisor:

If this is the case, you and Myra—and your workgroups—have a serious conflict in the way you want to operate. To begin with, your group will have to back off some. They can do all of the work they would normally do, but then they'll have to let you arrange any meetings with Myra's unit. They may also need to let you meet with Myra instead of the two units meeting. Make sure they understand that this isn't what you want to do and that you're working to improve the situation.

This is important: How strong is the organization's commitment to teams? Is "team" just another name for the traditional workgroup, so that you and Myra are both expected to manage as you always have, perhaps with a bit more emphasis on cooperation? If that's the case, you'll have to work closely with your unit to minimize any future confrontations with Myra or any other supervisors who want to remain in the traditional role. You and your unit should try to find a few other units whose supervisors are willing to let them have some autonomy and work as closely with them as possible.

Suppose, though, that the organization is really serious about strong teams with a great deal of autonomy. That means you and your team are doing what the organization wants. You can be more aggressive in trying to help Myra change. Work actively with her to let her unit have as much autonomy as possible with yours. (She can hold the reins in her unit's relations with other teams, if she wants.) Keep reminding her, as gently as possible, that what you're advocating is what the organization expects from both of you.

Keep demonstrating through all of this your understanding of the new management role. If you genuinely see yourself as a coach, teacher, and mentor and help her understand what this means, she may become more willing to move out of her traditional role.

Remember, though, that you're trying to make progress in team self-management at the same time that you're trying to maintain good relations with Myra and other traditional supervisors. Don't concentrate on either to the exclusion of the other.

SOMETHING TO THINK ABOUT

When an organization decides to make use of highly autonomous teams, first-level supervisors often see this as a threat. In one sense, it certainly is. Not only will the organization not need traditional supervisors, it will need fewer managers of any kind. First- and second-level managers often respond to this by opposing and even attempting to sabotage the movement to teams. In turn, this often leads organizations to fire these managers.

How do you prevent this? Even when an organization depends heavily on teams, it needs some managers to oversee the teams, coordinate their activities, and ensure that the teams are going in the direction higher management wants. As teams are being established, successful managers become teachers, coaches, and mentors. As teams become more effective, managers keep these roles to a certain extent, but also learn how to coordinate the activities of these autonomous teams.

The moral? Be prepared to change, and don't wait for someone else to tell you when or how. There are times it pays to stay ahead of the pack.

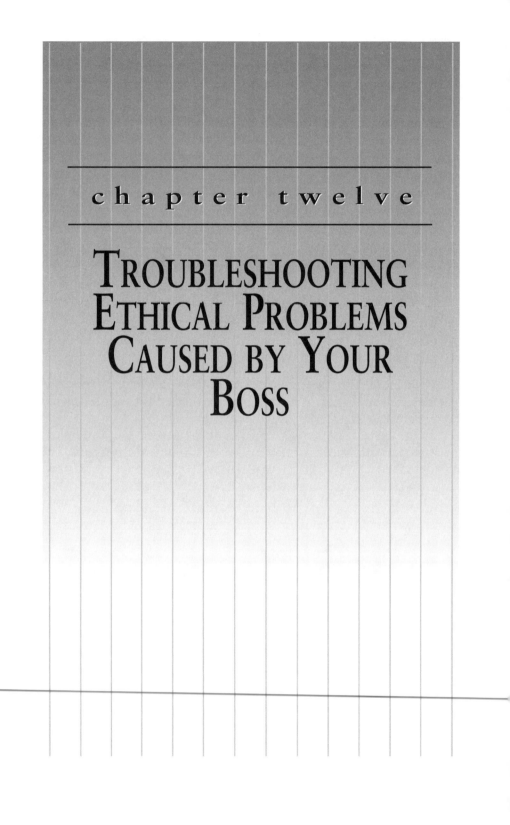

chapter twelve

TROUBLESHOOTING ETHICAL PROBLEMS CAUSED BY YOUR BOSS

12-1 THE PROBLEM

He tells you to "fudge" the figures on a report you prepare

THE SCENE

It's just not fair! You've been preparing production reports for as long as you've had this job, and every month things keep looking better and better—until now. One little downward "blip" in the charts, entirely explainable with the change in machinery and two new leaders in the group. But Walter, your boss, isn't satisfied. "Be creative," he said. Creative, ha! He wants you to cheat, no question about it. But he *is* the boss, and *he's* the one who has to give this report to the vice president, so maybe it would be okay to be a little "creative"—just this once.

POSSIBLE CAUSES

Your boss may believe that the figures themselves don't accurately reflect the true situation.

He may be concerned that *his* boss will react more to the negative figures than she should—ignoring the long-range improvements that will come from the new machinery and the replacement of mediocre leaders with some better talent.

Your boss may want to look good with his superiors.

He may be willing to sacrifice honesty for the sake of a good report.

Hint: Whether this is an "ethical dilemma" or not for you depends on the situation. If Walter wants you to change the figure in your production report to make it better reflect what's going on in your unit, his motives are essentially good and you may be able to find a way to accommodate him. If he just wants to make himself look better (or avoid looking bad), you'll need to make some hard decisions about how far you're willing to go to help him.

These aren't decisions we can help you with. They're based on your own internal code—about what your responsibilities are to your employer, about your responsibilities to maintain truth and honesty, about how far you can compromise without violating an essential part of yourself. You know what you're comfortable with and what you're not. You know when you have a "gut feeling" that you're about to cross the line. Pay attention to those feelings. They're usually right on target.

CURES

If Walter wants you to change the figures to make the report better reflect reality:

You can probably accommodate him without violating any of your principles, even if you don't agree that this is the best way to present the information.

Wherever you have to change figures to meet Walter's requests, just put a footnote in the margin to show that "These figures have been adjusted for . . ." That should satisfy Walter, but clearly indicate that you haven't done anything to disguise the truth.

If Walter isn't satisfied with the figures/footnotes approach, you can be sure that what he really wants is to look better with his boss. See below.

If Walter wants you to change the figures to make him look better:

This is much like the situation described in Problem 2 in this chapter, although the potential for harm to other employees is considerably less. See the discussion there for specific actions to take to protect yourself and the company.

SOMETHING TO THINK ABOUT

There are many times just in the course of day-to-day supervision when you're caught in ethical dilemmas. Often these are minor problems where it doesn't make a lot of difference either to the company or to you which way you go. But the decisions you make in these little things will influence how you respond when the tough questions arise, such as cheating on some figures or destroying a safety report.

If you're not sure how you'd react, or how you'd decide how to react, there is help available. Training organizations are beginning to develop courses to help you make ethical decisions. Find a course that seems to agree with the way you look at the world and see what they can offer you.

12–2 THE PROBLEM

He tells you to destroy a report that identifies serious safety hazards in the work area

THE SCENE

"You wanted to see me, sir?" you ask as you walk into Mr. Maxey's office.

"You know that shredder down in the mailroom? I want you to run this through it."

You look down in amazement at the papers he hands you. It's the report on safety hazards that the firm commissioned and that identified several dangerous conditions out on the floor.

Mr. Maxey looks at you intently. "I have to have your complete trust in this. We need to get rid of it permanently. If I can count on you for this, I think you can count on me to be quite helpful to you later on."

POSSIBLE CAUSES

The causes aren't significant here. Mr. Maxey may be scared because the report points out deficiencies he shouldn't have permitted. Or he may believe that it would be too expensive to fix them. Or if people found out about them the firm would be liable for large damages.

None of this makes a great deal of difference. He wants you to destroy a report that identifies dangerous hazards—hazards that people working in the area don't know about. They're in danger. Just as important, he's put you on the spot. How long until the next time he does that to you?

What matters isn't why he wants the report destroyed. It's what will happen if you try to go over his head with it. That dictates your actions.

Hint: Brace yourself—this is going to be *tough* no matter what you do.

CURES

If Maxey caused the problems or has another personal reason to hide the situation, and his superiors won't back what he did:

First, make sure this is really the case. It's unfortunate, but some organizations say all the right words, until a decision has to be made. Then they expect lower-level managers to "take care of things" without involving them. If that's the case here, you could find yourself without a job in a hurry.

The other side is that there are concerned firms who find what Maxey is doing completely reprehensible. The key is to find out what the real-world situation is in your organization. If you have contacts in other parts of the company, you can check with them.

Let's say that the company really does care and you see that the report gets to Maxey's superiors. They'll be profusely grateful. Maxey will hate you for it, but they'll probably fire him so that won't matter too much.

You may begin to find, though, that things aren't like they used to be. If you had good chances for promotion, you may find that they've faded away. If you used to get good assignments, you may find that they've dried up. Even if everyone knows that you were right and Maxey was wrong, they may not forgive you for going around him and exposing him. It'll never be anything you can put your finger on, but . . .

In other words, you won't be able to expose Maxey without risk, no matter how careful you are. If you happen to have a friend higher up in the organization, particularly if exposing Maxey makes him look good, he may be able to protect you. If you don't, you'll be taking your chances.

If Maxey will be supported by his superiors:

They may be expecting him to do just what he's doing, even though they'll never say so officially. Not only will telling them be occupational suicide, they'll probably see that the report gets buried at their level.

In short, there's nothing to be gained by trying to move the report further up in the organization. It may make you feel better, but it won't do much good.

If you have a good connection higher in the organization:

We mentioned above how helpful a connection higher in management might be. If you can trust him and know that he intends to do the right thing, he may be your best avenue. Take the report to him, preferably at home or some place other than his office. If he really does intend to act ethically, he'll see that the situation is corrected even though you may never hear about it again.

If you're caught, with no good avenue:

Of course, you can simply destroy the report. That's the worst possible thing. If nothing else, put it in a good safe place and lie to Maxey (we're playing *hardball* here!). You may need it to protect yourself against him later in case he decides to get rid of you to protect himself.

You must evaluate the danger to other workers if the hazards aren't fixed. If they're serious, can you live with yourself knowing that you could have prevented serious injury or illness but didn't? We have to leave that question to you and your conscience.

Another thought. Let's say that you agree to destroy the report. What will Maxey want you to do the next time? If this was a tough choice, how much tougher will that one be? And what happens to your self-respect if you *accept* this kind of behavior?

Finally, no matter what happens you may want to find yourself another job. You might get away from the situation somewhere else in the company. More probably, you'll have to go to work for another organization. (We warned you that this was a tough one!)

SOMETHING TO THINK ABOUT

The only good solution for this kind of dilemma is not to be there when it happens. If you have reason to think that your boss is dishonest and might pull something like this, find another boss. Don't panic, but work on it earnestly. Life is too short to let yourself be seduced into this kind of immorality. There are hundreds of companies and thousands of bosses who'll play straight with you. Find one of them.

12–3 THE PROBLEM

She asks you to lend her a large amount of money

THE SCENE

"I have a real favor to ask," Maria pleads at lunch today. "I have some doctor bills for the kids that have mounted up, badly. If I don't pay, they're threatening to take me to court. It's a thousand dollars, and I just don't know where I'm going to come up with the money. Could you help me out? Just this once?"

Maria's always been a good boss. She expects a lot and gives a lot. You'd really like to help her out. But you can't afford the money either. Still, she *is* the boss, so how can you say no?

POSSIBLE CAUSES

It really doesn't matter what the cause is—why Maria needs the money or why she's asked you for it. This is a bad position for her to place you in. Even if you want to help her out, the fact that she owes money to you can create some real conflicts of interest.

The need to reciprocate is almost irresistible. Once you've done a special favor for Maria, she's going to feel obliged to do one for you. If she can find a way of reciprocating outside the organization, that's great. But unless and until she does, she's going to be in your debt, literally and figuratively. So she's going to have a strong tendency to favor you over the other members of her unit, fairly or unfairly.

On the surface, that may be a tempting position to place yourself in. But in the long run, you know that's not the way to win. And if Maria *can't* find a suitable way to reciprocate (one that doesn't violate her own ideas about being a fair and objective supervisor) she may begin to resent the debt she owes—and the person she owes it to (namely, you). Then your position may not be so enviable after all.

CURES

The best way to handle this situation depends on the kind of relationship you already have with Maria. If you trust her and believe that she's not going to hold your refusal against you, you can be honest in your response. If you don't really trust her and aren't sure that your refusal won't come back to haunt you when it's time for your appraisal or the next promotion, you'll need to use a little more finesse.

If you have an open, trusting relationship with Maria:

Regardless of how good your relationship is with Maria—even if you're personal friends—lending her the money is a bad idea. The fact that you're now in a supervisory-subordinate relationship changes things. And you can't ignore that completely, even outside the office.

Make your refusal as direct, but sympathetic, as you can. Let her know that you appreciate the bind she's in, but that your lending her money is not the best way to get out of it.

Offer her other assistance in getting the funds she needs. Maybe you know of somewhere she can borrow the money at a lower interest rate than is usually available or someplace that loans money to people who've been turned down at other institutions. You might know, or be able to find out, programs that are available for people who have special medical problems and free support or counseling services they provide. Whatever you *can* do for her that doesn't compromise the supervisor-subordinate relationship, do it.

If you don't completely trust Maria:

It's even *more* important in this situation that you not put your-self in a compromising position by lending her the money. But it's equally important that you protect yourself as you refuse to do what Maria's asking.

Find out what your company's rules are about standards of conduct for supervisors. If there is a prohibition against supervi-sors soliciting employees for money, tactfully point that out to Maria. You can suggest to her that, much as you'd like to help her out financially, you're concerned that violating a company rule will hurt her more than the money will help. That's a refusal she can't get too upset about.

If your company has no such specific prohibition, you can probably still get out of this situation gracefully. One approach is to work around the issue. You can talk about your own finances and all the bills that are facing you without actually addressing Maria's request. Or you can talk about the difficulties in lending money and still maintaining an objective supervisor-subordinate relationship, again without actually refusing the loan.

If Maria presses, tell her that you're not in a position to lend her the money, again as tactfully as possible, and basing your refusal on reasons that have nothing to do with her personally. Depending on how likely you think it is that Maria will get upset and retaliate (overtly or covertly), it might be a good idea to talk to someone you trust at or above Maria's level. By getting the inci-dent on record with an objective observer, you may be able to pro-tect yourself against later reprisal.

If the chances that Maria will get nasty if you refuse are great enough, and if you don't expect managers above her to support your refusal (and protect you), *and* if you can afford it, it may be best to lend Maria the money. The only realistic alternative may be to start looking for another job. It's not necessary to take the first offer that comes along; chances are Maria won't do anything too drastic just because you refused to lend her some money. But in the long run, your chances for success here may be limited. It won't hurt to look around. If Maria takes the refusal well, you won't be out anything except a little time and effort. And if she takes the refusal badly, you'll have a head start toward a better sit-uation.

12-4 THE PROBLEM

He refuses to accept work from a senior worker because she's female

THE SCENE

"But, Mr. Weyant, Denise is *good*. If I give her this project, you'll get a real quality product."

"Now, now, I know she appreciates your loyalty to her, and so do I. But you know she just doesn't have the background she needs for the tough stuff. Give it to one of the men who came up through the ranks and really understands the in's and out's. Anything else?"

You shake your head and leave. Your boss just won't accept that a woman can do the really difficult work. It's always the same—"give it to one of the men." He supported you when you selected Denise, but now it looks as if that was just to make the EEO figures look better. Denise would probably never file a discrimination complaint, but you'd hardly blame her if she did. What can you do to help things?

POSSIBLE CAUSES

Mr. Weyant doesn't believe someone without the same background he and the other men have can successfully do the work.

Mr. Weyant has never seen that a woman can be good at this kind of work.

His ideas prevent him from ever being in a situation where he can see that he's wrong.

He is prejudiced against women.

Once you'd hired a woman into a senior position to meet a "quota," he had no interest in how well she could perform.

Hint: This is one of many situations in which you're trying to change your boss's attitude. Bosses can be effectively supervised, but it takes tact, skill, and a great deal of patience. It is, in short, one of those "character-building" experiences your mother used to tell you about.

CURES

If Mr. Weyant doesn't believe someone without his background can do the difficult work:

This mind set is fairly widespread. In many occupations, virtually everyone who enters them comes through one or a very limited number of routes. (For instance, a firm may hire all of its production planners from the shop floor.) Because everyone has the background, everyone assumes it's a necessity to get the job done. Weyant's feelings about Denise may reflect this more than the fact that she's a woman.

Again, this is circular reasoning. Since he doesn't think someone without his background can do the work, he won't let them, so he never finds out whether in fact they can. To be successful, you need to break the circle.

Any of the tactics in the next "cure" could be used for this one, too. You might also concentrate on the *process* a worker goes through to make the product. If Denise can show Weyant that she can perform the process successfully, he may loosen up some. It may help to show him that she knows what she's doing even though she doesn't have his background (for instance, if one of the difficult products requires intricate planning and she shows Weyant she can do it).

Your basic strategy, for this "cure" and the one below, is to give Denise all the exposure you can to Weyant. If she's really good, and his mind isn't completely closed, she'll eventually get through to him.

If he's never seen that a woman can be good at this kind of work:

There's a risky way to change this. Go on and give the project to Denise without telling Weyant. When you turn the project in to him, don't tell him who did it. Do this several more times. Then collect copies of all the work, give them to Weyant, and tell him what happened. When he sees the evidence before him, he may realize that he's been wrong. (On the other hand, he may just get madder than hell.)

A safer course of action is to give Denise the most difficult projects you can that won't antagonize Weyant. Assuming she does good work, point this out to him at strategic points. Over time, he may relent to the point that he'll let her work on something difficult. Then she'll have the chance to prove what she can do.

You might also try using a team made up of Denise and a male employee who works well with her. Weyant may agree to let them do the project jointly, confident that the male employee will keep them out of trouble. Then, after several successes this way, he may be willing to let her do one by herself.

If he's prejudiced against women, at least in this line of work:

It's unfortunate, but there's still a lot of feeling that women (like other minorities) belong in their "place." Weyant might have no problem at all with Denise in other occupations, even a profession like accounting. But he believes that women just aren't cut out for *this* line of work.

It's hard enough to deal with discrimination by employees against other employees, but dealing with discrimination when the guilty party is your boss becomes truly challenging.

It's imperative that as little of your boss's attitude as possible spills over into your group. Support Denise in every way you can (you may find some ideas in Problem 2–7). Make it clear to your employees that you support her and that you won't tolerate any discrimination against her.

Don't push too hard, but keep promoting Denise and her abilities to your boss. You might also want to suggest at times that "bringing her along" presents a good EEO image. You might even suggest that not letting her handle the toughest jobs might look like discrimination to some people. Even if he doesn't believe in women in the occupation and wishes you'd never hired Denise, he may go along with you just to keep out of trouble.

SOMETHING TO THINK ABOUT

It's often difficult to sort out a situation like this and decide just what the "cause" is. (Of course, there may be a combination of causes.) Remember what we've mentioned before in the book: Overt discrimination is largely dead, but more subtle forms of discrimination are all around.

12-5 THE PROBLEM

He tells you to fire a good employee whom he doesn't like

THE SCENE

Jimmy Csaki is a good, solid worker—not your best, but not your worst. Unfortunately, Norm, your boss, thinks he's a loudmouth, basically because he questioned a remark Norm made in staff meeting a couple of months ago about parking assignments. It was, admittedly, a dumb thing to do. (Norm doesn't take questioning well.) Jimmy apologized, though, and things seemed to be going okay. But now every time Norm sees Jimmy in the company cafeteria, he gets all worked up again. Finally, this afternoon, Norm decided he'd had enough.

"Get that troublemaker out of here," he stormed. "Two weeks—max. Then I never want to see his smirking face again. Got it?"

You got it all right. But it's not fair to Jimmy or to you. He *is* a good worker. One question two months ago (and not a big deal at that) shouldn't get him fired.

POSSIBLE CAUSES

Norm may have observed things about Jimmy's conduct or performance that aren't apparent to you.

There may have been other incidents where Jimmy was indiscreet in his dealings with Norm, incidents that you're not aware of. If these are serious or frequent enough, Norm may have defensible reasons for wanting to fire Jimmy.

Norm may have just taken a dislike to Jimmy.

There may be no objective justification for his dislike and no real reason to fire Jimmy, other than that Norm told you to.

CURES

If Norm knows things about Jimmy's conduct or performance you're not aware of:

Talk to Norm to find out what he's observed. Try to get specifics—times, dates, places, details of the incidents.

Given the information Norm's provided, what is *your* objective assessment of Jimmy now? Is this something you'd normally fire an employee for? If so, take the information you've received from Norm and talk to your personnel department about the procedures your company requires in terminating employees.

If the incidents Norm has observed aren't things you'd normally fire an employee for, talk to him about your concerns. Find out why Norm considers Jimmy's behavior so unacceptable. If you feel strongly that Jimmy shouldn't be fired, make your case to Norm. You might even suggest that Norm himself notify Jimmy that he's being fired. But as long as Norm has objective reasons for the termination, he *is* the boss, and this is one time when your appropriate response is "Yes, sir." You can register your objections, but in the end, it's Norm's decision.

After Jimmy's gone and things are back to normal, you should take the opportunity to talk to Norm about his reasons for wanting Jimmy fired. If you and he disagreed about the seriousness of what Jimmy did, you need to find out where the two of you disconnected. There will be other "Jimmys," and it's important for you to understand Norm's philosophy on acceptable and unacceptable behavior.

If Norm's dislike of Jimmy is irrational or unjustified:

Your first step should be to find out as much as you can from Norm about why he wants Jimmy fired. Depending on how reasonable a boss Norm usually is, you may be able to register your objections. But if Norm is likely to bear a grudge for your less-than-enthusiastic response, it's better to keep your objections to yourself.

Regardless of how unreasonable Norm's instructions are, he *is* the boss, and you're expected to follow his orders. Just as you expect your workers to obey your instructions and question them later, Norm will expect you to do as he tells you.

Depending on how unreasonable you think Norm's instructions are, it might be a good idea to document your objections in a memorandum or other similar document. Particularly if Jimmy fights his dismissal in a grievance or court of law, you'll be able to show that you were just following orders.

If the reasons for firing Jimmy aren't just bad judgment but instead are illegal, no amount of documentation will save you. Particularly if you believe that Norm's real motives for dismissing Jimmy are discriminatory, you're better off to refuse, keeping in mind the personal consequences. Let Norm's superiors know in advance that he wants you to fire Jimmy, and why. Then tell them how you intend to handle the situation. Keep in mind that you're taking a risk; they may not support you. In that case you need to weigh the risks of being fired yourself against the risks of civil penalties against you for engaging in discriminatory conduct. It's not a pleasant choice, but by checking with Norm's superiors first, you'll know better where you stand.

12–6 THE PROBLEM

He asks you for a date, even though he's married

THE SCENE

Well, it happened. Thad asked you for a date, even though he's your boss and even though he's married. In fact, he didn't just ask, he was insistent. You stalled him for the moment, but you know you'll have to deal with it again soon.

But how? You genuinely like him. Besides, if you turn him down he may take it out on you on the job. But he's married, and you've never gotten involved with married men. And you've never gotten involved with anyone at work, particularly not your boss.

POSSIBLE CAUSES

Thad genuinely likes you and is letting his emotions overrule his head.

You've established a very friendly but honest relationship with Thad, and he's misunderstood your signals.

He thinks you really want a "closer" relationship.

You've "come on" to Thad without realizing it or admitting it to yourself.

He's responding to you.

He thinks that since you work for him he can force his attentions on you.

Hint: Before you make any decisions, find someone you can talk with frankly, preferably someone who's at or above Thad's level in the organization. Tell him or her what's happened. Talk it over with the person and make sure he or she knows what you plan to do. Then, if the situation turns nasty, you'll have someone who can vouch for your side of the story.

CURES

If Thad genuinely likes you and is letting his emotions run away with him:

This is probably the easiest cause to deal with. If he cares for you as a person, he'll listen to your reasons for not wanting to date him (though this may take a little time). Point out the value of the relationship the two of you have and the dangers of getting emotionally involved in this way.

An effective and close working relationship is a different one from an emotionally charged one. Even if Thad weren't married, developing this kind of relationship would strain your work relationship. Then, if you ended the personal relationship, the strain at work could be even worse.

If Thad values the relationship as much as you do, he'll see the merit in these arguments. He may not want to, but he will.

If Thad has misunderstood your friendliness as something else:

The situation is much like the one above, but you have a bit more explaining to do. If he continues to mistake your friendliness, you may have to pull back from the relationship, and this could make it more difficult for the two of you to work together. It could also make your job less satisfying and enjoyable.

This requires some subtlety and tact. Simply telling him that he's wrong and you aren't attracted to him *that* way will probably damage the relationship. Be sure he knows that you do like him and enjoy his friendship but that you want to keep the relationship on a business level. All the reasons in the "cure" above are relevant here, too.

Even if you agree to keep the relationship as it is, things may be strained between you for a while (as they may in the "cure" above). Accept this as normal. If you've had a strong relationship, things will improve in a few days or weeks.

One word of caution: Emotions are tricky. Countless times, two people have worked through their feelings, decided to keep everything on a friendly, open level, and have then found themselves sabotaged later by feelings they had hidden. You both need to keep this possibility in mind.

If you've "come on" to Thad without realizing or admitting it:

Sure, we know you don't want to face this, but you have to. Emotions run by their own logic. In our heads, we may know the limits on our relationships. Our emotions may run in a different direction, but since we've "decided" not to do that, we hide them from ourselves. It's possible that you decided an emotional relationship with Thad was wrong, so you ignored your own feelings in this direction. But in one way or another, they slipped out. Thad is responding to them. Oops!

Obviously, you begin by being honest with yourself. You need to understand what's happening inside yourself before you can deal with Thad. If you have someone you trust deeply who can help you explore this, it will help immensely.

Then you need to be equally honest with Thad. It may be hard on both of you emotionally, but if your relationship is strong you'll both come through it. It may even help you develop a stronger, but still businesslike relationship.

If Thad intends to force his attentions on you because you work for him:

This, of course, is a dramatically different situation. You evidently can't count on a strong, honest relationship with Thad to pull both of you past this situation. In fact, whatever relationship you have has now been corrupted.

Did your mother ever tell you to say no "tactfully but firmly"? Well, this is where you put that to use. You don't want to ruin whatever is left of a real relationship with Thad, and you certainly don't want him angry at you. But the cost of giving in to him would certainly be high.

Here's where it would be helpful to talk with someone who's been in the same situation and handled it successfully. She may be able to give you some ideas on dealing with Thad.

If Thad remains insistent and begins to promise you job advantages or make job-related threats if you don't "cooperate," you have real, serious sexual harassment. This is where it's so important to have kept at least one disinterested outsider aware of the situation; you may have no alternative but to file a complaint of discrimination based on the harassment. If that becomes necessary, you'll need all the support you can get.

SOMETHING TO THINK ABOUT

We plainly haven't dealt with one aspect of the situation: Thad's relationship with his wife. That's really no concern of yours, no matter how strong your beliefs about the marital relationship. It's important to remember this, because Thad (honestly or otherwise) may talk about how unsatisfactory his marriage is and how much he needs your affection. As much as you may genuinely care for him, he needs to solve that problem in some other way.

Through all of this, you've probably been assuming that this is a situation between a female supervisor and her male boss. In this case, it is—but it needn't be. The female could be the boss, or they could both be the same sex. In all these situations, the basic dynamics are the same.

12-7 THE PROBLEM

She tells you to give a high rating to an employee who isn't very good

THE SCENE

"I'm afraid I can't sign this appraisal," Joan tells you after staff meeting. "Cecilia has done some special things for me, and I can't just ignore them. She needs to know that she's appreciated."

Sure, Cecilia needs to know she's appreciated—for running Joan's laundry to the cleaners and calling the florist on her husband's birthday and even typing Joan's speech to the school board. But that has nothing to do with her work, which isn't all that great. You have to send a lot of her stuff back to be reworked, and she tends to be surly with the staff. It just goes against your grain to give a good rating for performance like that.

POSSIBLE CAUSES

Joan may know something about Cecilia's performance that you aren't aware of—aside from the personal things she's done for her. She may also have done some special assignments for Joan that *are* work-related and performed better than when she's done work for you. That additional effort should be recognized.

Joan may be using the company's performance appraisal system inappropriately to reward Cecilia for personal business.

Her only motive for wanting Cecilia's rating raised may be these nonwork-related favors Cecilia has done for her.

Hint: The seriousness of this particular problem depends to some extent on the nature of your company's performance appraisal system. In some companies, employees are appraised just because someone along the line decided it was a nice idea, but the appraisal doesn't mean much because it's not used for anything. In other companies, the appraisal forms the basis for other actions. Pay raises and bonuses may be based on employees' ratings; promotion decisions and retention during layoffs may be affected by appraisal results.

If your company's appraisal system doesn't have any real "teeth," then this battle is probably not worth fighting. If appraisal *does* count for something, though, you have some decisions to make about how far you're willing to bend.

CURES

If Joan has information about Cecilia's work performance that you're not aware of:

Talk to Joan to find out what Cecilia has done that she believes justifies a higher rating. Discuss the incidents with her to try to come to some agreement on how much higher a rating Cecilia deserves. Once you've heard what Joan has to say, you may agree right away that the higher rating is justified.

If you still don't agree that Cecilia should be rated as highly as Joan wants, even after you know what work Cecilia has performed directly for Joan, you have some more discussing to do. Find out what Joan's basic philosophy is about rating employees—what kind of performance, in general, equates to what rating level. You and Joan apparently have a difference in basic approaches to rating, and your life will be a lot easier if you know what Joan is looking for in appraisals.

You should also take this opportunity to discuss with Joan the difficulties that arise when she assigns work to your people without your knowledge. Cecilia's work for you may have suffered because she had too much to do and thought it was more important in the long run to do well for Joan. If your boss bypasses you to your workgroup more often than you'd like, look at Problem 17–9 for some suggested solutions.

If Joan wants to reward Cecilia for personal favors she's done for her:

Talk to Joan about your perceptions of Cecilia's performance. If you have specific examples of her work, show Joan a few to illustrate why you think the lower rating is justified.

Depending on the level of trust and openness in your relationship with Joan, you may be able to discuss freely your objections to rewarding Cecilia for her personal favors through the company's performance appraisal process. But when (and if) you do question Joan's motives openly, it's a good idea to have some alternatives to offer. Maybe Joan could treat Cecilia to dinner, give her a gift certificate or some token present, send her flowers at home.

If you have contacts with someone at or above Joan's level in the organization, you might consider discussing your dilemma with that person. He or she should be able to give you some idea of whether you're likely to get support if you go head-on against Joan. And if you *are* likely to be supported, and the high rating for Cecilia will hurt other employees, it may be worth elevating your disagreement with Joan through channels.

In most organizations, though, you're not likely to arouse much management interest over one performance rating, unless management is looking for some excuse to "get at" Joan already. If you're not going to get higher-level support, you can document your objections to Cecilia's higher rating in a memorandum for your own files, or you can ask Joan to sign the rating herself since you're uncomfortable with it. But in the end, Joan *is* the boss, and it's in the interests of your continued employment to do as she asks.

THINGS TO THINK ABOUT

In all the problems we've discussed in this chapter, you're faced with a choice: You can do what your boss asks (often at the expense of your own principles), or you can take a stand against him or her (often at the risk of your continued employment). These aren't easy decisions to make. Only you know how much you can bend without breaking. Only you can weigh the risks of compliance against the risks of challenging your boss's demands.

We've tried to outline some actions you can take to preserve your integrity and protect yourself at the same time, but sometimes there's not much you can do to protect yourself. It's useful to remember, though, that unethical actions seldom occur in isolation. Environments foster ethical or unethical behavior, and you can usually tell fairly easily which kind of environment you're in. If things are going on around you that you're not comfortable with, it probably won't be long before you'll be caught personally in a difficult situation. The time to get ready is now—before you *have* to leave or do something you'll regret later.

chapter thirteen

TROUBLESHOOTING YOUR OWN PERSONAL PROBLEMS

13-1 THE PROBLEM

You let your boss get caught with a problem you should have warned him about

THE SCENE

"You knew that Sam Jonas was going to complain to the old man about my trip to Rochester?!"

"Well . . . he did say something about taking it higher in the organization . . ."

"And you didn't say anything to me?!"

"Uh . . . no . . ."

"Why in the world didn't you—oh, forget it. I don't want to hear anything more about it. Get back to work, and I'll talk to you later."

POSSIBLE CAUSES

You didn't think you needed to say anything to him.

After all, Sam didn't say for sure that he was going to talk to "the old man."

You meant to say something, but it slipped your mind.

Your boss can look out for himself.

You have problems of your own—you can't look out for him all the time.

Hint: Regardless of the cause, you are in hot water up to at least your eyebrows.

CURES

If you didn't think you needed to say anything to him:

Did you think that Sam was just "blowing smoke," that he would cool down? Or did you not think it was that serious?

It doesn't matter. In case you haven't learned it, here is one of the fundamental commandments of organizational life:

*No matter what else you do, **always** see that your boss knows about any matter that may affect him. Period. No exceptions. And doubly true if the "matter" is negative. Letting your boss be "blind-sided" by a problem you knew about is close to the top of employee mortal sins.*

There's a simple way to handle this. When your boss calms down, go see him. Tell him you goofed, that you should have picked up on Sam's comment and warned him. *Don't make excuses*; just apologize. Then promise him that it will never, *ever* happen again.

What if he's angry and yells at you? Let him. You deserve it. Again, don't make excuses. Do your best to direct his attention to the future—the future in which you won't ever let it happen again. With luck, he'll give you one more chance.

If you meant to say something, but it slipped your mind:

This is a first-class Oops! There's no excuse for it, and you should offer none.

Follow the suggestions in the "cure" above. Are you skilled at being abject? Good—you'll need to be good at it.

But you have an additional problem. How do you make sure that you don't forget to warn him again? There are dozens of ways. One of us makes lists; the other has an electronic scheduler and memo pad—complete with alarms. Use a pocket planner. If you're not sure what to do, find someone who does it right and copy him or her. But *do* it. Set up a system so that you never forget to warn your boss again. In this game, two strikes is out.

If you think your boss can look out for himself:

Bad misunderstanding! Apparently no one has taught you the first law of effective "subordinateship":

You have no responsibility greater than that of helping your boss be successful. None. Nada. Zip. Period.

Does this sound harsh and manipulative and scheming and otherwise unsavory? Stop and think a moment about what you expect from your employees. Don't you want them to help make you successful? Is there something wrong with that?

It really doesn't matter if you think there's something wrong with it—your boss probably doesn't. He just provided you with a useful learning experience. Take advantage of it.

When you talk with your boss, admit that you just didn't think. Tell him how much you've learned. Assure him that this failure was the "old" you, which he won't ever see again. Then make sure that you become and remain the "new" you.

SOMETHING TO THINK ABOUT

In many problems in this book, finding and using the right cure is difficult. Not in this case. It's as simple as realizing you fouled up, admitting it, and then making absolutely, lead-pipe-cinch sure it never happens again. There, that was easy, wasn't it? (And, with luck, your boss will still speak to you.)

13–2 THE PROBLEM

An employee accuses you of sexual harassment

THE SCENE

You answer what seems to be a routine telephone call from an employee. But instead you hear: "Mrs. Pierce, this is Bert Essmann from the EEO Office. I'd like to come over and talk to you tomorrow afternoon, if possible. Don Segali has filed a sexual harassment complaint against you."

Shocked and stunned, you replace the handset. What happens now?

POSSIBLE CAUSES

The specific cause of the sexual harassment charge isn't important here. There are only two possible conditions: Either you harassed Don Segali or you didn't.

A charge of sexual harassment is justified if you made unwanted overtures, either physical or verbal, to the employee making the complaint. It does not matter whether the actions or words were *intended* to have sexual overtones. What matters is that a reasonable person, objectively viewing the facts, would construe the actions or remarks as sexual in nature.

Likewise, confirmed sexual harassment does not require a superior-subordinate relationship. While the situation is worse if you supervise Don, particularly if he alleges that you threatened to take or withhold actions based on his cooperation with you, the absence of such threats or of a supervisor-subordinate relationship doesn't mean that sexual harassment hasn't occurred. Sexual harassment occurs *whenever* an employee is the object of unwanted overtures, regardless of the employment relationship between the employee and the person alleged to have harassed him or her.

So the first thing you need to do is find out the specific content of Don's complaint against you. As the person alleged to have harassed Don, you are entitled to know, specifically and in detail, what Don's alleging. You have a right to know not only what charge Don has made against you, but also what evidence he's offered in support of his charge. If he's cited specific incidents of harassing behavior, you have the right to find out the details of those incidents as he recounted them—names, dates, places, what happened.

Before you respond to any of Don's allegations, think carefully about what he's said. Did the incidents occur as he's described them? If not, in what respects do your recollections differ from his? If your recollections are essentially the same, do you see how Don could have interpreted the incidents as sexual harassment? What did you intend?

Only after you know what you're being accused of and have had some time to think over the situation can you respond appropriately to these *very* serious allegations.

Hint: Specific procedures for dealing with sexual harassment complaints differ somewhat from organization to organization. In general, though, you have the right to be represented in responding to the charges against you. Because sexual harassment charges, justified or unjustified, are so serious and potentially so damaging, you should find out what specific rights to representation you have before you answer any questions the investigator may pose.

If you have the right to be represented by an attorney or other representative, explain to the investigator or EEO counselor that you're very concerned about clearing up these allegations without damage to you or Don. Then defer answering any questions until your representative can be present. You need to protect yourself as much as you can. Even if you're completely innocent, you'll benefit from the assistance of an experienced representative.

CURES

Because the circumstances under which sexual harassment charges arise differ so much, there are only general guidelines we can give you in dealing with them. Most important is that you talk to your representative about the specifics of your case and follow her advice. If you're not comfortable with the advice your representative has given you, get a second opinion. But don't strike out on your own. Sexual harassment charges, justified or not, have much greater potential for ruining you personally than any other category of discrimination charge. Our best advice is "Watch your step!"

Your representative will want you to respond specifically and in detail to each charge and incident the complainant has raised. Any documents you have that were prepared at the time the alleged harassment occurred that would support your recollection of events will be particularly helpful.

Wherever you can, identify other people who may have witnessed the specific incidents that were alleged to have occurred. Even if no one was with you at the times Don claims you harassed him, you may be able to identify other employees who could make written statements about the general nature of your relationship with Don and with other men in the company that would help refute the charges.

You should *not* interview any of these witnesses personally. One of them could later claim that he or she was coerced into a particular position. It's much better if you provide the names to your representative or to an EEO investigator or counselor, describe the kind of information you expect the witnesses to provide, and then let someone else do the interviewing.

This is also not a situation in which you should approach Don yourself to try to resolve the complaint. If Don has filed a sexual harassment charge against you, it's clear that the relationship with you is badly strained. You cannot trust that anything you say to him informally about his complaint won't end up as a reprisal charge later on.

Once you've helped your representative assemble your defense against the charges, there's not much you can do except to sit back and wait as calmly as you can. Sexual harassment charges are difficult to prove if there are no witnesses and no previous history of discriminatory or unethical behavior. In those cases, the final decision depends greatly on the credibility of the people involved. If you've been an open, honest, trustworthy person all along, you have a good chance of refuting the charges even without witnesses who can contradict Don's statements.

In the meantime, treat your employees as you always have—fairly, impartially, and objectively. You needn't avoid Don, but you should exercise some prudence in how you talk to him (and where you talk to him). If you treat all of your employees fairly, you'll have little chance of a reprisal complaint in the future.

And what if, upon reflection, you decide that you did something that Don could reasonably interpret as sexual harassment? Let your representative know *right away*. Then follow the advice you're given to try to make Don "whole" without ruining your own career.

SOMETHING TO THINK ABOUT

If you decide that you did really sexually harass Don, there are two decisions you should make *soon*.

The first is a private decision that you will never engage in that behavior again and that you'll be on your guard against behavior that, however well intentioned, could be interpreted as sexual harassment.

The second is a career decision: If you've been found to have sexually harassed Don, intentionally or unintentionally, it's going to be difficult for you to function effectively in the future as a manager in your organization. You need to begin to look around for someplace where you can put your past mistakes behind you and start fresh. No one who's worked with you in this situation is likely ever to trust you again—the stigma of sexual harassment is *that* powerful.

13-3 THE PROBLEM

You missed the deadline on a major project

THE SCENE

"Millie, would you please see that Mr. Nomura gets this project summary?"

"The one for the general ledger update? Just a little late, aren't you?"

"Actually, it's less than six weeks behind. I think we'll have it up and running for real in another week or so. You know, that's not so bad for a project like this."

"Mr. Nomura isn't so nonchalant about it. When you told him you'd have it by two weeks ago without fail, he promised it to the controller by then. He's already been chewed out once—I'd try not to run into him for a year or so if I were you."

POSSIBLE CAUSES

One of your key programmers left you right in the middle of the project.

It took you over six weeks to replace him.

There turned out to be more coding than you expected.

The old system was in worse shape than you thought.

Several key managers in the controller's office were late reviewing the preliminary outputs and getting them back to you.

They have part of the blame for the system being late.

You did your best, but too many small things went wrong.

No one could have anticipated the sheer number of glitches you had to deal with.

Hints: None of the above matters. You promised to deliver a system by such-and-such a date. Your boss relied on you and made a commitment to his peers. Now the date has come and gone and there's no system. You've embarrassed your boss, not to mention fouling up the controller's plans. The excuses don't matter.

Now, let's get to what does matter:

- *Your planning was unrealistic.* You counted on everything (or most things) going right, and they didn't.
- *You didn't control the project effectively.* Even if your planning was okay, your execution was faulty.
- *You didn't warn your boss in advance that the project was in trouble.* This might at least have saved your boss the worst of his embarrassment, and let the controller revise her plans.

CURES

If your planning was unrealistic:

You'd better do a detailed "post mortem" quickly. What happened that you didn't anticipate? Where should you have known better? Where should you have built in some slack just on general principles?

If you don't have clear answers to these questions, you'd better find some first-class training in effective project planning.

If you didn't control the project effectively:

If your planning was realistic (and perhaps even if it wasn't), you let something get away from you. When did the slippage begin? Did anyone realize what was happening? If so, why wasn't it corrected? If not, how long did it slide before someone finally understood there was a problem? You'd better get the answers to these and similar questions in detail.

Again, it sounds as if you need some training in actual project management. It might be a good idea to find it and sign up for it as quickly as possible, preferably before you talk with Mr. Nomura.

If you didn't warn your boss in advance that the project was in trouble:

There's a lot we might say about this. Most of it is said in Problem 1 of this chapter. You probably want to look at that Problem and the suggested cures.

No matter what the cause is:

The most serious problem is the impact of this on your relationship with Mr. Nomura. You've let him down *badly*.

If you don't realize how badly, let us help you understand. One of the most valuable assets any individual can have is the absolute confidence of his boss. It doesn't matter whether you're an employee, a supervisor, or a senior manager. If your boss *knows* that he can count on you to produce what you promised, when you promised it, you're halfway home. If he doesn't know this— sorry, but you're not even on the team yet.

What approach should you assume when you approach Mr. Nomura? "Abject remorse" is one phrase that comes to mind. *Don't* even think of making excuses or offering explanations. You blew it, period.

What you need to do more than anything else is to direct Mr. Nomura's attention away from the past and toward the future—a much improved future. That's why it's important to analyze *why* and *how* the project failed, quickly and in detail. Then plan what

you need to do to prevent that kind of failure ever again. (Your
steps to prevent it should involve a significant amount of your personal time, not just on-the-clock time.) Get started on these steps
right away. If you're lucky, you'll be on your way by the time you
talk with Mr. Nomura. Then you can show him concretely what
you've learned and how you're going to see that nothing like this
ever happens again. Will it be enough? Who knows? We do know
that nothing less is apt to help.

SOMETHING TO THINK ABOUT

Stop and think. Aren't your really valuable employees the ones
to whom you can give a job and then never worry about it again?
You assign the project and—unless they warn you in advance—
they deliver what they promised. They're the people who make a
manager's life bearable (and occasionally even satisfying).

Do you have something more important to do than to be this
kind of person where your boss is concerned?

13-4 THE PROBLEM

*You've taken over a supposedly well-run
unit that's actually on the verge of disintegration*

THE SCENE

This is the third time this week you've found someone *almost*
doing something incredibly stupid, but managed to pull back in
time. First, John Bolling told the division chief's secretary there
was "no way" he could get her the materials she needed for the
chief's conference on Wednesday. (Luckily she complained to you
first, rather than to Mr. Simpson, so you could fix things up.)
Then, Gary Robinson deleted (but did not destroy!) most of his
supply orders. So you had to have data processing down to
"undelete" them.

Finally, yesterday afternoon Paula Chrisman "lost" a shipment of hazardous chemicals on their way to disposal (which, fortunately, someone found in a hallway, just before the trash pickup came).

That's just too many near misses, especially for what was supposed to be a "good" group.

POSSIBLE CAUSES

There may have been a lot of recent turnover in the unit.

The workers on whom the unit's good reputation was based may no longer work there, leaving you with a group of new people who don't know their jobs very well yet.

The group may have relied on their previous supervisor to keep things going.

Especially if the previous supervisor had a strong directive style and was technically very competent, she may have been the glue holding the whole operation together. The workers themselves may not be accustomed to being held responsible for their own work—they relied on her instead.

The unit's performance may have been deteriorating for quite a while.

The last supervisor got out just in time, leaving you to deal with the mess.

Hint: Early on, you need to decide just how bad things are in your group. Are there just a few key players who are doing poorly, but whose performance affects the entire unit's production? Or is almost everyone doing worse than you'd like? Is there likely to be "mission failure" if you don't step in immediately? Is there likely to be some noticeable "mission failure" even if you start working the problem right now?

If things are bad enough that you expect people outside the unit to begin noticing problems, then you need to let *your* boss know soon what you've found. This is delicate because you don't want to sound as if you're slamming your predecessor, or setting yourself up to look like a hero. But if there are likely to be complaints, he should hear about them from you first.

CURES

If there has been a lot of recent turnover in the unit:

To some extent, time will cure many of the problems you're facing now. But there are some actions you can take to speed the process along.

Review your files and ask other employees in the unit to see if there are standard operating procedures for the jobs that have been filled recently. Read over the procedures yourself and ask experienced employees to look at them also to be sure that they're still current and that they reflect a reasonable way to do business. If the operating procedures are usable, they're a good starting point for your training efforts. You can go over them with the new workers. Make sure they understand what they're supposed to do and then have them use the operating procedures as job aids when they encounter situations they're not sure about. With any luck, the standard operating procedures you have in place will cover much of the day-to-day work of the unit.

Ask some of your more experienced workers to work with the new people for a while until they're more comfortable in their positions. The more experienced staff shouldn't plan to *do* the work for the new people, but should be prepared to "look over their shoulders" for a while—to review work and answer questions when unfamiliar situations arise.

If the turnover has been especially heavy, leaving you with few people who know the operation, you may be able to arrange to borrow a few workers from other units. You'll be looking for people who have previously worked in your unit and know the work well enough to be able to get your new group off on the right foot. Ask to keep them for a few weeks, just long enough to get the new people started right, but not so long that they become dependent on the extra help.

If the group relied on its previous supervisor to keep things going:

You have a real challenge here, but one that can reap rewards if handled well. The key is to teach your staff how to accept delegation. This may not be pleasant at first. You'll be asking them to take responsibility for things they've never been personally accountable for before. But once they've tried it, most of them won't ever want to go back to the old way.

Sit down with your staff and talk to them about how your style differs from that of your predecessor. Without criticizing her style, explain what you see as the advantages to them and the unit of delegated responsibility. Stress the freedom they will have to run their portion of the process pretty much as they see fit, once they've demonstrated to you their competence and willingness to accept responsibility.

Then next step is just to jump in and do it. Begin by assigning specific tasks to individual workers. Agree on what you'll expect to see at the end of the assignment and when it will be due. Make a note on your calendar, and then *go away*. Don't initiate a contact with an employee again about the assignment until the day *after* it's due.

When employees come to you with questions about how they ought to do something, unless it clearly requires a policy or precedent-making decision, *do not answer them*. Respond with something like, "I'd have to think about that. How do *you* want to handle it?" You don't have to prove your technical competence. Your people know you know the work. They need to show you *they* know it. So resist the temptation to find answers for them. Their job is to come up with answers. Your job is to say "yes" or "no."

If you've explained your requirements clearly and stayed out of your employees' way as they've carried them out, they should begin very soon to deliver what you want. If not, a few repetitions of this assignment pattern, punctuated with reminders of your basic philosophy of delegation, should get the message across. What if repeated efforts don't result in a turnaround in your employees' willingness to accept responsibility for their own work and improvement in their products? You may need to talk to some of them about a career move—out of your unit.

If the unit's performance has been deteriorating for quite a while:

As we discussed in the problems dealing with individual poor performance, the longer performance problems go unattended, the harder it is to correct them. If performance has been deteriorating over a period of time and is just now reaching the critical point, you cannot afford to delay another day.

Although the situation is not quite as dire—yet—the cures presented in Problem 1–1 outline the basic steps you need to follow in dealing with ongoing organizational performance problems.

13-5 THE PROBLEM

You lied to your boss about finishing a project and now she's found out about it

THE SCENE

"Sit down," Ms. Braun, your boss, says. You sit. She is obviously mad, so you sit quietly waiting.

"You told me that you had finished the material for Mr. Lukas. He called me ten minutes ago and asked me where it was. First, tell me where it is, and don't you dare lie to me again."

"I really have almost finished it. It'll be in his hands by noon, I promise."

"Now, why did you lie to me about having it done?"

"I really thought I'd have it done soon enough that I could give it to him. But something came up and . . . ."

"Something came up, nothing! You lied to me! And I don't like having people around who lie to me. You get out of here and come back tomorrow morning at ten. And make damn sure Mr. Lukas gets what you promised." She looks back at her papers; you hesitate a moment and leave.

POSSIBLE CAUSES

You're performing poorly.

The fact that you're performing poorly doesn't justify your lying to your boss (or to anyone). But you may have felt that you needed to cover for the poor performance.

You felt pressured and lied your way out of the situation.

Individuals tend to make promises they can't keep and even to lie about what they have done when they feel pressured to deliver something they don't believe they can deliver. You may have felt this way because Ms. Braun was pressuring you very hard to have what Mr. Lukas needed to him. So, to get her off your back, you promised what you knew you couldn't deliver and then tried to lie your way out when you didn't deliver.

You don't take your commitments seriously.

Apparently you're not reliable.

Hints: The three causes don't exclude each other. In fact, all three could be true.

If you were working for either of us, you'd be one step away from unemployment. Ms. Braun probably sees the situation the same way. Act accordingly.

CURES

No matter what the cause:

You lied to your boss. You have a few hours to persuade her that this will never, ever happen again. If you fail to do that—well, you can figure out for yourself what will happen.

The three causes are listed to help you understand your own behavior. If you understand it and can explain to Ms. Braun why you lied *and how you will correct things so that you won't lie again*, you may keep your job. Just remember: The causes aren't excuses. They're conditions that you can change—that you will commit yourself to change—so you won't be tempted to lie again. Use them as such.

Don't even think of making excuses or trying to justify what you did. That's guaranteed not to work. Simply admit that you lied and that it was completely wrong. She'll almost certainly ask you if you've lied to her before. If you have, come completely clean about that too. Your only real chance is to own up to everything and then convince Ms. Braun that you can and will change.

If you're performing poorly:

When you and Ms. Braun consider your situation, you need to deal first with the fact that you lied and resolve that. Poor performance is no reason for lying, nor will promising to cure one cure the other. First you need to deal with the lying, then with the performance.

When you get to the performance, what do you do? You ask Ms. Braun to go over your performance and point out any deficiencies she's noted. Then you need to go over your performance, being even harder on yourself, until you're sure you understand just what you're doing (or not doing) and why.

Then make a clear improvement plan. Depending on Ms. Braun's preferences and your relationship with her, you may want to ask her to help. Remember, though, that the responsibility is totally yours (you can be sure she'll remember). Work out the plan, put some realistic milestones on it, and give it to her. Then do exactly what you say you'll do. (For more on this, see the last section of this case.)

If you felt pressured and tried to lie your way out of the situation:

Of course, this doesn't justify the lying either, but it may be something that needs to be dealt with when the truthfulness issue has been resolved. Do you believe that Ms. Braun puts too much pressure on you? Discuss it with her. Be specific about some of the consequences of the pressure.

Ms. Braun may pressure you because she believes that otherwise she won't get an appropriate amount of work out of you. How do you reassure her on that? She may believe you're unreliable; if so, look at the next section. Perhaps the problem's mostly with you, in which case you might want to go to some stress-management training and learn how to handle the pressure.

What you do need to learn, no matter what, is to not make commitments unless you're sure you can keep them. And that takes us to the next section.

If you don't take your commitments seriously:

This may be the key to the whole situation. If you want people to trust you and believe that you are dependable, you need to do two things. First, you make every commitment with the full intention that you will keep it exactly as made. Second, you either keep it or renegotiate it *well in advance of the due date.* That's all you have to do, and every one of us is capable of doing it.

Clearly, you haven't been doing it. Just as clearly, you need to start doing it immediately. And this is how:

- Whenever someone asks you for a commitment, or you volunteer one, think carefully before you make it. Can you realistically keep it? If so, by all means make it and then keep it. But what if you can't? Then don't make it. If Ms. Braun or someone else is pressuring you to make it, resist the pressure and ask for the person's help. Explain that you don't want to make a commitment you can't keep.

- As hard as it may seem, and no matter how great the pressure, don't make a commitment you don't believe you can keep—ever. If you have to, say something like "Okay, I'll agree that we'll do this by August 15th. But I don't believe we can. What are you going to say when I come to you on August 15th and tell you we need another ten days?"

- If someone wants a commitment you don't believe you can make, be as specific as possible about why you can't meet it. Go into detail if you have to. Use past records. Do whatever will help negotiate a reasonable deadline.

- Once you negotiate the commitment, keep it. If you can't? Well, that should happen only if something occurred that you couldn't reasonably anticipate. Renegotiate the commitment immediately. Don't ever wait until just before it's due and then announce you can't produce. Negotiate the change as soon as you can and make as small a change as possible from the original.

This may sound terribly difficult for you now. It may be, though you certainly have ample reason to practice it. As you begin to make and keep your commitments, you'll find it gets easier and easier. In part, this happens because people now see you're serious about keeping commitments so they're willing to trust you more. It's a virtuous circle.

SOMETHING TO THINK ABOUT

Nothing justifies individuals who need to work together and trust each other lying to one another. This is simply one of those things that needs not to happen, but to be dealt with quickly and firmly if it does.

No one will ever understand that lying is absolutely forbidden unless you set the example. You need to do so in order for your boss to trust you and give you some independence. You need to do so in order for your workgroup to be clear that you expect the same from them. And you need to do so in all your other job relationships.

Keeping commitments, making your word your bond, is only slightly less important. (Promising to deliver something and then not delivering it is very close to a form of lying itself.) If you insist on both in yourself and your workgroup and try to get the same from your boss, you will have taken a giant step toward building a successful workgroup with a great reputation.

13–6 THE PROBLEM

You often can't answer your boss's questions about work status

THE SCENE

"What's this I hear about your group having been asked to do some follow-on work on the Petersen project?" your boss asks after the staff meeting.

"I'm not sure," you reply. "I'll have to find out more about it."

"You mean you don't know what's going on in your own section? From what I hear, and it's all over the building, you've got a couple of real stars on that project. How could you not know what they're doing?"

POSSIBLE CAUSES

Your boss may want to know more details than you would normally be expected to keep up with.

Especially if she came from the area that you now supervise, and if she had a number of years of experience there, she may be interested in more of the guts of the operation. And especially if your technical strengths are *not* in that area, this puts you in a real bind.

Your people may not keep you informed about what's going on in their assignments.

They may be accustomed to working independently and seldom think to tell you about things unless there's a problem brewing.

You may be a "hands off" manager who doesn't want to know details.

Hint: How much do you *really* need to know about what's going on in your workgroup?

In general, you need to know enough to make reasonable work assignments (both kinds of work and amount of work each of your employees are currently assigned), to review work for overall quality and adequacy, to solve problems that arise, and to appropriately correct and reward your employees for their performance.

But, above and beyond that, how much you *really* need to know about the details is however much your boss is likely to want to know. Much of what your boss thinks of your performance as a manager is going to be based on two criteria: the feedback she gets from other sources (whether those are statistical reports or input from customers and other managers) and the reliability of what you tell her about what's going on in your group.

If she ever gets the impression that you don't know as much as she thinks you should about your group's work, you have a real problem on your hands.

CURES

If your boss wants to know more details than you would normally expect:

Now you know. After a couple of episodes like the one we've described, you should have a pretty clear idea of the kinds of things your boss is going to want to know about. Maybe she has a favorite area she always asks about (such as if she used to handle workers' compensation cases and asks periodically what the latest court decisions have said). Or maybe she wants you to know the exact status of each project in your section, rather than just that they're "on target."

But whatever her level of interest is, you should have a good idea fairly quickly what it is she's looking for.

So now learn enough about the details of those areas that you can answer most of the questions she's likely to pose. If this is an area where you don't have much technical expertise, sit down with the senior worker in that area and get some tutoring. Don't get in the habit of sending your boss herself to that worker for information, though. You'll just reinforce her impression that you don't know enough about what's going on.

But what if you're still stumped occasionally? It's probably not a problem if you don't know the answers only once in a while. Most managers realize that the reason you have a staff is so you can delegate the nitty-gritty work to them. And if your boss has a keen interest in one or two projects, so that she wants to know everything that's going on in them, you can sometimes take your senior worker along with you to give her periodic status updates.

What does all this probing do to your staff's morale? Especially if you've empowered them to run the project themselves? This can be a bit more tricky. So far, your boss hasn't asked you to *do* anything different; she just wants to *know* more details than you've been able to provide. Explain her interest to your staff and let them know that you'll try, by providing her all the information she could possibly want, to keep your boss's actual involvement in the accomplishment of the project to a minimum. If she gets enough information to reassure her that the project is running smoothly, she's less likely to want to intervene, and after a while she may even stop asking so many questions.

If your staff isn't keeping you informed:

As we discussed in Problem 11–4, both traditionally managed and empowered work groups are still responsible for keeping their managers informed about what's going on in their projects. Look at Problems 11–1 and 11–4 for ideas about how to manage your delegation of authority to ensure that you get the information you need from your group.

If you have a "hands off" management style:

In the next problem, we refer to the "if you don't hear anything, everything's okay" performance standard. Is that how you manage your workgroup? If so, then you really don't have enough information to manage well. Not only will your boss be disappointed that you can't answer her questions, you're also likely to have performance problems in your group unless you have an exceptionally talented and motivated group of people.

We've already outlined what you need to know to manage effectively: You need to be able to make work assignments, considering the skills and current assignments of your people. You need to be able to evaluate the adequacy of the work that your section produces. You need to be able to solve problems. And you need to be able to shape your workers' performance by rewarding and correcting them appropriately.

Do you know everything that everyone in your section is working on? Do you know whether everyone is fully occupied and whether anyone is truly overloaded? Do you know how they're doing with their milestones or whether production is at the level it needs to be? Do you know what the error rate is for production work? And whether there are certain kinds of errors that seem to occur over and over again? Do you know what your customers, internal or external, think of the work your group produces? Have you seen work samples lately? Or have you looked at copies of project reports or analyses your group has prepared recently?

If you can't answer "yes" to most of these questions, then you're operating as a "hands-off" manager. Even if your group is empowered to make decisions for itself, you have a continuing responsibility to ensure that the work is being accomplished according to the company's standards and expectations. And if you don't know, you're not managing.

SOMETHING TO THINK ABOUT

How much involvement is enough involvement is a tougher question than it used to be. But remember the distinction we mentioned earlier between *knowing* something and *doing* something. You can probably never *know* too much about what's going on. It's easy to *do* too much, to meddle with a team that's already functioning efficiently and throw it out of whack. It takes real self-discipline for most of us who became managers at least in part because we were good problem-solvers to know what's going on and yet not pitch in to "help" with the work. Resist the temptation. Knowing when to get involved and when to hold back is a lot of what makes the difference between being an ineffective manager and being a good one.

13-7 THE PROBLEM

*You never find out how your workgroup
is doing unless you get into trouble*

THE SCENE

"But I thought you and everybody else was happy with the way we were processing the high-value claims," you sputter.

"Whatever gave you that idea?" Eldridge Jones, your boss, replies.

"We haven't heard a word from you or from anyone else that anything was wrong. We thought we'd have the worst ones done this week and be handling them on a routine basis by the end of next week."

"Well, you can forget that. I have a list of problems longer than my arm with the last dozen you've done. I can't understand why you'd think this was okay!"

You end the conversation as quickly as possible and call a meeting of your workgroup. You might be upset, but it is nothing compared to the way they are going to react.

POSSIBLE CAUSES

The organization uses the "if you don't hear anything, everything's okay" as the basic performance standard.

The oldest and most pervasive performance standard in the book. Also the worst.

Your boss doesn't understand the importance of good feedback.

He may be so used to "no news is good news" that he never thinks of anything else.

Your workgroup doesn't attempt to get feedback from its customers.

Have they been assuming that they know what their customers want without asking? Always a very dangerous way to go about things.

You didn't negotiate standards for your work before you started the project.

If you knew you wouldn't get feedback, why didn't you at least talk to higher management or the customer or someone and try to define what successful performance by your workgroup would look like?

Hint: Not only *may* any and all of the four causes be involved, but all four of them probably are.

CURES

If the organization uses the "if you don't hear anything, everything's okay" as the basic performance standard:

Does this sound familiar? It's how most organizations seem to run. And now you're feeling how poor this standard really is.

What do you do about it? In terms of changing the organization, not much. If you take each of the next three causes seriously and follow the suggestions with them, though, you'll do a great deal to help the situation.

If your boss doesn't understand the importance of good feedback:

You start working on him today. You make it clear to him that you want every scrap of information on how your group might be falling short and you want it as soon as he gets it. You don't want him to "let things slide" in hopes the problem will go away. You want to hear it, you want to hear it without having him sugarcoat it, and you will listen to it and respond to it.

Now, make sure you mean this last commitment. "Respond to" doesn't mean "agree with." And it certainly doesn't mean "argue with" or "get defensive about." It means listen to the problem or complaint, understand it as fully as possible, and then do what's reasonable about it. If someone misunderstood something, help him or her understand. If the person's expectations were wrong, help him or her develop the right expectations. If you really did fall short, fix things as quickly as possible. That's what it means to respond.

When your boss passes on a negative to you, demonstrate responsiveness to the problem. Then demonstrate responsiveness to your boss. Report back on what you and the workgroup did. See if your boss is satisfied with your response. If not, find out what it takes and do it.

What does all this accomplish? It gives you great credibility with your boss, and it convinces him that you really mean it when you say you want feedback. And that will probably change everything, particularly if you couple it with the suggestions in this next section.

If your workgroup doesn't attempt to get feedback from its customers:

Time to change that, particularly if neither the organization nor your boss is concerned about good feedback. First of all, find out who your customers are. In this situation, who cares about how high-value claims are processed? There may be several units that care, and all of them may have different concerns. (It's simpler if you have only one customer, but don't be surprised if there are several.)

Then get organized to talk with your customers. In this case, you have a list of problems. You and a few members of your workgroup set the list in front of a customer and ask for more information on the problems. Do this with each customer. (If possible, take different workgroup members so that each one has at least one opportunity to participate in a customer visit.) Listen and take notes. Agree to respond by a specific date.

Then do what makes sense. If you need to change what your workgroup's doing, change. If you need to educate your customers, do that. Respond to every comment and respond in such a way that the customer sees you're responding.

Be prepared: This may be frustrating. You may have to go back and rework what you've done, though you can also try to negotiate changing future products, if that makes sense. But do it. In the long run, it will save you work, make you more effective, and make your customers far happier.

If you didn't negotiate standards for your work before you started the project:

Many workgroups never think of this, but that doesn't make it right. Feedback is most effective when you know what the standards are. It's a lot easier to respond to "You said you'd pay no more than 75 percent on the dollar" than to "Look, I think we're paying too much."

This doesn't mean that you can negotiate very specific standards. In many cases, you can't. But you can get the best standards possible up front, and then you can improve on them as you get feedback. For instance, a starting standard might be "We expect you to negotiate every claim down." That gives your workgroup a guideline. Then you get the feedback: "You're not negotiating them far enough down." This gives you a chance to work on a new standard, which may turn out to be "Negotiate no more than 80 percent on the dollar unless there are special circumstances."

That's more concrete, and future discussion may help define "special circumstances."

Get the feel? Negotiate expectations going in, then get feedback against these expectations. It isn't a precise process. It may be sloppy. But, boy, does it beat any other reasonable alternative.

SOMETHING TO THINK ABOUT

Now that you've learned all this about getting feedback, apply it to your relationships with your workgroup. Have you been working on the "If I don't gripe at you everything's okay" principle? Stop. Have you been letting them get by without feedback from their customers? Stop. Have you been letting them start projects with no agreement on the standard for a successful result? Stop.

Take every suggestion in this case and apply it within your workgroup. Give objective, straightforward feedback to each workgroup member. Does he not want it? Tough break. Give it to him and then discuss why he resists it. Expect equally honest feedback from the workgroup on your performance and don't dare get defensive when you get it.

What will happen? Do it, because if you don't do it now you won't believe how it will transform every relationship within your workgroup. Just do it, and see if we're telling you the truth.

chapter fourteen

TROUBLESHOOTING PROBLEMS WITH ANOTHER MANAGER

14–1 The Problem

A manager is trying to take over one of your functions

The Scene

"Mark, have you seen what Kim Heiss is doing now?" asks one of your team leaders. "She's offering something called a 'Customer/Client Mixmaster' that sounds an awful lot like our customer relations program."

You knew this would happen sooner or later. Kim and her group have been making inroads into your territory for the past few months. But this is pretty blatant. Customer relations is clearly your function, one of your bread-and-butter areas.

Possible Causes

There may not be a clear line between where your function stops and Kim's begins.

While Kim could have been more of a team player and discussed her plans with you ahead of time, what she's doing may not be clearly out of her area.

Kim may have been asked by someone higher than both of you in the organization to take on the project.

Again, she could have coordinated her work with you (unless she was asked not to), but she's basically following orders.

Kim may be trying to strip you of your function.

This could be something she's doing entirely on her own (perhaps with the support of her superiors, but not yours), which is intended to increase her influence and power at the expense of yours.

CURES

If there's not a clear line between your function and Kim's:

This is not at all uncommon, especially in large, complex organizations. It's often not very efficient for two or more groups to do the same things, but sometimes it is the better way, particularly if your customer bases are different. You may do customer satisfaction consulting with service industries, while Kim does the same kind of work with retail companies. There may be enough differences in your approaches, and the skills and knowledge required, to justify your separate involvement.

Whether this seems to be a reasonable division of labor or just a glitch in the design of the organization, if you think that fuzzy functional distinctions are at the root of Kim's incursion into your territory, your first step should be to talk to her. Describe what you see as the overlap and try to find out from her why she's performing the work and what she hopes to accomplish in this function.

She may not even have known that this was supposed to be your territory and began the work to fill what she perceived as a gap. She may not have thought you were doing the work as well as it needed to be done (although she may not put it quite so bluntly). Or she may believe that there's a legitimate role for both of you.

Try to work out the apparent duplication between your two units. Even if you'll need approval from your superiors for any accommodations you make, you'll be ahead to go forward with concrete proposals and with all the players in agreement. Of course, if this is a real baseline issue in your unit, you'll need to confer with your boss *first* to find out how she wants you to handle the negotiations.

Record your agreements in writing so there's less chance of another problem in the future. If your company has a formal organization and functions manual, make a change to that document too so managers all up and down the line know who's responsible for what.

If Kim was asked to take on the function by higher managers in the company:

This is another good reason to check with your boss before you begin negotiating with Kim. If someone at a higher level has already decided that Kim should be performing the work, you're certainly not going to be able to negotiate it back.

There are two reasons why Kim may have been asked to do the work instead of you: Your superiors may believe that the work more properly belongs in Kim's area *or* they may have been displeased with the way you've done work in the past. In the first case, Kim may have been looking at you for some time the way you're looking at her now, as if you've been trying to steal one of her functions. In the second case, you've lost the confidence of the people above you and you've got a lot of fence-mending to do.

In either case, Problem 16–3 addresses this situation in more detail and can give you ideas on how to work it out.

If Kim is trying to strip you of your function:

In this case, your basic line of defense is through your customers. Kim will be able to take away a function that is rightly yours only if others allow her to. If you can keep your current customers satisfied and continue to market your products, Kim won't have a chance to replace you.

That's true whether your customers are external to the organization or internal. Every function you perform has a customer. Unless top management decides otherwise (as in the second "cause"), your ability to maintain the mission and functions you have depends on how well you keep those customers satisfied. Do a good job, and they won't look elsewhere to have their needs filled. Do a poor job, and Kim will have your whole organization before you know what's happened.

At the same time that you're increasing your customers' satisfaction with the way you do the work (as opposed to the way Kim does it), you should subtly let Kim know that you're aware of her attempts to take over your function. It's probably better not to do this directly, since that kind of conversation can become a confrontation that would be difficult to work around later. It's much better if you can let the word get around the organization more informally—no threats, no confrontations, just for her information.

Depending on how far apart you and Kim are organizationally, it might also be a good idea to enlist your superiors' support in thwarting Kim's ambitions. Of course, the best way to get that support is customer-related. If it's apparent from the reports coming back from others that you're doing a good job, those above you will be less likely to consider letting someone else take over the function.

SOMETHING TO THINK ABOUT

While we've described this scenario as a takeover of one of your bread-and-butter issues, sometimes other managers try to take on things that are legitimately yours but that you don't really want anyway. You may be tempted to say, "Fine, let it go. It's more of a headache than it's worth." And maybe it is. But even in that situation, you can't foster the perception that you're a sitting duck for every ambitious manager that comes along. Regardless of how secretly thrilled you may be to get this monkey off your back, you need at least to let the other manager know that you're aware of what she's doing and that you will *permit* it to happen because you agree it's best for the overall organization. If it's not clear to the rest of the organization that you're in control of your functions, soon others will be raiding your group in more vital areas.

The best way to ensure the security of your own job and the maintenance of your function is to earn the confidence of your boss and those above him. If your boss is convinced that no one can do the job as well as you, then others' attempts to take over things you're assigned won't get anywhere. The other managers will look like fools for trying something so obviously futile.

14-2 THE PROBLEM

A manager keeps criticizing you to your boss

THE SCENE

"Max, I'm not sure what you're doing, but you certainly have Don Flores unhappy with you. He's complained about your unit and how you manage it twice this week already."

You finish the conversation and get out of your boss's office as quickly as you can. As if there weren't enough to worry about, now you have to find how to get Don Flores off your back.

POSSIBLE CAUSES

You and your unit are doing a poor job on work that matters to Don.

He's decided that talking to your boss is the only chance he has of getting you to improve.

Don doesn't like you and/or the way you run your unit.

He hopes that by pressuring your boss he can get her to make you change.

You've done something to make Don look bad, and this is his way of getting even with you.

Don wants your job.

He believes that if he complains enough about you, your boss will move you or get rid of you.

Hint: The most important factor here isn't what Don's motives are but what your boss's opinion is of you. If she has confidence in you and your abilities, she'll support you and perhaps even help you resolve the situation. What if she doesn't? Don may provide her the excuse she's been looking for to do something about you.

CURES

If you and your unit are doing a poor job on work that matters to Don:

Sometimes when a manager complains to your boss it's because he's concluded it's his only chance of getting you to produce the quality or quantity of work he needs. Perhaps this is Don's situation: He depends on your unit for work that he needs, and you don't provide what he needs when he needs it.

If this is the case, then the nature of the problem changes. The problem isn't that Don is complaining to your boss, but that your unit is producing work that doesn't satisfy him. There are three different responses you can make in this situation:

- You can change what your work unit produces so that it satisfies him. This means that you accept that you have a performance problem, and you solve it. Chapter 1 deals with work unit performance problems; chapters 4, 5, and 6 deal with individual failures to produce. You should find the answer to your current problem in one of these chapters.

- You can negotiate with Don (or any customer) for him to be satisfied with a different product. Perhaps you're providing Don with data his unit needs to develop production plans. He wants the data by the fifth of the month, but you physically can't produce it before the tenth. Since you can't change your production, you negotiate with him to settle for the tenth. If you're successful, he's satisfied and the problem is solved.

- Suppose you explain the situation but he won't change; it's the fifth or nothing. In this case, you may want to evaluate the third option: Get out of the game. If there's no way you can satisfy a customer, you may want to let someone else furnish him what he needs.

If Don doesn't like you or the way you manage your unit:

This is a very different situation, one that probably can't be cured by your unit doing a better job. So what do you do?

If the way you manage your unit is causing the problem, you may be able to change it, or persuade Don that he can accept it. For instance, you may be lenient about accepting tardiness of a few minutes, while Don is very strict about it and he feels that you're making it harder for him to maintain discipline. This is something the two of you can negotiate and perhaps find a solution to.

What if he just doesn't like you? You start by trying to find out why. If it's because you're a woman or Hispanic or a reserved person who won't respond to his "glad-hand" approach, there may be no real solution to it. But if you do things in a way that offends him, you may be able to change or to persuade him not to be offended. At least there's something to talk about.

Whatever the situation is, don't ever accept as final the fact that another manager doesn't like you. Both people and conditions change. If you keep an open mind to Don, he may begin to change his mind about you.

If you've done something to make Don look bad, and he's getting back at you:

The solution here is clear: Do what you have to do to make up for what you did. Perhaps you don't think it was so bad, or even think that what you did was justified. This doesn't matter if Don doesn't see things the same way.

Get together with him and deal with the problem openly and open-mindedly. You don't need to sacrifice your pride or integrity, but you can try to understand why he was offended and deal with that. You really didn't mean to offend him, did you?

If Don wants your job:

This is the most serious of the various causes, but at least potentially the easiest to deal with. In this case, it probably doesn't matter *why* he wants your job. What does matter is how your boss sees the situation.

Here's where there's no substitute for being an effective manager. If you've done a good job of supervising your work unit and doing what your boss needs done, you've probably got her support. If you can lead her to see what Don's motivation is, she'll side with you. (This may sound trivial, or even Pollyannaish. Take our word for it: It's not. Your best protection against a wide variety of organizational problems is doing an effective job for your boss.)

SOMETHING TO THINK ABOUT

We've already discussed the importance of your relationship with your boss, but it deserves one last mention. Every manager—you included—has people she can depend on and (usually) people she can't depend on quite so much. She's ready to go to bat for the ones she depends on; she needs them and doesn't want anything to happen to them. The ones she can't depend on quite so fully? Draw your own conclusions.

14–3 THE PROBLEM

A manager lets his unit keep giving you substandard work

THE SCENE

"Look here," points out Emil. "There's no way I can make a good assembly if the parts Jorge Ramirez's people machine aren't any good. And they usually aren't. Sometimes we catch them, but my people aren't technical experts in this. Sometimes we don't know they're bad until we get a complaint from a buyer. But Jorge's unit's poor quality work is making all of us here look bad too!"

POSSIBLE CAUSES

Jorge may not know that his unit is producing substandard work.

Since the blame falls on your unit, he may believe that what he's producing is perfectly acceptable.

Jorge may be producing substandard work for everyone.

He may not have good quality production systems in place to ensure that what goes out of his unit is good.

Jorge may have decided that your unit is lower on his priority list than some of his other customers.

Even if his work is generally good, he may not have sent a message to his people that *everything* should be a quality product. In that case, if you're not high on his list, your unit is one more likely to suffer.

CURES

If Jorge isn't aware of his unit's poor work:

Get some samples of poor products Jorge's unit has passed on to yours. Look them over to see if there is a pattern of errors or if they seem to occur randomly. When do the errors occur? Are there certain times of the week or month or certain parts of the production cycle when errors are more frequent? Get as much information as you can from your people about the kind, frequency, and timing of the poor products you're getting from Jorge.

Then go to see Jorge. Straightforwardly, but not accusingly, lay out the situation for him. Give him all the information you have about the substandard work you're getting and explain to him exactly how his poor products affect your unit's ability to do its work.

Enlist his support in developing a quality production mechanism that would be helpful for *both* of your units. Outline the benefits to him of not having to rework products either before they leave your area or after they've left the company.

As much as possible, try to set up systems that make the workers themselves responsible for the quality of their own work. Not only will you have fewer errors leaving the unit uncorrected, but you will, in time, reduce the base error rate.

If all else fails and Jorge fails to get his unit under control, set up your own inspection system for products entering the unit. Anything that you find to be substandard, send back! It won't take long for Jorge to get the message.

If Jorge is producing substandard work for everyone:

The cure here is much like that described above. Only your approach to Jorge need differ. In the first "cause" you were attempting to enlist Jorge's help in solving a problem of mutual concern. In this case, Jorge already knows he has a problem and probably wants desperately to fix it. But appeals to him aren't going to do any good, because he doesn't know *how* to solve his problem.

Your job now is *either* to find out as much as you can personally about quality production techniques so that you can make some useful suggestions to Jorge about how to improve his unit's work *or* to find someone else in the company or outside with whom he can consult to solve his problems. Instead of enlisting Jorge's support, your approach here should be to offer him yours.

If your unit's work has a low priority with Jorge;

Again, talk to Jorge about your concerns and the impact his poor production has on your ability to perform. Even if his regular work for you seems to be less important than the work he does for some other units, think of something you can do for Jorge or with him that would be of benefit to him or his unit.

When you talk to Jorge, discuss with him those areas in which you can benefit him and where you can work a "trade"—he'll produce better work for your unit if you will . . .

If the priority of your work is a real problem (which you'll know because several units are paying less attention to your needs), you may need to talk to your own boss about the problem. Is it necessary for *anyone* to do the function? Are there other ways the work can be performed without placing additional demands on other units? Could your unit be resourced to take on more of the work itself, cutting down on your reliance on other parts of the company? You may be able to get some support, particularly if this part of your work is something no one seems to get too excited about.

Whatever arrangements you are able to make with Jorge, be sure to follow through on your part of the bargain. While this function may be low priority, chances are that there's other work you do that's not. If you want cooperation in the big things when you need it, you have to prove that you can be counted on in the lesser things too.

SOMETHING TO THINK ABOUT

This is not just a problem between you and Jorge. Since it has to do with a quality issue, it affects the products and services of the company itself and the company's reputation with its customers. You can't do quality work if what Jorge gives you is substandard. While it's always best to try to solve problems at your level, this is one situation where you shouldn't hesitate to elevate. If all your attempts to get the quality of Jorge's work to improve fail, you can't just put up with the problem. Let your boss know what the problem is and what you've done to try to solve it. He'll want quality work from Jorge's unit at least as much as you do, maybe even more.

14-4 THE PROBLEM

A manager complains constantly about your workgroup's output

THE SCENE

"Can't your folks do anything right!" Jack exclaims. "Every single inventory list I get from your group has some inaccuracy hidden in it, usually in the most critical area. If your people can't even count right, I might as well contract with somebody outside for inventory help."

It's the same story over and over again. Jack is never satisfied. You've heard he complains like this about every other unit, but you still don't know what you could do to make things better.

POSSIBLE CAUSES

Jack thinks that if he complains loudly enough, you'll give his work higher priority.

He might not really be that dissatisfied with what you produce, but he believes that you're more responsive to other units than you are to his.

You and your unit really are doing a poor job for Jack.

He's trying to give you a chance to work the problem out yourself before he elevates it, but maybe you haven't been listening.

Jack complains about everyone.

He may be the kind of person who's never satisfied, or who thinks that no one else can handle any job as well as he and his unit can.

Hint: If you have good relations with other groups in the organization, you might check with some other managers to see if Jack complains about everyone (and what kinds of things he complains about). That should help you narrow down the cause of his constant complaining to you.

CURES

No matter what the cause:

Your first step needs to be to talk with Jack to get more details about why he's dissatisfied. Try to find out as much as you can about the specific problems he's having with your unit. Are his people finding errors in particular areas of the work they do? Are there certain of your workers who are causing Jack and his unit problems? Are his complaints about the quality of your unit's work or about the interactions between his unit and yours?

The more you can find out, the better. Not only can you pinpoint the source of Jack's complaints, you'll also make it clear to Jack that you're listening to his concerns. So even if it takes you some time to figure out how to solve the problem, he's more likely to work with you rather than against you.

If Jack thinks complaining will make you more responsive to his unit:

Find out what it is that Jack thinks other units are getting that he's not. Talk to him about the priorities you've established for assisting other units and how those priorities are set. If the work you do for him is truly lower priority than other work you're assigned, work with him to try to figure out how to meet his needs without hurting your production in other areas.

Maybe you can work out an agreement to allow some of his people to help yours when he's up against deadlines your group can't meet. Maybe you can shift some work back and forth between your units to meet both your work requirements. And if it appears that perhaps his work *ought* to be getting higher priority than it is, but your priorities have been set by higher levels in the management chain, talk to your boss about changing the focus of some of your work. Even if you can't change the level of priority you give Jack's unit, at least he'll know that you've tried within your own management chain to fix the problem. That will give him some ammunition to go up through his own chain to get extra help.

You can also look at Problem 6 in this chapter for ideas on how to deal with priority conflicts between units.

If you and your unit really are doing a poor job for Jack:

Don't dismiss this possibility out of hand. We can all stand to improve, and this may be one area where your unit needs improvement. Your doing poor work for Jack is the opposite side of the coin from the situation we talked about in Problem 3 of this chapter. Look at the causes we describe there and try to look at your unit from Jack's point of view. That should help you figure out why you're not performing for Jack and what to do about it.

If Jack complains about everyone:

This is probably the least likely cause. While we've run across many employees who are "recreational complainers," we've seen the breed much less often among managers, at least in complaining about peers. (*Everyone* seems to enjoy complaining about those higher up in the management chain.)

If Jack is the sort of person who believes no one can perform as well as his unit and who's vocal about that belief, your conversations with other managers will make it clear quickly.

Does anyone at higher management levels listen to Jack's complaints? If they've already written him off as a chronic complainer, you can too. If he does have the ear of a higher-level manager (who's in a position to affect your own career), try to talk to Jack to see if you can reach some resolution to turn down his noise level. But, if resolution doesn't seem possible, your best tactic is to make sure your own boss and the other managers with whom you deal are *very* satisfied with your work. Then Jack's naysaying will most likely be ignored and he'll look very foolish as the odd man out.

14-5 THE PROBLEM

A manager is trying to recruit your best employees

THE SCENE

You've always been suspicious of Tamara's "friendly visits" to your unit. The last time that happened, one of your best workers decided to transfer to Tamara's unit.

Sure enough, it's happening again. Ken Estes just told you that she's offered him a job with the promise of a promotion in three months. You need to put a stop to this—but how?

Possible Causes

There are really two sets of causes in this situation, and you need to take account of both of them. The first concerns you and your employees; the second concerns Tamara.

Where your unit is concerned, it may be that

- *You have the reputation for hiring and training excellent workers.* They have such a good reputation that other managers would really like to have them.
- *Your employees are unhappy, so it's easy for other managers to recruit them.*

Where Tamara is concerned, it may be that

- *No one has ever said anything to her about* not *recruiting other managers' employees.* She thinks it's okay, so she does it.
- *She's knows she shouldn't do it, but she's always been able to get away with it.*

Hint: You need to solve both problems.

Cures

If everyone wants to recruit your employees because you select and train them well:

This is a real bind. On the one hand, it's flattering that you and your employees have such a reputation. On the other, it makes you a hunting ground for everyone else. On the one hand, you should be happy that your people get ahead so rapidly. On the other, you *do* have to get your work done.

You need to deal with Tamara and anyone else who blatantly tries to recruit your employees. You also need to accept that if your people are that good others are going to want them and you don't want to block their advancement. You may find some ideas to help you hold on to them a little longer in the next "cure."

If your employees are unhappy and easy to recruit:

Even if your workers don't have a tremendous reputation, other managers may try to recruit them if they're known to be unhappy.

Are they unhappy because of the way you manage? This may be a hard fact to accept, but it may be true. In one way, though, it's good news: You can change the way you manage. Talk to other managers, people you trust, perhaps even your employees themselves. Find out what you're doing that they don't like. Then find a way to change the situation either by changing yourself or by persuading them that your management style isn't so bad after all.

What if you supervise them effectively but the work itself makes them unhappy? This is more difficult, but there may still be solutions. Can you reorganize the jobs so that individual workers perform more of a process or get to take more responsibility for the process (job enrichment)? Can you delegate more responsibility, so that employees have more freedom in how they do the work?

Are they unhappy because there aren't many promotion opportunities in your unit? If so, can you reorganize the work so that a few jobs can support a higher rate of pay? If your unit has a good reputation, can you get some additional work that's worth a higher rate? If neither of these is possible, resign yourself to a high turnover. You can also take some pride in the fact that you're doing a good job of getting effective workers into the organization.

If Tamara doesn't know that directly recruiting other managers' employees is poor practice:

No matter which situation you believe is the case with Tamara, you begin by talking with her (*not* with her boss). Tell her that you're not happy that she's recruiting your people without coming through you. See what her response is.

If she seems genuinely surprised, you should be able to resolve the situation then and there. Tell her what your expectations are (see the next "cure") and then negotiate what she'll do in the future.

If she knows she shouldn't do it, but has always been able to get away with it:

This is the time to put an end to it. Does this mean that she's never to talk to your employees, or encourage them to consider a job with her? No.

The important point is this: If she wants to recruit your people, she should work *with* you, not *around* you. You're responsible for the production of your unit, so you have the right to know when someone else wants to hire your workers away. Insist on this right.

If Tamara won't cooperate, this is one of the times when it's appropriate to take the situation to your boss. It's reasonable to expect him to talk to Tamara's manager and get the situation straightened out.

Does this mean you prevent Tamara and others from offering jobs to your employees? No. You have to find what you believe is the correct balance, but you don't want to stand in the way of your people getting ahead. Certainly the turnover causes you extra work in hiring and training and disrupts production. There is a silver lining, though. If individuals know that by coming to work for you they enhance their chances for promotion, your recruiting will be that much easier and that much more effective.

SOMETHING TO THINK ABOUT

All managers (both of the authors included) want to hold on to their best workers. As long as you can do this by offering them challenging work and a satisfying work environment, you and they both benefit. If you have to hold them by keeping other opportunities away from them, it's not so beneficial. Don't do it. If your employees know that you'll help them get ahead, they'll work much harder and more effectively for you. That's worth the extra time and trouble caused by higher turnover.

14–6 THE PROBLEM

A manager won't cooperate with you
unless you give his projects special priority

THE SCENE

"You know, Gene, I'd love to help you balance those expense statements for your department," explains Eric, "but it would be nice to get a little support from your folks too. I've had requests in to hire three accountants for the last two and half months, and from what I can tell, no one's done much of anything to recruit them for me."

Well, that's fine for Eric to say. His boss didn't just tell him to hire 50 new people for the shipping and receiving divisions by the first of next month. But that's the way Eric is: To get one little thing out of him, you have to make him think he's number one on your list.

POSSIBLE CAUSES

The cause isn't particularly important here. What is important is that Eric obviously isn't satisfied with the service you normally give him. Maybe his expectations are realistic and maybe they aren't. But you really have only one question to ask yourself: Is Eric important enough to your success to warrant making special efforts for him? Your answer to that will affect everything else you do.

Hint: Just because Eric wants to be treated as if his projects have special priority doesn't mean that you have to give them that treatment. All you have to do is convince Eric that he's getting special treatment. There are many techniques for doing that and still accomplishing your work in the priority order most advantageous to you (and your boss).

CURES

If Eric is worth special effort:

Talk to him about the other demands that have been laid on your unit. If this is one of a *very* few times you haven't come through for him, he may be understanding enough to let his work slip and still help you with yours.

If Eric isn't willing to compromise, assure him you'll get right to his requirements and do it. You've already asked yourself whether good peer relations with Eric were important enough to the success of your unit to warrant some accommodation for him. If they are, then satisfying Eric becomes one of your unit's regular, established priorities.

Make sure your workers know that Eric's work should come near the top of their lists and what that means in terms of day-to-day operations. Do they drop everything when he calls? When one of his subordinates calls? Do they let other work go to get his jobs filled? Or only the ones that are particularly difficult to fill? You'll probably need to specify in some detail how much special treatment Eric gets (or be prepared to work it out with your staff as individual situations arise).

Make a point of talking to Eric every once in a while to see how things are going with him. Check to see if there are projects or requirements he's particularly concerned about; then have your staff concentrate on satisfying those concerns. Check also to see if Eric's more satisfied with the general level of service he's getting from your unit. And if there are still areas where he doesn't believe he's getting the treatment he deserves, address them.

If being in Eric's good graces isn't that important to the success of your organization:

While you don't want to make enemies of any of your peers, there are some of them who just aren't that important to you or your unit. Their cooperation is nice, but it's not essential. The trick is to make them think you're concerned about them, without letting their requests get in the way of your "real" work.

Think about what happens when someone asks you or your unit to do something. How do you respond? "I'll get to it as soon as I can" (as you place the request on top of a stack of other papers)? Or, "I'll get on that right away"? You can almost always do *something* that takes just a few minutes to get the ball rolling so the requester feels somebody's paying attention to him.

Think, too, about your feedback mechanisms. Often when people want "special treatment" they already know there's not much extra you can do for them, but they *would* like to know what's happening along the way. If requesters know their work is being acted on (and isn't just sitting in a drawer somewhere), they'll have more confidence in you.

While you don't need to take time you don't really have, it wouldn't hurt to visit with Eric every once in a while to see how things are going with him. Without making any promises beyond those you'd make to any other manager, you'll still convey your interest and concern. Those cordial relations may stand you in good stead some other time.

Remember that your decision not to give Eric special treatment isn't final. Situations change. There may be a time when it's worth your while to do something special for him in return for help for your unit. On the other hand, bouncing him around in your priorities is probably worse than keeping him with the general run of work. He may come to expect favors when they aren't forthcoming and will be disappointed when nothing happens. Better that he knows what to expect and then gets it consistently.

Something to Think About

Eric obviously isn't satisfied with the level of service you normally give him—otherwise he wouldn't be pressuring you to give his work special treatment. Regardless of how well *you* think you're doing, you have a problem with the perception at least one of your peers has about your unit. Are there others? Does it seem that *everyone* uses your requests for assistance as an opportunity to demand more of you? You may have more of a problem than you realize.

Consider making regular visits to the managers you deal with most to see how you're doing with them. You don't need a specific agenda item—no special problem to work out or request to ask or service to offer. Just stop by for a friendly chat to let them know that you're interested in what they think. Once they find out that you're sincere in wanting to know, they'll tell you *exactly* how things are going.

chapter fifteen

TROUBLESHOOTING INTERNAL MANAGEMENT PROBLEMS

15-1 The Problem

The new employees you're getting aren't doing well

The Scene

"You know, Barb," reports Kit, "Marta just isn't working out the way I hoped she would. Somehow she's managed to scramble up mail Zena's already sorted—and lost an order from one of our best customers in the process. I don't know *how* many times I've gone over the steps with her—one, two, three. But the next time I look, she's screwed something else up. It's not *that* tough a job. I guess I shouldn't complain about Marta especially, though. She's no worse than the rest of the employees we've hired lately."

Possible Causes

Marta may not have the basic skills she needs to do the job.

She may lack such essential skills as basic literacy, or ability to alphabetize, or basic math skills. More and more of our entry-level workforce does.

Marta may not like the work.

She may have interests or aspirations in another direction and not be interested in the assignments you've given her.

Marta may be poorly motivated.

She may just be filling in the time until something better comes along, or she may not see any value in the work she's doing. But for whatever reason, she's really not motivated to do a good job.

Hint: If you're not sure whether the problems you're having with your employees are due to lack of skills or lack of interest, you can answer that question by asking yourself another. "If this employee's life depended on performing this job adequately, could she do it?" If the answer is "yes," then you have a motivation problem. But if the answer is "no"—if the employee couldn't perform, even if her life depended on it, then you have a problem with her skills or abilities.

CURES

If Marta lacks basic skills to do the job:

Talk with Marta and review her application and the other items in her personnel file to find out as much as you can about what skills Marta does have and the kind of work she's done in the past. Your training department may also be qualified to give basic literacy and computational literacy tests to find out what skills Marta has. If they can't help, you might try the testing services of your state's employment services department.

Check with your personnel department to see if there are any formal classes available that will teach the skills Marta needs. If there aren't, and if the skills deficiencies Marta has seem to be shared by a lot of your new workers, talk to the personnel department about developing courses or contracting with local schools or training vendors.

Try to identify a mentor for Marta to whom she can go when she has questions and who can check her work and help her correct her errors. She's more likely to consult another employee since she won't feel her job's being threatened when she admits problems.

If there are several parts of the job Marta needs to learn or isn't doing well in, parcel out some of the work to other employees. Then start teaching Marta the parts that are essential to the job. As she masters those, you can add in the rest later.

Encourage Marta whenever you can. By dealing with a skills problem early, you give the employee a much better chance of improving before she develops negative attitudes about the work or about working for you.

If Marta isn't interested in the job:

Talk to Marta to find out what kind of work she'd rather be doing. Then point out to her those parts of the job that are most similar to the kind of work she likes.

Let Marta know that if she does well in the job she's on now, you'll try to arrange for more of the work she finds interesting or help her find a job that's closer to what she's looking for.

At the same time, make it clear that Marta can't expect you to help her if she doesn't help herself. She's got to show you that she can do good work before you give her something more responsible to do or recommend her to another manager.

Make sure also that Marta is aware of the consequences of continuing to do poorly in this job. Regardless of how uninteresting she may find the work, she needs either to find herself a new job or face termination from this one for failure to perform.

If Marta is poorly motivated:

Different people are motivated by different things, but if Marta's level of motivation is typical of the new employees you're getting, you need to ask yourself some questions: Is the job set up to reward employees for doing the right things? Or are there rewards to employees for doing the wrong things (or for not doing the right things)? For instance, does your company reward quantity production exclusively without consideration of the quality of work? Do your employees understand how their jobs fit into the "big picture" of work that's done in the unit or in your company? Do they see the unit or company's work as worthwhile? Are there obstacles to doing good work here that discourage employees from even trying (like insufficient work space or materials)? The answers to these questions won't benefit just Marta—they'll benefit the whole workgroup.

If employees don't see any benefit in doing a better job, consider setting up an informal system of recognition for each job that's done well. This can be a public "pat on the back" or a more tangible form of recognition such as a certificate, a bonus, or a gift certificate. Set up systems also that make the employees themselves the ones who suffer the consequences of their poor work. Give your employees regular feedback on what they're doing well and not so well. When the work's not done well, make sure *they* do it over again until it's right. When new employees like Marta come on board, talk over with them your reward systems, so it's clear from the first why they should do good work.

If workers don't see the "big picture," put together an orientation program for your new employees that describes what each kind of job does, who the customer is (internal or external), and what impact the job has on other people or operations. Describe the company itself in some detail, identifying the services it provides or the products it makes. If it's not obvious, explain what value these products or services have. Then make sure everyone, including Marta, receives the orientation as soon as possible after joining your unit.

You might also consider revising your recruiting literature or your interviewing techniques to emphasize the contributions the company and your unit make. If employees are excited about the kind of work you do before they even start work, they'll be much more likely to perform enthusiastically (and well).

Review your work situation to see just what's getting in the way of doing a good job. Talk to your current staff. Examine the work flow and your organizational structure. Make any changes you need to see that tasks are done in a logical sequence and that segments once completed don't require rework farther down the line. Make sure someone is ultimately responsible for the quality of every product and that he or she sees the final result before passing it on. Do whatever you need to do to get your local supply department on your side. Workers who don't have the necessary equipment or supplies can't do a good job, no matter how well motivated they are.

SOMETHING TO THINK ABOUT

When we've talked about some of the basic skills Marta may need to acquire to do her job, it's been in terms of skills that make up the content of the work (like reading, writing, and similar skills). But there is another whole class of skills that Marta may not have—basic work discipline skills. These include things like knowing that you have to come to work each morning—on time, knowing that you don't spend your day on personal telephone calls or out in the hall chatting with friends, or knowing that when you make a commitment to do something you're expected to follow through.

Many of our newest entrants to the workforce lack even these basic skills. They weren't taught them in school, and they haven't picked them up anywhere else. Appalling as that may seem, it's a situation we're going to encounter more frequently in the years ahead. So we'd better start now thinking about how we're going to train those *very* essential areas.

15–2 THE PROBLEM

You can't promote a talented, ambitious employee who is already looking for jobs outside the company

THE SCENE

"Don, I know there's nothing you can do about this," begins Tony, "but I think I owe it to you to let you know that I'm looking around. I think I've taken this job about as far as I can go. There don't seem to be any new challenges to meet, and it's all getting pretty routine. But it doesn't look as if there's anywhere for me to go as long as I stay with Smart Systems. I know it's not your fault—there just aren't any openings higher up right now. But it doesn't look as if there are going to be any soon either. And I think it's time for me to move on."

You're not surprised. Tony's right. He's gone about as far as he can with the job he has, and it doesn't look as if anything's going to open up you could promote him into. But he's such a good worker! Isn't there something you can think of to get him to stay?

POSSIBLE CAUSES

Tony may not feel appreciated in this job.

He knows he's done well for the company, but he believes the company hasn't done well by him. He believes that the contributions he's made ought to buy him some recognition, preferably a better job with more money.

Tony may not feel challenged in this job.

He's mentioned that he thinks he's taken this job as far as he can go. If there are no new worlds to conquer, doing the same old work day after day can get pretty boring. Tony's looking for something where he can regain the excitement and challenge.

Hint: The best way to find out the cause of Tony's dissatisfaction is to ask him. He's been honest with you about wanting to leave. He'll probably also be willing to tell you specifically why.

CURES

If Tony doesn't feel appreciated in this job:

Even if you can't promote Tony, chances are there are forms of recognition you can offer him—a bonus, a gift certificate, mention in the company newsletter, recognition as "Employee of the Month" or "Employee of the Quarter." Identify those things you can do, and choose one that you think Tony will like and that's appropriate for his contributions.

You may be able to change Tony's title or stature in the office without giving him a real promotion. Maybe he could be a lead worker or a "special assistant." This "no-cost" promotion, accomplished with a significant amount of fanfare and accompanied by a more tangible bonus or reward, may let Tony know that his employers do appreciate him.

Finally, make sure Tony understands the way promotions work in your company and what you are able (and willing) to do to help Tony get promoted, either within your section or elsewhere in the organization.

If Tony doesn't feel challenged:

Identify special projects or assignments you could give Tony that aren't a regular part of his job but that would give him a chance to expand his skills. Be careful in what you assign Tony. Don't give him anything *too* much higher than what he's doing now. If he gets mad at you later, he could sue you for giving him work he's not being paid to do.

Talk to Tony about his long-term career goals. Would he like to continue to expand his technical expertise, completing progressively more demanding assignments? Or would he prefer to complement his technical skills with managerial assignments? Try to structure additional responsibilities around the things he's most interested in.

At the same time that you're enhancing Tony's assignments to give him greater challenges, look into taking away from his job some of the more routine work (or work he's mastered so that it's become routine). Assign those duties to someone else in the organization who you believe will be able to perform them creditably. It's not fair to Tony to keep piling work on him without relief. While a good employee consistently looks for greater challenges, he also resents being overburdened because "you can always count on Tony."

What if there *is* no more challenging work in the organization you can offer Tony? In that case, you need to have a straightforward discussion with him and explain that he's already doing the most interesting work the unit has to offer. Then do what you can to help Tony find the kind of work that will satisfy him, preferably retaining his skills within the company, but going elsewhere if that's what he needs.

SOMETHING TO THINK ABOUT

There are some things you can do to encourage Tony to stay, at least for a while, and we've talked about them in the "cures" above. But you also need to ask yourself at some point if the effort's worth it. If you can't give Tony what he thinks he wants—a promotion—the things you *can* give him may not satisfy him for long. Or he may be becoming so resentful of the company's failure to recognize him that he's not going to do as good a job for you as he has in the past.

In either case, his dissatisfactions will surface again—possibly before very long—and he'll resume his job hunting. If that's likely to happen, then your best course of action is to express your understanding of the difficult situation Tony is in, acknowledge your inability to satisfy him, and offer your help in finding him something better elsewhere. You can't be all things to all people.

15–3 The Problem

One of your best employees has asked to go part time so she can attend college just as an important project is starting

The Scene

Why did Maria have to do this to you now? A year ago you'd have been happy to give her a leave of absence for college. Eighteen months from now, you'd be happy to give it to her. But six weeks from now, the week after you start reviewing every company operation to see whether it could be contracted out? Ow!

If it were anyone but Maria, the answer would be simple: No. Maria, though, has been with you for five years, and she's an excellent worker. If ever anyone deserved help getting through college, it's her. How in the world can you tell her "no"—but how can you tell her "yes"?

Possible Causes

The causes aren't the critical elements. Whatever Maria's reasons are for wanting to go to college, you support them. Your real concerns are (1) how you can help her get college courses without totally disrupting your operations and (2) how useful those courses will be to the company.

Cures

If Maria's education will make her more valuable to the company and you expect her to stay with you:

In this case, both you and Maria benefit. You want to do everything you can to help her get her college courses. No matter what arrangements the two of you make, though, you need to keep these two points in mind:

- If possible, the company should provide financial assistance. This shows your support for her ambitions and will probably help her concentrate on her studies. If the company has a program for this, use it. If not, talk with your boss and anyone else who can help arrange it.

- Make all your commitments contingent upon successful performance at work and at college. The two of you should make your agreements on a quarter-by-quarter (or semester-by-semester) basis. At the end of the quarter, you look together at how she's doing and make a decision about the next quarter.

Here are some of the options the two of you can consider:

- *Maria converts to part time.* For instance, could she take off only a few hours each week for the courses themselves and do all of her homework at night and on weekends? This would keep her on the job, and if she's really that good she may accomplish more on part time than a replacement could working full time.

You have a strong motivator working here. If Maria sees that you've really made an effort to support her college goals, she'll probably work even harder during the time she's on the job.

- *She does some work at home.* If you really need her full time, would it help if she did some of her work at home? Perhaps she could take off time during the day for college and then make it up by doing work at home at night or on the weekend.

This doesn't give her the additional time for college. It does give her more control over her schedule, and that may be enough to make it practical.

- *She attends college at night.* If you just can't spare her, can she attend college at night? This may put quite a strain on her, particularly if she's a single parent or has to care for her own parents. Look at it carefully, though, because there are steps you can take to make it easier for her.

For instance, you might work out a flexible work schedule for her. If she has a late class, she might start work an hour or two later than normal the next day. If she needs a class that starts in late afternoon, perhaps she can start work that day earlier than usual.

Working at home can also help, for the same reasons that we mentioned above. If she has a job that permits this, using it liberally could be a major help to her.

If you can agree that she'll go to school at night, at least while the project is "hot," you should provide her as much financial assistance as possible. If she's really that good and your company will allow it, could you pay even for babysitters and parking if that's what it takes?

- *She puts off attending college.* This is a last resort. If none of the alternatives we've looked at work, would she be willing to wait a year or 18 months to start?

Don't make the effort one-sided. If you're going to ask her to wait on something as important as this, there needs to be some commitment on your side, too. For instance, you might make a firm commitment that she can start part time in a year, no matter what. Does that make you nervous? You've given yourself a year to plan to handle it; isn't that enough?

If Maria's education won't make her more valuable to the company:

Suppose she wants to become a nurse, but you're an accounting firm? Or she wants to prepare herself for a job where you already have plenty of well-qualified applicants. In other words, the education she wants may pay off for her but it doesn't pay off for you.

The list of alternatives here isn't as long. One of the first is to talk with her about taking courses that *will* help the company. If you're an accounting firm and she doesn't want to become an accountant, could she study human resources management? The company might be able to use that skill.

What about reducing the number of hours she works over several years? The first semester or two, she works full time and goes at night. Then she shifts to half time for a few semesters as she trains a replacement. When she finishes her education and moves to a new career, she leaves a fully trained replacement behind her.

These aren't realistic? Is there another way that you could support her desire for education and still act responsibly for the company? Do your best to find it.

SOMETHING TO THINK ABOUT

Education is a very precious possession in America in the 1990s. We need every college-trained person we can get. It benefits us all to support Maria and everyone else as fully as we can. Even if there's no immediate pay-back to the firm, it's probably worthwhile to help Maria get to college.

There's also a very practical reason to help. If you won't let Maria shift to part time (or otherwise help her), she has another option. She can leave you and go to work for a company that will help her get a college education. If she's good, that probably won't be too hard. Most firms are delighted to have employees who're putting themselves through college. It may be a hardship to shift her to part time, but is it more of a hardship than losing her?

15-4 THE PROBLEM

One of your best employees has asked you to make an exception to a rule for her

THE SCENE

"I know this is a little irregular, Ben, and I know I was off on the day after Thanksgiving last year, but I really need to be off again this year," Fran says. "It's important to be consistent, I know, and this policy of 'one year on, one year off' is a good one, but my parents are coming in this year. The kids and I haven't seen them for three years, and I'd really appreciate being able to spend some time with them. Couldn't you make an exception, just this once?"

Fran's always been somebody you could count on—to stay late, to work over, to cover for somebody else who got in a crunch. You can sympathize with her wanting to spend some time with her family. But if you make an exception for her, what about the rest of the group? Are they all going to come in wanting off the day after Christmas? And if you make an exception for Fran, how can you deny anybody else?

POSSIBLE CAUSES

If we assume that Fran's reasons for wanting you to make an exception are legitimate, then it doesn't matter much beyond that what they are. The real questions here have to do with the rule itself and the importance of applying it consistently. To decide what to do when an employee requests an exception to a work rule, ask yourself the following questions:

- *How important is the rule?* In this case, Fran's asking you to make an exception to a rule that's clearly discretionary (determining who gets to take off the day after a major holiday). But if the rule were something affecting workers' safety (like a requirement to wear a hard hat in certain areas) or it if affected the quality of your unit's products or services (like a request to skip a checking step to meet a customer's production requirements), your flexibility in granting exceptions would be more limited.
- *How much discretion do you have in granting exceptions?* Is this a rule you made, or is it a part of your labor agreement? Is it something your superiors require, that they consider "sacred" even if you don't? What are the bounds of your authority to make exceptions?
- *What message do you want to send to your employees about this rule, or your application of it?* It doesn't matter *what* kind of exception Fran is asking for, or how discreet you and she are about granting the request. You can almost guarantee that *someone* else in the unit is going to find out that you've made an exception. Is it important that you be as consistent as possible in how you treat this rule, or this particular group of workers? Will granting the exception make you look like a humane

and concerned manager? Or will it make you look like a wimp? Will granting this exception make it harder to enforce the rule next time?

CURES

If the rule isn't critical to the success of your unit and if allowing Fran the exception won't set a precedent for the rest of the group:

Allow Fran to take the time off she's asked for. Explain to her what prompted your decision so she (and other workers who may ask the same favor) will know under what circumstances you consider the exception appropriate. If possible, arrange for Fran to reciprocate (perhaps by working another day that she would normally be permitted to have off).

If the rule itself is important, but some flexibility in your application of it is appropriate:

Ask Fran for her suggestions of ways you can meet the spirit of the rule, while still granting her the exception she wants. Maybe she could trade days off with another worker. Or maybe she could work part of the day after Thanksgiving—the hours when her presence is most critical, then take the rest of the day off. Between the two of you, you should be able to come up with some accommodation that will preserve the integrity of the rule itself, but without being rigid in applying it.

If you *can't* come up with a way even to meet the spirit of the rule, then you'll need to rethink how important it is. If it's really important to conform in some measure to the requirements, then you'll have to deny Fran's request.

If the rule itself isn't that important, but it's critical that you be consistent in its application:

Consider Fran's request in light of other requests for exception you may have received. Can you make a policy decision that would permit these exceptions for all workers who meet specified criteria? Maybe employees who have seniority could be permitted to select the days they'll work or request exceptions? Maybe employees could be allowed to switch with co-workers as long as both people agree?

As above, if you can't come up with a set of criteria that you could apply across the board, then think again about how important it is to be consistent. Will it really do that much damage to your ability to enforce the rules if you grant an exception to a good employee? Are there extenuating circumstances you could cite to make it clear that you *won't* grant exceptions just to suit each employee's whim? If consistency is that critical, and if you can't think of a way to grant Fran's request without undermining that consistency, then you have no alternative but to deny Fran the time off she wants.

If the rule is one over which you exercise little or no control:

Explain to Fran that you don't have the authority to grant her request. Let her know who in the supervisory chain she should see about her request and the kind of back-up information or arguments she'll need to have it approved.

SOMETHING TO THINK ABOUT

Consistency isn't as great as it sounds. While you may think that granting a request for one employee means you have to do the same thing for others, that really isn't so. Nor is it practical in many cases to come up with a policy that will cover all the possible situations and reasons for exception that may arise. Most employees will understand why you've given someone a special exception (as long as you don't favor certain employees consistently over others) and won't try to take advantage. They'll be much more impressed with your humane, reasoned approach to requests for exception than a mechanically consistent application of every rule.

15-5 THE PROBLEM

Your unit's supplies are being pilfered, but you don't know who's doing it

THE SCENE

Tina brings you the third loss report on a missing calculator this month. Then there's the power stapler that no one can find. And the boxes of disks and printer ribbons that can't be accounted for. Nothing big is missing—yet—but you're getting concerned. How can you stop all this before it gets really bad?

POSSIBLE CAUSES

Your employees think it's okay to take small equipment and supplies to use at home.

Over the years, this has become an informal "fringe benefit" for them, one they count on.

Someone in the unit has a substance abuse problem.

Most theft in this country is committed to support drug habits. That may be happening in your unit.

You have a thief in your unit.

Security in your office is too lax.

Someone who doesn't work for you is stealing from you, because you don't have control of visitors in the work area.

Hint: This is a good time to be careful, systematic, and rational. Don't jump to conclusions or take rash steps without getting the facts. See if there's any office gossip about the thefts, but don't act on it until you've verified it for yourself.

CURES

If your employees think it's okay to take small equipment and supplies for personal use:

This may seem strange, particularly if you're used to an office where supplies are strictly controlled. It does happen. It may be a practice of long standing. It may simply have grown up without anyone authorizing it; employees have been taking small items simply because no one told them they shouldn't.

You might start by talking with other managers and see what they believe the firm's practices are. One or two of your senior workers might be willing to talk with you about it. You'll also need to find out what the formal company policy is.

If the company doesn't intend for employees to take equipment and supplies, you need to stop your employees from doing it. *Don't* start by being judgmental and demanding. Explain how the situation developed and that you expect it to stop. If you know what the cost is to your unit and/or the company, tell them that. Most employees will understand. If one or two of them don't, and you've made what you expect clear, treat them as thieves. The next three "cures" will help you with this.

If someone in the unit has a drug abuse problem:

If the supplies and equipment are being stolen by one person and if they're items that could be resold, there's a good chance that person (or someone close to him or her) has a drug abuse problem. This doesn't make the theft permissible; it just gives you a specific place to start.

Talk to some of the employees you trust the most. Have they noticed that someone is behaving differently or showing other symptoms of an abuse problem? Combine this with your own observations. Someone who's abusing drugs enough to start stealing to support the habit is probably showing his habit in other ways, too (late for work, increased errors, and so forth).

If it appears that an employee is abusing drugs, deal with the problem promptly. You can find suggestions on how to do this in Problems 2–2, 3–2; and 4–3.

If you have a thief in your unit:

If one of your employees is a thief, catching her may be very difficult. First of all, she's probably had experience at it. Second, she can pick her times and places; if necessary, she can hold off for a few weeks until you and everyone else relaxes. Finally, she knows that you have to be very careful about accusing anyone, to keep from offending innocent employees.

If there are several employees in whom you have complete confidence, solicit their help. If two or three people are watching constantly, it's much harder to pilfer. Remember the paragraph just above, though; don't let up just because a week or so goes by without a theft.

If your situation permits, you may want to lock up the items that could be stolen. Then they can be checked out to employees when they're needed and checked back in at the end of the workday.

If security is too lax:

Perhaps the problem isn't with your unit at all. It may be easy for someone from another work area, or even from outside the company, to slip in and walk off with small items.

This is often the easiest situation to deal with successfully. There's almost always something you can do to improve security. At the least, you can have your people keep their eyes open and notice anyone from outside the unit immediately.

This need not be negative in any way. It's courteous to greet individuals from outside the work unit and ask if you can help them with something. If they have business with your unit, they'll appreciate the attention. If they don't belong there, this will help them decide to leave.

Even if one of the other causes seems to be the right one, you should check out the security of your work area. Is it easy for outsiders to get in without being noticed? If it is, change your security. You don't need to keep people out, just to make sure that you know when and why they're there.

SOMETHING TO THINK ABOUT

If your employees aren't taking small equipment and supplies because they think it's okay, look carefully at the possibility that drug abuse may be behind the thefts. Many people who develop a drug habit can't afford to pay for it with their salary. They have to "augment" their pay by stealing.

chapter sixteen

TROUBLESHOOTING PROBLEMS THAT YOUR BOSS CAUSES

16–1 THE PROBLEM

He assigns you a high-priority project that you have no one capable of working on

THE SCENE

"But Mr. Paulson, I don't have anyone who can do this."

"Then train someone to do it, or hire someone—just get it taken care of! Everyone else is overloaded, so yours is the only unit I can give it to. You have three weeks to get it done, and I want it done well. Any more questions?"

You shake your head, turning toward the door. No one in your organization has any experience at this, and there's not enough time even if someone did. It's going to be a disaster!

POSSIBLE CAUSES

Your boss has tremendous confidence in you and your unit.

As difficult as the project seems, it's a show of confidence in you that he gave it to you.

He's looking for an excuse to reassign you or get rid of you.

He's not happy with you in the job, so he wants to replace you with someone he has more confidence in.

He is desperate.

Your unit is the best alternative he has.

Hint: Worry about *why* your boss did it second. Worry about how you're going to get it done successfully first.

CURES

No matter what your boss's reasons are, you need to make sure the job gets completed successfully. Here are some ideas:

Check first with each of your employees. Perhaps one or two of them actually know something about the project you've been given. You may be able to get it done with your own people. If you can, free them to concentrate on it.

Does another manager have someone qualified to do the project that you could borrow? Here's where the time you spend developing good relationships with other managers pays off. Perhaps a manager owes you a favor she can repay this way. If not, make it clear that if you can borrow one of her workers, you know you'll owe her one.

If no one in the organization can handle the project, can you hire someone temporarily to do it? This may not be as farfetched as it sounds; a tremendous range of talent is available for temporary work. If the person needs organizational knowledge, can you assign one of your employees to work with him and furnish this knowledge?

None of these will work? What can a team of your employees—perhaps with you as part of it—accomplish? Clearly, it will stretch all of you. You'll probably have to work nights and weekends. Look on it as a challenge; no matter what your boss's motive was, successfully completing the project in-house will be a real victory. (If you complete it successfully in-house, reward your people lavishly for their efforts. They'll have earned the reward.)

If he did it because he has tremendous confidence in you and your unit:

No matter how you complete the project, finishing it successfully will justify your boss's confidence in you.

There's another side to this. If you keep completing "impossible" projects, your boss may conclude that you and your unit can do *anything*. That's a great reputation to have—just make sure you and your employees are prepared to live up to it.

If he's looking for an excuse to reassign you or get rid of you:

You certainly don't want him to get away with this. It doesn't matter what you have to do (generally within reason, of course)—get the project done successfully.

The larger question is why he wants to move you out of the job. If it's because you've been managing poorly, this is your chance to turn things around. Then you may want to keep referring to this book to help you deal with the other challenges you're going to handle successfully, starting now.

Perhaps it has nothing to do with your performance. Maybe he needs to place someone else he feels loyalty to; maybe his boss is behind it. Get the project done successfully, then have a heart-to-heart talk with him. If he really wants you out of the job, see if you can't negotiate a mutually acceptable way to accomplish it. For instance, he might give you a day or two off each week to do job hunting and provide you with good references.

In other words, if nothing you can do will make him want you in the job, don't try to hang on. Negotiate the best solution you can, then get a job somewhere they want you.

If he simply is desperate:

Here's your chance to show that you can indeed come through for him. No one warms a manager's heart more than someone he can depend on in a real crisis. Use this occasion to demonstrate that he can always depend on you and your people.

SOMETHING TO THINK ABOUT

No matter the reason, this is a real opportunity if you approach it as one. Certainly it's going to be difficult, perhaps almost impossible. Don't let that defeat you. Make up your mind to succeed, no matter what—and then succeed. If you and your unit have been having problems, this could be the event that turns the situation around.

16–2 THE PROBLEM

She gives you a poor performance rating

THE SCENE

"But, Mrs. Morales, this is the lowest rating I've ever gotten."

"I expected that you wouldn't like it, but it's the rating I'm giving you. If your performance improves, I'll be happy to give you a higher one next year."

There's obviously nothing you can do to change her mind. You pick up the paper and head for the door wondering what to do now.

POSSIBLE CAUSES

Mrs. Morales has been directed to give lower ratings this year.

Organizations often decide that ratings are too high in general, so they direct managers to give lower ratings to everyone.

She can give only a certain percentage of good ratings.

Your performance wasn't that bad, but it wasn't as good as that of several others who're getting the higher ratings.

She's setting you up to get rid of you.

If you have a poor rating, this will be easier for her.

Your performance really was that bad.

There's nothing wrong with the rating. Perhaps it's even a little generous.

Hint: These aren't four equally important causes. The fourth one is probably the right one. You need to look at the other three first, though, to make sure you don't waste effort unnecessarily.

CURES

If she's been directed to give lower ratings this year:

This requires some real sensitivity on your part. She may feel that it would be disloyal to the company to tell you this. She may also feel embarrassed that she had her authority limited. No matter what, she may not tell you what the situation is.

One way to find out whether this is the case is to ask her how you could have gotten a better rating. If she answers the question in great detail, you can be fairly sure that she developed the rating herself. If she's vague or evasive, she may be following directions from higher management.

If you conclude that this is the reason for the poor rating, let the matter drop. Accept the poor rating and then do the best job you can this time around. (It may help to tell yourself that your performance really was okay and that this is just a bad break.)

If she can give only a certain percentage of good ratings:

This is a lot like the situation above. The difference is that she's been told that only a certain *percentage* of her ratings can be high; the others have to be average or even lower. This happens often in organizations that believe that ratings should follow a "normal" distribution.

If this is the situation, there's no point in fighting the rating this year. Just make sure that your performance improves to the point that next year you'll get one of the high ratings. (You can console yourself with the same thought as in the situation before this one: Your performance really was better than your rating.)

If she's setting you up to get rid of you:

You're in a serious predicament, and you need to make a sound decision concerning what to do about it.

In Problem 1 of this chapter, we suggested that if your boss doesn't want you in your job you should start looking for another one. That's one option here. If it sounds like a workable alternative, read that part of Problem 1.

What if you don't want to leave, if you think you're being treated unfairly? Probably the first step to take is to have a frank and honest discussion with Mrs. Morales. Why does she want to get rid of you? Is there something you can do to change the situation?

If you decide that you can't look for another job and Mrs. Morales sticks by the rating, you need to fight it however your firm permits. It will help if you've not only done a good job but can *show* that you've done it. This is a risky course, but if you succeed you may prevent Mrs. Morales from doing anything like it again.

If your performance really was that bad:

As we suggested above, this is the most probable cause. You may not think your performance was that bad, but *she* does. Your job is to perform effectively this year and make sure that she recognizes how effectively.

The first step is to find out how your performance fell short. This is a perfectly proper question to ask Mrs. Morales, as long as you're honest about it and not defensive. If she tells you, *don't argue with her*. If you believe she's wrong, leave it alone for now. Concentrate completely on finding out what she thinks.

Suppose she won't tell you what you need to do to improve? That's certainly not helpful, but it may happen. Accept it, and then see if someone else can give you useful information. Perhaps her secretary or clerk knows what Mrs. Morales expects from you and can tell you. Another manager who works for her or with her may be able to give you suggestions. If you know her boss and can't get information any other way, you might very discreetly see if he can find out for you. It doesn't matter whom you talk to, as long as you get accurate information.

Once you've found out what's wrong, correct it. You really were performing well but she didn't realize it? Do whatever you must to see that she realizes it this year. You weren't performing as well as you should? You know what to do about that. (Using this book and others like it throughout the year may help you improve significantly.)

SOMETHING TO THINK ABOUT

There's one situation we didn't deal with. Suppose you and your boss disagree on just *what* you should be doing or *how* you should be doing it? What then?

Start by asking a question: What's at stake here? If there's a principle or a matter of vital interest to you, it may be worth the disagreement and the low rating. Otherwise, it seems best to do what she wants done the way she wants it done.

Suppose you have a vital interest. Suppose she wants to reduce your authority or limit your freedom to make decisions. This is the time to have an honest discussion with her about your concerns. Perhaps you misunderstand her intent. Perhaps she didn't realize what's troubling you and is willing to change. Perhaps you can work out an alternative together. At the least, you'll have the matter out in the open, where you may be able to resolve it at some time in the future.

16–3 THE PROBLEM

He gives a major new project that should have been yours to another section

THE SCENE

You slam down the quarterly status report in disbelief. Joan Jordan is working on the performance support enhancement that *you* suggested to your boss six months ago. Who does she think she is, taking over *your* project? But, then, she didn't do this on her own. Bud Turner, your boss, must have given her the assignment. She's not the sort of manager who builds her own empire by stealing from others. So why didn't Bud give the project to you? And what can you do about it now?

POSSIBLE CAUSES

Your boss may have had to make a decision between two close functions.

There may not have been any intention to keep you out of the project. Your functions and Joan's just happen to overlap in this area, and Bud made a choice to go with Joan.

Your boss may believe that Joan's group will do a better job.

In this case there *was* a conscious decision not to give the project to you. You've got a problem.

Hint: Turf battles are seldom productive. You will probably never, by sheer strength of personality, be able to convince another manager (or your mutual superiors) that an assignment proper-

Troubleshooting Problems That Your Boss Causes

ly belongs to you. So fighting it out isn't usually a useful response to your boss's assignment of a project to another section. The way you get functions—and keep them—is by *demonstrating* that you can do the work, satisfy your customers, and meet your boss's needs better than anyone else can.

CURES

If your function and Joan's overlap in this area:

Talk to Joan to let her know you're interested in the project and to offer her your assistance. Make it clear to her that you're not trying to take over. It's an area in which you're interested, and you'd like to do what you can to help her out.

Assuming that Joan trusts you and accepts your offer at face value, give her whatever assistance she needs. In the course of this project, meet with her to work out specifically what the two of you believe are the limits of your respective organizations. Put your agreements in writing so there's less chance in the future that Joan gets a project that should have been yours (or vice versa). If your company has a formal organization and functions manual, draft changes to that too. Then go, with Joan, to your boss to present your proposal for splitting up the work.

If Joan refuses your help and seems pleased to have an assignment that would normally fall in your area, your problem is more like that described in Problem 14–1. Look there for hints on how to handle a manager who's trying to take over your projects.

If your boss believes that Joan's group will do a better job:

Your real problem isn't the project that got away. It's your poor performance record. You'll need to do some soul-searching about the causes for your boss's low opinion of your group. And once you know *why* your boss thinks less of your group than he does of Joan's, fix it.

Chapter 1 deals with organizational performance improvement. Chapters 4, 5, and 6 cover various aspects of individual performance improvement.

Your boss is sending you a clear message here about his lack of confidence in you and your organization. Listen to it. For whatever reason, you've failed to produce as well as he'd like in the past. The only way you'll get the projects you want in the future is to show him *now* that you can perform.

SOMETHING TO THINK ABOUT

It's possible that it wasn't your boss who decided that the project should go to Joan's group rather than yours. Maybe someone higher than Bud in the organization decided the question for him. Maybe a customer specifically requested that Joan work on the project (or that you *not* work on it)! While the source of the decision differs, the root causes are the same as those described in the second "cause" and "cure" above.

It's also possible that your boss gave Joan the assignment because it's a high-visibility project and he's grooming her for advancement in the company. That's good for Joan and too bad for you, but the question still remains: Why is he grooming Joan for advancement and not you? Maybe because of the level of confidence he has in you and your unit? Sound familiar? See the second "cause" and "cure" again. There's no substitute for good performance.

16–4 THE PROBLEM
He isn't clear about assignments

THE SCENE

You walk out of your boss's office shaking your head in puzzlement. After 20 minutes of listening to him expound, you're still not sure what he wants. It could be anything from a marketing strategy to a technical report—all you know for sure is that it's something written and it's something about the new mutual fund accounts. But what? And by when? More and more your assignments come like the plots of a detective novel, a clue at a time and sometimes too late to prevent another fatality.

POSSIBLE CAUSES

Your boss may not know what he wants.

He may be thinking aloud and relying on you to put substance into his ideas. But even if he doesn't know exactly what he wants, he'll know it when he sees it, and he'll know it when he doesn't!

Your boss may have received the assignment from a superior, and maybe he's not sure what she wants.

The instructions he received may have been even less clear than the ones he's given you. He's added as much substance as he can, but basically you're both flying blind.

He may not be able to articulate his ideas clearly.

He may know *exactly* what he wants, but he's not good at conveying those ideas to you for execution.

Hint: Sometimes, being a good subordinate means being a good mind reader. That's nothing unique to managers. You may have run across the same problem when you were doing technical work. The difference is that back then, if you misinterpreted your boss's assignments, you were the only one whose labors were wasted. Now, if you misinterpret your boss's assignments, your whole unit may waste its time on unproductive efforts.

CURES

If your boss doesn't know what he wants:

If you can pull it off without making your boss impatient with you, ask him for the details he *can* provide about what he's looking for. Perhaps he's seen a product similar to the one he wants you to develop, or perhaps he knows of someone in another organization who's worked on something similar. Be careful about pressing for details, though. Your boss has probably told you as much as he knows of what he's looking for. Your pushing for more information than he has available may embarrass him and will certainly irritate him.

Talk to other people whom you trust in the company about how they've handled similar situations. What kinds of things are usually important to him? Substance? Presentation format or style? Orientation to a specific audience? Then try to gear your products to those things you've identified as usually being important.

As soon as you have a concept and approach roughed out, go back to your boss for confirmation of the direction you're taking. Listen carefully to his criticisms. He may still not know exactly what he's looking for, but his initial reactions will tell you something about the things that strike him most forcefully. Then try again, and again, and again—until you get it right.

Don't be discouraged by this lack of specific direction. Things are going to be tough for a while, and you may begin to believe you can't *ever* please him. But little by little, you'll begin to get a feel for what your boss is looking for.

If your boss received vague instructions from his superiors:

As above, try to work out as many details with your boss as you can. Focus on the objective and goals of the assignment and on its intended audience. If there are people you know and trust in the company who've done work for the manager who's ultimately going to receive your products, consult with them for advice and hints on how to proceed.

Review company reports and formats to see how top management is used to seeing information presented. Look particularly at those portions of annual reports or publications that relate to the subjects you're dealing with. Model your product after the published items you've found.

Try to arrange to accompany your boss when he presents your proposals and drafts to his superiors. That way you can get first-hand feedback on how your product measures up to expectations.

Rely also on your boss's advice as you proceed. *He's* the one higher-level management tasked with this assignment. You're the vehicle for getting it done. But if what you produce isn't what they want, he'll look just as bad as you do. So this is one time where it's clearly in your boss's best interest to help you succeed.

If your boss can't articulate his ideas clearly:

This situation is a little trickier than the first two, since in this case your boss *does* know what he wants and probably thinks you should too, since he's explained it to you. Chances are very good that he doesn't realize that he communicates poorly.

If your boss is someone with whom you have an open and trusting relationship, you can tell him directly that you don't know what he's asking for. Then make pointed inquiries until you get what you need.

If you don't trust your boss enough to be able to admit your confusion, go to trusted co-workers for advice. They'll probably know what kind of things are usually accepted. What you've been asked for may be a routine report or product that you can put together easily once you know what it is.

For the long term, listen carefully as your boss gives assignments to *other* managers. Then talk to them about what they developed in response to the assignments. In time, you'll have picked up enough clues about what your boss's instructions mean to be able to interpret them accurately.

SOMETHING TO THINK ABOUT

Whenever you're having a communication problem with another person, whether it's your boss, a coworker, or someone who works for you, you should at least consider that the problem may be yours—not his. Perhaps you're not asking the right questions. Or maybe you're filtering his answers through your own view of things so that you can't see the other person's point of view. Especially if there seem to be *lots* of people with whom you have communication difficulties, it's a possibility certainly worth considering.

16–5 THE PROBLEM

She keeps pitting you against another workgroup you need to work closely with

THE SCENE

"Well, this is the third month in a row that Andretta's workgroup has out-produced yours. What do you have to say for yourself?"

Your boss, John Savage, is visibly upset. This is the fourth time in the last two months that he's called you in to talk about your production compared to several others. "I keep telling you, John, we just can't be competing with them. We rely on them too heavily, and the moment they think we're out to beat them they're going to make life really difficult for us. If you want us to compete, I can tell you about a couple of other workgroups we'd be glad to compete with. But we need to leave Andretta's group alone."

"No way! If you're not willing to get out there and compete with them, I'll find someone who will. Now you go back and think it over and come back in here tomorrow and tell me how you're going to beat them next month."

POSSIBLE CAUSES

Your boss is competing with Andretta's manager for a promotion.

He believes that if his workgroups maintain a higher productive rate than Andretta's workgroups he'll have a better chance at the promotion.

Your boss is naturally competitive.

No matter what situation he's in, he'll try to find someone to compete with.

There is an opportunity for healthy competition between workgroups.

Not all competition among workgroups that also have to cooperate with one another has to be destructive.

CURES

If your boss is competing with other managers for a promotion:

No matter how conscientious your boss is, if he thinks he can influence his chances for promotion he will probably do so. He has a powerful reason for looking better than his competitors for the job.

You cannot ignore this situation. Look carefully at the suggestions in the third section, to see if you can set up a healthy competition with the other workgroup, remembering that Andretta's boss may be pushing his workgroup to produce for the same reason your boss is.

Suppose that healthy competition won't work. What then? You need to figure out the least harmful way to compete. Your planning will be easier if you have an idea when the job your boss wants will be filled. Are you going to have to compete for a month or two, or for no one knows how long? That makes a difference, perhaps quite a difference, in what you do.

Do you know Andretta and can you work with him? Talk with him. See if he's in the same situation you are. Perhaps the two workgroups can engage in out-and-out competition if you and he meet regularly to ensure that events aren't getting out of hand. Try to find any way that will let each of you compete with the other that won't destroy the cooperation you need from each other.

If your boss is naturally competitive:

How is this different? Your boss isn't looking for a specific payoff (a promotion) from the competition. He just thinks he will get higher productivity from your workgroup if you're competing with Andretta.

Again, look at the next section for possible ideas. But also take a different tack at the same time. You have a meeting scheduled with your boss. Set the stage by assuring him that you want to give him what he wants. Then find out, in as much detail as possible, why he thinks your workgroup should be competing with Andretta's.

Is there some flexibility despite his rejection of your offer to compete with other workgroups? Explore it. Identify the other workgroups and suggest why competing with them would be a good idea. Perhaps the two of you can negotiate effective competition that won't interfere with necessary cooperation.

If there isn't flexibility, then lay out for him the disadvantages of competing with Andretta's workgroup. Perhaps you're dependent on it for data or material, and it can disrupt your operations by delaying either. Or you have to work together on certain projects that require skills from both your workgroups. Don't sound as if you're making excuses; present the case strongly but objectively. Then if he says, "Compete," you compete. (But when the harmful effects of the competition start showing up, you'll probably want to make sure he knows about them.)

If there is an opportunity for healthy competition between workgroups:

Even when workgroups must cooperate with one another, there may be some room for healthy competition. How do you find and define this room? Here are some suggestions:

- The two workgroups must agree that neither will do anything to make the other look bad. Without this basic confidence, the competition will become harmful in a hurry. Let each team do its best and win or lose on its own merits.

- The two workgroups must define as clearly as possible where they will compete and where they will not. In general, whenever one workgroup is a supplier or customer for the other, or reviews the other's work or performs in a similar role, competition needs to be strictly prohibited. In general, the more that either workgroup performs one of these roles vis-à-vis the other, the harder it will be to keep the results of competition from overflowing into the relationship.

- The two workgroup managers or other representatives must agree to meet regularly, to meet quickly if either thinks the other is breaking an agreement, or both. Even very minor events can begin to erode trust rapidly if they're not put on the table, discussed, and resolved. Conversely, even what would be major problems can be resolved if they are caught and dealt with quickly enough and with good will on both sides.

Something to Think About

Over and over, we stress that your first job is to enable your employees to be successful since they get the work of the unit done, and your second job is to contribute to your boss's success. Often you can accomplish the two of them together, often but not always. What do you do then?

Of course, the best answer is that you work very hard to find a solution that accomplishes both goals: Your employees and your boss both come out as winners. Don't take this one lightly; with a reasonable amount of work and imagination, you often can find a solution that works for everyone.

What about the situations when you can't? Stop and ask yourself if you're really sure what your boss wants won't work, or if you're just not used to doing things that way. He or she may be right, and you may be objecting just from habit. Don't ever do that. If you're going to disagree with your boss, make sure you've examined yourself and your response, thought the matter over, and decided that it's worth it. Then do what you have to do.

There's one final point. What happens next when you sit down across from your boss and say "I'm sorry, I just can't do this" will depend on the relationship the two of you have created. If he knows that you have consistently worked to help him be successful in the past, he may cut you some slack. If you haven't, if you've consistently ignored his need to be successful—well, the discussion will be far different.

16–6 THE PROBLEM

He chews you out in front of other managers

THE SCENE

"You screw up like this once more, and you're history!" Your boss bangs the desk for emphasis, then turns and stalks out of the room.

The three other managers in the room with you look at each other and follow him out without a word. Joyce is the last one out, and she looks back at you and shrugs as she leaves.

This isn't the first time your boss has chewed you out, but this is the first time he has done it in front of your peers. Joyce and Mike were embarrassed; Bernie kept a straight face, but you know he was delighted at the whole thing.

You drop your head into your hands, wondering how to overcome this.

Possible Causes

Your boss doesn't have the self-discipline to wait until he can talk with you alone.

He just lets go without considering its impact on you.

He was dissatisfied with others as well as you and wanted to make an example of you.

He expected the others to learn what might happen to them if they failed him.

He was so angry that he paid no attention to the fact that you weren't alone.

Normally, he'd talk with you alone. This time, things looked so bad to him that he exploded.

He thought that chewing you out in public was the only way to communicate how blatant he thought your failure was.

This is a step beyond any of the previous causes. He did it because he didn't think anything less would get through to you.

Hint: No matter what his reason was, getting chewed out in public is a tremendous blow to anyone's ego. It may take you a while to work through your hurt and angry feelings. That's okay; give yourself the time you need to recover.

Cures

No matter what the cause is—maybe:

When you've recovered, can you talk with him? That's the best way to find out what the cause was. Then, if it's appropriate, you can tell him how you feel and ask that he not chew you out in public again.

Be careful with this one. It may be days or weeks before he's willing to talk to you about the situation—if he ever is. This is where you have to use your judgment. Talk with him if you can; otherwise, try to work things out on your own.

If he doesn't have the self-discipline to wait until he can talk with you alone:

How you handle this one depends on your relationship with him. Is the relationship basically a strong one? If so, you can probably level with him about how the public chewing out made you feel. You may even influence what he does next time. The relationship isn't so strong? This is probably an excellent time just to take what he did and work quietly to restore his confidence.

If he wanted to make an example of you:

If this was the case, he can probably tell you so. (At least if we did it for this reason, we'd call in the poor victim and let him in on the secret.) This may help salve your feelings a little.

If he was so angry he paid no attention to the fact that you weren't alone:

The two previous "causes" weren't necessarily too serious. Your goof might have been a relatively small one. Not so with this and the following one. If he was so angry that it overrode his better judgment, he was *angry*. And you need to act.

Do you know why he's angry? If you do, even if you don't know all the details, start to work fixing it immediately. Then, if you have to ask him for more information, you can show him what you're already doing to fix the situation. (If you have to ask him, it may be best to wait a day or two or even a week or so for him to calm down. Then ask him. Don't be defensive, don't argue with him, don't try to justify yourself. Just find out exactly and completely why he was so angry.)

Then, fix it—quickly—and make sure it never happens again. If the problem was one of those described in this book, look it up and use the suggestions we provide. If this book doesn't cover it, or if you need more information, find some other book to help you. Talk to your friends. Attend a training course. Do whatever you have to do and then make it clear to your boss that you did it.

If he thought that chewing you out in public was the only way to communicate how blatant he thought your failure was:

The problem isn't at the Wolf level any more; this is an Elephant, perhaps even a Shark. He's sending you a strong, strong message. You can't afford to ignore it.

Most of the suggestions in the previous "cure" are applicable here, but more urgently. Take quick, *visible* steps to correct the problem (if you can) and ensure that it never happens again.

It's absolutely essential that you transmit a strong, positive message to your boss. He should be able to see that you're capable both of dealing with the situation and preventing it from ever recurring. This may be your last chance to do that.

SOMETHING TO THINK ABOUT

You've probably noticed that we don't have as much to say on this one as on many of the others. Unfortunately, there's not a whole lot to say. When your boss chews you out in front of your peers, it hurts and it's embarrassing. Because of this, you would never even *think* about chewing one of your employees out in public, would you?

A final thought. If this situation starts to happen to you again, try tactfully to prevent it. Perhaps you can stop your boss and the two of you go to a private room. If not, maybe you can signal the others to leave quickly and quietly. You may not succeed, but it's definitely worth the effort.

chapter seventeen

TROUBLESHOOTING PROBLEMS WITH YOUR BOSS

17–1 THE PROBLEM

He wants one of his people in your job

THE SCENE

"Marv, are you absolutely sure that's what you heard?"

"No question about it. He told Phyllis that if she'd keep doing what he told her, he'd have her in your job by April. And, I tell you, he *meant* it."

"Marv, I really appreciate your telling me this. Now I see why he's been leaning on me the way he has. All I have to do is figure out what to do . . ."

POSSIBLE CAUSES

He wants to take care of a friend by giving her your job.

It doesn't have anything directly to do with you or your performance.

He isn't comfortable with you and/or the way you manage.

He wants to deal with someone who'll do things the way he wants them done, and he's decided that someone isn't you.

You've been doing a very poor job, and he wants someone who will do a good job for him.

He believes that Phyllis is a much better manager than you are.

Hint: Do we need to tell you how critical this one is? We didn't think so.

CURES

If he wants to take care of a friend by giving her your job:

Let's assume in this "cure" and the next one that you've been doing at least a satisfactory job. Your performance isn't an issue so you can't help the situation by performing better.

Essentially, you have three alternatives:

- You can avoid dealing with the situation head-on. You can work hard, do nothing that might get you in trouble, and hope the crisis blows over. That doesn't sound very "strong," but it may be the best solution for you. Situations like this do blow over. Even if it doesn't, if you perform well enough your boss may decide that it's not worth the trouble and pick on someone else.

- You can start looking for another job. If you can find another job that pays as well but doesn't have this strain, it may be worth it to take it and leave. Since this makes it easy for your boss to put Phyllis in your job, he'll probably be glad to give you a good reference.

- You can fight the situation. Don't do this unless you're prepared to follow wherever it takes you. If you decide to go this way, start by talking with your boss. Be careful to protect Marv—you certainly don't want to get him in trouble. Let your boss know that you know. See what his reaction is. At that point, you have several options. You can threaten to take the issue as far as you need to—his boss, the EEO system, the board of directors. Or you can offer to leave if he's willing to help you get another job (either inside or outside the company). Make it clear that you're holding the cards and that his success depends on what he's willing to do for you. (We told you not to think of this one unless you were willing to take it all the way, and we were serious.)

If he isn't comfortable with you and/or the way you manage:

Unfortunately, of the three alternatives in the first "cure," two of them won't help here. Doing nothing will get you nowhere but out, and you don't hold any chips to bargain with your boss. You can take the second alternative and start looking for another job.

Probably the best alternative of all, though, is to have an honest talk with your boss. *Why* isn't he comfortable with you? *What* does he want from you that you're not giving him? *How* could you change the way you're managing, to make him more comfortable?

The answers to those questions will point the direction in which you need to move. If you can do what he wants you to and are willing to, simply do it. If you're unwilling to do it, you might try to find a middle ground both of you find acceptable. If you can't? Your best move is probably to see if he'll help you find a job elsewhere or at least give you acceptable references.

You may resent the way he wants you to manage. That's normal, but not necessarily relevant. If you can reasonably change to manage the way he wants, you may learn something from it. If the way he wants is really uncomfortable, go somewhere where your boss will be comfortable with your style. If he seriously expects you to act immorally or illegally, leave as soon as possible. (See Problems 12–1 and 12–2 for more information on this last situation.)

If you've been doing a very poor job, and he wants someone who will do a good job for him:

This makes your alternatives even sharper: Shape up or ship out.

Make sure you know what he expects (see Problem 16–4 for suggestions on this). If you can, start giving it to him immediately. If you're not sure you can meet his requirements, start looking for a job elsewhere.

It's worth asking for his help in finding another job. At worst, he'll know you intend to leave, even if he's not willing to help you. At best, he'll give you decent references and possibly even open a door or two for you.

SOMETHING TO THINK ABOUT

Sometimes it's difficult to tell which of three situations you're in:

- You're performing poorly.
- Your performance is okay, but your boss doesn't like your style.
- Your performance and style are adequate or better, but for personal reasons he wants someone else in your job.

Difficult or not, it's important to find out which is the case. Then you can take the proper action.

17-2 THE PROBLEM

He's talking about abolishing your job

THE SCENE

"Don, could you come in here a minute," calls Mr. Elizondo. "I've been looking over all these charts for the proposed reorganization, and the only one that seems to make sense to me is this one right here. But, see, it requires that your unit be split up between these other two sections. Gary would take one, and Georgia would take the other. I might be able to reassign you to a staff position. But when I'm getting so much pressure to flatten the organization, keeping your unit separate is just a lot of wasted overhead."

POSSIBLE CAUSES

Your boss may believe that the work will be accomplished more efficiently elsewhere.

He may have decided that the current organizational structure doesn't meet the company's real needs. Your job doesn't fit in.

The company may be faced with serious cutbacks.

Your job may be one of several that is being abolished. The downsizing that affects your unit may also affect your specific job.

Your boss may not be satisfied with the way you're doing the work.

If he doesn't want to confront you about your failure to meet his performance expectations, he can sidestep the issue by abolishing your job. That gets you out of the way, but without unpleasant confrontations.

Hint: This situation looks extremely serious at first glance—and maybe it is. But the fact that your job is being abolished doesn't necessarily mean that you're going with it. Before you panic, take time to find out what's really going on. If your boss considers you a valuable employee, he'll do his best to find you another job.

CURES

If your boss believes that the work will be accomplished more efficiently elsewhere:

Talk to him about how the new organizational structure will work. What kinds of supervisory jobs will be available? Which ones could you be a serious candidate for? Which ones would you like to work in?

Make your bid for the jobs that you'd like under the new structure. Talk to your boss about your qualifications for the work and point out the strengths in your management style that have made you successful in your current job. (Your boss will know those already, but it doesn't hurt to do a little self-promotion right now.)

Whatever job you're assigned, accept it gracefully. If it's something you don't want, you're still free to look elsewhere. But it's a lot easier to find a job when you have a job. And by doing good work wherever you are, you'll get a better reference from your boss when you find a position you like better.

What if there is no position for you in the new structure? It may be because there just isn't enough money to support it. If there are five managers in your section and only four supervisory jobs in the new structure, someone's going to be left out. You need to find out why it's you. Do the workers who were placed have greater seniority? Are you not qualified for any of the new managerial openings? If you are qualified and have comparable seniority, what makes you a less desirable selection than your peers?

If there are sound reasons for your not getting one of the available jobs that aren't within your control (like qualifications or seniority), your situation is the same as for any other cutbacks. See the second "cure" below.

If the problem is your performance or your ability to work comfortably with your boss, the problem is much more serious. Not only are you out of a job, but you're not likely to get much help from your boss in finding another one. See the third "cure" below.

If your company is coping with serious cutbacks:

Take comfort in the fact that there isn't anything "personal" about the situation. Lots of managers have been through this before, and many others will go through it in the years ahead. That doesn't find you a new job, but it does relieve you of any guilt you may feel.

Ask about outplacement services your company offers to help displaced workers find new employment. Talk to your personnel department about your entitlements upon separation (such as severance pay, pay for unused sick days or vacation time, early retirement buyouts available). Do some financial planning, with a professional consultant perhaps, to figure out how you could get by without your salary for a while.

Make a systematic plan for finding a new job. Identify commercial placement services if your company doesn't have outplacement help available or to increase your chances of finding a job quickly. Rely on friends and business acquaintances to help you find openings for which you can apply. Use the network you established during your employment to help you now in pending unemployment.

Don't panic! If potential employers think you're desperate, they're much less likely to consider you seriously. They'll figure you're going to take *anything* now just to get a job—and jump ship as soon as something better comes along. Stay calm, and plan your strategy. With a little planning, you may come out of this with an even better job than you left (honest!).

If your boss isn't satisfied with your performance:

It may be too late to save yourself, but it's worth one last try.

Talk to your boss about what he wants and expects and about what he isn't getting. Problem 16–4 has ideas on how to find out what your boss wants when he isn't clear in telling you. Then give it to him. Ask for feedback on how you're doing and what you could do to improve. Let your boss know you're serious about doing better work, and he may hold off on the decision to abolish your job until you've had a chance to prove yourself.

If you don't think you can meet your boss's requirements, or if he's not willing to give you another chance, it's better to quit than to be fired, since it will be easier to find a new job without the "black mark" of a previous firing on your record. Use the ideas in the "cure" above to find a new job. Then resolve to perform better in your new organization.

SOMETHING TO THINK ABOUT

It's scary to think about being out of work, whether it's your fault or not. Even in these days of two-income households, many families rely on both incomes just to break even. Loss of one income may mean financial disaster. But it's important to realize that *no* job is absolutely secure. So it's best to plan ahead for financial setbacks. The six-month rule still applies. (Save at least the equivalent of six months' salary for a "rainy day.") And with the help of a financial consultant, there are even more things you can do to make your family more secure. You may not be able to avoid a decline in your standard of living, but with a little prior planning you can avert financial disaster.

17–3 THE PROBLEM

He complains about you to your peers and his boss

THE SCENE

"I don't know what you did to upset Bill Grumledge," Jerry remarks, "but he sure was hot this morning. And he's usually such a low-key supervisor. But he complained about the Brigsley report all the way to staff meeting—and about what a terrible job you did getting the team together to work on it. I read the summary, and it didn't look that awful to me. There were a couple of areas I would have approached differently, but nothing to get Grumledge all fired up like that. In front of the rest of the staff too. I sure wouldn't want to be in your shoes right now!"

Possible Causes

This is one of those cases where it doesn't make a lot of difference *why* your boss is complaining about you. The fact that he is means that he's not satisfied, and it's up to you to find out why. The question of whether this is appropriate behavior for your boss or not (in general, it's not) is really irrelevant. He's not happy, and other people know it. So your job is to do what you can to redeem yourself.

Cures

Regardless of the specific cause of your boss's complaints:

Talk to him about his dissatisfactions. Don't worry that he didn't tell you directly. The fact that he so openly criticized you to your peers probably means that he wanted the story to get around to you. (Maybe he didn't want a messy confrontation.) Find out why he's unhappy and what you need to do to fix things. If he's not clear about what he wants, look at Problem 13–7 for help.

Then as soon as you find out what you're doing wrong, fix it. It doesn't matter whether *you* believe you're doing that badly or not. Your boss does. (The exception, of course, is if he wants you to do something illegal or immoral. In that case, look at Problems 12–1 and 12–2 for advice.)

Make sure your boss knows that you're making serious efforts to improve. The way to do this is *not* just by telling him, although a report of the steps you've taken to correct the problem may be a useful early step. But you also need to demonstrate by improved performance that you've fixed whatever he was unhappy about.

How well do you get along with your boss in general? And how much do you trust him? Once you've fixed the immediate problem and he's satisfied with your work again, you might make an opportunity to talk to him about how he treated you. Let him know how embarrassing it was to find out from someone else that he was unhappy. Then reassure him that you won't get defensive if he approaches you directly the next time he's concerned about something.

If he continues to complain about you to your peers and others, particularly if he hasn't been able to identify specific performance problems, you're probably dealing with a conflict of styles. The real problem has little or nothing to do with your performance. Your boss just isn't comfortable with the way you operate. Problem 17–1 has some ideas on how to work this one out.

SOMETHING TO THINK ABOUT

One other possibility we haven't discussed is that this may just be the kind of person your boss is. Maybe he complains about *everyone* to anyone who'll listen. Regardless of how nice he is to you when you're around, you never know what he's saying about you to someone else. Do you really want to work in that environment? If this is an ingrained habit of your boss's, chances are he's not going to change. Maybe you should look around for a better place to work.

17–4 THE PROBLEM

He thinks you're out for his job

THE SCENE

". . . and, furthermore, I intend to stay in this job until I retire or someone promotes me. You'll just have to wait until then to get it. If you want a promotion that bad, go find a job with a supervisor who's easier to fool!"

You stumble out of your boss's office, dumbfounded. Twenty minutes ago you made what you thought was an exceptionally good presentation to the corporate staff. You thought your boss would be proud of you; instead, he was furious—because he thinks that you did it as another step to get his job.

POSSIBLE CAUSES

You've been presenting yourself so that it makes you look good and your boss look bad.

He's drawn the logical conclusion that you want to get him out of his job and yourself into it.

You're innocent, but you haven't been paying any attention to how you're making him look.

Not quite as serious, but still bad.

You keep trying to make him look good, but he distrusts you.

No matter how hard you try, it always ends up this way.

Hint: We've mentioned this before, but it bears repeating. One of the fundamental jobs of any employee is to make her boss look good. It doesn't matter what you think of him or how he reacts to it; doing it is extremely important for your long-term success.

CURES

If you've been presenting yourself so that it makes you look good and your boss look bad:

Oh, no—you couldn't be doing this. Before you jump to that conclusion, make an honest review of the matter. Do you talk to other managers so that it sounds as if you're succeeding despite your boss? When you make presentations, does the same thought come through? How do you *feel* about your boss? (For instance, scorn and arrogance show through pretty clearly.) Are there other ways you imply that you'd be even more effective if it weren't for him?

If there are, then stop. Stop now!

How you feel about your boss's competence is your own affair, but what you convey about it to others isn't. He may get in your way, veto your best ideas, drive you crazy with nitpicking. That's your burden to bear, and it can be a heavy one. It's not one you can share with the world in general.

Loyalty to one's boss is a fundamental rule of the organizational world. It may seem feudal, even dishonest. No matter, it's still the rule. You don't have to give him phony credit or flatter him, but it won't hurt to let him share the credit you get and to build him up. Who knows, if you start treating him like an effective, supportive boss he may begin to become one.

If you're innocent, but you haven't been paying any attention to how you're making him look:

All of the thoughts on loyalty in the previous "cure" apply here. Presumably, you already knew how important loyalty is. You just forgot for a while.

Now it's time to concentrate on it again. Demonstrate loyalty clearly, but don't overdo it. The last thing you want is for your boss to think you're insincere about it. Make subtle changes in the way you present yourself and your work. Include him quietly but positively in the credit. Start slowly, then build on it until it become automatic.

It might also be appropriate to apologize to him for having created the misleading impression. That depends on the relationship between the two of you, but if the relationship is at all strong an apology is proper.

If you keep trying to make him look good, but he distrusts you:

This is tough, so treat it as a challenge. Be as sensitive as possible. Are there particular times and/or situations that seem to reinforce his distrust? Can you modify what happens so that it's less threatening to him? Keep working the problem; a number of small changes may start to turn him around.

You also need to have another concern: Is he undermining you? If he believes you're after his job, he may try to undercut you in the organization. Loyalty works both ways. If you give it, you have every right to expect it.

Is it possible to have a frank discussion with him? If you can, you might be able to negotiate out what both of you expect as loyalty from the other. That would certainly be desirable from both of your points of view.

SOMETHING TO THINK ABOUT

It's sometimes tempting to try to "show up" your boss, even to try to get his job. It may work, but it's dangerous. Even the manager who puts you in your boss's job will distrust you; if you were disloyal once, won't you be disloyal again? Disloyalty is an almost sure way to trade short-term career success for long-run career stagnation.

The other side of that is the danger in working for a boss who doesn't show you loyalty. If he doesn't, you may not have much job security, and what you have may be up for grabs every time he gets mad at you. If this is your situation, you need to evaluate it carefully. A job change may be disruptive, but it might be the best step you could take to achieve your long-run career objectives.

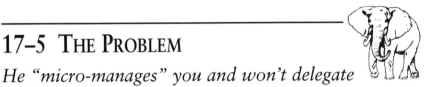

17–5 THE PROBLEM

He "micro-manages" you and won't delegate

THE SCENE

"I just wondered how things were going on that Sylvestri case," Carl says as you walk into his office. "Have you had Lois look into those precedents I told you about? And have you been making Charita record all the time she's spent on the phone for this one? What about those statistics I gave you to review? Oh, and one other thing; let me look at that letter to the PrestoPop people before you send it out. Anything else you wanted to discuss?"

Not really, you're tempted to reply—just what I have to do to get to run my own unit! But instead, you depart with a smiling, "No, sir" and go off to do Carl's bidding while the things *you* know need to get done sit for another day.

POSSIBLE CAUSES

Carl may have come up through your unit and still identifies with it.

This is a common problem. You know by now that supervisors tend to get very attached to the organizations they run. It's hard to give them up, even when the supervisor's promoted to a higher-level job.

Carl may think that he's operating the way a manager should.

He may be reacting to the abuse of delegation he's seen by going too far in the direction of "hands-on" management.

Carl may not think you're doing a very good job managing by yourself.

This is another case where he perceives you as a poor performer.

Hint: Although this is a difficult situation and *may* reflect Carl's dissatisfaction with your performance, it's much more likely that this is just the way Carl operates. That doesn't make it any easier for you to manage around him, but it should reassure you that Carl's probably not out to get you. You just have a difference of opinion about management style.

CURES

If Carl came up through your unit and still identifies with it:

You have two tasks facing you: Convince Carl that you can do a good job running "his" unit (recognizing, of course, that you'll never match his achievements) and wean him away from the substantive work in the organization.

Begin by letting Carl know in advance every move you plan to make, before he has to ask. You're not asking his *permission* to take specific actions; you're letting him know because you are aware of his interest. Gradually begin to let him know about some less important items after the decision's been made and the action taken. Continue to discuss many items with Carl in advance, but offer to "take care of the details" so he won't have to be bothered. As time goes on, you should be handling more and more of the "details" without consulting Carl first. Let him know when your efforts are particularly successful—tactfully, since you don't want him to feel that you're outshining his performance in the same job.

In order to achieve full delegation for running your unit, you will probably need to divert Carl's attention with other matters. (This is known as "managing your boss.") Bring problems to him that properly belong in his sphere—organizational issues, administrative matters, questions of interrelationships among units or with outside organizations. If you can keep him busy with these "big picture" issues (many of which will *never* be solved), he won't have time to meddle in the affairs of your unit.

If he still insists on getting involved to any appreciable degree in the substance of your work, try to limit his participation to specific areas. Maybe there's a cross-functional project team he'd like to head. Maybe there's a pet area he'd like to do some basic research in (research that you may or may not have a need for later). You'll very likely be able to channel his interests into areas that aren't an integral part of your unit's work.

And if he still insists on "micro-managing" your assignments? He's still the boss, and if he has the time and energy to do his job and yours too, there's probably not much you can do about it. You could make a tactful suggestion that he not work so hard, and leave more of the "grunt" work to you. But if he wants to get involved, you really can't stop him. Decide whether you can operate comfortably in that environment and, if not, start looking around for something better.

If Carl believes that he's operating the way a manager should:

Recognize that Carl's instincts aren't altogether bad. There are a lot of "high flyers" who are more interested in getting ahead and making themselves look good than in producing something of real value. Carl's "hands-on" approach shows he has a sincere interest in the good of the organization, and he's to be commended for that. At the same time, he's doing the job you're paid to do, and that makes your job even harder.

Much of what we said in the first "cure" about convincing your boss that you can do a good job with the unit applies here too. Gradually assume more of the details of running the organization, at the same time that you direct Carl's attention to issues that are more properly handled at his level.

How well do you and Carl get along? Does he trust you? If you think he won't be threatened by the conversation, talk to Carl about his management style. Point out the extra burdens it places on him to do two managers' jobs and the difficult position you're in by not being allowed to make your own decisions. That little talk, coupled with your demonstration of your competence and willingness to attend to detail, may convince Carl to delegate more.

As above, the final decision about how much to delegate is Carl's. If he's not comfortable giving you greater freedom, it's a situation you'll have to learn to live with, or find another situation elsewhere.

If Carl doesn't think you're doing a very good job managing by yourself:

Your job is to prove to him that you can, and will, do much better. We've talked elsewhere about ways to demonstrate improved performance to your boss. See especially Problems 16–2, 16–3, 16–6, 17–1, 17–2, and 17–4 for ideas.

This is going to take some time. You can't just promise to do better and expect that you'll suddenly have full delegation. You'll need to demonstrate by continuing good performance that you can handle the job. You've already done something to raise questions in Carl's mind about your abilities. You need now to reearn his confidence.

SOMETHING TO THINK ABOUT

One of the real classics of management literature discusses this problem of delegation at great length. It addresses both ways you can use delegation to increase your leverage as a manager and techniques you can use to obtain greater freedom and delegation from your supervisor. *Managing Management Time* by William Oncken is a "must" for any supervisor who wants to increase her effectiveness without increasing her toil.

17–6 THE PROBLEM

He refuses to support your decisions when they're unpopular

THE SCENE

"Now, Madeline, I know you mean well. I'd like to see your people produce more, too. But it's just not wise to fight over an extra ten or fifteen minutes at lunch. You can encourage them to get back on time, that's certainly okay with me. Writing them up for it, though, or docking their pay—that's just going too far. I want you to go back and tell Scott you're reconsidered and you're going to pull the warning out of his personnel file. I think everybody'll be happier that way."

It happened again! This is the third time *this month* that he's made you back down from an action because it was unpopular. How in the world does he expect you to maintain discipline and productivity if he undercuts you like this?

POSSIBLE CAUSES

He believes that you rely too heavily on negative supervision.

He wants to see you develop more positive ways of motivating your employees.

He doesn't like to make employees angry.

For whatever reason, he believes that this isn't an effective way to handle them.

He doesn't want your unit to cause him any problems.

From his point of view, he has enough to worry about without your adding to it.

Hint: One of the facts of organizational life is that your boss's managerial style puts limits on what you can do. If you push these limits too forcefully, he may lose confidence in you (as in Problem 17–1). The limits may be frustrating, but you can't avoid them if you want to keep his confidence. The challenge is to modify your style so that he's comfortable with it and still deal effectively with your unit.

CURES

If he believes that you rely too heavily on negative supervision:

Look carefully at this alternative. If you think it may be the case, talk with him about it. You may have been leaning too heavily on "showing them who's boss" or "shaping them up." Ask him to suggest alternatives; then think them through carefully. Try them out and see what happens.

At the worst, you'll learn some new ways to supervise. They may not work in the current situation, but they might be just the ticket another time. At the best, you'll find they really do make your job easier.

We all prefer to handle situations in familiar ways. Unfortunately, the preference can all too quickly become a rut. Regardless of your boss's style, it's an excellent idea to try new ways of handling situations ever so often. It keeps you flexible and growing.

If he doesn't like to make employees angry:

There might be any of several reasons for this. He may believe that you lose more from the anger than it's worth. He may need employees to like him. He may see himself as a kind person who doesn't make people angry.

It doesn't matter why he reacts this way. If he doesn't want employees angry, you need to find ways to supervise effectively without making them angry enough to complain to him.

We don't have the space to talk at length about positive ways of supervising. Here are a few brief ideas.

- Make sure that employees get rewarded for doing good work, and not otherwise. Use praise lavishly for a job well done; spend a minimum amount of time criticizing poor work.

- Give clear assignments with clear standards for successful completion. That will be enough for most employees to do a good job. When one doesn't, provide objective criticism based on the standards.

- Be a leader. We know—that sounds hackneyed. It's not. A leader sets goals and gets employee commitment to work toward the goals. A really effective leader does this *with* his people; they become everyone's goals, not just his.

- Above all—and this is hackneyed, too—set the right example. Everything else you do is more effective if your employees see that you believe it enough to live it yourself.

If he doesn't want your unit to cause him any problems:

Some managers believe that they shouldn't have to handle problems from subordinate units. If a problem reaches them, the supervisor of that unit fouled up somewhere. If no problems come to them, their subordinate managers must be supervising effectively.

If that's what your boss believes, that's what you do your best to give him. It's difficult. At the same time, it gives you the opportunity for real freedom in managing your unit. If you can keep problems out of his office, you can manage pretty much as you want. How often do you get a better deal than that?

The suggestions in the "cure" before this one are applicable here. You also need to let your employees know discreetly that they'll be in big trouble if they complain to your boss before they've talked to you. That gives you the chance to take care of the problem (which, of course, you'll do).

Something to Think About

You can't build effective supervision around the idea that you'll never make employees angry. On the other hand, if you *consistently* make them angry you'll never have a really effective unit. What's the answer? Your management style ought not make employees angry often; when it does, the issue should be an important one. The goal, though, isn't to keep them from being angry. The goal is to manage so that they do their jobs without the kind of intervention from you that makes them angry. That's good management.

17–7 The Problem

She doesn't like you

The Scene

"Mario, you really don't know why you have such a hard time with Ms. Estridge?"

"No. I do everything the way I think she wants, and it's never right. Nothing ever satisfies her. I'd love for you to tell me why."

"It's simple. She just doesn't like you."

"Why? What have I ever done to make her dislike me?"

"That I don't know, but I know she doesn't like you. I heard her in the cafeteria last Tuesday, telling Mr. Harris how much you irritate her."

"That's a hell of a note! What am I supposed to do about that?"

POSSIBLE CAUSES

The problem is caused by a cultural difference.

Mrs. Estridge expects people to behave in a certain way, but you were brought up to behave differently. Just by acting normally, you're irritating her.

She finds your personal style offensive.

This isn't a matter of ethnic differences, but of your own personality traits. She dislikes you because of the way you act as an individual.

What she really meant was that she doesn't like the way you manage.

This is a very different matter.

Hint: We're going to suggest some ways to approach the situation, but there may not be anything you can do about it. Living with it or leaving may end up being your only two alternatives.

CURES

No matter what the situation is:

Talk with Mrs. Estridge. Carefully plan what you're going to say.

If you think the direct approach will work, tell her that you think she doesn't like you. Ask if she can tell you why. Then listen; don't try to make points. You want the clearest picture you can get of why she feels as she does. You can try to deal with any wrong ideas of hers at a later meeting.

If you don't have confidence in the direct approach, you'll have to try to find out the same information indirectly. Perhaps you could work through her secretary or another manager who gets along well with her. If that won't work, try this: The next time she criticizes some of your work, ask her in detail how she'd have preferred you to do it. Don't argue; just listen closely to what she says. It may give you clues to some of the reasons for her uneasiness with you.

If the problem is caused by a cultural difference:

Whether you can solve it will depend on how willing each of you is to learn what the other expects. For instance, you may be used to expressing yourself forcefully (perhaps even loudly), while she believes that it's unprofessional to raise her voice. You may be very deferential and quiet, while she expects you to be friendly and talkative.

If you're both able to talk about the differences, you may start to reach an understanding. Don't expect it to be quick or easy. If you both want genuinely to build a good working relationship and are willing to really listen, you can make progress. You'll know you're succeeding if you can each joke about the other's culture without offense.

If you can't discuss it openly, not too many choices remain. You can try to adapt to her expectations, and you may do it successfully. If you can't, you'll just have to accept that it's an unpleasant state of affairs. The remaining alternative is to move to another job.

If she finds your personal style offensive:

This feels much like the first situation, though the cause is somewhat different. She simply doesn't like people who act the way you do.

Again, if the two of you can talk it out you may reach an understanding. Even if you never become fond of each other, you may be able to work successfully together.

There's an "up" side to this. We've stressed in other problems the importance of finding a variety of ways to deal with people and problems. Most of the time, the way you act and manage may be fine with people. Other people, though, may be put off or irritated by it. Why not use this as an excuse to learn some new ways of dealing? You don't have to change, or "give in" to anyone. You simply develop a broader range of ways to relate to people. Then you use the one that's most appropriate for the person you're dealing with.

If what she really doesn't like is the way you manage:

This is probably the easiest problem to resolve. ("Easiest" doesn't necessarily mean "easy," though.) There's really no "best" way to manage, and you may learn some valuable skills if you can change to a style she's more comfortable with.

Once again, if the two of you can talk honestly with each other about what she wants it will be much easier. Problem 1 in this chapter has some specific suggestions for dealing with this type of situation.

SOMETHING TO THINK ABOUT

It's disappointing, and often irritating, when someone dislikes you. If the reason is your management style, that's bad enough; if it's your personality or your culture, it's worse.

Our basic advice is simple and straightforward: Don't take it personally. There's no rule that says you have to like everyone else, or that everyone has to like you. It may be inconvenient—even hard on your career—when other people don't. It's not an attack on you, or a judgment on your worth as a person. Simply accept the fact that the person doesn't like you. Try to find out why. Then, if you can and are willing to, change the behavior that offends her. If you can't, put up with the situation or move out of it. Just don't let it "get to you."

17-8 The Problem

She's a good friend of one of your hard-to-manage employees

The Scene

You enter Ms. Grimsley's office apprehensively and take a seat, wondering what kettle of hot water you've fallen into this time.

"Jon," she begins, "I've been hearing complaints that you're picking on Harold Schweibeck. Is there something wrong with the way he's doing his work?"

You *knew* this was coming. Ms. Grimsley and Harold Schweibeck have been friends since long before you came to this company. But Harold's been a problem for as long as you've been in the company too. And his continual bragging that "you can't touch me" makes it hard to demand anything of anybody else in the unit. But this is the first time Ms. Grimsley has actually confronted you about your attempts to tame Harold, and you're not sure *whose* side she's on.

Possible Causes

The question here isn't *why* Ms. Grimsley and Harold are such good friends (although knowing the answer *may* help you to view Harold in a somewhat different light). The real question is how you can get Ms. Grimsley to back your attempts to manage Harold without damaging her own relationship with him.

Hint: A little empathy on your part will make it easier to understand this situation. Ms. Grimsley is in a difficult bind. She's caught between the demands of the workplace and the expectations of the personal relationship she has with Harold. Unless things are orchestrated *very* carefully, she's going to lose on one side or the other. Either the work of your unit will suffer, or her relationship with Harold will suffer. Since the latter causes her more personal pain, it's not hard to see which way she's likely to go, is it?

CURES

Regardless of the reason for the friendship between Ms. Grimsley and Harold, you still have a job to do. These suggestions may help you make things more palatable to Ms. Grimsley:

Make sure Ms. Grimsley knows exactly what problems you're having with Harold and how they impact on your unit's ability to do the work. She may know Harold *primarily* from a social perspective. And if no one's complained to her before (with hard facts to back them up), she may not know what the problems are. Her attempts to protect Harold may spring from her lack of knowledge rather than a conscious decision to sacrifice your unit's productivity for the sake of her friendship with Harold.

In explaining the problems you have with Harold, focus on the impact they have on productivity and morale in your unit. Make it clear that these are not just differences of style or personality conflicts; they're problems that affect the unit's bottom line.

Suggest ways of dealing with Harold that won't require Ms. Grimsley's direct involvement. If you agree to take the heat from Harold, and arrange for Ms. Grimsley to be a sympathetic listener, she may be more willing to let you deal with the problem. Many managers have a stated policy of requiring their subordinates to deal with issues at their level without intervention. If Ms. Grimsley makes it clear to Harold that her involvement would violate a policy that she (or her superiors) have already established, he may not blame her personally for all the "nasty" things you're doing to him.

If you can't gracefully arrange for Ms. Grimsley to remain uninvolved, you might suggest that Harold be reassigned to another unit that's not under her supervision. That would allow his new supervisor to deal with his problems without intervention and would take Ms. Grimsley entirely out of the line of command. The company could work out the problems with Harold, but Ms. Grimsley's friendship with him would remain intact.

What if Ms. Grimsley doesn't *want* to be uninvolved? What if protecting Harold, even at the expense of the company, is *exactly* what she's trying to do?

In that case, there's not much you can do about the situation except grin and bear it. If Harold's behavior or performance are intolerable, you *might* consider going over Ms. Grimsley's head. But you should weigh the consequences first. Ms. Grimsley will certainly be dismayed at your lack of personal loyalty to her and may remember that during later key events—like appraisal time, or when the next promotion comes up, or when unpleasant assignments have to be handed out. If she's angry enough, she may even try to get rid of you.

If it's Harold's performance that's at issue, there are probably some things you can do to minimize the damage he causes that won't upset him or Ms. Grimsley. Remove him from critical assignments; give him special projects to work on that will have high visibility with Ms. Grimsley, but with few other people. He may not do you much good in those assignments, but he won't do you much harm either.

If it's Harold's conduct that's the problem, you need to evaluate just how bad his behavior is. Has he alienated key customers or suppliers? Is there potential harm to the safety or well-being of himself or others? In those cases, the problem is important enough to elevate. Keeping on Ms. Grimsley's good side is *not* more important than the safety of your workers.

You may still be able to take some action without specifically involving Ms. Grimsley or openly ignoring her directions to you. Can you arrange for one of the other managers in the company, preferably at Ms. Grimsley's level or above, to observe Harold in action and put pressure on you, through her, to resolve the problem? If Ms. Grimsley sees that others are unhappy with Harold, particularly others who have influence over *her*, she may see the political necessity of dealing with the problem regardless of her social relationship.

If Harold's behavior is not intolerable, just annoying, do what you can to minimize its ill effects and put up with him as best you can. Your job isn't *only* to produce for the company, it's also to keep your boss happy whenever you can. So look on this as just part of the day's work.

Something to Think About

One of the advantages of a small company is the solidarity and "family" feeling that are easily fostered among managers and employees. One of the disadvantages is that those feelings frequently lead to friendships that extend beyond the office and can complicate management. In a larger organization, such friendships still develop, but when they do, there are more options. You can move people around to avoid potential conflicts of interest without damaging either person's career or opportunities for advancement. If personal relationships get in the way of company management more often than you'd like, maybe you're in the wrong environment. But if you like the feeling of being "part of the family," you should recognize that these conflicts are a price you may occasionally have to pay.

17–9 The Problem

He bypasses you to your workgroup

The Scene

"Eleanor, why aren't you out in the bindery? You know that we have to get the pageant brochures out today."

"Oh, no—first we have to get the 1000 Club certificates printed."

"What ever gave you that idea?"

"Mr. Schultz. He came by about an hour ago and told me to switch over to the certificates."

"Okay. Go ahead." You turn away, swearing under your breath. Once again, Schultz has gone straight to your people instead of telling you what he wants done. It's a wonder that any of them pay any attention to you any more!

Possible Causes

Mr. Schultz doesn't believe you relay his instructions accurately.

He's concluded that the only way your people are going to get the right directions is for him to give the directions to them personally.

You're often not around, so he's given up trying to find you to tell you.

It's easier just to find the employee and tell her what to do.

He doesn't realize how disruptive what he's doing is.

He's not used to being a second-level manager.

He still thinks in terms of managing employees directly.

Hint: This circumstance may reflect a broader lack of confidence in you. Keep that in the back of your mind while you're dealing with the specific problem. If he does lack confidence in you, that's by far the more serious problem.

CURES

No matter what the cause is:

Instruct your people that if Mr. Schultz or anyone else in higher management gives them instructions they're to tell you as soon as possible. They're to do what they're told, but they're to see that you know about it quickly. That way, you can at least keep up with what's going on. You won't be surprised when they're doing something different from what you told them to do.

Try to talk with Mr. Schultz about the situation. See if you can find out why he bypasses you and how he looks at it. Remember that your primary objective is to listen; you can defend your position in a later conversation.

If he doesn't believe you relay his instructions accurately:

This one may take some work, but the solution is easy. It's probably best not to approach it head-on. Try to intercept Mr. Schultz, so that it's awkward for him not to give you the instructions. Then listen carefully, repeat the instructions back to him, and make sure you understand them exactly. Then pass them on exactly. If you do it right, he'll begin to get the message and start dealing with your people through you.

You should also look at the reasons why you weren't getting the instructions right before. Did you get defensive if he seemed to be critical of you? Did you listen haphazardly, so that you got things confused? Just why did it happen? Is it happening in other situations, with other people?

Not listening carefully and fully is one of the worst habits a manager—or anyone—can have. If it's a habit you have, take advantage of this situation to rid yourself of it completely.

If you're often not around, so he's given up trying to find you to tell you:

He may have started off wanting to give instructions through you. Because you're so often not there, he's gotten in the habit of going directly to your employees. It saves him time and frustration.

The simplest solution, if it's practical in your situation, is to have an employee who generally takes over when you're gone. Ask your boss to deal directly with him if you're not around. He can pass any instructions on, then see that you know about them when you return.

If this isn't acceptable, having your employees tell you what instructions they received is the next best solution. You might also be able to time your absences from the work area so that you're less apt to be gone at the times Mr. Schultz usually visits the area.

If he doesn't realize how disruptive what he's doing is:

He may have gotten into the habit of bypassing you and other supervisors because no one ever complained to him. He thinks it's okay with you. Or he may understand that you don't like it but not believe it interferes with anything.

This is where a good relationship with your boss is important. If the two of you can be honest with each other, you can bring the situation up with him. You hope he'll see how disruptive it is and agree to change.

This is another one of the many situations in which your ability to listen carefully and ask effective questions is important. Of course, this automatically means that you've learned not to be defensive.

If he's not used to being a second-level manager:

This is almost the same problem as the last one, but with a small twist. Probably no one has told him that bypassing you is disruptive because he's been doing it so short a time. That makes it even likelier that he'll listen if you bring it up to him.

There is one caution, though. If he's new, he may be very sensitive to any criticism of his supervisory style. You need to make it clear that you know he's just being conscientious. All you're asking is the chance to show him that he can come to you and get what he wants done.

SOMETHING TO THINK ABOUT

You have one solid argument for having him deal with your employees through you—no matter why he doesn't do so at the moment. If he passes his instructions through you, you can see that they're carried out. If he doesn't, you may not know exactly what he wants, and it may not get done. In other words, it will be easier for him to do his job if he works through you instead of bypassing you.

PROBLEM-SOLVING CHECKLISTS

PROBLEM-SOLVING CHECKLISTS

Whenever you have a problem that doesn't exactly fit one of the situations we've described in the previous chapters, look here for hints on how to solve it yourself. These checklists will walk you through the problem and show you the steps to take to solve it.

We've included seven different checklists that cover the spectrum of "people problems" you're likely to encounter as a manager:

Checklist #1: Performance Problems (either individual or group)

Checklist #2: Conduct/Behavior Problems (either individual or group)

Checklist #3: Acceptance Problems (when one or several of your employees isn't accepted by the group)

Checklist #4: Problems with Your Peers

Checklist #5: Problems with Your Boss

Checklist #6: Your Personal Problems

Checklist #7: Substance-Abuse Problems

THE GENERAL CHECKLIST

Whenever you have a management problem, these are the general steps you should follow to solve it successfully:

❑ State the problem specifically in terms of

- its source (who's responsible for causing the problem, *not* who's responsible for fixing it) and

- the kind of problem it is (such as performance, behavior, and so forth).

❑ Ask questions and gather all the facts you need to make a decision.

❑ Identify the options available to you for solving the problem, now that you know exactly what the problem is.

❑ Choose an option that you'll follow (or a series of steps if that's the best way).

❑ Consider writing down why you chose the option you did, particularly if you think you'll be called on to defend your actions later.

❑ Act. Implement your decision.

❑ Evaluate how well your decision worked. If the solution is one that's implemented over a period of time, evaluate its success at specific points along the way. If it doesn't seem to be working out as you expected, go through the steps again to see if you can find a better approach.

The patterns that follow take you through the first three steps of this general problem-solving procedure. It's up to you as the manager to make the final decision, implement it, and evaluate its success.

GOOD LUCK!

CHECKLIST #1:

Performance Problems

Answer each of these questions:

❑ Exactly what is the nature of the performance problem?

❑ Does the employee have basic self-management skills such as skill in organizing and prioritizing work and in sticking to deadlines?

> If not, look for formal training courses that will teach those skills. Coach the employee. Set short, progressive deadlines to help the employee manage his work as he assumes greater responsibility for managing it himself.

❑ Does the employee have the technical work skills needed to complete his assignments?

If not, teach the skills through training (either formal or on the job), supplemented with practice and feedback. Assign a mentor to review the employee's work and provide continuing coaching. If the procedures are hard to remember or seldom used, consider devising a job aid to list the directions in narrative or a diagram. (Standard Operating Procedures [SOPs] are a kind of job aid too.)

❏ If training, practice, and feedback don't yield significant improvements, decide if the employee has the *ability* to learn the work. (Your personnel department or training department may be able to help in this assessment.)

If he doesn't, transfer the employee to a job you believe he *can* do or terminate him.

❏ Does the employee have the interpersonal skills required to establish and maintain effective work relationships?

If not, use formal training to teach the skills or coach the employee. Provide regular feedback on his progress. If coaching and regular feedback and counseling don't result in improved performance, terminate the employee.

❏ Does the employee/organization have the tools necessary to do the work (such as supplies, materials, equipment, sufficient time)?

If not, remove the obstacles or devise ways to work around them.

❏ Does the employee/organization have a positive incentive for doing the work correctly and on schedule?

If positive incentives don't exist, design them into the system to the extent you can. At the least, remove any disincentives and make sure employees understand how their work contributes to the overall goals of the organization. (If you're not sure what disincentives might exist, ask your employees, "What gets in the way of your doing the best job you possibly can?" They'll tell you—maybe more than you want to know!)

Note: Look also at Checklist #7, Substance-Abuse Problems, to see if that could be the source of an individual employee's performance problem.

CHECKLIST #2:

Conduct/Behavior Problems

Answer each of these questions:

❑ Exactly what unacceptable behavior is the employee/organization exhibiting?

❑ Is the behavior serious or merely irritating?

> If it's merely irritating, caution the employee (or group) that the behavior isn't appropriate and that you may have to take stronger measures if the situation doesn't improve. Be prepared to live with most irritations, though, unless the behavior worsens or it begins to have a noticeable effect on the productivity of the unit.

❑ Is the employee/organization aware of the rules in this area?

> If not, let her/them know what the rules are and warn of the consequences for not following those rules. Make a written record of the warning.

❑ Is the behavior critical to the organization or to the safety/well-being of other people?

> If so, your first action should be to stop the behavior. That may mean calling in your company's security office or the police. After the immediate situation is taken care of, decide on the penalty for the misbehavior. In a situation this serious, termination is the most appropriate remedy unless there are unusual or strong mitigating factors.

❑ Does the behavior undermine your authority or the basic supervisor/subordinate relationship?

If so, consider terminating the employee or moving her out of your unit unless there are strong mitigating factors.

❑ Is the behavior deliberate?

If so, and if it's serious (even though it's not critical to the organization or to employees' safety and doesn't undermine your effectiveness), you still need to take action strong enough to stop the employee and others from repeating the behavior. Appropriate measures include suspensions without pay, writing up the employee in her official records, or moving her into a lesser position.

Note: Look also at Checklist #7, Substance Abuse-Problems, to see if that could be the source of your employee's conduct or behavior problems.

CHECKLIST #3:
Acceptance Problems

Answer each of these questions:

❑ Exactly what problem is occurring?

❑ Are others failing to accept a worker because she is a woman or a member of a minority group?

If so, first make sure your workers know your policy, and the company's policy, on discrimination. Explain how you expect your employees to behave toward all their co-workers (for instance, including them in meetings and discussions that are relevant to their assignments). Model the behavior you expect of your workers, so that it's clear you practice what you preach.

Then work on changing the underlying attitudes that caused this problem. Examine off-the-shelf training materials. Discuss individual differences and individual contributions at staff meetings and other appropriate occasions. Arrange positive experiences for people of diverse cultures and backgrounds to work together.

❑ Are others failing to accept a worker, not for discriminatory reasons, but because he irritates them?

> Encourage your employees to work together harmoniously. Make the establishment and maintenance of positive relationships a part of each employee's performance discussions and see that all your employees understand the negative effects on performance (and their appraisals) of failure to nurture those relationships. Then follow through.

❑ Has one of your workers been accused of discriminatory behavior (including sexual harassment)?

> If so, first get the facts. Talk to the employee who made the allegation, any witnesses he names, and the worker who's been accused. Take notes of your discussions. If you believe the employee is innocent, talk to the worker who made the accusation to explain why you believe he misunderstood the situation and advise him of the right to file a discrimination complaint. If you believe the accused worker *did* discriminate, take appropriate action, even if it means firing him.

CHECKLIST #4:

Problems with Your Peers

Answer each of these questions:

❑ Exactly what problem is the other manager causing you and/or your unit?

❑ Is what this manager is doing (or failing to do) important to your effectiveness or the effectiveness of your unit?

If it's not, you have your solution. Just live with what she's doing. You have other, more important problems to worry about.

❑ If what she's doing (or not doing) is important, are good relations with her important to your personal effectiveness or the effectiveness of your unit?

If they are, forget trying to force her to change what she's doing. Instead, pick one of the following alternatives, which doesn't require you to confront her or try to compel her to change. If none of those alternatives will work, just live with the situation.

❑ No matter how important good relations are, do you *have* good relations with her?

If so, your best alternative is to work out a resolution with her.

❑ If you don't have good relations, or can't work out a resolution, do you have something to offer her in exchange for her cooperation?

If so, see if you can't strike a bargain with her. Even if your relationship isn't that good, you can probably make a deal.

❑ If you don't have anything to offer, is there another way beside confrontation to get what you want or need or to minimize the effect of what she's doing?

If so, try to get around the problem she's causing without forcing the issue.

❑ If you have no good alternatives short of forcing her to change, can you rely on your superiors and peers to support you if you try to force her to change?

If so, it's worth trying to pressure her into changing.

If not, your only good alternative is to live with the situation.

CHECKLIST #5:
Problems with Your Boss

Answer each of these questions:

❏ Exactly what problem is your boss causing you or your unit?

❏ Is it a problem because it will harm the company, harm you, or require you to do something immoral or illegal?

> If it's not one of these, why is it a problem? It sounds like a disagreement, which means that you may try to persuade your boss to do otherwise, but if you can't, you do what he wants.

❏ Is the problem that he wants to take (or wants you to take) an action that will harm the company?

> If so, and if you trust your boss, discuss your misgivings with him. If he still wants to take the action after you've said your piece, do what he says.
> If you don't trust him, decide whether it's important enough to force the issue. If not, do what he wants. If it is, use the following suggestions.

❏ Is the problem that what he wants to do will harm you (hurt your career, make you look bad, and so forth)?

> If so, and you trust him, discuss it with him.
>
> If you're not satisfied with the results of the discussion, or if you don't trust him, see the following suggestions on forcing his hand.

❏ Is what he wants to do (or wants you to do) immoral or illegal?

> If so, and if you have effective connections with your boss's superiors, go to them with the situation.
>
> If so, but you don't have effective connections, is what he wants to do serious enough to risk loss of your job? If not,

do what he wants and then start looking for a job somewhere else, because his next request may be more serious.

If so, and the matter is serious enough for you to risk your job, you have no choice but to refuse to do what he wants and threaten to make the issue public. Needless to say, you also need to start looking for another job—quickly.

(*Note*: There is a significant difference between an action that is immoral because it violates widely held moral standards and one that is immoral because it violates your personal standards. If it violates community standards, it may be easy for you to get support from others. If it violates your personal standards that most others don't share, they probably won't help you.)

CHECKLIST #6:

Your Personal Problems

Answer each of these questions:

❑ Exactly what is the problem?

❑ Is your boss dissatisfied with your performance or generally unhappy with you?

> If so, talk to her about what she wants to see changed. Then, if it's something you can fix, fix it. If it's something you believe you can't fix, or are unwilling to change, you should know by now that your boss will come out the winner. It's time to look around for another job or prepare to live with your boss's continuing dissatisfaction.

❑ Are personal problems interfering with your work?

> If so, talk to your boss to let her know that there are outside influences that may affect your performance for a while. Let her know how long you expect the situation to

last and try to work out some temporary accommodation that's acceptable to both of you.

Don't try to tough it out on your own. Your boss will notice the difference in your work, and she may assume you've just lost interest.

❑ Are you burned out on the job?

If so, try to find an interest, either on the job or in your personal life, that will revitalize you. Take some time off (no one's indispensable) to relax and reassess where you want to be and what you want to be doing. If you already have outside interests and the combined demands are overloading you, ease off. Give yourself some time to unwind and contemplate. If your dissatisfaction doesn't diminish in time, then consider whether this is really the right job for you. Get some professional help in identifying a career that will be more personally rewarding.

CHECKLIST #7:
Substance-Abuse Problems

A growing concern in the workplace is the impact of alcohol and drug abuse on employee productivity. Tremendous costs (many of them hidden) result from poor quality work, absenteeism, interpersonal conflicts, and other by-products of substance abuse.

There are several keys to identifying a substance-abuse problem, but the primary indicator is *change*—

- change in an employee's behavior
- change in his patterns of work and absence
- change in the way he relates to others
- change in the quality of his work
- change in the amount he produces

Most of the time, you *won't* be able to identify impaired employees by physical symptoms—

- the odor of alcohol
- dilated pupils
- slurred or incoherent speech
- disorientation
- lack of muscular coordination (staggering, dropping things, shaking)

The clues will be much more subtle. And you won't recognize them if you don't already know what the employee's *normal* patterns are. Here's the checklist to follow:

❑ Get to know your employees' characteristics and patterns— the way they typically act or react.

❑ If you notice a decline in work behavior or performance, talk to the employee about it right away. Evasion and denial are classic responses of employees with substance-abuse problems.

❑ Look for changes in other areas. If an employee has been calling in sick frequently, has his performance also deteriorated? Or is he more irritable in dealing with co-workers or customers?

❑ Identify the specific performance or behavior problem(s) affecting the employee, then confront him. Make sure he knows exactly what will happen if his performance and/or conduct don't improve. Having related the problem(s) to work requirements, you should then offer the employee assistance or referral if he believes he needs it. Don't accuse! Your concern is getting the work out. If the employee recognizes that he has a problem, he'll need your understanding and support. If he doesn't recognize it, none of your accusations will help.

❑ If your company has an employee assistance program office, consult the coordinator for help in confronting the employee. If you have no employee assistance program in-house, talk to your personnel department for help.

❑ Then follow through. Whether the employee gets help or not, make it clear that you expect him to improve his performance and/or behavior. If he does, congratulate him and offer your continued support. If he doesn't, take whatever measures are appropriate—including discipline or termination.

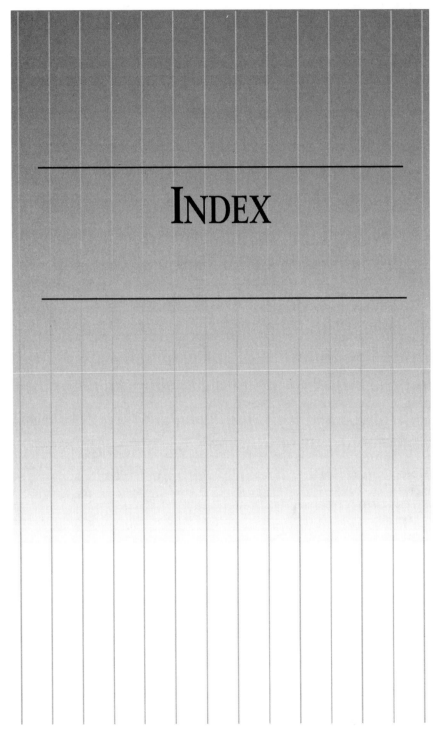

INDEX

A

Acceptance rate, 19-20
Alcohol use/abuse, 64-67, 69-71,
176
 cures for problem, 65-66, 71
 possible causes of problem, 64-
 65, 70
Anger:
 about deadlines, 97
 about downsizing, 203, 205-6,
 215-16
 about employee's embarrassing
 comments to boss, 163-66
 boss's, toward you, 401-4
 at employee stubbornness, 22
 at suppliers, 75-78 163-66
Annoyance bickering, 13
Anxiety, and downsizing, 203

B

Babysitter problems, *See* Child-care
 problems
Badmouthing of competitors, 122-
 26
 cures for, 123-24
 as habit, 125
 and insecure salespeople, 124-25
 possible causes of, 123
"Bad press," overcoming, 24-26
Basic skills training, 92-94
Boring jobs, improving, 57-59
Boss:
 abolishment of your position by,
 409-12
 bypassing by, to workgroup,
 430-33
 complaints to peers about you,
 412-14
 cultural/personality differences
 with, 423-26
 disastrous projects, assignment
 of, 386-88
 dishonesty with, 332-36
 distrust of, 416
 employee's embarrassing comments to, 163-66
 fear of employees' anger, 422
 friendship with hard-to-manage
 employees, 427-30
 getting chewed out by, 401-4
 handling problems with, 405-33
 interference with workgroup
 empowerment, 275-80
 keeping informed, 319-21
 lending money to, 302-4
 loyalty to, 416
 making look bad, 414-17
 manager criticizes you to, 350-
 53
 micro-management by, 417-20
 ouster from your position by,
 406-8
 poor performance rating from,
 388-92
 problems caused by, 385-404
 sabotage of, by employee, 194-
 97
 supportiveness of, 420-23
 taking credit for subordinates'
 work, 258-61
 unclear assignments by, 394-97
 unfair project assignments by,
 392-94
 workgroup-workgroup competition, 397-401
 See also Ethical problems
Boss-employee friendships, 191-94
 cures for problem, 192-93
 possible causes of problem, 193-
 94
Burnout, 82, 83-84, 112

C

Call-backs, from layoffs, 215
Casual dress policy, and employee
    appearance, 53, 54-55
Challenges to authority, 178-201
    boss-employee friendships, 191-
        94
    cooperation with manager, lack
        of, 182-85
    emergency overtime, refusal to
        work, 197-201
    end-runs, 185-89
    public criticisms, 189-91
    refusal to follow orders, 179-82
    sabotage, 194-97
Change:
    learning curve for, 6
    resistance to, 20-23
    of title, 373
Child-care problems, 43-47
    and "company manners," 45-46
    cures for, 44-46
    on-site day care, 44
    possible causes of, 44
    work-at-home assignments,
        arranging, 46
Clear assignments, 422
College education needs, 375-78
Commitments, taking seriously,
    335-36
Communication:
    clarity of, 95, 98
    importance of, 95, 98
    problems, 133-36, 183-84
Company information, misuse of,
    223-26
Company property, misuse of, 171-
    73
    company policy on, 171-72
    cures for, 172-73
Company rules, violation of, 113-15

Compensation system, examining,
    19
Competition among workgroups,
    397-400
Competition vs. cooperation, 236-39
    cures for, 237-39
    possible causes of, 236-37
Competitors:
    badmouthing of, 122-26
    employment negotiations with,
        203-6
Confidence:
    boss's, maintaining, 254
    employee lack of, 146-47
Conflicting goals of units, 9, 11
Conflict resolution, 288
Continued downsizing:
    fear of, 225
    rumors of, 207-9
Cooperation skills, learning, 236-
    39
Credit, misappropriation of, 258-
    61
Criticism:
    from other managers, 350-53
    public, 189-91
        cures for, 189-90
        possible causes of, 189
        public retraction for, 190
Cultural differences with boss, 423-
    26
Customer(s):
    educating, 12
    expectations of, failing to meet,
        24-25
    playing customer with salespeo-
        ple, 124

D

Deadlines, 94-98, 132
    anger about, 97

missed, 325-28
  cures for, 131-32
  possible causes of, 130-31
  setting, 96-97
Delegation:
  boss's resistance to, 417-20
  empowerment vs., 264-65
Demoralized workgroup, 15-17
  cures for, 15-17
  possible causes of problem, 15
Destruction of report, ethics of, 299-302
Deteriorating performance, 99-102
  cures for problem, 100-101
  possible causes of problem, 99-100
Disagreement, infighting vs., 14, 197
Disastrous projects, assignment of, 386-88
Discipline, purpose of, 173
Discrediting a coworker, 169-71
  cures for, 170-71
  possible causes of, 169-70
Discrimination, 281, 310
  sexual, 305-8
Discrimination accusations, 39-43
  cures for problem, 40-42
  possible causes of problem, 40
Dishonesty, 34-35, 159-62
  about completed assignment, 166-68
  with boss, 332-36
  cures for, 160-62
  expectations of, 159-61
  possible causes of, 159-60
  pressure to lie, 161-62
  as self-protective measure, 160, 162
Disillusionment with job, 99-102
Disincentive for low level of production, 19-20

disinformation, countering, 26
Disintegrating unit, 328-32
Disloyalty to boss, 416-17
Dismissal, 173, 205
  for failure to learn job, 92-94
  of good employee, 308-10
  reasons for, 182
Disorganization, 130-33, 136-37, 173
Displaced workers, 219-23
  and mentors, 221-22
  separating simple work for, 222
  training, 220-21
Distrust of boss, 416
Downsizing problems, 202-34
  anger about, 203, 205-6, 215-16
  competition vs. cooperation, 236-39
  continued downsizing:
    fear of, 225
    rumors of, 207-9
  displaced workers, 219-23
  grievances, threats of, 209-13
  and increased workload, 247-50
  job hunts on company time, 226-30
  loss of best workers, 254-57
  misappropriation of credit, 258-61
  misuse of company information, 223-26
  negotiations with competitors, 203-6
  new functions, 217-19
  new manager, 230-34
  nonperformers, 250-54
  performance levels, 213-16
  stress, 239-43
  and unreasonable quality/quantity demands, 243-47
  work, 203, 205-6, 215-16 202-34

Dress codes, 54
See also Employee appearance
Drug abuse, 34-36, 64-67, 83, 176
  cures for problem, 65-66
  employee report of, 34-36
    cures for, 35-36
    possible causes of, 34-35
  possible causes of problem, 64-65
  and theft of supplies, 382, 383

E

Education:
  of customer, 12
  employee education needs, 375-78
EEO regulations, 10, 11
Emergency overtime, refusal to work, 197-201
Emotional problems, and negative attitude, 150
Employee appearance, 53-56
  acceptable norms, defining, 53-56
  and casual dress policy, 53, 54-55
Employee education needs, 375-78
Employee performance, *See* Performance problems
Employee problems, 2-29
  demoralized workgroup, 15-17
  in-group fighting, 12-17
  low production bogey, 18-20
  poor reputation of workgroup, 23-26
  promotions, resentment about, 26-29
  resistance to change, 20-23
  unacceptable work, 2-3
  workgroup:
    and internal customers, 8-12

  and new methods, 5-8
Employees:
  boss-employee friendships, 191-94
  competition vs. cooperation, 236-39
  dishonesty, 34-35
  embarrassing comments to boss, 163-66
  expectations of, 56-60
  fear of anger of, 422
  good, dismissal of, 308-10
  hard-to-manage, boss's friendship with, 427-30
  lack of confidence of, 146-47
  limits to authority, 263-68
  limits to employee authority, 263-68
  misconduct, *See* Misconduct
  need for feedback, 120, 121
  personal problems:
    alcohol abuse, 64-67, 69-71
    drug abuse, 64-67
    excessive time off, 67-69
    health, 62-64
    office romance, break up of, 71-73
    and slipping performance, 87-88
  refusal to help, 88-91
  sabotage of boss by, 194-97, 205-6
  stubbornness of, 22
  team leader-employee affair, 37-39
  See also Employee appearance; Performance problems
Employee stubbornness, anger at, 22
Employment negotiations with competitors, 203-6
  cures for, 204-6

possible causes of, 203
and self-protection, 204-5
Empowerment:
    definition of, 276
    leveraging resources through,
        276-78
Empowerment problems, 262-95
    boss's interference with imple-
        mentation, 275-80
    joint projects, 268-71
    limits to employee authority,
        263-68
    self-managing teams, achieving,
        271-75
End-runs, 185-89
    cures for, 186-88
    possible causes of, 186
Equipment, filling needs for, 2-3, 4
Ethical problems, 296-317
    destruction of safety hazards
        report, 299-302
    dismissal of good employee,
        308-10
    "fudging" figures on reports,
        297-99
    lending money to boss, 302-4
    and poor performance, 314-17
    sexual discrimination, 305-8
    sexual harassment, 310-14
Example, setting, 422
Excessive time off, 67-69
    cures for problem, 67-69
    possible causes of problem, 67
Expectations:
    about promotions, 27-28
    about work-at-home schedule,
        126-27
    customer failing to meet, 24-25
    employee, of social environment,
        56-60
    of employee performance, 79
    and training, 2-3, 4

F

Failure to prioritize, 110-13
Falsified work hours, 107-10
    cures for, 108-9
    possible causes of, 107-8
Favoritism, and promotions, 29
Fear:
    of continued downsizing, 225,
        227-28
    of employees' anger, 422
    of new technology, 118
Feedback:
    employee need for, 120, 121
    lack of, 340-44
    positive, 81
Flexibility:
    and personal commitments, 198-
        99
    reorganizing life for, 199
    and second job, 200
    special plans vs., 199
Flexiplace, 127
Flextime:
    benefit to employees, 108
    and falsified work hours, 107-10
"Fudging" figures on reports, 297-
        99
    cures for, 298
    possible causes of, 297-98

G

Grief, 67-68
Grievances, threats of, 209-13
Grudges, 164

H

Habitual lateness, 174-77
    as bad habit, 176
    cures for, 174-76

and family responsibilities, 175
as personal problem, 176
possible causes of, 174
Hands off management, 337, 339-40
Hard-to-manage employee, boss's
   friendship with, 427-30
Harrassment, sexual, 31-33
Health problems, 62-64
   cures for situation, 63-64
   possible causes of, 62-63
Help, employee's refusal of, 88-91
High-quality work:
   low volume of, 145-48
      cures for, 146-47
      possible causes of, 146

I

Ignorance vs. stupidity, 79
Ignored work procedures, 104-7
Illness, 68
Immigrants, and language difficulties, 47-49
Inappropriate dress, See Employee
   appearance
Increased workload, and downsizing, 247-50
Inequity, in-group fighting about,
   13-14
information campaign, 26
In-group fighting, 12-17
   about real/perceived inequity,
      13-14
   cures for, 13-14
   possible causes of, 13
Instructions:
   ignoring deliberately, 183, 185
   refusal to follow, 105
   to new employees, 92-94
Intentional performance problems,
   103-28

badmouthing of competitors,
   122-26
failure to prioritize, 110-13
falsified work hours, 107-10
ignored work procedures, 104-7
new technology, refusal to use,
   115-18
substandard work, 119-22
violation of company rules, 113-15
and work-at-home schedules,
   126-28
Internal customers:
   educating, 12
   organizational stress on, 8, 9-10
   and workgroup, 8-12
      cures, 9-11
      possible causes of problem, 8-9
Internal management problems:
   employee education needs, 375-78
   inability to promote, 372-75
   new employees, poor quality of,
      368-71
   rule exceptions, 378-81
   theft of supplies, 382-84

J

Jealousy, 169-70
Job enrichment approach, 84
Job hunts, on company time, 226-30
Job training, basic skills training,
   93-94
Job unsuitability, 155-57
   cures for, 156-57
   possible causes of, 155-56
Joint project problems:
   cures for, 269-71

and manager cooperation, 268-71
possible causes of, 268-69

K

Keyboarding skills, improving, 117

L

lack of cooperation with manager, 182-85
cures for, 183-85
possible causes of, 183
Language difficulties, 47-49
cures for, 48-49
possible causes of, 47-48
Lateness, habitual, 174-77
Layoffs:
continued:
fear of, 225, 227-28
rumors of, 207-9
Leadership, 422
by example, 282
Learning curve, 99
for change, 6
Learning saturation point, 99, 100
Lending money to boss, 302-4
cures for, 303-4
possible causes of, 302-3
Listening skills, 6
"Lone" worker problems:
cures for, 282-84
possible causes of, 281
and teams, 280-84
Loss of best workers, 254-57
cures for, 255-57
possible causes of, 255
Loss of income, 412
Loss of production, and new methods, 7

Low production bogey, 18-20
cures for, 19-20
possible causes of problem, 18-19
Low-quality work:
cures for, 143-45
high volume of, 142-45
possible causes of, 142-43
and quality standards, 143
rewarding quality, 144-45
speed vs. accuracy, 144
Loyalty:
and lying, 160
to boss, 416
Lying:
about completed assignment, 166-68
cures for, 167-68
possible causes of, 166-67
and loyalty, 160
to the boss, 332-36
under oath, 159-62
cures for, 160-62
possible causes of, 159-60

M

Managers:
and demoralized workgroup, 15-17
lack of cooperation with, 182-85
lack of support by, 15-17
marginal, 15-16
new, disinterest in unit, 230-34
substandard work, acceptance of, 16
Marginal managers, 15-16
Marginal work, informal leader as, 151-54
Mastery of skills, 141, 147
Mentors, 80
and displaced workers, 221-22

Micro-management by boss, 417-20
  cures for, 418-20
  possible causes of, 417-18
Minority group member, poor performance of, 50-53
Misassignment of blame, 24, 25-26
Misconduct, 158-77
  discrediting a coworker, 169-71
  dishonesty, 159-62
  embarrassing comments to boss, 163-66
  lateness, habitual, 174-77
  lying about completed assignment, 166-68
  misuse of company property, 171-73
Misperceived pressure, as reason for lying, 160, 162
Missed deadlines, 130-32, 325-28
Misuse of company information, 223-26
  cures for, 224-26
  possible causes of, 223-24
Motivation, importance of, 3
Motivation problems, 78-81
  cures for problem, 79-81
  possible causes of, 78-79

N

Negative attitude, 148-51
  cures for, 149-50
  and emotional problems, 150
  possible causes of, 148-49
Negative supervision, 421-22
New employees:
  instructing, 92-94
  and lack of motivation, 78-81
  poor quality of, 368-71
  refusal of help by, 88-91

New functions:
  following downsizing, 217-19
  and heavy workload, 218-19
  trading, 218
New job, systematic plan for finding, 411
New methods:
  implementing, 5-8
  and loss of production, 5, 7
  resistance to learning, 5-8
  timetable for learning, 7
New technology:
  employee refusal to use, 115-18
  fear of, 118
  and workforce reduction, 117-18
"No-cost" promotions, 373
Noncompetition contracts, 204
Nonperformers, manager's refusal to fire, 250-54

O

Office romance, break up of, 71-73
Office technology, employee refusal to use, 115-18
One-on-one tutoring, 93
On-site day care, 44
Other managers, 345-66
  attempt to take over function, 346-50
  complaints about workgroup output, 356-59
  criticism from, 350-53
  lack of cooperation from, 363-66
  recruitment of your best employees by, 359-62
  substandard work from other units, 353-56
Outplacement services, 411
Outsiders, loners as, 281

P

Peer review system, establishing, 153
Performance:
    and downsizing, 213-16
    of minority group member, 50-53
    and work environment, 2-3
Performance problems:
    deteriorating performance, 99-102
    intentional, 103-28
        badmouthing of competitors, 122-26
        failure to prioritize, 110-13
        falsified work hours, 107-10
        ignored work procedures, 104-7
        refusal to use new technology, 115-18
        substandard work, 119-22
        violation of company rules, 113-15
        work-at-home schedules, 126-28
    and motivation, 78-81
    new employees, instructing, 92-94
    and offensive manner with supplier, 75-78
    refusal of help, 88-91
    substandard report, 85-88, 94-98
    unacceptable performance level, 81-84
    unintentional, 103-28
        communication problems, 133-36
        failure to deliver on promise, 136-39
        high volume of low-quality work, 142-45
        informal leader as marginal worker, 151-54
        job suitability, 155-57
        low volume of high-quality work, 145-48
        negative attitude, 148-51
        poor organization skills, 130-33
        stress/pressure, 139-42
Periodic episodes, 240, 241-42
Personality differences with boss, 423-26
Personal problems:
    dishonesty with boss, 332-36
    disintegrating unit, 328-32
    feedback, lack of, 340-44
    keeping the boss informed, 319-21
    missed deadlines, 325-28
    sexual harassment, accusations of, 321-25
    work status questions, failure to answer, 336-40
Personal style, boss's dislike of, 424, 425-26
Poor organization skills, 130-33, 136-37, 173
    cures for, 131-32
    possible causes of, 130-31
Poor performance by organization, 2-4
Poor performance rating from boss, 388-92
    cures for, 389-91
    possible causes of, 389
Poor reputation of workgroup, 23-26
    cures for, 24-26
    possible causes of, 24
Positive feedback, 81
Pressure, 139-42
    and promises, 138
    to lie, 161-62
Priorities:
    failure to prioritize, 110-13

setting, 85-87, 95, 96-97
Problem-solving checklists:
   Acceptance Problems, 438-39
   Conduct/Behavior Problems,
      437-38
   General Checklist, 434-35
   Performance Problems, 435-37
   Problems With Your Boss, 442-
      43
   Problems With Your Peers, 439-
      40
   Substance-Abuse Problems, 443-
      45
   Your Personal Problems, 442-43
Production goals, recognition for
   reaching, 19
Project control, 327
Promotions:
   and favoritism, 29
   resentment about, 26-29
      cures for problem, 27-29
      possible causes of problem,
         27
Public criticisms, 189-91
   cures for, 189-90
   possible causes of, 189
   public retraction, 190

Q

Quality, rewarding, 144-45
Quality/quantity demands, unrea-
   sonable, 223-26
Quantity vs. quality, 145

R

Racism accusations, 39-43
   cures for problem, 40-42
   possible causes of problem, 40
Recognition, 2-3
Recognition systems, 3, 19-20, 373

Recruitment, of best employees by
   managers, 359-62
Refusal of help, 88-91
Refusal to fire, manager's, 250-54
Refusal to follow orders, 105, 179-
   82
   cures for, 179-82
   possible causes of, 179
   and safety, 179, 180
Refusal to work overtime, 197-201
   cures for, 198-200
   possible causes of, 198
Reputation of workgroup, 23-26
Resistance to change, 20-23
   cures for problem, 21-23
   possible causes of problem, 20-
   21
Retention bonuses, 256
Retraining, 144
Rewards, 2-3, 422
   for personal favors, 314-17
Rule exceptions, 378-81
   and consistency, 380-81
   discretion to make exception,
      379
   flexibility in application of rule,
      380
   importance of rule, 379
   message sent by, 379-80
Rumors, 169-71

S

Sabotage:
   of boss by employee, 194-97,
      205-6
      cures for, 195-97
      possible causes of, 194-95
   of coworker, 169-71
"Sacred cows," 278
Safety, and refusal to follow orders,
   179, 180

Second job, impact on flexibility, 200
Self-managing team:
    creating, 271-75
    exercising initiative for, creating, 273-74
    workgroup as, 271-75
Setting priorities, 85-87
Sexism accusations, 39-43
    cures for problem, 40-42
    possible causes of problem, 40
Sexual discrimination, 305-8
    cures for, 306-7
    possible causes of, 305-6
Sexual harassment, 310-14
    accusations of, 321-25
    cures for, 311-13
    possible causes of, 311
Sexual situations, 31-33
    employee brags of affair with supervisor, 31-33
    team leader-employee affair, 37-39
Six-month rule, 412
Skills training, in new technology, 117
Social environment, employee expectations of, 56-60
Social environment problems, 30-60
    child-care problems, 43-47
    drug abuse, 34-36
    language difficulties, 47-49
    poor performance, of minority group member, 50-53
    racism, accusations of, 39-43
    sexism, accusations of, 39-43
    sexual situations, 31-33
        employee brags of affair with supervisor, 31-33
        team leader-employee affair, 37-39

sloppy dress, 53-56
Speed, importance to operation, 148
Star performers, and job suitability, 155-57
Stress, 139-42
    of downsizing, 239-43
    falling to pieces as learned response to, 141-42
    reducing, 140-41
    and work overload, 242-43
Substandard report:
    due to time constraints, 94-98
    as sign of poor performance, 85-88
        cures for, 86-87
        possible causes of, 85-86
Substandard work, 119-22
    cures for, 120-22
    feedback, need for, 120
    and ongoing review process, 120
    possible causes of, 119-20
    reputation for, 24-25
Superior-subordinate relationships, 72-73
    team leader-employee affair, 37-39
Supplier, employer's offensive manner with, 75-78
Supportiveness of boss:
    lack of, 420-23
        cures for, 421-23
        possible causes of, 421
    and negative supervision, 421-22

T

Team leader-employee affair, 37-39
Teams, 123
    accountability of, 121
Teamwork problems, 280-95
    authority in other units, 292-95

customer relationships, 288-92
disruptions, 284-88
"lone" workers, 280-84
Temporary roadblocks to learning, 99-101
Termination, *See* Dismissal
Theft of supplies, 382-84
catching the thief, 383-84
cures for, 382-84
and drug abuse, 382, 383
possible causes of, 382
security, increasing, 384
Time off, excessive, 67-69
Title changes, 373
Total Quality Management (TQM), 59
Training, 117, 135, 273
in basic skills, 92-94
displaced workers, 220-21
and expectations, 2-3, 4
in new technology, 117
retraining, 144
Trust, 3, 21
distrust of boss, 416
Turnover, 230, 329, 330

U

Unacceptable performance level, 81-84
burnout, 82, 83-84
cures, 3-4, 82-84
discussing with employee, 82-83
job enrichment approach to, 84
possible causes of, 2-3, 82
Unclear assignments, 394-97
Unfair project assignments, 392-94
cures for, 393-94
possible causes of, 392-93
Unintentional performance problems, 103-28

communication problems, 133-36
failure to deliver on promise, 136-39
high-quality work, low volume of, 145-48
informal leader as marginal worker, 151-54
job unsuitability, 155-57
low-quality work, high volume of, 142-45
negative attitude, 148-51
poor organization skills, 130-33, 136-37, 173
stress/pressure, 139-42
Units:
conflicting goals of, 9, 11
and deadlines, 16
Unrealistic planning, 326-27

W

Work-at-home assignments, arranging for employee, 46, 68-69
Work-at-home schedules, and poor performance, 126-28
Work environment, and performance, 2-3
Work flow, examining to encourage good work, 4
Workgroups:
boss's bypassing to, 430-33
challenging, 249
competition among, 397-400
demoralized, 15-17
in-group fighting, 12-17
and internal customers, 8-12
conflicting goals of units, 9, 11
cures, 9-11

possible causes of problem, 8-9

workgroup standards, 9, 10-11

low production bogey, 18-20

and new methods, 5-8

cures, 6-8

possible causes of, 5-6

poor reputation of, 23-26

resistance to change, 20-23

as self-managing team, 271-75

Workgroup standards, 9, 10-11

Workgroup-workgroup competition, 397-401

Workload increase, rumors of, 210-13

Work output, measuring, 127

Work procedures, ignored, 104-7

Work status questions, failure to answer, 336-40

Write-ups, 173